WHEN CAESAR WAS KING

The Center Theatre, final home of *Your Show of Shows*, October 21, 1953.

WHEN CAESAR WAS KING

HOW SID CAESAR
REINVENTED AMERICAN COMEDY

DAVID MARGOLICK

SCHOCKEN BOOKS   NEW YORK   2025

FIRST HARDCOVER EDITION

PUBLISHED BY SCHOCKEN BOOKS 2025

Published by Schocken Books,
a division of Penguin Random House LLC,
1745 Broadway, New York, NY 10019.

Schocken Books and the colophon are registered
trademarks of Penguin Random House LLC.

Library of Congress Cataloging-in-Publication Data
Names: Margolick, David, author
Title: When Caesar was king : how Sid Caesar reinvented
American comedy / David Margolick.
Description: First hardcover edition. | New York : Schocken Books, 2025. |
Includes bibliographical references and index.
Identifiers: LCCN 2025009695 (print) | LCCN 2025009696 (ebook) |
ISBN 9780805242553 (hardcover) | ISBN 9780593804384 (ebook)
Subjects: LCSH: Caesar, Sid, 1922–2014. | Comedians—United States—
Biography. | Television actors and actresses—United States—Biography. |
Sketch comedy television programs—United States—History
and criticism. | LCGFT: Biographies.
Classification: LCC PN2287.C22 M37 2026 (print) |
LCC PN2287.C22 (ebook)
LC record available at https://lccn.loc.gov/2025009695
LC ebook record available at https://lccn.loc.gov/2025009696

penguinrandomhouse.com | schocken.com

Printed in the United States of America
1st Printing

The authorized representative in the EU for product safety
and compliance is Penguin Random House Ireland,
Morrison Chambers, 32 Nassau Street,
Dublin D02 YH68, Ireland,
https://eu-contact.penguin.ie.

To Amy

I'm proud of you. You know, you *really* know, you *really* understood, the show. Now you're going to do this book, and people are going to say, "Gee, this is really good and really interesting. Just one question, David: Who's Sid Caesar?" You're going to get that. "Who was Sid Caesar?"

—MEL BROOKS TO THE AUTHOR

To be Jewish is to harbor a psychic defect and thereby be gifted with instincts for transcendence. It's a blessing and a curse to be a Jew. You takes your choice.

—NORMAN MAILER TO PETER MANSO

My boy, you will some day write about Jews. Well, I ask you to remember this advice. When you write about Jews, write with humor. Make jokes.

—SHMARYA LEVIN TO BEN HECHT

Lucille Kallen   Mel Brooks   Imogene Coca   Sid Caesar   Mel Tolkin

Howard Morris   Max Liebman   Bambi Linn

Carl Reiner   Bill Hayes   The Billy Williams Quartet

"Your Show of Shows" Company   1952–53

CONTENTS

WHEN CAESAR WAS KING

"This Is Your Story," April 3, 1954.

INTRODUCTION

On the evening of Saturday, April 3, 1954, during a commercial for Griffin Microsheen Boot Polish ("Your 'Shine of Shines' on *Your Show of Shows*"), Sid Caesar quietly made his way down an aisle in New York's Center Theatre and slipped into the seat set aside for him, the only empty one in sight. It was hard for the bulky, muscular Caesar to be inconspicuous, but in this barn of a place, more cavernous even than the nearby Radio City Music Hall, few in the audience would have noticed him. But they'd always remember what he, and they, were about to pull off: the longest and lustiest laughter, before or since, in the history of television.

That night, Caesar felt cocky, rambunctious, liberated. After more than four years on the air, *Your Show of Shows*, the program on which he'd made his name, the one that had set the rules, and the standard, and the contours, of television comedy for years to come, was winding down. Soon, he'd launch his own show, bearing his own name, where, with the greatest team of comedy writers ever assembled, he could set *his own* rules and, presumably, ascend even higher. Now, though, he had to pull off an intricate eleven-minute-long sketch, one centered on him, live on national television. Once the commercial ended, the cameras would roll, and twenty million people would watch a wicked takeoff of another mainstay of early TV, as lachrymose as Caesar's show was irreverent: *This Is Your Life.*

On one level, "This Is Your Story," as the spoof was called, was an orgy of kissing, hugging, and slobbering as Caesar's hapless character, one Al Duncey from Darling Falls, Montana, is dragged kicking and screaming up to the stage and reunited with various figures from his past, most notably his beloved Uncle Goopy, played by Howard Morris, the third banana on the show. But on another level, Carl Reiner, the second banana, later said what they saw that night was "the greatest sketch ever, ever done in the history of television." "Such a glorious muddle of bawling humanity does more than gladden the soul," a critic from *The New York Times* would write about it. "It leads me to think that on certain Saturday nights *Your Show of Shows* may have been the laughter of the gods."

The takeoff was also a clinic in the elements of classic comedy and an inventory of what had made *Your Show of Shows* unique. "That sketch *says it all:* the inventiveness, the freedom, the insanity, the brilliance, and yet the control," said Bill Persky, the Emmy Award–winning comedy writer and producer for *The Dick Van Dyke Show,* one of many TV shows, movies, and plays that *Your Show of Shows* and its successor, *Caesar's Hour,* had spawned. "The business you want to go into is based on a foundation and this is it," he'd tell his students at Yale, Columbia, and New York University before playing it for them. "These are the people who set the stage. We didn't know it at the time, but what they did was *impossible.*" The screening came with a guarantee: If what he was about to show them wasn't one of the funniest things they'd ever seen, he'd turn it off after a minute. This he never had to do.

Television was still young when "This Is Your Story" aired, and so was Caesar: only thirty-one years old, though he'd already put five years into the enterprise. In that time, he'd become TV's initial homegrown star, the first without a long apprenticeship in vaudeville, radio, or the theater. In TV's original colonies—the big cities, mostly in the Northeast, to which it was limited in its earliest days, shortly after World War II—watching Caesar and his co-stars—Imogene Coca, Reiner, and Morris—on *Your Show of Shows* had become a grand ritual. Thanks to them, folks could now stay home Saturday nights without feeling like wallflowers. What proved a bane to Broadway theaters, movie palaces, night-clubs, bowling alleys, and babysitters had been a boon to Caesar: By the spring of 1954 he was making an unthinkable $25,000 a week—more, an irate NBC shareholder complained, than David Sarnoff, the man running the network, was collecting. At least publicly, Sarnoff wasn't perturbed. "I have no doubt there is more public interest in Sid Caesar than in David Sarnoff, so he prob-ably is worth more than I am," he said.

"You are young and talented and intelligent," the man who'd brought Caesar to NBC, Sylvester L. "Pat" Weaver Jr., had writ-ten to him a few weeks before the sketch was aired, part of a campaign to keep him from straying to another network or going off to Hollywood. "You are gifted in a way which is rarely seen during a lifetime. If you handle yourself right you have a career ahead which will be hard for anyone in our time to top." And for a while, it was true. Caesar off camera was remote and noto-riously hard to read, but entertainment writers and Broadway columnists also recognized his uniqueness and newsworthiness, forever monitoring his latest triumphs, his residences, his waist-line, his ratings, his contracts, his diet, his respiratory system, and his mental health.

In some ways Caesar peaked that night. Though *Caesar's Hour*, his next show, produced a new body of distinguished work, within a few years Caesar was largely off the air, giving him two additional distinctions in the annals of television: becoming its first great victim and suffering its most precipitous fall. "Much too front-loaded" was how Larry Gelbart, the writer in Caesar's stable he might have respected most, once described his career. But as invisible as Caesar himself would become, his imprint remained enormous, his disciples ubiquitous.

His influence was felt in every branch of comedy: movies, sit-coms, stand-up, sketches. "No Sid Caesar, no Mel Brooks," Mel Brooks liked to say, and it was true, for Caesar had discovered, protected, tolerated, and nourished Brooks for a decade. Lenny

Bruce's biographer called Caesar "the only comedian who had a real decisive influence" on Bruce. Woody Allen, who'd worked for Caesar toward the end of his great run, was flabbergasted when, in a conversation with his old boss in the early 1990s, Caesar predicted *he'd* be a footnote to *Allen's* career. "You're Sid Caesar, and you're not appreciating what a genius you were and what an influence you are on everybody!" Allen thought to himself. "You're one of the greatest comedians that we've ever had!"

Not just *The Dick Van Dyke Show*, but *The Andy Griffith Show*, *M*A*S*H*, and *All in the Family*; *Bananas* and *Annie Hall*, *Blazing Saddles*, *Fiddler on the Roof*, *The Odd Couple*, *Hello, Dolly!*—all were written by people who wrote for Caesar first. A generation of leading comics acknowledged their debt to him. The young Johnny Carson knew all of his sketches and ripped off one of the most famous routines for his act at the University of Nebraska. The young Carol Burnett passed up precious tickets to *My Fair Lady* to watch Caesar rehearse and patterned her own TV show after his. The young Dick Cavett played hooky from Yale to go to New York and watch him perform. Jonathan Winters, Richard Pryor, Conan O'Brien, and Al Franken were all inspired by him. "He was just somebody you couldn't take your eyes off of, even as a five- or six-year-old," said Billy Crystal. Larry David watched Caesar as a kid and has called him "easily the best sketch comedian I've ever seen, without a close second." "My dad would watch Sid Caesar, and *literally* fall off his chair," the actress and comedienne Louise Lasser remembered. "*Literally*. He would be on the floor." In Richard Lewis's fractured family (and lots of others), a truce was declared when Caesar's shows came on.

Even when, before VCRs and DVDs and YouTube, Caesar's work was hard to find, the comic cognoscenti tracked down, pored over, and emulated it. Robin Williams recalled how, after watching a collection of classic Caesar sketches at a movie theater in the 1970s, the old woman seated next to him turned and told him he'd never be that good. "We all lost our grandfather today," Jon Stewart declared on *The Daily Show* the night Caesar died. Then, in the program's "Your Moment of Zen," there was Caesar once again in one of his most familiar roles: his down-and-out but know-it-all German professor, dressed in his customary crushed top hat and rags, this time playing "Dr. Ludwig von Snowcap," authority on mountain climbing, who'd fallen 17,780 feet from a Himalayan peak—and lived.

"Were you *badly* hurt, Professor?" his ever-faithful interlocutor, played by Reiner, asked him.

"See that?" replied Caesar in a thick, ersatz-German accent, pointing to the tip of his pinkie. "That's the original me. All the rest is *new*!"

HE WAS THE UNLIKELIEST of comics: introverted, ill at ease, tongue-tied. "Extremely smart but completely inarticulate," as another notable Caesar alum, Neil Simon, described him. Buddy Hackett called Caesar "the most quiet man I know and the only quiet comedian I know." "The first thing I noticed about Sid Caesar was he wasn't funny," recalled Tony Webster, a writer whose own alcohol-fueled relationship with Caesar was especially combustible. Reiner said he never heard Caesar tell a joke; another Caesar writer, Joe Stein, said he never heard him laugh. A photograph of the New York comic fraternity (taken in December 1953 at a bachelor party for early television comedy's other titan, Milton Berle) captured how anomalous Caesar was. While all the others—Red Buttons, Joe E. Lewis, Sam Levenson, Morey Amsterdam, Henny Youngman, Jan Murray, Joey Adams, and Berle himself—mugged, clowned, or wisecracked for the camera, Caesar smiled wanly, looking as if he'd rather be anywhere, or anyone, else. Much of comedy stems from rage, but Caesar was more conspicuously angry than the others. "Comedy comes from animosity and frustration," he once said. "You want to get back at something but you're afraid to do it in a big way because you'll get in trouble."

But as Simon said, Caesar could be funnier without telling a joke than any man he'd ever seen. "Like seeing a new country" was how he described watching Caesar for the first time, in *Tars and Spars*, a 1946 film that became, for aspiring funnymen of his generation, part of the comic catechism. "All other comics were basically doing situations with farcical characters," Simon remembered. "Caesar was doing life." Caesar demanded more elevated material than the usual stuff—the "my mother-in-law" jokes, the "my wife is so fat" jokes—everyone else did, said Stein. Caesar "had a radar for truth—truth in comedy," he added. "It could be exaggerated truth, upside-down truth, nutty truth, but there had to be truth. And if Sid didn't *feel* it, he wouldn't give us a lecture about truth, he'd say, 'Ah, it ain't funny.' But we knew he smelled something false." "He knew intuitively how people behave," Reiner observed. "He had a perfect pitch about the human condition." "Sid was a great mimic, but he didn't do Humphrey Bogart," as Brooks put it. "He simply mimicked humanity" and had his writers write "mini-plays about mankind."

Larry Gelbart was once asked to describe Caesar's personality. "Zero," he'd replied. "Sid's personality could be described as 'non-existent.' It's one of the reasons Sid was as good as he was." With so little of himself to get in the way, Gelbart reasoned, Caesar could become whoever or whatever he wanted, or needed, to be. However opaque, and even baffling, he could appear, inside him were all the tools—insight, imagination, discipline, and what Howard Morris called a *"meshugana* energy"— that the instantaneous, insatiable new medium of television demanded. His wide-ranging comedic skills—including pantomime and monologues—were tailor-made for small screens in big wooden boxes in living rooms. Though Caesar never got past high school himself, he had a sophistication born of native intelligence and curiosity that resonated with early television's urbane audiences. But even if you'd never seen *On the Waterfront* or *The Bicycle Thief*, or eaten (or tried to eat) at a health food restaurant, or heard Grieg's Piano Concerto, he could make you laugh about them. And though you might never have seen a silent movie, his meticulous re-creations of them could make you laugh *and* cry.

For ninety minutes over thirty-odd weeks for more than four years, and an hour a week for three years after that, Caesar presented life *live*, a feat of endurance and brinkmanship no one else ever attempted, before or since. One of his writers likened it to "walking across Niagara Falls" every Saturday night. An ever-present sense of danger lent the shows an intensity and precariousness in which viewers felt almost complicit. And with the primitive cameras—the size of Volkswagens, Persky recalled—zeroing in on Caesar several times every show, viewers came to know him, or at least to think they did, in a way they'd come to know few stars before him. Comics generally came smaller and more fragile than Caesar; as the architect of *Your Show of Shows*—its director, Max Liebman—once said, to have succeeded as he did, Caesar had had to overcome his size. And his good looks: Had television had its own Silent Era, Brooks once said, Caesar might have starred in that, too. Most comics *looked like* comics, one of Caesar's most faithful students, Nakhman Zalowitz of the Yiddish *Forverts* once observed; no one could have mistaken Groucho Marx for a steel magnate. But by his appearance, his clothing, his manners and mannerisms, Caesar, Zalowitz wrote, "could be taken for a U.S. Senator, or a successful lawyer, or a Park Avenue doctor."

Traditional comics generally got away with single characters or routines, tweaked periodically. But aided by his uncanny ear for accents and a knack for mimicry, Caesar could play everyone and everything: imperious German general, Italian cobbler, Stalinist diplomat, American corporate chieftain, British aristocrat, mobster, concert pianist, pasha, gunslinger, silent film star, samurai warrior. He could be a bully or a schlemiel, a boy at his first dance or a paranoid schizophrenic, a duke or a drunk. And should mankind prove too confining, he could become an animal (a trained seal, lion, alley cat, puppy), or a fly crawling on a piece of feta cheese, or various inanimate objects: a punching bag, seltzer bottle, telephone, or gumball machine, to name a few, each with its own sounds and, remarkably, neuroses. His very versatility proved a curse: While viewers cherished comedians whose quirks were limited and predictable, like Jack Benny and Bob Hope, Caesar's were varied and elusive. The only character he couldn't play was himself, and for a simple reason: As Reiner put it, "He didn't know who Sid Caesar was."

· · ·

FOR MANY VIEWERS CAESAR *was* television, coming with their first DuMonts or Admirals in the way new Maytags came with boxes of Tide. "The pioneer TV set owner was a courageous fellow," noted a television writer of the time. "He not only had to invite in the entire neighborhood; he had to provide popcorn and beer as well as Sid Caesar." Eggheads who disdained TV and succumbed to it only reluctantly—like Newton Minow, the chairman-to-be of the Federal Communications Commission who dismissed it as a "vast wasteland" (but only after Caesar had grown scarce)—used Caesar as their excuse. "Satire is what closes on a Saturday night," the comedy writer George S. Kaufman memorably said, but Caesar's satires were what Kaufman stayed home Saturday nights to see.

Albert Einstein watched Caesar, as did Isaac Asimov and Norman Mailer. By teaching him to savor the sound of a foreign language (even if it was all gibberish), Caesar helped make Robert Pinsky a poet. Before becoming a playwright and gay activist, Larry Kramer had wanted to write for Sid Caesar. Leonard Bernstein limited his TV viewing to "newscasts, documentaries, late-night movies, and anything involving Sid Caesar and Imogene Coca." As the comedian Shelley Berman later argued, by choosing an intense and sophisticated introspection over blandness and superficiality, Caesar (and Jackie Gleason) advanced comedy during a perilous time. "In a world in which comedians were not talking, these guys were *feeling*," Berman wrote. "And they let us feel inside of ourselves."

For a comedy writer, winning a job with Caesar was like a coronation. "I was on the most important and popular television show," remembered Lucille Kallen, among the rare women in the fraternity. "Television itself was new. I was new. The world was new." "Except for the fact that we were all white and Jewish, we felt like we were in Duke Ellington's band," said Gelbart. With Gleason, you'd slip your jokes under the door and get them back the same way. But Caesar was always with his writers, rather than, as he once put it, upstairs hitting golf balls. "There was something more than just talent, some gift that Sid possessed that obeyed none of the rules and regulations I'd learned at Yale," said Mike Stewart, whose job it was on *Caesar's Hour* to nab the shards of brilliance flying around the writers' room and get them down on paper. Caesar's writers considered themselves not merely a cut above writers for Gleason or Steve Allen and everyone else but, as Brooks put it, "in a different ballpark, completely." They not only brought out the best in one another, but, though their respective contributions are hard to trace, elicited better work from at least some of them than anything they subsequently did on their own; not *always* is it good to be the king. But the job, pressure packed and competitive, was hardly the wisecracking frolic of revisionist lore. "Absolutely the happiest and worst time of my life" was how Caesar's longtime (and long-suffering) head writer, Mel Tolkin, recalled the experience.

As intensely as he worked with his colleagues, Caesar remained an enigma to them. "We used to sit around and talk about what makes Caesar tick, talk about that more than anything else," Reiner recalled. "I don't think anybody ever really figured him out." Because he was so inscrutable, he was easily underestimated. "His knowledge and intuition could surprise you," Reiner said; at any given moment, "he could be twice as smart as you." While onstage, Coca felt a spooky kind of telepathy with Caesar; offstage the two barely spoke. On a train ride to Washington together to perform at Dwight Eisenhower's first inauguration, "We rode for eight hours, and I didn't even say hello to her," Caesar recalled in a joint interview with Coca. "Just stood there like that, for eight hours. Right next to her." "And it seemed perfectly natural," Coca chimed in. But as oblivious as Caesar could be, and as frustrating and infuriating, he was also inspiring. If he'd created anything of value in his career, Morris said late in his life, he had Caesar to thank for it, "because he had the nerve to break the rules."

Reporters attempting to "get" Caesar didn't have it any easier. One newspaper devoted six separate installments to plumbing his psyche. *TV Guide* tried more than once. "Zany, frustrated, unhappy, tragic," it called him one time, and "shy, introverted, extravagant and often inarticulate," another. Long before people even acknowledged their psychoanalysis, Caesar described his incessantly.

Even Caesar couldn't quite believe what he was pulling off.

Nor could he believe it would last: Some otherworldly force had given him a great gift, and it could just as easily, and capriciously, take it away. "I seemed to be waiting for the evil eye or some mystic power to come down and say, 'He's got too much happiness, now let's give him a little misery,'" he recalled. Whenever someone complimented him after a show, he'd cringe. "Shhh . . . don't say that; luck might hear you," he'd plead. One night, eavesdropping outside Caesar's dressing room, Neil Simon heard Caesar castigate the man staring back at him in the mirror. "Go!" Caesar told himself. "Go make a fool of yourself in front of America!" He felt bad for him, Simon said, but two minutes later he was on the floor, laughing at his antics. Among his fellow comics, it became a kind of macabre sport, an amalgam of wonder, envy, and schadenfreude, to guess how long Caesar could last before he either cracked up or burned out.

As television's reach expanded, the television audience changed and, at least in Caesar's world, coarsened. "As the price of sets went down so did the IQ of the watchers," Gelbart once said. It was the bandleader and accordionist Lawrence Welk whose program knocked Caesar off the air (and not, as Reiner joked, because "he was funnier than Sid"). When Caesar fell, television lost its innocence; only then did people realize it was governed by the same laws, human and economic, as everything else. "These people would have much rather seen bubbles coming out of Lawrence Welk's ass than Sid Caesar doing a takeoff on *Rashomon*,"* said Gelbart. But "if your time slot's not paying the rent, it doesn't matter how gifted you are. They would have canceled Michelangelo if no one came to the Sistine Chapel."

But even without Welk, Caesar was running out of gas. "Nobody's talent was ever more used up than Sid's," said Brooks. "I don't say that it wasn't used well. But over a period of years, television ground him into sausages—one sausage a week—until, finally, there was little of the muse left." Early on, when television remained an iffy proposition and Caesar weighed whether to go on it at all, Brooks warned him that the tube violated the

* The 1950 film directed by Akira Kurosawa.

Second Commandment, the one against worshipping graven images: TV, Brooks cautioned, might rob Caesar of his face. "It sounded funny then, but ultimately that's pretty much what happened," Brooks later observed. "It hurt more to fall from that high," said Reiner. "He was king of the world. My God, his name was Caesar."

ONE NIGHT IN DECEMBER 2000, I found myself in the Grand Ballroom of the Pierre in New York, a short walk from where the theaters from which Caesar's shows had originated had once stood. Caesar had always been too busy, or anxious, or superstitious, or incredulous, or impaired, to savor his success. But now, in his late seventies, he finally could. The most prestigious prizes, like the Kennedy Center Honors, had eluded him. But on this night he was the third recipient of something called the Alan King Award in American Jewish Humor, named for the famous stand-up comic and handed out by the National Foundation for Jewish Culture.

Like most people my age (I was born in 1952), I had seen and knew very little about Caesar. Built around sketches of irregular lengths, and poorly preserved on primitive kinescopes (films made off television monitors), his shows had never enjoyed the eternal life of filmed sitcoms like *I Love Lucy* or *The Honeymooners*. Clueless about their historical significance, NBC had discarded its own set of Caesar's shows; the few remaining sets moldered on wagon wheels of deteriorating stock in a couple of closets, a fire or flood away from obliteration. From his home north of Sunset Boulevard (his friends regularly compared him to Norma Desmond, the aged and embittered star in the film), Caesar tried cutting and pasting his old shows into chunks suitable for syndication, only to watch them get relegated to the wee hours on triple-digit channels.

Even those who remembered Caesar might have found this particular prize—and specifically the "Jewish Humor" part of it—puzzling. True, Jews had always constituted a disproportionate share of Caesar's audience. ("Gentlemen, gentlemen, we've got to get something done!" Tolkin would implore his writers as they put together their next show. "Jews all over America will be watching!")

But nothing on Caesar's shows had been explicitly Jewish. Like so many of his generation, Caesar and his peers, most of them the children of Jewish immigrants, were simultaneously infused with and confused by their Jewishness—among themselves proud of (and even chauvinistic about) it, while publicly reluctant even to acknowledge it, let alone to attribute anything good about themselves or their work to it. In their minds, the worst thing they could do would be to admit they were different from everyone else (even if, on some level, it was something all of them believed), lest they appear parochial or play into anti-Semitic stereotypes or seem like anything less than full-fledged, unhyphenated *Americans.*

Never was the word "Jew" or anything even close to it uttered on any of Caesar's shows. Almost reflexively, and for years afterward, the people who created them would insist their humor was "New York" rather than "Jewish." Christmas and Easter were always enthusiastically observed on Caesar's shows, and Jewish holidays ignored. Yiddish words were almost totally verboten, surfacing only in the takeoffs on Japanese movies. (Words like *schmatta** and *chazerai*[†] sounded oddly apt coming from Japanese princes.) A trace of *Yiddishkeit*—what the critic and cultural historian Irving Howe called a "wave to the folks back home"—could occasionally be discerned, but never anything blatant; Brooks's 2000 Year Old Man, né the 2000 Year Old Jew, had been born in Caesar's writers' room but until recorded many years later was let out only for what Reiner called "Jews and our non-anti-Semitic Christian friends." Along with the crumpled paper cups by the watercooler, at day's end all the Jewish jokes, or Jewish anything, were swept up and thrown away. Apart from declaring their own independence, Caesar and his writers were also in search of laughs. "We wanted more universal humor," Brooks explained. "We wanted people in Cincinnati to laugh."

---

* Rag; also slang for garments.
† Junk, trash, bad food.

Yet in multiple ways, Caesar's humor *was* Jewish, and Jews read it as such. "I always, *always* used to look forward to Saturday night," Larry Gelbart said in the video tribute he'd sent in for the award ceremony. "To me, *Your Show of Shows* was the cherry on top of Shabbos." Its point of view—literate, detached, irreverent, skeptical of conventional wisdom, conceit, certitude, or authority of any kind, and faith in the fairness of the universe—was Jewish. In it, the privileged and stuck-up always look ridiculous, snobs get theirs, the cocksure are shaken, phonies are unmasked, the overly ambitious and pretentious ridiculed. There is resentment toward the Establishment and sympathy for the underdog, whether it's a baby or a housefly or a much-abused gumball machine in a sub-way station. The humor was Jewish in its worldliness, featuring Caesar's double-talk in fake French, German, Italian, Russian, and Arabic, and foreign movie spoofs. It was Jewish in what the cartoonist Jules Feiffer called "the smartness of it, the smartass-ery of it," the same ethos that led a different group of young Jews to create *Mad* magazine around the same time and only a few blocks away. And Jewish in the New York–ness of it, some-times explicit—Professor von Snowcap's expedition to Mount Everest nearly ran aground in traffic at Twenty-Third Street and Broadway—but more often implied.

It was Jewish in its obsession, born of privation, with food in all its forms and stages: craving it, getting it, *not* getting it, getting enough of it, or enough of the right kind of it, or too much of the wrong kind of it, or getting it too slowly, or getting less of it than the other guy, or savoring familiar forms of it, or struggling with new and unfamiliar forms of it, or gorging on it, or digesting it, or not digesting it, or savoring it as it went down, or paying the price for it once it landed.

Coming at a time when the Jewish place in America remained precarious, it was Jewish in its caution, instinctively avoiding anything topical, political, off-color, risky, or risqué. For all of Caesar's apparent strength—he was comedy's version of the baseball star Hank Greenberg, or, as the writer Albert Goldman called him, "the model of the handsome young Jewish *shtarker,*[*]

---

[*] An extremely tough guy.

the kind of big strong boys the Yids had turned out in *Amerike*"—
Caesar, as Reiner put it, "was very afraid to offend *goyim*."* "He
would be very elegant when *goyim* would come into the room,"
Reiner said once with uncharacteristic candor, for on this subject
he, too, trod carefully, even after achieving great eminence of his
own. "Not *elegant*, but polite and nice. It permeated a lot of his
behavior. Wild-eyed comedy, fine. . . . But he was very aware that
he was Jewish and that 'they' were 'better.' I think we all felt that:
that 'they' are better than us; 'they' own the property and we're
just renting." The Holocaust and the Red Scare of the 1950s,
both of which had touched several people in Caesar's circle, were
two more reasons to lie low.

Finally, their humor was Jewish in its very strenuous insistence that it wasn't. When it was acknowledged at all, it was done
so hesitatingly, begrudgingly. Lucille Kallen tied herself all in
knots when asked once what distinguished *Your Show of Shows*
from *I Love Lucy*. "Smarter," she said. "More talent. A different kind of talent. I mean, *Show of Shows* was basically . . . basically . . . *Jewish*."

Still, Caesar's shows were the product of an extraordinary
time and place in Jewish history—New York City in the years
immediately after World War II, when Jews were both still
excluded from the American mainstream in some, but numer-
ous enough, ways and free enough to come together and create as they had never done anywhere else before and, with the
European wellspring from which they'd come no longer around
to replenish their ranks, never would again. The Jews themselves
wouldn't have dared to note their impact on the New York of
Caesar's heyday, but others could. "No one can estimate what the
Jews have contributed to New York," Brooks Atkinson, the eminent drama critic of *The New York Times*, wrote just as *Your Show
of Shows* hit its stride. "They have enriched the life of New York;
they have kept it alert, broadminded, flexible, and hospitable
to ideas. New York would quickly lose its drive, its spontaneity,
and its cosmopolitan flair if the Jews were not every day pouring

---

* Non-Jews.

warmth and vitality into it." At Caesar's creative peak, two of his three co-stars and all seven of his writers were Jews—"very, very gifted, neurotic young Jews, punching our brains out," as Gelbart put it. Their individual genius only intensified as they struggled to top, or even to wipe out, one another. As in Los Alamos a few years earlier, Caesar's team reflected what liberated, brilliant Jews could accomplish together, only *their* Manhattan Project was actually in Manhattan.

GETTING THE EVENING UNDER way, Alan King, who'd once called Caesar "probably the greatest comic talent we've ever had," read something Woody Allen had just told *The New York Times:* that working with Caesar had been one of his proudest credits, and that Caesar continued to influence his work. King then ticked off the Jewish greats in the arts: Jolson and Cantor, Gershwin and Berlin, Horowitz and Bernstein. "In this pantheon, this bearded old Jew is right up there with the gods," he said, pointing to Caesar. "*Really.*"

It was that "really" of King's that really said it all. To anyone younger than fifty in the room that night, it was hard to imagine that the shrunken man with a white goatee before them had ever been funny; Mel Brooks, whom Caesar had discovered living "underneath a hovel" in Greenwich Village, was the evening's real star. It was a role that under normal circumstances Brooks would have taken over. But whatever modesty, generosity, and gratitude resided in Brooks, Caesar was uniquely able to summon. Brooks had come tonight, he explained, "not to bury Caesar, but to praise him and to love him." And to present the award. Whatever he'd written for Caesar, Caesar had made so much better, which was why "I fell madly in love with this guy," he said. Then he invited him up on the stage.

Haltingly, Caesar made his way up. His very name had long inspired endless puns on grandeur and power, ego and empire; now it connoted decline and fall—ancient ruins, even. When Caesar finally arrived, the two embraced. Brooks kissed him, then placed a medal around his neck, then yielded the stage; this was not *his* night. Caesar then reached into his blazer and removed a small, rectangular piece of paper, containing four columns of names: French ones (for example, Pasteur, Madame Curie, Maurice Chevalier), German (Max Planck, Lili Marlene), Italian (Michelangelo, Mamma Leone), and Japanese (Hitachi, Toyota). When he'd been in charge, he'd banned cue cards: If you read from them, you couldn't look your fellow performer in the eye. But nowadays, he needed cues.

"Bonjour, Mesdames et Monsieurs," Caesar suddenly said, in what sounded like pitch-perfect French. And instantly, the anxiety in the room gave way to relief and laughter. Doing his double-talk, Caesar was Caesar once again. As he moved on, speaking his fluent gibberish in one language after another, the audience hooted and cheered. But when, having wrapped up his shtick, Caesar had to play Caesar again, and offered some lame comments on the Middle East, no one laughed. Suddenly, awkwardly, the evening was over. And I wondered, What had made this man so titanic a figure? What accounted for the affection, and gratitude, that people still felt for him? And what had happened to him? How had he gone from "This Is Your Story" to *this*?

CHAPTER I

ORIGINS

The Navajo begin measuring a lifetime from a child's first laugh. If, within the tribe of comedians, the clock started when someone gets his first laugh, Sid Caesar could be quite precise about when and where his own life began.

It was in 1933, and he was ten or eleven at the time. He was onstage at Nathaniel Hawthorne Junior High School in Yonkers, New York, poised to play Saint-Saëns's "Swan" on his saxophone. He'd been blinded momentarily when the spotlight fell on his music stand, so he moved it—and the audience laughed. When the spotlight followed him, he moved it again—and there were more laughs. He kept doing it, and every time he did, the laughs got louder. "It was the first time I felt people laughing, and I could *make* them laugh," he remembered. Laughter and a sense of control—in his young life, both had been in short supply.

Caesar hadn't begun talking until he was three. That words came so begrudgingly to him made him devise alternative means of communicating: facial expressions, gestures, sounds, silence. From the start, he was different: He seemed impaired. "I used to worry about his future," one of his teachers later recalled. If he really applied himself, she thought, maybe he could be a truck driver. "We used to call him Silent Sidney," recalled a machinist who'd rented one of the rooms upstairs from the restaurant Caesar's father ran. "He wouldn't even say good morning. He would just look right past you." In grade school he'd been consigned to an "opportunity class" for impaired children. "Hey, Dopey!" his classmates would shout at him.

At the height of his fame, journalists trying to decipher Caesar invariably returned to his childhood, with Caesar gladly escorting them through it. "Caesar himself feels that he was driven into comedy by a desire to express in some other character feelings he could not otherwise safely reveal," a profile in *Redbook* concluded. "I grew up angry," he told the magazine. "I kept quiet because I didn't know what might happen if I let loose." His father, Max, had come from Poland as a boy; his mother, Ida, arrived from Odesa when she was a baby. Later, everyone—including Caesar's family—assumed his perfect, and perfectly pronounceable, surname had been made up, cleaned up, shortened from something else, or conferred upon them at Castle Garden. In fact, steerage records show that when Caesar's paternal grandmother pulled into New York Harbor in 1881, the family name was Ziser—pronounced ZEE-sir. (In Yiddish it means "sweet person.") Only the spelling was changed.

Born on September 8, 1922, Sidney was the couple's fourth and final son, fifteen and ten years younger than his brothers Abe and Dave. (Another brother had died in childhood.) "I was what they called a 'makeup child,'" Caesar later wrote, "meaning, I assume, that they were mad at each other for a long time, then made up, and I was the result." Caesar's mother, who was considerably taller than her husband, bequeathed her height to her sons. She was the more tenderhearted of his parents, the one who would sing to him in Yiddish and feed him oatmeal. He grew up in exile from exile, not in Jewish Brooklyn or the Bronx or the Lower East Side, places where Jews could delude themselves into thinking they were the center of the universe, but twenty miles or so away in largely industrial, polyglot Yonkers.

With his parents struggling to make a living at the luncheonette and rooming house they ran, he got little attention from either, and learned to steer clear. "The first lesson I learned at my mother's knee was to stay out of the way of her flying feet—or I'd get a belt from my father's hand," he recalled. His parents packed him off to school at age four—to get him out of their way, he said. Around that time, Sid later remembered, his father put him on a train with a sign saying, ASBURY PARK—the New Jersey town where his maternal grandparents lived, and to which his mother had stalked off during her latest marital spat—around his neck. He arrived just in time to spot her on the New York–bound train pulling out across the platform. "If my mother and father had beaten me with baseball bats, they couldn't have hurt me half as much," he recalled. Caesar withdrew into his own world, always awkward with others; "he didn't develop those social skills that most people have," Carl Reiner later said. But with distance came a knack for scrutinizing and mimicking other people.

Nor did he get much companionship from his brothers, who also worked in the family business. "It was like being in solitary at Sing Sing," Caesar said of his life at home. The middle brother, Dave, was more of a father to him than his father was, though sometimes Dave could be sadistic, tying a rope to Sid's baby carriage, then letting it careen down the steep street by their house, only to yank it back at the brink. It left Caesar with a lifelong feeling of vulnerability: What if, suddenly, no one's hands were on the rope? School, too, was a problem. Caesar was outnumbered by children from other places who didn't cotton to his kind, and there were so many fights, and bloody noses, that his parents had him transferred.

In such a world, movies at RKO Proctor's in Yonkers, to which Dave would take him on Fridays and Saturdays, became a blessed refuge. Sid preferred the films of Charlie Chaplin, Buster Keaton, and Laurel and Hardy, comedy that told a story or, really, *two* stories, one that tickled and another that touched, to the slapstick and pie throwing most kids liked. "Working both sides of the street," Caesar called it. Much to his father's annoyance, he'd pass entire days watching and absorbing such films.

Coming of age in a melting pot rather than in a reconstituted shtetl accounted for one of Caesar's greatest comic gifts. The St. Clair Lunch, the one-armed joint his father ran, did more than teach Caesar the pleasures of authentic, abundant grub. It catered to laborers, many foreign-born, employed by the nearby elevator or hat or sugar factories. Busing their tables, Caesar couldn't understand whatever language they spoke—German, Italian, Hungarian, French, among others—but in fifteen minutes or so he absorbed its sounds and sensibilities; every language, he liked to say, "has its own song." For authenticity's sake, it helped to sprinkle a genuine word into his gibberish occasionally, though a few were more than enough. "I knew '*poulet*' was chicken. That's about it," he once said of his double-talk "French."

"It's a gift, or he's a little crazy," Neil Simon once said of Caesar's strange knack; like the sound effects (mostly of machines) he also mastered, "double-talk" was a means of communicating beyond conventional speech. Albert Goldman likened Caesar to a stammerer: Because he was frustrated by his inability to express himself, there'd be "this tremendous pressure building up behind this verbal nozzle," and out would come "some mad dislocation of language." That same discomfort with words also led Caesar to mimic gestures, which attracted him to the dying art of pantomime. And to music. And, for that matter, to television, which both gave him a mighty audience and walled him off from everyone except those in the theater. Double-talk outlasted all the other devices, handing Caesar an escape hatch—a *life raft*—until the very end of his life.

Two languages Caesar rarely "spoke" as a comedian were the two he actually did speak, at least a little: Hebrew, which he picked up in the synagogue and in Hebrew school, and Yiddish, which he heard at home. "I don't want to make fun of my own," he once told the *Forverts*. But he hated the coercive, rote, and alienating routines of Hebrew education; while everyone else practiced writing Hebrew letters, he made grotesque doodles of Frankenstein's monster. "Is that nice, for a Jewish boy to draw always monsters?" the rabbi would complain. Furtive quests for World Series scores were as much a staple of Caesar's High Holidays as prayer. Like so many Jews of his generation, his Jewishness mattered most to him only when non-Jews made something out of it. Jewish culture and traditions—day trips to the Lower East Side, eating at restaurants like Ratner's and Dubiner's, and *shvitzing** with his father at the Eighth Street baths—were far more appealing. Surviving on the steamy top shelf in the baths marked his passage to manhood more meaningfully to him than his bar mitzvah. (It was thanks to an attendant there that Caesar added Russian to his portfolio of double-talk.)

In public school Caesar loved history and science, especially astronomy and physics, with Albert Einstein becoming a personal hero. But he kept his enthusiasms, and aptitude, to himself. "He showed no marked ability in any subject," recalled one of his teachers, who saw him ending up as a counterman at the St. Clair Lunch. Like many lonely children, Caesar loved animals and was sensitive to any cruelty to them; his mother recalled how frequently he brought home strays, once climbing to the top of a tall tree to rescue a cat.

When Caesar was nine or so, a deadbeat boarder in one of the rooms upstairs from the luncheonette left behind a fine Selmer Super Cigar Cutter tenor saxophone. When no one claimed it, Max Caesar gave it to Sidney, who began taking lessons at the nearby Hebrew National Orphan Home. It quickly proved to be the perfect vehicle for his abilities and frustrations; he played it incessantly and passionately. Luckily for him, Caesar later said, that boarder hadn't left behind a shotgun.

Crushed by the Depression, Caesar's father had to sell the restaurant, creating in his youngest son a lifelong belief that success of any kind was freakish and fragile. (He'd then opened Caesar's Smoke and Trick Shop, a candy store that doubled as a bookie joint. Both of Caesar's older brothers worked there; each was arrested at least once for bookmaking.) Music offered Sidney a way out. While still in junior high he joined a dance band; soon he was playing all over town, then all over Westchester County, then all over "the Mountains," the Jewish resorts in the Catskills. As one Yiddish paper put it, his parents considered his making music preferable to a life spent serving drunks at the restaurant. He was serious about his music. "While the rest of us were hors-

---

* Sweating.

ing around, Sid would be practicing," a bandmate recalled. "If he hit a sour note, he'd smack his fist hard against the wall." Caesar got good enough to join orchestras led by Charlie Spivak, Claude Thornhill, and Shep Fields. He even played briefly with his first musical idol, Benny Goodman. Classical music also intrigued him, especially after hearing Marcel Mule play a concerto for alto saxophone by Jacques Ibert. He studied with a member of the NBC Symphony and crashed classes at Juilliard.

It was in the Mountains—specifically at Vacationland in Swan Lake, New York—where Caesar branched into comedy. He'd study comics performing there, picking up tools of the trade like rhythm, timing, discipline, and improvisation. The hotel's social director, a playwright and actor named Don Appel, spotted something funny in him: With his stage whispers and mugging, he had his bandmates "in stitches" during rehearsals. Though he literally needed a good shove to go out on the stage the first time, Caesar was soon doing comedy regularly, earning an extra $4 a week for routines of his own devising, built around his observational skills, mimicry, sound effects, and imagination, like conjuring up the inner thoughts of a pinball machine. People clamored to see him, though grown-up Jews, he quickly discovered, were tough taskmasters. "These people didn't laugh easy," Caesar recalled.

When Appel decamped to other resorts, like the Avon Lodge in Woodridge, Caesar followed him. Caesar had once been engaged to Appel's niece, until her family put its foot down. ("A sax player in the family?" her mother complained. "Who needs it?") At the Avon Lodge in the summer of 1942, Caesar met, and fell in love with, Florence Levy, whose uncle owned the place. She was beautiful and then some—"like a showgirl out of the Copacabana," someone later remembered. Both were nineteen. Florence attended Hunter College in Manhattan, and was far more worldly and political than he. "I couldn't think of anything intelligent to talk to her about, so I didn't say anything" was how he remembered their first date. "I just took her for a walk." "He was a tall, quiet fellow with an anxious, wistful look on his face and his eyes a million miles away," Florence recalled.

Sid quickly knew she was the one; Florence wasn't nearly so sure. But Caesar was persistent, and serious about broadening his horizons; on his own, he'd studied Bach and Stravinsky, and read John Steinbeck and Clifford Odets. A year later, in July 1943, the two were married at Moskowitz & Lupowitz, the venerable Lower East Side restaurant where, it boasted, "the finest Jews come to eat."

In some versions of Mel Brooks's recollections, it was also at the Avon Lodge—again, through Appel, whom Brooks knew from Williamsburg, Brooklyn—that he first met Caesar. "Sid was the Apollo of the Mountains, the best-looking guy since silent movies," said Brooks in one account. "He would stretch himself out on a rock near the lake and we'd all stand and look at him." Far more likely, they met several years later, in New York. When the weather turned cold, Caesar worked at the Capitol Theatre just north of Times Square, first as an usher, then as a doorman. To warm him up on wintry nights, his mother brought him hot noodle soup in a thermos all the way from Yonkers.

With the United States already at war, Caesar soon enlisted in the Coast Guard and was sent to Brooklyn, where he spent a year guarding the docks and delousing German POWs. At the urging of the composer Vernon Duke ("Autumn in New York," "I Can't Get Started"), who was then a Coast Guard lieutenant, Caesar put together shows on the base. In one, he played both halves of a conversation between Hitler and Donald Duck; in another, he played an English commander, an American pilot, and the planes themselves. "The war was great for me," Caesar later said. "I found myself." Soon he was cast in a service revue called *Tars and Spars*, which Duke had written with the lyricist and librettist Howard Dietz. Directing the show, which would open in Palm Beach and then tour the country, would be Max Liebman. Everyone in the Borscht Belt, Caesar included, knew of Liebman: He was the Ziegfeld of the Poconos, the "social director" of Camp Tamiment since 1933. More than anyone else, Max Liebman made Sid Caesar Sid Caesar.

.   .   .

ON THE ITINERARY OF stops in American comedic, and Jewish, cultural history, Tamiment, nestled in the hills midway between New York and Philadelphia, is now largely forgotten, with nearly every physical trace of it erased. But for the decades flanking World War II, Tamiment was an important stop on the cultural road map, a place where legions of aspiring writers, actors, singers, dancers, musicians, stagehands, and directors gathered every summer to hone their crafts and where waves of intellectually curious and artistically ambitious young people, most of them Jewish, eager to escape the heat of city summers and the parochialism of their greenhorn parents (yet still too poor to travel very far from home), would come for a week or two to take in the shows, and the country air, and, maybe, one another.

Alongside the glitzier resorts of the Catskills, Tamiment was positively spartan: It lacked the highest hills, the steepest waterfalls, the tastiest food (and the largest portions), the fanciest facilities, or the gaudiest entertainers. Its roots lay in progressive activism rather than allrightnik hedonism, though by the late 1930s its mission had become more cultural than political, with a ferocious singles scene (depicted by the novelist Herman Wouk, a Tamiment alum himself, in *Marjorie Morningstar*, where he called the place "South Wind." Marjorie's mother calls it "Sodom").

When it came to the entertainment, the clientele was discriminating, or, as the Viennese-born Liebman put it, was "wised up and intelligent and far from a pushover"; lodgers "would forgive bad service, but not a bad show." "Emergency theater," he called his hastily assembled but impeccably crafted weekly productions. Liebman was barely five feet tall and unprepossessing, with sad eyes, "bird-like hands and feet," and a hairpiece often described as the world's worst. "The theater at Tamiment is all business," Liebman declared in 1941.[*] "It has Broadway standards and a unique method of operation—no socializing, mixing, or life-of-the-party stuff. . . . The demands are tough, the attitudes hardboiled and the sweat runs freely." Never, he liked to say, would he settle for the usual "drool."

* In an article he wrote with Sylvia Fine (later Mrs. Danny Kaye).

Liebman's weekly revues featured comedy, song and dance, solo performances, and sketches, all meticulously ordered. Anything corny was canned; marital infidelity was a more likely theme than boy meets girl, though only rarely was anything too blue. When the curtain came down on one show, planning began for the next. The shows could be recycled (most guests could afford to stay only a week or two) but had to be good, to entice people back. No other summer resort spawned so many famous alumni, including Danny Kaye, Jerome Robbins, and Carol Channing. "He was the oracle," said Channing. "If he approved, you were in show business."

Despite the demographics, Liebman steered clear of the easy, stereotypical Jewish stuff. His goal, as he described it, was "to banish forever the conception that a summer resort entertainment features a pair of idiots sitting in a lake of sour cream, throwing herrings at one another." The old standbys—the Jewish mother saying, "You're going out with a *shiksa*? That's OK with me. All I can do is stick my head in the oven and kill myself . . . don't worry about me"—were spurned. Jewish material still abounded, but of a more subtle and sophisticated cast.

A representative musical number called "I Play Hamlet in the Catskills" neatly captured American Jewish culture as it marched—appreciatively and affectionately but resolutely—from one sensibility (old-world, parochial, religious) to another (hipper and more secular). The performers were "Howard" (supposedly as in Leslie), "Gielgud" (as in John), and Epstein (as in Epstein).

HOWARD: *I play Hamlet where the tropic sun is glaring;*
GIELGUD: *I play Hamlet in the North, where men are daring;*
EPSTEIN: *And I play it where they live on pickled herring,*
   'cause I play Hamlet in the Catskills.

GIELGUD: *I am one the critics will never admonish;*
HOWARD: *My diction is so clear that I astonish;*
EPSTEIN: *And mine is just a bit Galitzianish,**
   'cause I play Hamlet in the Catskills.

---

* The dialect of Jews in southern Poland and northwest Ukraine.

There were also numbers about the burgeoning leisure pastimes of Jews:

> *Sadie Salowitz likes to play bridge;*
> *Rosie Rosen gives teas;*
> *Beckie Beckowitz goes in for golf;*
> *Pearl has a Pekingese;*
> *Mollie Maltz goes to Carnegie Hall;*
> *Sally Schmaltz likes to sing;*
> *Gertie Gillis likes traveling a lot,*
> *She's crazy for Paris in Spring.*

And when war was brewing in Europe, fascism was on the march, and the New Deal under fire, sketches were steeped in the progressive politics appealing to Jews. Whether it was anti-Semites, demagogues, appeasers, or garden-variety reactionaries in general (or Father Charles Coughlin, Huey Long, William Randolph Hearst, Neville Chamberlain, or Joseph Goebbels in particular), everyone recognized the targets and relished the barbs. From one representative song:

> *Now Adolf and Benito*
> *Are really lovely boys*
> *What if they and Hirohito*
> *Are partial to the Goys?*

There was also a "Yiddish Mikado," set in a Hasidic town in Japan. "I didn't understand a word anybody was saying but I have never laughed so much in my life," remembered Imogene Coca, who had come to Tamiment in the late 1930s. (To conform to local norms, Gentiles performing there had to learn some Yiddish: In one sketch, in which a man was threatening to stab himself, Coca had had to shout, "Neyn! Neyn! Dos iz der putermeser!" ("No! No! That's the butter knife!")

Born in 1908 to a bandleader in Philadelphia and a dancer, the tiny, rubber-faced Coca was already a veteran vaudevillian when she reached Tamiment, someone who could sing, dance, act, and mug. Somehow, she exuded innocence and impishness, vulnerability and grit: She was at once irrepressible and shop-worn. She'd been in Liebman's troupe when he brought his show, retitled *The Straw Hat Revue,* from Tamiment to Broadway in September 1939, attracting notice of a sort she hadn't had before. "Miss Imogene Coca is a young lady with the face of a junior gargoyle, the shape of a suspender strap and a name so appropriate that if a national contest were held to find a name for Imogene Coca, the name Imogene Coca would win," declared *Collier's.* The show itself got mixed notices, but proved that if sufficiently bowdlerized, depoliticized, and de-Judaized, a Liebman show could appeal to a wider and more diverse audience.

LIKE JUST ABOUT EVERYONE in his generation, Liebman never forgot his first glimpse of television. It happened one day in 1939 on Broadway and Ninth Street, in the New York branch of John Wanamaker, the famed Philadelphia department store, where he spotted a crowd gathered around a small box with a flickering screen. While everyone else there saw the future, he saw *his* future: He'd been doing television, only without the cameras, all his life.

But there was a war to fight first. Liebman's contribution to Fortress America was to become a civilian director and sketch writer for the USO and Coast Guard. That was why Vernon Duke had asked him to go to Florida to work on the embryonic *Tars and Spars,* in which the young Sid Caesar was to appear. When the assembled cast auditioned for Liebman that night, Caesar stood out, clearly gifted but needing work. "He made a lot of sounds, did a lot of things, but it was formless," Liebman recalled. No one else could have cooked up or pulled off as incredible a display of raw, unhinged energy and talent as his reenactment of an aerial dogfight, for instance, but it needed to be shaped and made more consistent from one performance to another. So Liebman took it apart, then put it back together, then got it down on paper. For Caesar this was something new: He had never had to follow a script, nor do anything the same way twice. Repetition bored him. He burst into tears at Liebman's commands. Caesar was a kinetic, anxious performer, often throwing up before going onstage; he didn't know if he could follow Liebman's formula, or if he even wanted to.

For his part, Liebman realized that Caesar wasn't your classic stand-up comedian, not that he aspired to be one; if a straight joke was any good, anyone could do it, he figured, so why should he? "He had to distill his material through his own sieve," Liebman said. "No matter how it went in, it had to come out Caesar." But Caesar was "on fire with talent," a great mimic, great actor, great *re*actor. Many likened him to Liebman's other great discovery, Danny Kaye, but to Liebman, Caesar had an emotional depth, sincerity, and originality Kaye lacked. Liebman hadn't a clue where that technique of his had come from. Caesar couldn't come up with all of his material—he needed "writers on writers on writers"—but would then "Caesarize" whatever they fed him. Liebman knew to keep his touch light; while he could dismantle and reassemble his routines, to do more than tinker with such a talent would be vandalism. Rather than remake Caesar, Liebman refined and domesticated him.

From opening night in Palm Beach in March 1944, when Caesar's aviation routine (now called "Wings over Bombinschissel") brought what the *Miami News* called "tears of laughter to the eyes of even the most blasé playgoer," to Portland, Oregon, where the national tour closed ten months later, Caesar—rather than the show's headliner, Victor Mature—was the star of *Tars and Spars*. "Complete newcomer, but surefire pro postwar," *Variety* wrote after catching him in New York. Caesar saw his future. "I smoked a twenty-five-cent cigar, and thought for the first time in my life, Hell, maybe there's something to this kidding around—maybe I can make it pay me a few bucks," he recalled. Liebman left the tour early, but buttonholed Caesar on his way out. "After the war, I want you to come see me," he said.

Life on the road wasn't all standing ovations. Performing six times a day for a week, week after week, was debilitating. "I was building up to my first mental breakdown," Caesar remembered. One morning in Buffalo, with only a handful of people in the audience, Caesar slashed the aviation sketch in half. His furious superior officer—Caesar *was* still in the service—ordered him to go back out onstage and do it right. Instead, Caesar picked up and heaved a fifty-pound bag of sand at him, barely missing his head. He was hauled off to the hospital, where he was given a shot to calm him down and then examined by a psychiatrist. He could have been court-martialed.

Caesar was in bed the next morning when two marines entered, deep in conversation. "All they were talking about was Jews, Hebes, kikes, sheenies—and how yellow they were," Caesar was to write. Never had he heard such anti-Semitism. The men then inspected the chart hanging from the bedpost, which identified Caesar's religion. "I *told* you this one was a yellow Jew," one said to the other. Caesar went off again, this time smashing a glass water pitcher and, while one of the men fled, holding the jagged edge against the neck of the other. "Now, how yellow are these Jews?" he asked him. Sympathetic higher-ups in the Coast Guard who'd seen Caesar perform got him off the hook, and after ten days in the hospital and another ten at home he rejoined the tour. Only now, Florence was with him.

Once the road show ended, Caesar huddled with Liebman on Columbia's film version of the show. It would star Alfred Drake and the actress and singer Janet Blair, with Caesar playing Drake's loyal, fast-talking, New York wise-guy pal. "Cute, tall, and blond, terribly shy, and green as grass" was how Blair found him. To make the film, Caesar paid his first visit to Hollywood. ("All I could do was stand and gape at the low buildings," he joked.) He was paid $1,000, which he took in $1 bills, which he and Florence scattered like confetti in their bungalow. The buzz on the film—actually, the buzz on *him*—was enormous. The head of Columbia, Harry Cohn, had been poised to cut out the airplane sketch altogether until everyone started asking him about the fabulous blond sailor who performed it.

Tars and Spars opened in early 1946. Unlike the sappy romance at its core, Caesar's solo cadenzas—another was a paean to mess hall scrambled eggs—were thunderbolts. His newly refined airplane number now lasted eight frenzied minutes, with

Caesar playing the stuffy, unintelligible British colonel, the various members of the squadron, two flying aces, American planes (they sounded nice, like buzzing bees, and smiled as they went in for the kill) and German ones (whose engines ranted like Hitler in the Reichstag), the blazing guns, the Messerschmitts getting pulverized, the bombs falling.

To *Time*, Caesar was a "likable blond zany," while the famed gossip columnist Hedda Hopper called him a "four-way threat": "He writes, sings, dances and makes with the comedy." "Sid Caesar is the boy to keep your eye on," advised Jack Gaver of United Press. "One, two years from now you'll be bragging that you tagged him for a comer." In London, Kenneth Tynan wrote of "a young blond boy called Sid Caesar who out–Danny Kaye's Danny in a delirious burlesque of any aviation film," adding, "I go to the West End cinema every night this week at 8 p.m. to see this delicious monologue again." But some spotted possible perils. "Sid Caesar, funny the first time he does his routine, wears thin after the third or fourth," wrote one. Another called him "as exhausting to watch as he is funny." But that's not what the young men who, unbeknownst to them, would soon work for Caesar were thinking. "Like the first time you see the girl that you fall in love with for the rest of your life," recalled Neil Simon, who watched *Tars and Spars* on an army base in Biloxi, Mississippi. Carl Reiner beheld someone "whose mouth moved like nobody's mouth in the whole world." "Extra-planetary—he was just so gifted," Larry Gelbart recalled.

When the film played in midtown Manhattan, Caesar's father, dying of cancer, was too ill to go. So Caesar arranged for a screening at a movie theater close to Yonkers, during which, following the airplane number, the audience broke into applause—something that, for all his moviegoing, Caesar had never witnessed before. He hadn't caught a single frame, so busy was he watching his old man watching him. (Max Caesar, who squirreled a positive review of Sidney's performance under his pillow, died four months after the film opened.)

Caesar now gave his first interviews, in which he articulated his comic credo. "Every gag that can possibly be told has already *been* told," he said, but "there's something funny in everything, even the way a man opens a door or sits down to read a newspaper." He pledged to remain modest about fame, having only "a little house in Bel Air"—"no swimming pools and tennis courts." But based on his experience making *Tars and Spars*, he worried about all the time wasted waiting around in Hollywood, plus the prospect of a life spent playing the pumpernickel sidekicks of white-bread leading men, and not as "Sid Caesar" but with a more mainstream moniker—something like "Ron Roland," which some Hollywood types were trying to foist on him. More enduring than anything Caesar accomplished in Hollywood was the filmed reenactment of an experience he had there, when he punched the horse that had rolled over, and very nearly crushed, Florence during an equestrian outing in Griffith Park. It was a story Mel Brooks heard about, and remembered, and immortalized in *Blazing Saddles*.

Monte Proser soon signed Caesar up for his storied New York nightclub, the Copacabana. Caesar had never been to, let alone performed at, such a place, so Liebman helped him assemble and polish an act. In late 1946, Caesar road tested his show five times a day between showings of *The Thrill of Brazil* in a Chicago movie house. "Highly entertaining," the *Chicago Tribune* called his routine, "but must be very tough on the vocal chords [*sic*]." New Year's nights at New York nightclubs were generally slow, but when Caesar opened at the Copa, there were lines around the block. "Boffola," *Variety* called his act. But a sketch in which Caesar contrasted British and Russian actors led some observers to detect communist sympathies in him, a ridiculous notion that reinforced his lifelong aversion to political material.

At the Copa, Caesar was either reunited with or, more likely, first united with Mel Brooks. Eager to break into show business, a dazzled Brooks watched Caesar perform and instantly felt a kinship. "Sid had this terrific anger in him; he was angry with the world—and so was I" was how Brooks explained their bond. Afterward, under the auspices of Don Appel, Brooks went backstage and began auditioning for the role of Caesar's sidekick, acolyte, jester, mascot, irritant, stooge, muse, gofer, and groupie. He won the part. "Sid viewed him as an amusing kid," Brooks's first wife, Florence Baum, recalled. "Mel made him laugh." Brooks put his own considerable ambitions on hold. But already, Caesar had spared him the fate of so many other working-class Jews: a life sentence in the garment district, where Brooks's own mother had long labored. "I always thought I was destined to push a rack of clothing from a dress company to the Post Office," said Brooks. To secure his position, Brooks started smartening up. "Mel began to burn up the books, reading voraciously to make up for all the years he spent rejecting them for egg creams and laughs at the corner candy store," one of his older brothers, Bernie Kaminsky, recalled.

A MONTH AFTER OPENING at the Copa, Caesar was yanked back to Hollywood by Columbia to add some comic spice to a *Best Years of Our Lives* knockoff called *The Guilt of Janet Ames*. It featured another frenzied Caesar solo, this time as a demonic Viennese psychiatrist. Caesar returned east to entertain the incumbent and future presidents Truman and Eisenhower at the White House Correspondents' Association dinner in early March, then to appear at the Roxy in New York (capacity fifty-five hundred) between showings of *Boomerang*. "The best looking young comedian to hit the Broadway scene," wrote Ed Sullivan of the New York *Daily News*, who, in a prelude to the television show he'd soon have, emceed the production in the theater. Sullivan quickly became one of Caesar's great champions.

Janet Ames opened in early March. Caesar then went back on the road, honing his nightclub act. Local reviewers liked him, but more provincial local audiences, looking for wisecracks, not so much. Caesar found their inattentiveness infuriating. "Some guy comes in with a dame and sits there wondering how much liquor the dame can drink and what's in it for him and what he's going to tell his wife when he gets home," he griped. "He's not watching me." So frustrated did he become in Baltimore that he tore a sink off the dressing room wall when the show was over.

By the fall, Caesar had returned to more hospitable New York, and the more appreciative Roxy; *Variety* noted "heavy mitting" following his performances there. Caesar was now making $3,500 *a week* (nearly $50,000 in 2024) at a time when, as he put it, if you made a hundred bucks a week you got married. He promptly treated himself to his first Cadillac, which quickly became a key prop in Caesar lore. Finishing his show one night, he sailed his new boat down to Greenwich Village (Zero Mostel was performing there), parking it on the street by the theater. As he walked away, he heard the sound of someone shimmying into the adjacent spot, nudging, and re-nudging, the bumper of Caesar's car. When Caesar demanded he stop, the man told him where to go. That was when Caesar grabbed the driver through the vent window, then tugged. Did he remember being born? Caesar shouted. Because he was going to be born again! (Only the intervention of Dave Caesar kept him from inflicting serious harm.) The story was so good that Brooks adopted it, placing himself in the middle of the action, though he hadn't been. In later iterations, he transplanted the story, and himself, to Chicago.*

Next up for Caesar was a starring role in a revue called *Make Mine Manhattan*. It would bring him less than a tenth of what he was making at the Roxy, but, Liebman argued, he'd be on Broadway. Liebman helped him fashion some new material, including a long musical monologue—another feat of memory, mimicry, and lung capacity—based on Caesar's courtship of Florence, called "Five Dollar Date." In it, Caesar conjured up an evening out in Manhattan in 1939, when $5 bought a French (*and* an Italian, *and* a Chinese) dinner for two, *and* a movie, *and* free dishes and silverware, *and* a live show (with Benny Goodman, Bing Crosby, Bob Hope, *and* Jack Benny), *and* a hansom ride through Central Park, *and* taxis, *and* boundless solicitude from everyone. He then contrasted that night with far more expensive and abrasive nights on the town in prosperous postwar New York.

The United Nations, then rising on the East River, proved a boon for Caesar, enabling him to portray the various delegates

* In that rendition, the fracas took place after a Chicago cabbie, driving a DeSoto and "wearing—I'll never forget it—a little yellow cap and a black, shiny bow tie," cut off Caesar in traffic. "I had to bite Sid's hand, because Sid would have pulled the entire cabdriver, like a snake, right through that window," Brooks "remembered" (Mel Brooks interview for the *A&E Biography* "Sid Caesar: Television's Comedy Genius").

(English, French, German, Persian, Russian) gathering at a luncheonette across the street. He also reprised his role as an innocent gumball machine that turned to crime after being kicked around by frustrated or sadistic subway riders. And played an overbearing British film director who devolved into a Yiddish-accented glove maker when provoked. All told, Caesar played twenty-three characters in the show, in addition to simulating hunting calls, a bugle, a rifle bullet, a telephone dial, a siren, and a horse. After watching a triumphant tryout in New Haven, the playwright and director Moss Hart, who was checking on his investment in the show, decided that nothing needed fixing. "You'll never have another poor day, my boy," he told Caesar.

When the show opened at New York's Broadhurst Theatre in January 1948, the reviews were rapturous. Among those taking notice was a young, aspiring comic named Lenny Bruce, who signed on as an usher just to watch Caesar perform. But at a time when the remnants of Popular Front radicalism still lingered in the culture, Caesar's apoliticism rubbed some, like Philip Hamburger of *The New Yorker*, the wrong way; to him, Caesar's depictions of the agonies of the inanimate objects were bathetic, reactionary, and insincere—a gimmick. "Vending machines, he implied, were far more miserable than Okies or children with rickets, and their suffering hurt him deeply," he later wrote. He called the routine "perhaps the least funny thing I had ever seen anywhere," and dismissed Caesar as "a misplaced comic with a heart of Cream of Wheat." He never could have imagined there was no fakery involved—that in Caesar's mind gumball machines really did have souls.

At the Broadhurst, Caesar introduced Liebman to Brooks. "Do for Max what you did for me," Caesar commanded Brooks. The three then entered the empty theater, where Liebman took a seat and Brooks got onstage and broke into a number he'd developed *tummling* in the Catskills:

> *Hello, hello, hello*
> *I've come to start the show*
> *Just a ham who's minus looks*

But in your heart I'll grow
I'll tell you gags
I'll sing you songs
Happy little snappy tunes that roll along
I'm out of my mind
Won't you be kind?
And though I'm not much on looks
Please love Melvin Brooks!

And with that, Brooks, on one knee and arms outstretched, made a "Mammy-type gesture" in the manner of Al Jolson. Afterward, the dumbfounded Liebman had but one question: "Who is this *meshuggener*?"

Newspaper stories portrayed Caesar as a thinking person's comic—an intellectual. "You get the idea he really would be more at home with Rachmaninoff's Second [Piano Concerto] on the vic* and a volume of Kant at hand," one journalist wrote. At the same time, he could be a tough guy. "Comedian Sid Caesar is nursing a bruised hand because two muggs [*sic*] accosted his wife on Central Park South," went his debut in Dorothy Kilgallen's Broadway gossip column. There were awards (one presented by Henry Fonda) for best Broadway debut, a feature in *Vogue*, an appearance in *Ripley's Believe It or Not*, and interviews from Lindy's (the famed New York showbiz hangout) and the Stork Club. "Look at me now," he said in one. "I'm getting laughs with the show every night and they've got me in Helen Hayes's dressing room. And I'm the guy who only wanted to grow up and play the saxophone!" After catching his show at the Waldorf Astoria, Dwight Eisenhower asked Caesar where he'd learned his excellent Russian. The *Forverts* reported that students at New York University had named Caesar Comedian of the Year. More people wondered how long Caesar could, or should, keep up his breakneck pace.

Physically and emotionally, the show *did* take a toll on him,

---

* Short for "Victrola," or the generic name for the record player manufactured by the Victor Talking Machine Company in the early twentieth century.

which he eased with scotch. Apart from watching his big brothers hurl nasty drunks onto the sidewalk outside the St. Clair Lunch, Caesar had mostly avoided alcohol; in the service, he had been just about the only one in his unit not to get soused while on liberty. But now, after rehearsals and especially after performing, he'd begun hitting the bottle, hard. "I don't know why I did it," he later said. "I never got to like the taste. It was just that after I forced down the first two drinks, I *thought* the whiskey made me feel good. It didn't really. It just anesthetized me temporarily from tensions and fears I didn't want to face." And those tensions would only intensify. "Be careful," a colleague cautioned. "It's a tough life. The day after you get to be a star, you have to start worrying about staying there." Caesar wasn't listening.

When Liebman returned to Tamiment for the summer of 1948, it wasn't just to entertain guests but to position himself for television, which by now was expanding with Malthusian speed: From fewer than 10,000 sets produced in 1946 (many of them landing in corner bars), the number jumped to 800,000 in 1948 and 7 million two years after that. Legions now got to see the 1947 World Series, the 1948 political conventions, Harry Truman's inauguration, Princess Elizabeth's wedding, and the Joe Louis–Jersey Joe Walcott fight, all courtesy of DuMont, Philco, Crosley, and Admiral. Caesar first encountered the "box"—still, essentially, a big piece of furniture with a screen on top—in a store near the St. Clair Lunch. Reiner's introduction was catching a Kid Gavilán fight at the home of a friend. Tolkin was supposed to be watching Milton Berle but saw only a "flickering mess" through the window of a Sixth Avenue bar. In 1948, as John Crosby of the *New York Herald Tribune* put it, "television was a seedling, just barely planted."

WORLD WAR II HAD conferred new confidence and optimism on American Jews. More than half a million of them had served; eleven thousand of them were killed. In what became a storied episode of ecumenism, one of them, Rabbi Alexander Goode, read psalms with three Christian clergymen as all went down together on the SS *Dorchester*, torpedoed by a German U-boat. "We are fighting for a new age of brotherhood," Goode had written to his wife before the ship left port. "Justice and righteousness dreamed of by the prophets who gave the world the democratic spirit will cover the world as a torrent." And so returning Jewish veterans like Caesar (and Brooks, Reiner, and Morris) would have hoped.

For many of them, especially the New Yorkers among them, military service marked their first excursions out of semi-protective ethnic cocoons and their first brushes with virulent Jew hatred. It's hard to imagine, or to overstate, how sheltered from America they had been. Brooks's world, for instance, was "mostly Jews and a few strange people." Jewish veterans returned stateside more worldly, emboldened, ambitious, and accepted than before—more "persona grata," as Reiner put it. Their service, plus the nascent State of Israel, belied stereotypes of Jewish weakness and malingering. A new "Judeo-Christian" era beckoned; at major civic events, like when television first came to Boston in June 1948, rabbis routinely joined ministers and priests. America's Jewish community was now the world's largest and strongest. And, as *Look* magazine put it, "Hitler made anti-Semitism disreputable"; nowadays, it reported, "you seldom hear words like 'kike,'" which, it noted, the banker and philanthropist Otto H. Kahn had once defined as "a Jewish gentleman who has just left the room."

But Jews, or at least the Eastern European kind, remained sufficiently exotic, or alien, in the United States that an article about Manhattan's Stage Delicatessen in *Collier's* in 1951 felt compelled to define both pastrami ("highly spiced beef plate") and bagels ("a hard-boiled, varnished doughnut without sugar, jelly, grease, or taste"). More generally, the Jew hatred that had effectively barred Jews from entering the United States immediately before, then during, the Holocaust lived on. The Red Scare of the late 1940s and early 1950s, and accusations that Jews were communists as well as warmongers, stirred up the embers. Posters appearing in Harvard Square in 1951 highlighted Jewish involvement in atomic espionage, blamed Jews for making Hollywood "immoral," "ruining" New York, and dragging Harvard down to "their level." Only Nazi Germany, they declared, had had "guts enough to kick them out."

Meanwhile, more genteel kinds of anti-Semitism had persisted; *The New Republic* found it stronger in the United States in 1947 than in Germany in 1933, pointing to restricted resorts, communities (Bronxville, New York; Litchfield, Connecticut), and universities (Yale, Princeton, Amherst, Williams, Dartmouth, Haverford, Bryn Mawr, Mount Holyoke). More than a third of those polled by *Fortune* in October 1947 believed Jews had too much economic power. Viewers complained that too many of those bright youngsters on the television program *Quiz Kids* were Jewish. Mindful of such things, Jews lay low even where they held sway, as in Hollywood.

"Were the Jews a totally extinct race surviving only as a few Passover cups and saucers in the Metropolitan Museum, they could have hardly less representation" in American movies, Ben Hecht observed; only Jewish comedians and musicians remained visible. "The Jew, like the hunchback, is permitted always the part of jester and troubadour in all the courts—even those run by Jews," he wrote.

The conflicted state of postwar American Jewry was neatly captured in Laura Z. Hobson's bestselling 1947 novel, *Gentleman's Agreement*, and the Oscar-winning film made from it, starring Gregory Peck. Peck's character, a Gentile reporter named Phil Green (full name: Philip *Schuyler* Green), goes undercover, pretending to be a Jew as he investigates worsening American anti-Semitism. He encounters it *everywhere:* from cabbies, soldiers, his doctor, fellow journalists, his sister, and even his new girlfriend. *Gentleman's Agreement* catalogs not only Jew hatred but, inadvertently, Jewish self-hatred, something Hobson (who was Jewish herself) was peculiarly well suited to capture. If Jews are scorned, the book suggests, they have only themselves to blame, for their aggressiveness, vulgarity, bad taste, and self-importance—all the "Chosen People" stuff.

But like the movies before it, television proved unusually hospitable to Jews. They were available and good at precisely what television needed: filling in all those empty hours with material. In the case of television comedy, that work began, reflexively, with retreads: formats and performers recycled from radio and vaudeville. (*Variety* even coined a term—"vaudeo"—for such warmed-over, hybrid stuff.) The prototype was Berle, whose show, *Texaco*

Star Theater, premiered in June 1948. It was a weekly helping of warmed-over shtick, filled with cheap stunts, crazy costumes, and slapstick, but riveting for those who'd never seen it onstage, or welcomed the chance to see it again, or loved anything that came into their living rooms or favorite bar for free.

Berle couldn't be bothered de-Judaizing his material; he knew nothing else. There were Yiddish puns and Jewish references galore—characters named Professor Mischa Gos and Princess Latke, words like *hamantaschen** and *shvitz* and *sheitl*.[†] When Rita Hayworth married Prince Aly Khan in 1949, Berle had to correct his mother: "Mom, it's not the same Kahns who lived in the Bronx." *Tummling* went electric; when Mel Brooks later asked, "Is television an electronic Jew?" he might have had Berle in mind. Jews laughed knowingly and non-Jews just laughed, while executives at NBC, many Jews themselves, squirmed until they looked at the ratings.

To an industry still finding its way, Berle proved that a comic *could* produce a show weekly, and that the public would keep watching it. But where to find the material? The New York radio personalities Tex McCrary and Jinx Falkenburg had a suggestion: Max Liebman's magical trunk, the one in which he'd secreted all of his sketches from Tamiment. In fact, Liebman was already on his way. While *Make Mine Manhattan* ran its course, he talked TV with his agents at William Morris. And with Sid Caesar to sell, he wasn't just peddling old merchandise in newfangled form. In him, Liebman saw the finest comic talent since Charlie Chaplin. "If I can't be the greatest, I don't want to be anything," Caesar confided to the head of the agency, Abe Lastfogel.

"Your husband is going to be a big, big star," Liebman told Florence Caesar.

"Couldn't he just be a *little* star?" she responded.

So Caesar, the boy who'd gotten his first laughs in a shifting spotlight, would now have another, far brighter one shining on him. Only this one wouldn't budge.

---

* Triangular pastries prepared for the holiday Purim.
† A wig worn by married Orthodox Jewish women.

CHAPTER 2

ON TO TELEVISION

When Max Liebman first mentioned TV to Sid Caesar, Caesar was skeptical. "Television only goes from here to New Jersey and that's the end of it," he said. Admen and network executives, however, had no such reservations, hoofing it to Tamiment to see, and try to sign up, Liebman. The way in which they approached him was, as Liebman put it, "about what a courier gets when he arrives with a serum in a plague-stricken village." "We were the most coordinated army of craftsmen and artists to enter the TV arena," he recalled. "We couldn't miss."

Among those traipsing to the Poconos was Sylvester L. "Pat" Weaver, then an executive at the New York advertising firm of Young & Rubicam, whose client General Foods was looking for a show to sponsor. Weaver, who emphatically wasn't Jewish, certainly stood out at the place; "a tall, immaculately dressed goy," one camper later called him. Seeking to allay any concerns that he could produce a weekly show for an entire season, Liebman urged Weaver to come back to Tamiment the next week, and then the week after that. General Foods ended up passing. The Admiral Corporation, makers of TVs and other appliances, signed up Liebman instead. Liebman then turned to Caesar, who in turn turned to Brooks for his thoughts. "Don't do it!" Brooks had exclaimed in one of his several, increasingly elaborate versions of their conversation. "It's trafficking in graven images, and there are strict Jewish laws against that." At the very least, he said, Caesar would be sterilized by the cameras. Caesar went ahead anyway.

The new show, set to start in early 1949, was originally christened *Friday Night Frolic* but was soon reborn as *The Admiral Broadway Revue*. It would be broadcast more widely than anything in the medium's short history, running live from 8:00 p.m. to 9:00 p.m. on twenty-four stations in sixteen cities, primarily in the Northeast, on both NBC and the smaller DuMont network. Viewers in fourteen other places would see it on kinescopes two weeks later.

The program represented the first television show with a permanent "stock company" (of about twenty-five people); the first with large chunks of original material; and the first to originate in a legitimate theater adapted for television (the International Theatre on Columbus Circle in New York, holding 375 people).* The female headliner would be the singing comedienne Mary McCarty. Imogene Coca landed only a short-term, secondary role, and only at Liebman's insistence; while the sponsors thought her over-the-hill, Liebman was convinced she'd be a star. Of course, Caesar was the *real* star. He'd collect $900 a week, a quarter of what he'd been making onstage (Coca earned a quarter of that), but he was investing in his future, and television's. Each production would have a theme—"Radio City," "Night Life," "Cross Country"—with related sketches, songs, and dances.

Though both of the show's principal writers, Mel Tolkin and Lucille Kallen, were Canadian (Tolkin by way of Ukraine), they'd help define American television comedy. Tolkin believed foreignness helped: "If you're an insider—so runs the thinking—you lose the detached perspective necessary to see the absurdity, the

---

* When William Randolph Hearst bought it in 1923 it seated 1,500 people, but chunks of it had been removed for the orchestra, control booth, and cameras. One thing it didn't have was air-conditioning, which was simulated by placing gigantic fans near more gigantic blocks of ice.

lunacy, the plain *mishugas* of the human comedy that a man from Mars would observe," he explained. Born Shmuel Tulchinsky in Odesa in 1913 (and thus nine years older than Caesar) and raised in the small town of Gaisin, Tolkin had been steeped both in Jewish culture (reading Sholem Aleichem, whom his father had once met) and in anti-Semitism: Periodic pogroms in his town left him forever convinced that catastrophe was around the corner. "The pressures made heroes of some, and poets and violinists of some," he said. "But it made for a lot of broken human beings, too. It created the condition where humor becomes anger made acceptable with a joke." At twelve, he'd come with his family to Montreal. Embarrassed by his broken English, for two years he barely said anything, and ever afterward he spoke it with brittle, vaguely archaic precision and the remnants of a Russian accent; coming out of his mouth, even the foulest curses sounded courtly. He became an accountant, but music and politics were his passions: On the family piano he composed satirical songs for left-wing revues, and learned jazz well enough to play in local bands. Hiding such pursuits from his parents and clients led him to a streamlined new name, chosen because its cadence resembled "Cole Porter."* Though it sounded like a joke, Tolkin spent World War II playing the glockenspiel with the Canadian Army Band. That he, like Caesar and several of his writers, was musical was no accident; as he once explained, in going from conflict to development to resolution, sketch comedy resembled a sonata.

Like many immigrant Jews in Montreal, Tolkin found he'd exchanged one brand of anti-Semitism for another, this strain more benign but two-headed, with both snooty Anglophile and ultraconservative French Catholic components. It made him want to flee anew, this time to cosmopolitan, tolerant, unapologetically Jewish New York. "The war, for me, will end not on the day of my discharge, but the day I walk down Broadway," he wrote to a friend. With his pedigree (foreign-born, left-wing), entering and staying in the United States proved tricky. But he

---

* Years later, Tolkin hung on his office wall a framed letter from J. R. R. Tolkien to Tolkin's son in which the author speculated on the shared origins of their last names.

got to New York with a typewriter and a rhyming dictionary, pur-
chased a piano before a bed, and settled into the "beautiful seductive" city. Through a friend he landed a job at Tamiment, where
he met Max Liebman. A song he wrote around then, crammed
with all those hard-won English idioms, celebrated his glorious
new situation:

> *Come on out, the sun is hidden,*
> *Everything's right that's not forbidden—*
> *Get your kicks from*
> *Night Life in New York.*
>
> *Out of Towners, heavy spenders,*
> *Midwestern Babbitts out on benders,*
> *Leave the sticks for*
> *Night Life in New York.*
>
> *Night time, night time—*
> *Gay and bright time—*
> *Some folks find the day time*
> *Only good for hit-the-hay time.*

But the freedom, and sense of belonging, took him only so
far. "Anchorless. Rootless. A perpetual immigrant" was how
Tolkin described himself. At least subliminally, G-men replaced
Cossacks in hot pursuit. "You've been told in your formative years
that you were born into the wrong race, in the wrong economic
class, that there are bad guys out there to hurt you and your loved
ones, and you begin to think of happiness as a frivolous pursuit."
Or, as he put it another time, "If you like what's going on in the
world, if you're part of it, you'll find little comedy in life. Happy
people are idiots."

Tolkin, too, saw *Tars and Spars* and spotted Caesar's genius.
When they'd met, he'd taken Caesar, with his fair hair, blue eyes,
and beautiful wife, to be Greek (or so he said), learning otherwise
only when, in casual conversation, Caesar tossed off a familiar line
in Hebrew from the Passover Seder. Equally alienated and awk-

ward, Caesar and Tolkin formed a durable but uneven and mutually uncomprehending bond. They needed each other, though
Tolkin needed Caesar more; in photographs of the two together,
Tolkin, invariably looking anxious or supplicating, is never very
far away. The two men shared one goal: to show "them," whoever
"them" might be. Sitting in the audience on show nights, Tolkin's
wife, Edith, always found the laughter reassuring: At least temporarily, she knew, it would tamp down her husband's turbulent
soul.

Kallen's background, too, was musical: She'd trained as a
concert pianist. She'd begun writing in high school, including a
novella in which a rival of hers—blond, good-looking, wealthy,
popular, and Christian—wound up impaled on a wrought-iron
fence, and her erstwhile beau was suddenly smitten with the
dark-haired Jewish her. She, too, was politically left, and had
fled Canadian parochialism and anti-Semitism—in her case, the
Toronto strain. "This was what you lived for: to get to New York
and Broadway and the lights and the glamour and everything,"
she recalled. "It was Utopia."

And if New York was utopia, Tamiment was the gateway to
New York. Liebman had been looking for another Sylvia Fine to
help him write his shows, and since Kallen, too, was short, dark,
female, clever, creative, musical, and Jewish, she seemed to fit the
bill. In the summer of 1948, she and Tolkin became Liebman's
writing team. Taken so soon after the slaughter of countless
young people every bit as talented and promising as they, a photograph of the two exulting at a Tamiment banquet captured just
how capricious history could be, and how blessed they must have
known they were. Kallen had arrived at Tamiment frightened
and alone that first summer, but when it came time to leave in
September, she wrapped her arms around a tree and wouldn't
let go.

With Tolkin and Kallen on hand, the writing staff of *The
Admiral Broadway Revue* was officially complete. But at Caesar's
urging, Mel Brooks showed up one day at the International
Theatre. Caesar's manager shooed him away, but at least as
Brooks told the story, he planted himself on the sidewalk beneath
Caesar's dressing room and then, knowing Caesar liked cats,

meowed loudly and repeatedly. "And he looked out the window, and instead of a cat, he saw a little Jew," Brooks recalled. Caesar let him back inside, and he never left.

Liebman, though, was a problem. To him, Brooks was inelegant and uncouth, a ghost from his own unmourned Yiddish past, a *tummler*—that is, one of those roving characters employed by Catskill resorts to entertain guests and distract them from the bad food or accommodations. "Mel was everything he hated," recalled Florence Baum. "Liebman was *Hochdeutsch* as opposed to this Middle European peasant. Everything he wanted to escape, Mel personified." Brooks could see Liebman's point; whenever Max looked at him, he said, "he saw an arrogant, obnoxious little shithead who thought he knew everything." Worse, Brooks belonged to Caesar, not to him. "Sid's private court jester," Liebman called him, or "Sid's valet." ("Sid's pet" was also apt.) More squatter than staffer, Brooks clung close to Caesar, plying him with the two things Caesar needed most: devotion and jokes. He told him he'd work for nothing, but because Caesar pitied him, and Liebman refused to dig into his own pocket, Caesar gave him $40 a week. Liebman let him "stalk the corridors" but barred him from anything official or important.

Caesar's first writers' room, above the old Guild Theatre on West Fifty-Second Street, doubled as the male dancers' changing room, forcing Tolkin and Kallen to sit and work amid "sweaty jockstraps and discarded tights." Brooks was banned. Instead, he waited in the hallway until Caesar stuck his head out the door and said something like "We need three jokes," and three jokes Brooks would give him. Snobs of a sort themselves, Tolkin and Kallen saw Brooks as an interloper from the Catskills; while Brooks considered its humor "glorious and majestic," to them "Borscht Belt" meant "coarse" and "primitive." Caesar landed somewhere in the middle, hoping, perhaps, that by injecting the rawness and raucousness of the Mountains into Tamiment's more cerebral sensibility, Brooks would enliven Caesar's work. Brooks wore down Liebman as he had Caesar, burrowing his way into the writers' room and onto the payroll, though not into the credits at the end of the show, at least not right away.

Around the same time, another short New York Jew entered

the picture, a young actor named Howard Morris who'd heard that Liebman needed a flyweight whom Sid Caesar could lift up and throw around for his new television show. To Morris, all of 106 pounds, TV was schlock work, something to do only if there was nothing better around. He'd never heard of Caesar, but because he needed the money, it was an easy call. "I was either going to do that or get the bus and go home," he remembered.

He soon met Liebman, and then Caesar, who struck him as "a Jewish god . . . tawny and tanned." They rehearsed a bit, with Caesar playing a mob boss and Morris his henchman. Caesar threw him around as advertised. "Max! Him. Get," he said. From then on, whenever Liebman needed a man to be manhandled, Morris got a call. "When in doubt, rip Howie's clothes off" was how Morris described his portfolio. "Or have him climb over Sid. Rip, climb. I didn't mind. It got laughs." (Also on hand that first day was one Monsieur Bruit, described to Morris as a young Frenchman in town to learn about American television. Just how wasn't clear, since he seemed to speak little English. After three days of gesticulating, Morris and Bruit found themselves standing at adjacent urinals. "Hi, Howie! How're they hangin'?" the "Frenchman" suddenly exclaimed in fluent Brooklynese. Howard Morris, meet Mel Brooks.)

The Admiral Broadway Revue "opened"—without a vocabulary of its own, television freely expropriated from the theater— on January 28, 1949. The premiere had all the trappings of a Broadway opening: a Coast Guard band, searchlights crisscrossing the sky, New York's mayor, William O'Dwyer, and other celebrities on hand. Backstage, there was chaos. There'd been no rehearsal with the cameras in place; the lore afterward claimed they'd been brought in at the last minute from either Ebbets Field, the Polo Grounds, or Yankee Stadium, though why cameras were in baseball stadiums in January no one explained. Four hours before the start, part of the stage was still being built. But at the appointed hour the orchestra sounded a fanfare, and a curtain with "Admiral" sprinkled around it appeared on the screen. "*The Admiral Broadway Revue* . . . brought to you by your Admiral dealer," a voice declared. "It's *The Admiral Broadway Revue:*

Nightlife! Starring Sid Caesar, with Mary McCarty, Imogene Coca, Marge and Gower Champion. Ring up the curtain!" Five singers—three women flanked by two men, all in maritime garb—then marched out onstage, saluted, and burst into song. The words, uncredited but surely Tolkin's, were quaint, sweet, endearingly awkward—a chorus by thesaurus:

> *The top of the evening to you!*
> *It's time for your* Admiral Revue,
> *To make each Friday sweeter than a honeycomb,*
> *We try to bring Broadway*
> *Right into your home,*
> *The top entertainment for you,*
> *A topical musical that's new.*
> *But just before we clear the floor*
> *And ring up the curtain,*
> *We'd like to be certain*
> *You know where to shop.*
> *And Admiral is wonderful*
> *The cost is low*
> *But the quality's always on top.*

Against a backdrop of cardboard skyscrapers came another Tolkin paean to New York ("You'll find Fifth Avenue exquisite / It's not to live in, just to visit"). And then the action moved to the same greasy spoon near the UN featured in *Make Mine Manhattan*, with Caesar reprising its cosmopolitan clientele: a Persian pasha; a dotty English aristocrat; an imperious Soviet commissar seeking Stalin's permission to put gravy on his roast beef. Coca then did a spoof on *Afternoon of a Faun*. Caesar's expectations for the new show were modest; neither he nor Liebman knew anyone who owned a television. "If it flopped, who would know?" he later asked.

"Admiral Bows Sock Revue with Top Artists, Yocks, Sizzling Pace Comparable to Best Broadway Hits," crowed *Variety*. To *Time*, its costumes, decor, and choreography were superior to those found in "any nightclub and many theaters." Paul Denis

of the *New York Post* called Caesar "forceful, versatile, agile."
"A Caesar Rises in Television: Comic Named Sid," the *Chicago
Tribune* proclaimed; Caesar might not only entice bigger stars
onto television, but was, in and of himself, "one of the soundest
arguments for buying a television set." Very quickly, said Liebman,
everyone involved considered Caesar "the fountain from which
we all drank." And, after receiving glowing reviews, Coca soon
displaced McCarty as the show's female lead. To Liebman, who
felt he'd failed to push for Coca enough in her career, this recti-
fied his greatest mistake. It also sprang Coca from the penury
that once forced her and her husband to spend two nights on the
benches at Grand Central Terminal. Now she could even buy her
mother a television set—on time.

Like others before them, the two most important chroniclers
of broadcasting, Jack Gould of *The New York Times* and John
Crosby of the *New York Herald Tribune*, worried about things
like Caesar's originality and longevity. Though "a hard-working
gentleman of considerable versatility," Gould noted, could he
produce something *new*? Crosby, for whom Caesar's face was
"as malleable as wax and expressive as a small child," wondered
whether he could do it every week. But "for an hour's entertainment I can't think of anything better in New York's expensive
night clubs," he noted. "Come to think of it, there isn't anything
much better on Broadway, either."

Wise, lively, urbane, and stylish, personifying the literacy
that made the *Herald Tribune* the preferred destination for New
York journalism's most writerly writers, Crosby was among the
first to study Caesar and to see his fate, and television's, as intertwined. "Sid Caesar, who is twenty-six years old and preposter-
ously talented, is perhaps the best laboratory specimen available
of a new species of entertainer," he wrote. "It is a very human
humor. He takes the normal responses of people to life's little
vexations, exaggerates them a little and comes up with something
wonderfully funny. His is a television face. It can run the gamut
from delight to horror like a pianist runs up a keyboard." Bob
Hope, yet to adapt the more labored style of radio to a visual
medium's brisker pace, could learn a lot from him, Crosby said.

And perhaps Hope did, for though he wasn't much impressed with television, he loved Sid and Imogene and watched them with his family.

On another point, Crosby proved equally acute. Trade publications were already cautioning that by making certain programs too racy or ethnic or abrasive—code for "too New York," which was code for "too Jewish"—television was being extremely short-sighted. This kind of thing worked okay for now, with broadcasting still largely confined to eastern cities, but wouldn't for long. As one industry journal put it, comedy "built entirely upon Broadway humor (or frequent references to the borscht circuit, the Brooklyn Dodgers, the Palace Theatre, or even famous New York nightclubs) will find an indifferent audience in Kokomo, Indiana, and in the hundreds of Kokomos around the country." Elitist and Manhattan-centric, the Admiral show was, in its own cosmopolitan way, parochial. (Admiral certainly knew its prime audience, advertising a model requiring "no installation and no landlord permission.")

A sketch that April, recounting the saga of a ditchdigger turned film idol named Mike Schlump, highlighted the problem. Along with Schlump's Yiddish moniker, at one point he gripes about the hapless authors of his scripts: Eugene O'Neill, Moss Hart, and William Shakespeare. "Get me some *writers!*" he demands. Equally alien beyond the Hudson were recurring jokes about psychiatrists, as in a sketch from March: So alarmed is a junior mobster ("Weasel," played by Morris) when his boss ("Boss," played by Caesar) buys tickets to a policemen's ball that he urges him to see a shrink. "I ain't nuts!" the boss insists. "Who says you're nuts, Chief?" Weasel replies. "You ain't nuts! You're neurotic. You got a slight case of hypertension, an Oedipus Rex complex, and a dash of schizophrenia!" Caesar's show was nonetheless the third most popular on the air, behind only Milton Berle's and Arthur Godfrey's.

Weekly themes on the show included a round-the-world cruise, Hollywood, and a county fair. A mélange of sketches and leitmotifs built around Caesar's varied talents emerged. One was "Nonentities in the News," in which a trench-coated reporter questioned assorted oddball characters from foreign climes as they disembarked at (the newly named) LaGuardia Airport. Caesar played "Signor Ravioli" of Spumoni, Italy, winner of an international spaghetti-eating contest, and the world's greatest bullfighter, Señor Enchilada of Hot Tamale, Mexico, and Gon-Gon, a boy reared by animals in the jungle and wearing a loincloth. Brooks later claimed that Gon-Gon was the first character he created for Caesar—chosen, he explained, because "Sid was like a Jungle Boy" himself.[*]

Then, appearing as often as every other week, there was Caesar's scatterbrained and disheveled professor, newly arrived from Vienna (though always described as German), blathering to the same reporter on his varying areas of bogus expertise. In monologues, Caesar also dissected various cliché-ridden film genres (gangster movies, Westerns, boxing pictures), playing each of the characters and supplying all of the sounds. Caesar continued to plumb the souls of a subway turnstile and other inanimate objects, though they gradually yielded to living creatures, generally, though not always, human, with a wider range of emotional possibilities.

Former nightclub comics like Berle (who loved sexual double entendres) and Morey Amsterdam (who once poked fun at stutterers) posed headaches for network tastemakers. "Could you brief the talent on keeping away from jokes on personal afflictions?" NBC's chief censor, Stockton Helffrich[†]—official title: "manager of continuity acceptance"—pleaded to colleagues in 1951. But Caesar gave Helffrich little to do, partly because he was so prudish and skittish himself. "He was very conscious of not making waves," Kallen said. The sponsors had other concerns. Evidently fearful that it reflected TV's pernicious effects on everyday life, Admiral scotched a sketch portraying life "B.T." (Before Television)—children coming home from school and

---

[*] What aired in Gon-Gon's brief and unmemorable debut (see page 72) bears little resemblance to Brooks's later descriptions of the sketch.
[†] The man who later decreed that when Elvis Presley appeared on *The Steve Allen Show* it would be only from the waist up.

greeting their parents, friends coming by to play bridge, and so on—and "A.T.," once life had been reconstituted around the tube and social life and civility disappeared. When informed of their decision, Caesar tore another sink off the wall.

Viewers quickly learned the constituent parts of this Gulliver who filled their Lilliputian screens. They knew the mole just east of his nose; his hair, which lost altitude whenever he got exercised; and the sweat of his brow, and back, and underarms, five or six pounds' worth every show, prompted by the pressure as much as by the primitive lights. But nothing about him was as distinctive, or talked about, as his cough, the most conspicuous, and chronic, and chronicled in the annals of both broadcasting *and* medicine.

Technically, it wasn't a "cough" at all, but a one-shot, quarter-note clearing of the throat. It could come at any time, or multiple times, during a given show. People debated its etiology—whether it stemmed from nerves or allergies or overly strenuous rehearsals or a long-running cold, or if, as Caesar sometimes suggested, it was purely tactical, a way to give himself an extra second or two to think or speak. (Brooks said he would sometimes write "cough, cough" into a script specifically to provide him with such an interval.) To the reporters forever tracking it, it never stayed the same: It was always getting better or worse. From time to time, it was declared "cured," including by Caesar himself. "That was a psychological thing," he told *The New York Times* in 1950. "I was plain scared." The past tense was premature.

To commentators, Caesar's cough was variously annoying, disconcerting, disgusting, jarring, infuriating, mystifying, alarming, or entertaining. Once, Steve Allen began his program with *his* cough, then said, "Welcome to the Sid Caesar show." In the same line of comedian squeeze dolls that had "Desi Arnaz" shouting "Loo-see!" and "Jackie Gleason" saying "Pow!," "Sid Caesar" coughed. Jack O'Brian, radio and television columnist for the Hearst papers and the cough's most compulsive chronicler, called it "one of the few things on his show we wish wasn't"; whenever Caesar hacked away, "we forget what he's been funny about and worry a little." Even Reiner, loyal but persnickety, was annoyed that Caesar never excused himself after doing it. For all Caesar's gifts, Reiner liked to say, he'd been "shortchanged on charm."

At the same time, such touches of verismo humanized Caesar far more effectively than his periodic, ham-handed attempts to reach out to the audience more directly.[*] One thing Caesar's cough was, was unique. And with the advent of videotape, which allowed TV to cover up such imperfections, it always would be.

BONDS QUICKLY FORMED BETWEEN Caesar and Coca, and between Coca and the audience. The pair had not known each other before *The Admiral Broadway Revue*. Thrown together by Liebman a few weeks into the show for a pantomime, Coca sensed Caesar's wariness. "I thought 'Dear God, he's already suspicious—like—it was good for her in a show—how can it also be good for me?'" she recalled. In fact, the match was a great gift to them both. Their physical contrast served both well. "One of the subliminal sources of Sid's humor," Albert Goldman wrote, "was simply the repeated spectacle of this big, enormously loud and powerful and over-wrought man brought virtually to a stand-still by this tiny gnat of a woman." Their very different strains of introversion and awkwardness somehow bonded. Coca, too, couldn't tell a joke, favored comedy based as much on movement as on words, thought it should be both believable *and* poignant: She'd never forgotten watching Fanny Brice play a poor woman whose husband had just paid off the rent with what turned out to be a winning lottery ticket. "She wasn't *acting* poor, she *was* poor," she marveled decades later.

Offstage, Caesar and Coca quite literally had *nothing* to say to each other. After each show, they went their separate ways—in Coca's case, only a couple of hours afterward, once she was sure all the fans awaiting her outside had given up the ghost. But onstage, they communicated instinctively—via alpha rays, Caesar once said, and probably believed.

---

[*] "We had a suggestion that [you] want to meet us. So here we are," went one early attempt (*Admiral Broadway Revue*, Feb. 18, 1949).

Like Caesar, Coca was versatile. Howard Morris said Coca "knew where the fun was," whether as Cinderella, Pocahontas, or Scheherazade, a princess, pixie, burlesque star, striptease artist, torch singer, water sprite, diva, dancer, drunkard, child, model, gypsy, flirt, flapper, or tramp. Like Caesar (who always carried a bullet in his pocket and left a certain tuft of hair unshaven), she had her quirks: She refused to ride elevators, disliked eating out, always rehearsed in the same clothes (old jeans, checked shirt, sneakers), never looked in a mirror, never watched herself on the kinescopes. You could never whistle in her dressing room, Caesar learned, and if you touched her on one shoulder, you had to touch her on the other. She, too, was fully at ease only in character. Though she was nearly fourteen years older than Caesar, onstage they became contemporaries. Liebman didn't tamper too much with either. "They were great before they knew me," he said. Only in the foreign-language sketches—for which foreign phrases had to be written out phonetically—did Coca come up short; as she saw it, her role was principally to say "oui" or "nein" seductively.

Coca quickly developed her own passionate following, especially among women. "Sid Caesar is a fine pantomimist, but week in, week out, it's Coca who's the polished, the disciplined, performer," wrote one of Caesar's earliest and greatest champions, Harriet Van Horne of the *New York World-Telegram*. Coca's connection to viewers was more visceral than Caesar's; while he could seem elusive and confounding, her vulnerability was relatable, and there for all to see. Coca gave Caesar a measure of class he hadn't had, and elicited a degree of affection and warmth from fans he never did, which became a source of strain—for Caesar. "People *loved* Imogene," recalled Howard Morris. "They respected and admired Sid. You couldn't love him. Gleason *you loved:* his characters were totally human and hurtable. But not Sid."

At the close of *The Admiral Broadway Revue* for June 3, 1949, the five sailors once more marched out onstage and sang the show's theme song for the last time, modified slightly for the occasion:

The top of the evening for you
The clock tells us that we're nearly through
We hope we made a little bit of Broadway zoom
Right over the footlights and into your room
Your Admiral dealer bids all
A happy farewell until the fall
Tonight's show is the last but don't forget to remember
In early September we'll be back with you.

LIEBMAN RETREATED TO TAMIMENT to recuperate, put on another summer's entertainment, and prepare for more Admiral shows. "If, a year ago, some guy came to me and said, 'How'd you like to do 10 Broadway musical shows in 20 weeks?' I'd yell, 'Scat, man! Back to your booby hatch!'" he wrote in *Variety*. TV, he'd learned, was "the toughest, back-breakingest, ulcer-breedingest entertainment medium in existence—a fascinating monster that devours material, tortures talent, sears souls and paralyzes the participant."

And, he might have added, broke hearts: Surprising everyone, in midsummer, Admiral declined to re-up for another season. Demand for its sets had shot up so much—from 50 to 100 a week to 5,000 *a day*—that the company was pumping its money into production rather than programming. "We're being dropped because the show was too *good*?" an incredulous Caesar asked the head of the company. But Liebman and his team wouldn't remain idle for long, not with Pat Weaver having become vice president for television at NBC.

A man with big dreams, and guts, Weaver saw TV as a "capacious instrument"—a tool not just, or even principally, for entertainment but for enlightenment, education, and understanding, one that, in the right hands, would "make the average man the uncommon man." Weaver was forever expounding such lofty thoughts, often in language so opaque—"intellectual yoga," Jack Gould called it—that even he couldn't always follow it. "Whenever your TV set is behaving badly, don't blame sunspots," John Crosby wrote. "More probably, Sylvester L. (Pat) Weaver is thinking again."

Weaver promptly launched something he'd called "Operation Frontal Lobes" (so named because he'd read somewhere that the enlargement of that part of the brain was what differentiated human beings from chimpanzees), designed to use TV to make complex social issues more digestible. His version of nirvana would have the cowboy star Roy Rogers taking kids to the Supreme Court, and Milton Berle introducing them to Einstein and Toscanini. Crosby dismissed it as NBC's "somewhat starry-eyed attempt to con the public into absorbing a certain amount of culture along with the jokes." But Weaver wasn't all pie-in-the-sky: *Today* and *The Tonight Show* were his ideas, too.

"Used for good, used intelligently, this medium can communicate an upthrust to the mental level, the maturity level, the knowledge level, the alertness level of this nation that will bring about almost a mutation in us," he once told bewildered network affiliates. And in TV's prelapsarian days, he didn't dream alone: In 1949, the chairman of the FCC proclaimed that thanks to television "the day of the hinterland, the provinces, the backwoods, the sticks has passed."

On a more prosaic level, Weaver set out to colonize Saturday nights. For TV programmers it had long been, as he put it, a "dog night," when any red-blooded American hoping to hold his head high Monday morning wanted out of the house. Liebman, Weaver figured, was the man to keep them in their living rooms— making money for NBC, to be sure, but also to smarten them up in the process. Even as it laughed, America would eat its spinach.

Weaver quickly shed two straitjackets handed down from radio: an undeviating half-hour format (which discouraged more adventurous programming), and shows with single sponsors (giving particular corporations complete, and stultifying, control over content). He proposed a two-and-a-half-hour variety show called *Saturday Night Revue*. Thanks to limited capacity on the cables carrying TV out of New York, the first hour would originate in Chicago, with the stand-up comedian Jack Carter as host. It would be the stepchild of the package. Ninety minutes would go to Liebman and Caesar in New York, at their insistence. They were the main event, and the classier act. "There is a vast tendency to underestimate the intelligence of the general public," said Liebman, who'd sneak in classical music and opera around the entertainment but not too much, lest viewers think they'd be "stuck with it for the whole evening." Morris, for one, saw the possibilities. "We had *matured* to the point where we wanted to say certain things about society, about ethnics, about relationships, about human beings, and hope to bring some sense of revelation—the thing that you loved about *Death of a Salesman*,"* he recalled.

Like everyone else, Weaver wasn't sure how the protocols for watching television would evolve, and how undivided people's attention would be. At least initially, he envisioned the new show coexisting with traditional Saturday night pursuits rather than supplanting them. That meant that folks might take in pieces of the show either before or after a movie; if they threw a party, perhaps they'd keep it on in the background. The NBC executive Michael Dann recalled how the network gave ten-inch sets and $40 to staffers to entice bigwigs into their homes to watch it.

Multiple sponsors would allow for a more generous budget: $64,000 a show. Two thousand of those dollars would go to Caesar, a salary no other television comic his age could claim. None of the enlarged budget went toward hiring additional writers; Tolkin and Kallen remained, while Brooks, still uncredited, continued to lurk. Bill Hayes, a handsome young "pop baritone," would croon on the new show, while the Hamilton Trio would dance. Presiding, and participating in some of the sketches, would be whatever celebrity guest from Broadway or Hollywood could be enticed into slumming on TV.

Without an Admiral, Texaco, or Kraft to stamp its name on the proceedings, and Caesar and Coca still too obscure, what would the new program be called? Liebman's choice, *Your Show of Shows*, had a connoisseur's ring, some biblical overtones, a precedent—the 1929 Warner Bros. variety show movie *Show of Shows*, which had also offered a Liebman-like mixed bag of different levels of culture—and what Albert Goldman called "Barnum-like bravado." Even Caesar later said the show had been named

---

* Arthur Miller's seminal play had opened on Broadway in February 1949.

"optimistically and somewhat arrogantly," not that he much cared. As Larry Wolters of the *Chicago Tribune* wrote, they might have gone with "Greatest Show on Earth" had it not already been taken. Network flacks touted Caesar as the first actor ever to spurn movies for television, and insisted he had enough material to go on for seven hours at a time.

Weaver was inexplicably vacationing in St. Moritz in February 1950 when someone on the home front fired off a telegram. "Must come back for *Show of Shows* opening. Promises to be biggest thing ever on television," it declared. Commercial time for the entire season had sold out within a few days. So overwhelming was the demand for seats from ad agencies and their clients that ordinary guests were relegated to the dress rehearsal. It, too, played to a packed house.

Caesar seemed surprisingly calm when *Newsweek* caught up with him on the Wednesday before the Saturday opening, even though he was simultaneously working a four-week engagement at the Waldorf Astoria's Wedgwood Room, where he earned approving nods from the Duke and Duchess of Windsor. By now Caesar could memorize whole paragraphs, but he had yet to see the script for the opening show. He wanted people to know who he was, he said, and television was the way to do it. "The camera can get right on your puss," he explained. Anyone studying Caesar could see how tightly wound he was; at rehearsals, he shifted constantly from one foot to the other, and kept his pencil and paper poised. He was up until three in the morning, which meant no rehearsals until early afternoon. "He does chew gum like mad and drums his fingers on the tablecloth the same way," the *Newsweek* reporter noted.

"Tonight! Premiere of the biggest show in television," declared the ad in *The New York Times* on the morning of February 25, 1950. "In about a minute, your living room will become the greatest theater, the grandest night club, the biggest circus in town," viewers were informed just before the show aired. At precisely nine o'clock, the orchestra sounded and the dancers began dancing. And then the chorus broke into a glorious new song.

CHAPTER 3

YOUR SHOW OF SHOWS

Stars over Broadway,
See them glow,
Get ready to take in
Your Show of Shows,
Show of Shows,
Show of Shows,
Show of Shows*!*

Come on and step lightly,
And walk brightly,
And join Broadway on parade,
See that happy, fabulous throng,
Get their fill of rhythm and song,
It's a great gay-time,
A late play-time,
The night's right for escapade.

It's wonderful to behold,
All that glitters as good as gold,
Sheer magic that scintillates and glows,
It's Your Show of Shows*!*

The words and music were, once again, Tolkin's, but rather than a jingle for appliances, it was a paean to a city and a time and way of life, an ode to optimism and fresh starts. It hardly mattered that between the primitive microphones and speakers the lyrics were muffled; the spirit came through. New York was Tolkin's *goldene medina*,[*] and he'd composed an anthem to its magic, promise, and tolerance. New York in 1950 was just about the safest and happiest place Jews had ever been. The trumpet fanfare at the outset sounded triumphant, and the strings that followed connoted comfort, luxury.

Save for a few weeks, every program of what came to be known colloquially as *The Show of Shows* started out with Tolkin's jaunty tune. Against a papier-mâché backdrop of blinking lights and primitive signs—CLUB, HOTEL, THEATRE, CAFÉ, RESTAURANT, SUBWAY—as the opening credits wobbled up the screen, the dancers, cast as cops and sailors and firemen, reached for those stars over Broadway. For Caesar, the song came to signal that Liebman's marvelous creation was once again springing to life. He tingled when he heard it. Now you got to do it. It's real, it said to him.

The veteran actor Burgess Meredith hosted that first show, and was at once tentative, dignified, extravagant, and intense. He talked about the "great galaxy" of performers waiting in the wings and all offerings on tap: comedy and tragedy, ballet and music, grand opera. Caesar then took the stage as a goofy small-town suitor in some indeterminate past, courting a demure and innocent Coca. It was a suitable keynote to a show that for its bursts of high culture and cosmopolitanism—the opera singers Marguerite Piazza and Robert Merrill, who'd be regulars on the show, singing a duet from *La traviata* and Coca saluting the smorgasbord—was often corny and cautious; Max Liebman would go heavy on the Currier and Ives. "The vast majority of people who watch television seldom see a Broadway show," he explained to *The New York Times*. "You can't feed them the same sophisticated comedy." Caesar kept himself busy, playing Professor Kurt von Wolfgang, authority on pain avoidance; Christopher Columbus (who'd landed in America solely to ensure there'd be a Columbus Day, Columbus, Ohio, and Columbus Circle); and a timorous groom before his wedding.

[*] Golden land.

The show was technically ragged (Meredith had read from a crib sheet), creatively uneven, and only intermittently funny. Despite its hefty budget, John Crosby complained, Caesar's show didn't sport a single original idea. But he praised Caesar as "a truly natural comic" who could "make you laugh before he says anything," and predicted "he will eventually be first-class if he isn't there now." The bartenders where Fred Rayfield of the New York *Daily Compass* had hoped to catch the show had gotten fed up with Carter's lackluster show beforehand and changed channels for the wrestling matches, sending Rayfield into the bitter cold in search of another saloon. There he saw a program good enough "to eventually replace even wrestling matches in bartenders' affections."

Something about Caesar, probably his silent, brooding mien, began tempting people to psychoanalyze him. Val Adams of the *Times* wrote that with his cerebral approach to comedy Caesar was "operating in a vastly uncrowded field." "Fundamentally, Caesar is a serious young man who will never be the life of any party," Adams observed. "When the curtain goes down, he withdraws into a shell which he is not likely to leave until the curtain goes up again." Such moodiness and seriousness were even leading some to deem him "high hat." "Because the angels have been with him every step of the way, it is not easy for Caesar to keep his head out of the fog," Adams wrote.

Meredith hosted the second show, too, then yielded to the actors Macdonald Carey, José Ferrer (twice), and Cedric Hardwicke and the singer Rudy Vallee. Because of the pay—as much as $4,000 a show—and the exposure it afforded, the show lured some bigger stars, though others accustomed to doing multiple takes on everything steered clear. When the cameras started to roll, Rex Harrison, who'd chosen *Your Show of Shows* for his TV debut, confessed he was "terrified" (he also carried notes), but explained that "just dropping dead and letting Sid Caesar do it all" simply wasn't right. Guest performers had to promise not to "ad lib or add any 'mugging,' gestures, or grimaces, nor deviate in any other way from your material shown to us in rehearsal, and approved by us." On such unfamiliar turf, all of them very dutifully complied.

The program quickly fell into a pattern. Each began with a domestic sketch featuring Caesar and Coca—shaking hands with the audience, Caesar called it. Then came the culture, generally short, savory, and accessible. The operatic selections, sung by Piazza and Merrill, were from Puccini and Bizet, not Wagner.* "Some of my friends said they're going to go to the toilet during the operas and the ballets and I said, 'I don't think so: not the way I do them,'" Liebman later boasted. Less snooty and far more typical were the production numbers, often set in cheery foreign locales—Parisian cafés, Alpine meadows, and the like; for his first several weeks on the show, Hayes later wrote, "all I did was sing in Lederhosen." No one better captured the all-American image Liebman sought than the boyish, likable Hayes, a native of Harvey, Illinois, who'd gone to college in Indiana. Thanks to two years of singing for hire at a synagogue on Chicago's South Side, he was far more exotic to the Jews on *Your Show of Shows* than they were to him. Marveling at its crisp efficiency and all-American sound, both Caesar and Brooks (who'd had to fabricate his own two-syllable name) loved calling Bill Hayes "Bill Hayes."†

There were also regular trips to cowboy country, filled with roundups, hoedowns, and cardboard cacti, and repeat retreats to the Gay Nineties, set to chestnuts like "In the Good Old Summer Time," "Let Me Call You Sweetheart," and "The Band Played On." Assorted puppeteers, acrobats, and ventriloquists made everything go down even easier.

Comedy, from Caesar and Coca, jointly and separately, was of course the key. The two appeared as Samson and Delilah and, in what quickly became a painfully tedious feature on the show, as a pair of hicks (Caesar a slightly effeminate one) from places like "People's Creek, Nevada," and "Beaver Falls, Iowa," who encounter each other in the big city and trade clichés. Most of the early sketches, including those incorporating guest hosts, were unoriginal or forgettable; the show was still too busy stay-

---

* That ads for recordings of Toscanini conducting Beethoven were mixed in with pitches for Snow Crop frozen orange juice and Chiquita bananas attested to the audience for such highbrow acts.

† Hayes, who had a pop hit with "The Ballad of Davy Crockett," went on to soap opera stardom on *Days of Our Lives*.

ing upright to experiment or grow. It was often at the end of the
show, with Caesar alone on the bare stage performing his monologues and pantomimes, that the program peaked.

For all his heft and brawn, Caesar was capable of great deli-
cacy and poignancy. He would depict the interior thoughts of
a six-month-old, or the family dog, or a man about to ask for
a raise, or a soon-to-be first-time father (as Caesar himself had
been a few years earlier, when his daughter, Michele—named for
his father, and called Shelly—was born). Such solos were never
cloying or saccharine; in fact, they could be quite the opposite.
Caesar's baby, for instance, was a kvetch. ("Don't kiss me with the
beard!" "Go get the formula! Ever taste it? Ech!") And since it
had his genes, it, too, coughed.

Unlike that of so many other comics, Caesar's goal was not
just to endear himself, to charm and beguile, but also to unsettle.
"You know, in almost every marriage, there comes a time when
the two people stop looking through the rose-colored glasses
of romance," he declared in a monologue from February 1951.
"And they start to look at each other as two ordinary plain human
beings. And when this happens, you know that the marriage is
starting to collapse." It brought laughs—*knowing* laughs. In
another monologue, he awakens to hear his wife screaming, "I'll
kill you, you rat! Get out of the house! I'll kill you. I can't stand
you, you're a rat." Wake up! he pleads; you must have been having a bad dream. "Who's dreaming, you rat!" she shrieks. "I'll kill
ya, you nut! I'll murder ya!"

Despite concerns from the censors about giving people
ideas—"The world is a little sick these days and until it starts getting better our hunch favors avoidance of a rash of plots having
to do with people throwing in the sponge," one cautioned—talk
of suicide popped up inordinately in Caesar's routines. Exhausted
from dissuading a despondent Coca from jumping from the
Empire State Building (or, another time, into the Seine), Caesar
gives the next sob sister he encounters a shove—or jumps himself. He also was fixated on the ostensible American Everyman
who was actually crazy, or cruel, or both. Take his portrayal of a
paranoiac, convinced he's being dissed or had or both, who talks

to himself, eyes everyone else suspiciously, and is always poised to pounce. "You give me your word of honor this is chicken salad?" he snarls at a waiter. "You're lying in your teeth! This is tuna fish!"

For a couple of hours once, Caesar had followed around and studied such a guy; his own psychoanalysis had informed his portrayal. But the sketch so disturbed New York's assistant commissioner for mental hygiene, James Brussel, heretofore a fan of the show, that he wrote directly to David Sarnoff. By capturing with "agonizing accuracy" a paranoid schizophrenic "overwhelmed with multiple and unsystematized delusions of persecution," he declared, Caesar had hit "a new and horrifying low in distasteful comedy." "I fail to understand where so-called humor encompasses man's mental and physical afflictions," he continued. "I presume that in the weeks to come we can anticipate Mr. Caesar portraying a consumptive coughing through a pulmonic hemorrhage to death, or a blind man walking out of a ten-story window, or a G.I. amputee helplessly fumbling with his prosthetic appliances in lieu of arms and legs he has lost. These, in the eyes of experts on wit, must be dandy sources of material for laughs."

"In many private and public institutions some patients are granted special privileges as awards for improvement," Brussel concluded. "This may be realized in allowing them to stay up Saturday nights for the SHOW OF SHOWS. What a slap in the face and what a clinical shock Mr. Caesar's thoughtless effort must have been for those patients!" Caesar never played the man again, and it was a pity: Never did he portray someone so troubled so convincingly. To Howard Morris, Caesar better exemplified Method acting than Marlon Brando did. "I learned that from Sid," he explained. "Get into yourself, and find out where the reality comes from."

Then there were Caesar's pantomimes of the differing ablutions of men and women, or of teaching Coca how to drive, or of taking her to the movies or on a picnic, or of fighting over what to watch on their new TV. Caesar loved pantomime because it made audiences participate and *imagine*, rather than merely sit and watch; it sidestepped television's aggressive literalism and brought back the magic of the radio of his youth, when, as he put it, "they couldn't build a castle as big as the one I had in my mind," nor "make a princess as beautiful." (And, as Chico Marx pointed out, it spared Caesar from having to memorize *even more* lines every week.) Reiner marveled at how Caesar gave nonexistent objects height, breadth, and heft. Caesar could don an imaginary overcoat, Liebman once said, and you'd know whether it was a raglan or a chesterfield, and made from either camel's hair, herringbone, flannel, or tweed. Coca was equally adept at, and absorbed by, the craft: All the imaginary popcorn, ice cream, and hot dogs she ate on their simulated trip to Coney Island made her feel genuinely like throwing up afterward. Here, as always onstage, they were perfectly in tune. In rehearsal once, Caesar couldn't resume tossing a nonexistent salad until Coca had handed him back the nonexistent salad bowl.

Television was called a "medium," Fred Allen, the much-respected radio wit (and hero to Caesar and other thinking comics), once quipped, because nothing on it was well done. But Allen exempted Caesar from his broadsides. He lived around the corner from the International Theatre and would often drop by for dress rehearsals. "A casual observer might have assumed that Allen, the master, had come to instruct Caesar, the apprentice," *Collier's* noted. "Actually it was the other way around. Allen was embarking on his first television show and *he* had come to learn from *Caesar.*"

Before long, Caesar rued the day when he and Liebman had taken all ninety of the minutes Pat Weaver had offered them. "For the birds," he called that last, agonizing half hour. But it was then, when he was most depleted, that he was also at his most ingenious, reflective, autobiographical, and exposed, that he bonded with his audience, and that his peculiar suitability for TV became most apparent. "Caesar seems to be the ideal comic for television," Jeanne Loughlin noted in *The Daily Compass*. "His spontaneous, adroit facial expressions—wonderful in television close-up—might be lost on a theater stage. His comic material, drawn mainly from perceptive observations of everyday life, might not be broad enough buffoonery for the movies. At night clubs, perhaps much of his comic creation of the adventures of an average man might be wasted." But "for home consumption," she noted, his antics were "just about perfect."

There was drama at the start of every show unmentioned on the printed program. It came when Caesar introduced the week's guest host, or tried to. When he first appeared onstage—"Ladies and gentlemen, *Sid Caesar!*" the announcer would shout as the last note of "Stars over Broadway" faded—he was all business. He'd hold up his hands peremptorily, almost imperiously, to cut off the applause, not out of modesty, but because it prolonged his agony. He'd then start speaking, in an affected, actorly, slightly stilted manner. Much as he hated (and even banned) cue cards, so inimical to authenticity, spontaneity, and connectivity (to the audience as well as to the other performers), it sounded as if he were reading off one of them.

"Good evening, ladies and gentlemen, this is Sid Caesar," he'd say, as if on radio rather than standing there for all the world to see. "Welcome to *Your Show of Shows.*" But only rarely was that how the words came out. Tolkin once assembled the forty or so different ways they actually did, among them "Woolkim to the shoo," "Wilcome to the shaw," "Wulcum to da shee." Caesar's stock line when presenting the evening's guest presenter—the correct phrase was "star of the week and host for this evening"— seemed formulated to trip him up. Getting through the visitors' latest credits also proved an ordeal. "Our star tonight has just finished a picture where he co-starred wis . . . with Miss Betty Hutton, in the Cecil B. dePicture, *The Greatest Show on Earth*" was how he presented Charlton Heston in October 1951. Once finished, Caesar would dash off the stage, ostensibly to prepare for the opening sketch but also to play someone besides himself. Reiner attributed it all to fear. "His feeling is, I'm just an ordinary guy whose folks ran a luncheonette in Yonkers," he theorized. "Who am I to be up here, having all these people watching me and listening to me?" Caesar kept trying—it was, he once explained, "the way I practice being me"—but it never got any easier. Hugh Downs, brought on later to spare Caesar from such agony, likened Sid's struggle to "the stark, evident terror of a kid in a high school play."

Viewers actually enjoyed the "fluffs," Caesar observed: They gave them "a sense of participating." (A week *without* a flub was novel enough for *Variety* to note.) The sheer brinkmanship of his performances was part of the show's power. As the critic Andrew Sarris later put it, "their opening nights were not only their closing nights, but also their eternal incarnations," lending an "exquisitely wrought emotional tension" to the experience of watching them.

Every show was recorded, though hardly for posterity; practical concerns, rather than intimations of immortality, explained why, unlike so much of early television, *Your Show of Shows* was preserved: The kinescopes allowed for last-minute reprises of old sketches—say, when something else wasn't funny or had suddenly fallen through. "Better a good old thing than a bad new thing," Liebman liked to say. Whenever that happened, he'd ask his young assistant, Len Kanter, to fetch a particular "kinny" containing something tried and true, which the principals would then review and recommit to memory. But posterity's hold on the show was fragile: Periodically, another of Liebman's assistants, Natalie Goodman, would fill the metal tray beneath the reels of film with water to keep them from drying up and disintegrating.

Even without the repeats, there were complaints of predictability. As early as April 1950—barely two months into the show—*Variety* was calling the program "tired and pedestrian." But with television spreading, lots of folks were still seeing Caesar for the first time. And Caesar kept collecting kudos. Groucho Marx congratulated him at Toots Shor's. *Look* called him television's best comic, *TV Guide*, a "clown of majesty." *Cue* magazine compared him to Chaplin and W. C. Fields, and said that how good television was in any given week "depends on how funny Caesar has been." That he was so often likened to Chaplin only made Caesar more tongue-tied the two times the two men met. (Running into Jack Benny once, Caesar hadn't known what to say to him, either.)

For all the talk about joining "Broadway on parade," the show brought jitters to the Great White Way. "Ticket demand is almost as hot for this one as for *South Pacific*," Larry Wolters of the *Chicago Tribune* reported. The managers of Radio City Music

Hall begged NBC to move *Your Show of Shows* to Thursdays. Robert Taylor complained that he could no longer get his wife (Barbara Stanwyck) to go out on Saturday nights because she was home watching Caesar, and Ida Lupino had the same beef with Howard Duff. Ordinary people had to make adjustments, too. Because foot traffic from the nearby movie theater had dried up on Saturday nights, Myron Lipsy, who owned a shoe store in Syracuse, closed up then. Caesar's few detractors reconsidered. Philip Hamburger of *The New Yorker,* who had found Caesar's portrayal of a gumball machine in *Make Mine Manhattan* so offensive, now hailed him as "one of the two or three funniest men on television" (and Coca as "far and away the funniest" of the comediennes).

Caesar was among the few television comics to impress Mack Sennett, the man who'd directed Chaplin, W. C. Fields, and the Keystone Cops. To those who said television comedy would come of age only once the "big boys"—Hope, Benny, and Jimmy Durante among them—came on board, *TV Guide* had some news: "The big boys are too late." NBC gloated. "Now we own Saturday night," George McGarrett, who supervised the production of the show for the network, wrote to Weaver in April 1950. Liebman took his bows. If they'd had to put out half what he did, the producers Moss Hart and Max Gordon told him, they'd "be ready for the guy with the big net." *Billboard* suggested, "NBC oughtta build a statue of Max (Sat. Nite) Liebman" "smack dab in the middle of Rockefeller Plaza."

CAESAR NEEDED NO COVER from the blacklist then proliferating; he was no more vocal about his politics than about anything else. Colleagues assumed he was a liberal, but never really knew. He took no chances, staying on the good side of Jack O'Brian, television columnist of the conservative Hearst papers and pal of Roy Cohn, Senator Joseph McCarthy's closest aide. Bishop Fulton Sheen praised Caesar on his show (and Caesar praised him back on his), providing an additional layer of insurance. Politics was something the show continued to avoid (were it not for blood drives and reminders by the kindly folks at R. J. Reynolds of the free Camels they were sending to the front, the Korean War would have passed unnoticed), not just because it was politic, but because it was transitory. "Our comedic attack was human behavior, from the caveman to the guy in apartment 29A," Brooks once said. For Tolkin, it was a matter of status, too. "We were snobs," he said. "We didn't want to do things off the headlines because it would die, and we were immortal."

But inevitably, the rancid tenor of the time intruded on the show. In March 1950, Melvyn Douglas—one of Caesar's boyhood idols, who'd co-starred in *The Guilt of Janet Ames*—was guest host. Simply asking him on was a statement: His criticism of the House Un-American Activities Committee had prompted Representative John Rankin of Mississippi to remind everyone that Douglas was born "Hesselberg." Caesar only accentuated Douglas's politics by introducing him as "the husband of Congresswoman Helen Gahagan Douglas," the so-called Pink Lady whom Richard Nixon would red-bait, and defeat, in a contentious Senate race that fall. "Thank you for that introduction," Douglas ad-libbed. "And just for that, I'll be happy to check your loyalty test any time you want it." Liebman invited Douglas back twice more that year.

Less happy was a visit by the cartoonist Al Capp, creator of *Li'l Abner*, who guest-hosted in May. Capp was a great Caesar fan, modeling a character named Sam the Centaur after him and creating a place called Caesar Siddy on the isle of Bagle-Bagle, just off the coast of Lower Slobbovia, where most of *Li'l Abner* took place. (Caesar reciprocated: In a proto-*Flintstones* sketch the week before Capp's appearance, he and his caveman wife, Coca, read *Li'l Abner* on stone tablets.) When, on the program, Capp introduced a nostalgic piece on lawn tennis, he situated it "back in the nineteen hundreds, before our lives were threatened by the H-bomb and by comic books and by Faye Emerson's neckline, and all we had was peace." Thus, in a single sentence, Capp managed to touch on three separate television taboos: politics, cultural controversy, and sex. Capp was not invited back.

Liebman took additional risks: At least five of his guest hosts (Burgess Meredith, José Ferrer, Lena Horne, Marsha Hunt, and

Henry Morgan) appeared in *Red Channels*, the June 1950 compendium of alleged communists in the entertainment business that became the bible of the blacklist. And despite their left-wing pasts, he kept on Reiner, Kallen, and Tolkin. Liebman himself wasn't beyond suspicion. "The people at NBC were scared to death that Max would be investigated," Coca said. At one point, network officials asked Coca whether Tamiment was "Communist." In such a climate, doing no harm was perhaps as much as could be expected; *The Daily Worker* praised the show for "its complete absence of red-baiting." (Network publicists took care to purge the paper from their mailing list.)

ON MAY 20, 1950, *Your Show of Shows* concluded its first half season. And this time, they *knew* they'd be back. "Does Sid Caesar have to worry where his next yacht comes from now that 'The Saturday Night Revue' already has nine sponsors for next fall, and not a spare minute left?" Jack O'Brian asked. When Mayor O'Dwyer declared "Television Week" in New York in July, Caesar was among the featured attractions.

Rather than take a break, Caesar booked *another* gig for himself at the Roxy. By this point he was important enough to be interviewed by Saul Pett, the master portraitist of the Associated Press. Like everyone else, Pett found Caesar silent, sullen, angry, wary, humorless, and inarticulate, even though he was living it up: driving *two* Cadillacs, smoking fat cigars, sporting fifteen suits, lavishing "monster" tips on delivery boys, and enjoying $10,000 worth of guns, including the pistol he brought with him to the Roxy, which he took apart and put back together for relaxation. (Remarkably, he'd stayed in his $175-a-month, five-room apartment in Forest Hills, and still came to the theater by bus.) "You can go nuts from too much money, too," Caesar told Pett. "Everybody is slapping your back. Everybody pulling at you, everybody on the bandwagon now. You got to keep your head."

On the day when Pett visited Caesar, six thousand people awaited him outside the Roxy. Meanwhile, surrounding him in his dressing room was a collection of "camp followers," including a manager, two writers, a minder from NBC, a buddy from the Coast Guard, and his mother, who'd actually bought a ticket to his show. ("So why should I bother Sidney?" she asked. "Maybe he's lying down or sleeping.") Caesar was in a reflective mood, talking about his childhood. "I was always running away," he said. "I guess I'm still running away. Everybody has something driving them. You know, something happens in your life and you want to get even." He didn't elaborate. Even praise left him looking pained.

But Mel Brooks was ebullient during Pett's visit. For months he had remained in internal exile, with the writing credits reserved for Tolkin, Kallen, Liebman, and Caesar, who, while never wielding a pencil, "was as much a writer as anyone else," Liebman insisted. (Caesar soon removed his name.) But Brooks had persisted, and Liebman persistently let him. "When you fire somebody four times a day it means you haven't fired him," he explained. Finally, in April 1950, Liebman sort of promoted him, on the wings of an imaginary bird.

In the show of April Fools' Day 1950, Gon-Gon, the jungle boy introduced a year earlier, returned for another airport interview. Stuck once again for a few good lines, Caesar had turned to Brooks, who had the boy recount how he foraged for his jungle breakfasts: by pulling a bird out of midair. Gon-Gon's description came complete with the sound of the doomed bird cawing agonizingly as he was captured and consumed; it was that blood-curdling caw, along with an airport interview the following week featuring Caesar as a Russian disciple of the famed acting teacher Konstantin Stanislavski, that seems finally to have gotten Brooks into the credits, though only, in Liebman's sadistic formulation, under "additional material by."[*]

As Pett interviewed Caesar, and as Caesar's Coast Guard pal played the harmonica, Brooks jumped around like a monkey. "Do

---

[*] Even this second, more elaborate incarnation of Gon-Gon wasn't the crowning sketch Brooks repeatedly described in later years. Only in his imagination (and never, it appears, on an actual show) did Gon-Gon wage war with those creatures he feared most: Buicks.

the introduction number, Mel," Caesar asked him. "Mel obliged," wrote Pett. "He started singing, crooning, bellowing, hopping, shuffling and finally, on one knee a la Jolson, ended with 'I'm out of my mind, so please be kind—to Melvin Brooks.'" Caesar, and then everybody else, laughed.

CHAPTER 4

WEEKLY RITUALS

William L. Laurence of *The New York Times* was confounded by his new television set. Laurence was no technophobe: He'd won the Pulitzer Prize for describing the development of the atomic bomb. But so flummoxed was he by his TV that he'd asked a colleague at the paper to diagram which dials to turn where to get a decent picture. After two days of fiddling around, he'd finally figured things out. "It worked," Laurence crowed. "Saw Sid Caesar. Great."

For Laurence and its millions of fans, after its four-month run earlier in the year, *Your Show of Shows* entered its first full season in September 1950 with colors flying. Though the show remained at the International Theatre, Liebman's company had abandoned the jockstraps and grunge above the Guild Theatre for four floors in the City Center, the former Shriners Temple on West Fifty-Fifth Street. "The U.S. Steel of television," Kallen called the new setup. As the show resumed, reporters from four different magazines were following Liebman around. Caesar was now earning $4,000 a week, which would soon be upped to $5,000. NBC could afford it: Ad rates for the show had tripled. *Variety* complained of commercials following almost every number, but television was still so young, and viewers still so enamored, that they considered all the huckstering a fair price to pay for what they were getting. Not so long ago, the writer Paul Gallico observed, he'd forked out $18 to see Sid Caesar; now, simply by looking at a beautiful new refrigerator or a toy polar bear hawking frozen peas for a few minutes, he got him for free.

It wasn't just NBC that was getting fat: so was Caesar, who'd taken on a blocky, almost rectangular look. *Cosmopolitan* detected "the beginning of a comfortable bulge" around his waist. Caesar's poundage would now be tracked as closely as his ratings. "My, Sid Caesar's been putting on weight, hasn't he!" Dorothy Kilgallen wrote in mock horror. Acknowledging his client's "avoirdupois problem," Caesar's publicist assured Kilgallen that his client was "trying to peel it off," though a few months later, one reporter called him "Tubby." In fact, Caesar had picked up (or intensified) binge purges. He'd have his usual trencherman's breakfast, come into the office, then head for the bathroom to puke. Sometimes it happened on its own, and sometimes he helped it along. After lunch, the ritual was reenacted. So second nature did the routine become that after a while the regulars didn't even notice. But to new arrivals, the sounds coming from the bathroom raised eyebrows, and questions. "Oh, Sid just came in," someone explained matter-of-factly to one of them.

THE ACTOR ROBERT CUMMINGS was the new season's first guest host, on September 9. But the program's most significant new face was Carl Reiner, who appeared in an otherwise tired sketch in which Caesar's Dr. von Wolfgang had been brought in to help make a "neurotic picture" called "For Three Weeks I Was a Murderer." Reiner played the studio executive in charge.

Liebman had seen, and liked, the twenty-eight-year-old Reiner on Broadway in a show called *Alive and Kicking* as well as in another television program, *The 54th Street Revue*. Brooks, too, had spotted him, and seen "a great foil, a great second banana, a great Abbott to Sid's Costello." "We can't just keep taking people from the chorus to work with you," Brooks told Caesar, referring to the incumbent interlocutor on the airport interviews, a dancer and supernumerary on the show named Tom Avera, whom Bill Hayes later described as "a Southern boy who did not really fit in with the kind of wonderful Jewish comedy that we featured."

Reiner, in turn, had followed Caesar's career, and was yet another awestruck fan. "I heard Sid Caesar, and I said, 'Wait a minute. If I'm a comedian, what's *that?*'" he remembered. But he'd be quite content to sit in the second chair, knowing that it was alongside a throne. Reiner brought intelligence, versatility, charm, stability, and sanity to the ensemble. As cool as Caesar was hot, as poised as Caesar was wired, as steady—and *normal*—as Caesar could be freakish and unhinged, Reiner would both enhance Caesar's genius and help keep it on track. Caesar's "sturdy supporting oak," one writer called him. With someone so grounded by his side, Caesar could fly; should he fly off too far, Reiner would yank him back. "Without him, the show would just have spun off the planet," said Bill Persky, who studied Caesar as a young man and wrote for him later.

Reiner was a more evolved, housebroken, presentable kind of Jew than Caesar, and more ebullient, upbeat, assimilated, and accommodating, well suited to smooth Caesar's jagged Jewish edges—a universal maître d'. Even his toupee fit comfortably and (at least as these things go) convincingly on his head. That rarest of qualities in Caesar's circle—a certain Waspishness—made Reiner perfectly suited to play the twits and Brits, the pompous Hollywood directors, the insufferable butlers, and the supercilious waiters Caesar loved to mock. But he could just as easily do ingratiating game show hosts, lecherous sweatshop operators, harsh television interrogators, and hayseeds. In the Jewish culinary vernacular, he was "parve"—neither meat nor dairy, going down easily and acceptably with just about anything. While his doubletalk wasn't quite up to Caesar's, he could play Parisians, Prussians, and Italians with him. And no one was ever better suited to play the roving reporter in those airport interviews. Reiner was by nature a listener and facilitator, coaxing still more out of what the officially funny guy said. He even looked the part, someone for whom a trench coat and spiral notebook were perfect accessories.

A watchmaker's son raised on the Grand Concourse in the

Bronx—he claimed his father had patented the first battery-operated clock—Reiner had been drawn early to acting, learning good diction and how to mask his accent from listening to Claude Rains. During World War II, and thanks to Howard Morris, whom he'd known in New York, he'd done Shakespeare in Maurice Evans's entertainment troupe in the Pacific, only to conclude that comedy was a better fit. Liebman honored the old vaudeville saw that a straight man should be taller than the comedian he served, which wasn't so easy when that comedian was six feet one. Even here, Reiner fit the bill—by an inch. When Liebman offered him six weeks of work, Reiner grabbed it.

Like Caesar, the real Reiner was hard to read, though in his case mostly by choice: his carefree, imperturbable facade was largely an act. "He measures himself out" was how the writer Lawrence Christon described him. "He's an affable, layered man whose genial surface occasionally yields a glimpse of the solitary man watching from the shadow." "I put on the face for people," Reiner acknowledged. "I give them the smile. They don't have to know what I'm feeling. I like to make people happy."

Like Tolkin, Reiner had been raised in a fear-filled household. His mother, originally from Bucharest, had been frightened all her life, first of pogroms (during one, she'd been hidden in an oven) and then of the authorities in New York, for she'd never got past kindergarten and had worked while underage. Reiner's protectiveness toward her nurtured in him a lifelong desire to care for people. Hitler had murdered most of his father's family. Asked once what it meant to him to be a Jew, Reiner replied, "It means to have extra antennae out. It's that kind of feeling that we are a breed apart, we are not safe in the world. People call us overly sensitive. I think we're just the right amount of sensitive to stay alive." "Let's not buy any statues," he'd advise. "You can't carry them when the Nazis come."

Also in his baggage was left-wing politics. As a young man, Reiner had read *The Daily Worker*, though more to follow Negro League baseball stars like Josh Gibson and Satchel Paige than the party line. He'd worked in the same left-wing summer camp in upstate New York as Abel Meeropol, the former communist who, as Lewis Allan, wrote Billie Holiday's antilynching anthem, "Strange Fruit."* That was also where he'd met his wife, Estelle (who was more political than he). A benefit Reiner had emceed for Spanish Civil War refugees in early 1949 prompted a visit from the FBI. While Caesar *couldn't* play himself, Reiner *wouldn't* and *didn't*. Even his personal papers were purged of anything sensitive or disagreeable. "Carl acts mostly off-stage," Larry Gelbart once said. "He acts like everything's OK, and it's not." Like other newcomers, he spent his first few weeks in hallway exile, hard labor for someone who'd always kept himself in the mix. But he quickly became indispensable, even inevitable: How, Kallen once asked, had they ever gotten along without him? Far more quickly than Brooks, he gained entry—*sashayed*—into the writers' room, where he designated himself "writer without portfolio," much to the annoyance of writers *with* portfolios, especially the territorial, status-conscious Tolkin.

AS THE SHOW'S FIRST full season got under way, Jack Gould noted Caesar's evolution from boisterous but repetitious dialectologist to a more subtle and variegated artist. While much of the program dragged, he wrote, "so long as Mr. Caesar is around, *Your Show of Shows* is not to be missed." John Crosby was even more effusive, calling Caesar "one of the wonders of this modern electronic age." Again, there were worries about overexposure. Larry Wolters of the *Chicago Tribune* warned that NBC was exhausting Caesar, Coca, *and* their audience; long before June, he predicted, viewers would have had their fill.

On the new season's second program came its first woman guest host: the actress and comedienne Arlene Francis. (She'd be back, because, as she put it, "there's no business like 'Show of Show' business.") Other visitors that season included Ralph Bellamy, Nanette Fabray, Geraldine Fitzgerald, Douglas Fairbanks Jr., Veronica Lake, Sarah Churchill, and Joan Bennett. (Liebman had

---

* Meeropol and his wife, Anne, later adopted the two orphaned sons of the executed atomic spies Julius and Ethel Rosenberg.

hoped Greta Garbo would make her television debut on the show; she didn't.) MGM's head of production, Dore Schary, forbade his stars to go on television; it watered down their mystique, he said, and with its primitive lighting, cutting, and camerawork made them look less attractive. But the chance to appear before twenty-five million people was hard to resist, and the show became, as one television columnist put it, "probably the foremost lure to skittish Hollywood stars to take the TV plunge."

Though, by one count, only 18 of 240 routines that season were repeats, it seemed like more. In October, Caesar went through his one-man rendition of a boxing movie for the third time (and, a year later, the fourth). In various guises of a goon, Caesar inserted himself between Coca and elegant guest hosts on a subway car, bus, and plane, as well as at a wrestling match and in a restaurant, movie theater, casino, shoe repair shop, and opera house, his boorishness in the same full flower. For a brief time, complaints about too many repeats were probably equaled by complaints about too few. "How many times have you heard someone mention the 'funny sketches of Sid Caesar and Imogene Coca' which you had missed seeing?" griped one reader of the *Brooklyn Eagle*, who suggested that networks operate a "Re-Run Theater" during some as-yet-uncolonized part of the schedule, like Saturday or Sunday afternoons or nights after 10:30.

While some of his material grew stale, Caesar did not. Even the famously curmudgeonly humorist Henry Morgan, who guest-hosted the show in November 1950, joined the chorus. "Now I have to introduce a guy who, ah . . . is a comedian," he said. "*Real* comedian. Maybe there are five; I doubt it." While more East Coast people grew fatigued, novitiates in the hinterlands were still discovering Caesar. To viewers in Des Moines and other points west of Chicago, who only in late September 1950 got something besides travelogues, industrial films, test patterns, and wrestling matches on their TVs, Caesar's arrival occasioned "some figurative throwing of hats into the air," Paul Cotton wrote in *The Des Moines Register*. In thousands of homes in and around Iowa during the winter of 1950–51, he noted, "watching [Caesar's] show Saturday night became a habit."

For such viewers, Caesar became synonymous with New York, and his show, a primer on the place. "This is for the benefit of all you *lucky* people who live in the country," the guest host Madeleine Carroll declared in October 1950, before Caesar and Coca portrayed straphangers competing for a seat on the A train. In a "Clichés" sketch the following week, Caesar told his fellow hayseed Coca how New Yorkers drink from 2:30 in the afternoon to 2:30 in the morning (and spend cocktail parties showing off how smart they are). Sophisticated city folks liked foreign movies, which, with Reiner double-talking back to him, Caesar could now spoof. One of the first, a send-up of *The Bicycle Thief*, aired in December 1950. A takeoff on *The Blue Angel*, in which a bookish scientist (Caesar) falls for a boa-wearing nightclub singer (Coca), followed a few months later. New Yorkers also knew about psychiatrists, and if viewers elsewhere didn't, the program would teach them. "A few years ago, the word 'psychoanalysis' would have meant very little to the general public. But today almost everyone knows about the psychiatrist's couch, the interpretation of dreams and so on" was how the guest host Coleen Gray introduced a dance number in May 1952. One of Caesar's Professors, an authority on animal psychiatry, was brought in to treat a depressed tiger in the Central Park Zoo and a manic monkey in the Bronx.

In a wave of profiles in national magazines, Caesar underwent a bit of cracker-barrel psychoanalysis himself. "In private conversation, he has two disturbing habits," *Cosmopolitan* observed in January 1951. "He is likely to start grimacing and making strange noises because this is a simple, natural method of communication for him. Also, he may stop in the middle of a sentence and seemingly become enchanted with a chair, a bush, or a tree. This means he has thought of an idea for a skit and is kicking it around in his mind." Or, perhaps, having a conversation with it.

Apolitical though it was, politically oriented magazines also took note of *Your Show of Shows*, as if its very sophistication were a political act. To the jazz writer Leonard Feather, appearing in *The New Statesman*, Caesar was something he'd never heard on radio or seen on television before: a genius. Saul Carson of *The*

New Republic exempted Caesar's show from the run of television comedy, "created solely to prove that life is one big guffaw," filled with either cream pies (heaved), tomatoes (squished), or seltzer bottles (squirted). Carson's critique would surely have extended to the Chicago portion of *Saturday Night Revue*, and on that NBC's boss, David Sarnoff, would have agreed. "The Jack Carter Show on Saturday night is consistent if nothing else," he griped to Weaver that October. "It is consistently lousy and the lousiest thing on the show is Jack Carter himself." (Carter was soon axed.)

Touting Caesar's latest award became as much a staple of *Your Show of Shows* as Piazza's arias or Bill Hayes's ballads. It was after collecting such a prize one snowy evening at the Waldorf Astoria that Caesar, preparing to leave, spotted his mother across Park Avenue, standing beneath a streetlight. When he walked over and invited her to come inside, she demurred. "I'll be OK," she insisted. "At least, Ma, let me put you in a car to send you home." "No, no, no, no. It's all right. You'll be with your friends. Go ahead. They want to talk to you." And then she walked away. It was a scene he'd remember, and one day reenact in one of his most affecting sketches. Ida Caesar, aged sixty-five, died on January 21, 1951, a day after Jack O'Brian had come on the show to announce that the Hearst papers had voted her son the best comedian on television. The *Times* ran a short item on her death.

The same month, Caesar took out half a page in *Variety* to thank "everyone for everything." Then he headed to Miami Beach for two weeks. The legendary sports columnist of *The Washington Post*, Shirley Povich, was alongside him when a crowd gathered around his Cadillac convertible outside the Lord Tarleton Hotel and Caesar stood up on the back seat and offered them a menagerie of characters for the next hour. Also at the Tarleton, Caesar had the thrill of hanging out and horsing around with Harry Ritz, the long-forgotten comic whose high-energy antics with his brothers—eye-rolling, double-talk, depicting how people walked, talked, and even urinated—had inspired Caesar and many others. As much as he praised Chaplin and Keaton, "Maybe I liked Harry Ritz most of all," Caesar said.

Caesar and Coca left their highly paid competitor on CBS

that season, Frank Sinatra, reeling. The *Saturday Review* described the mismatch: "two very funny people" against "the likeable kid from New Jersey trying hard to find his place in the television sun." While Caesar was hip, Sinatra, still playing to the bobby-soxers, was already old hat.[*] In early November, the editor of the New York *Daily Compass* griped when NBC preempted part of Caesar's show for a speech by President Truman. Taking in Judy Garland at the Palace Theatre, Coca's great-aunt noticed how people couldn't stop staring at her niece, then besieged Coca for autographs long enough to hold up the show. One night Nick Kenny of the *New York Mirror* witnessed something he'd never seen before for any artist: When Caesar walked into Lindy's, everyone stood up.

LENA HORNE, JUST BACK from a European stay, appeared on the show in January 1951, after Liebman and Caesar mollified network executives and advertisers jittery over having a Black guest host. "When I took a look at one of the brightest spots on television," she told the audience, "and when they asked me to be a hostess on that particular show, then I was doubly glad to be home again." Walter Winchell praised Horne's "shelectricity" on the show, which of course was what made the network suits so skittish.[†]

Liebman was better than most on racial matters. "Color-blind and quality obsessed," Caesar said of him. But there were limits. *Variety* had reported beforehand that Horne would "sing, emcee and do a sketch with Sid Caesar," but the third item could

---

* "I don't think anyone tuned in except Ava Gardner," wrote Paul Cotton of *The Des Moines Register*, referring to Sinatra's actress girlfriend at the time (*Des Moines Register*, Sept. 28, 1951).

† Horne's appearance on the *Colgate Comedy Hour* a few weeks later—and, specifically, the cut of her gown—showed the perils she posed. "My wife and children should not be subject, in our own home, to such outrageous effrontery," a North Carolina lawyer wrote to NBC. "This Horne woman may be a good singer but if I am not mis-informed she is the woman that married a white man and we still have a large number of states that make such a marriage a crime" (Letter, Feb. 26, 1951, box 129, folder 5, NBC Records).

never have come to pass: Blacks could not interact with whites in sketches. According to Caesar, the North Carolina–based R. J. Reynolds Tobacco Company vetoed Black performers of any kind on those portions of the show it sponsored. "The singing of 'Love,' incidentally, had some of the animalian distinctiveness that frequently marks Miss Horne's singing, but it was toned down considerably for greater effect," *Variety* wrote of Horne's appearance.

The Billy Williams Quartet—or, as the program cards NBC prepared internally after each show called it, "The Bill Williams Quartet (colored)"—was conspicuous, but circumspect. Impeccable in matching light suits and ever smiling, the group performed two songs per program, almost none of them "race music." *Variety* urged that the men be integrated into the cast, but that was wishful thinking: Only during curtain calls did that happen. Black performers were always introduced from a different part of the stage, allaying concerns of any interracial interactions; even panning from the foursome to the sleekly clad white dancers who sometimes followed them onto the stage brought angry letters. As much as the Black press enthused about the quartet, many of its fiercest fans were white. "A bunch of little Jewish girls from Brooklyn" was how one member of the group, Claude Riddick, described them.

Other shows, *not* run by Jews, were actually more progressive racially than *Your Show of Shows;* Jewish caution trumped Jewish progressivism. When, in January 1952, Governor Herman Talmadge of Georgia enumerated in his family's newspaper three television shows offending southern sensibilities, *Your Show of Shows* wasn't among them. What especially perturbed Talmadge was Arthur Godfrey's weekly program, which featured a mixed-race (two whites and two Blacks) quartet called the Mariners; a Christmas special in which Black and white children "mixed indiscriminately," and a third show in which performers of both races "exchanged badinage on a purely equal social basis." Talmadge *praised* Liebman's show for keeping Billy Williams and his singers—"a great group," he conceded—cordoned off. An unbowed Godfrey noted that at that very moment Black and white Americans were dying together in Korea. When, in a subsequent Godfrey show, the Mariners sang

"You're a Nobody," Godfrey sang along—and dedicated the song to Talmadge, something Liebman and Caesar would never have dared to do.

Though there'd been talk of having Harry Belafonte on the show, it never happened. When one network executive suggested that Duke Ellington appear, another replied, "Let's forget." "There would probably be some mention of United Negro fund work . . . are your sponsors any problem?" Weaver cautioned another NBC executive who'd asked about having the Hampton Institute Choir on the program. Such selectivity still didn't placate one St. Louis businessman. "If you must have negroes, then have an all negro performance," he wrote to NBC. Race reared its head again when the dancer Arthur Mitchell, who later starred in the New York City Ballet and founded the Dance Theatre of Harlem, auditioned, spectacularly, for the program but wasn't hired. "Arthur was a better dancer than most of us," the dancer and choreographer Bambi Linn, then a regular on the program, remembered. "I think Max just didn't want the controversy."

There were other sensitivities. Not every Italian American found Caesar's Italian double-talk amusing. Incensed by a sketch in March 1951, a past national commander of the Italian-American World War Veterans charged that Caesar's "pseudo-comedy" subjected him and people like him to "unjust ridicule and contempt." The NBC censor, Stockton Helffrich, thought such routines "without malice," but after another complaint, this one from the Italian-American Congress—and with congressional hearings into organized crime then under way—he counseled caution. "Maybe with so many Italian gangsters under fire these days it is a good point at which to space Caesar's spoofing of Italians further apart," he advised.

It didn't help. "Sid Ceasar [*sic*] may not know it but he's lost a flock of admirers who object to his 'unnecessary, uninspired and unrealistic portrait of Italians, which seem more than anything else to hold the race up to public ridicule,'" Al Salerno of the *Brooklyn Eagle* complained that October, calling Caesar's spoofs "a crude burlesque, a mumbo jumbo of words that mean nothing in any language." To him the real villains were Caesar's writers, who must have "lost their marbles" to turn out such stuff, and his producers, for letting them. At the same time, the waiters in Coca's favorite nightclub, all of them Italian, told her how magnificently Caesar spoke their mother tongue. The show's scenic designer, Fred Fox, recalled watching an Italian bartender in Philadelphia telling his patrons what Caesar was saying—"translating," Fox marveled, "and not a word made sense." Enough Italians claimed Caesar as a *paisan* that Jay Grayson of the Yiddish *Forverts* felt bound to remind his readers that he wasn't. "Every race wants to claim Sid Caesar," he wrote.

Though Caesar's own Yiddish was spotty—when the Caesars, Reiners, and Tolkins took in Yiddish theater on Second Avenue, Caesar laughed only after Reiner had translated the joke for him—the Yiddish dailies (New York had four of them in the early 1950s) *kvelled* over him. And unlike the anemic and marginal English-language Jewish press of the time, they didn't have to worry about Gentiles thinking it unseemly. So it was in the Yiddish press more than anywhere else that feelings of curiosity about and pride in Sid Caesar found fullest flower. In the *Morgn Zhurnal*, under the headline THE JEWISH TELEVISION ACTOR WHO IS CONSIDERED A SECOND CHARLIE CHAPLIN, M. Kantor traced Caesar's rise from poverty to Catskills *komedianshtshik* (jokester) to someone far superior to Milton Berle and Danny Kaye. "Sid Caesar no longer uses slapstick routines," Kantor wrote. "He has no need to resort to such cheap effects. These are only for comedians without any talent." Like Chaplin, said Kantor, Caesar was "a melancholic poet rather than a comedian who puts on a crazy shtick."

His story prompted a letter from Caesar's boyhood rabbi, David Shohet of Congregation Agudas Achim in Yonkers, in which he recounted Caesar's rigorous religious education and his spectacular performance at his bar mitzvah, when he read the Hebrew passages "like an old hand." Young Sidney's speech that day made clear that "here was a great artist in the making . . . everyone watching was enthralled by his oratorical skill, which flowed from within a good Jewish soul." On the anniversary of his father's death, he noted, Caesar always came to the synagogue to say the Kaddish (the Jewish prayer for the dead), and perfectly at that. "I've seen him in shul many times on Rosh Hashonah and Yom Kippur wearing a tallis," he added. And Caesar had kept in touch with him, the rabbi said, even inviting him to see *Make Mine Manhattan*.

But Caesar's principal chronicler in the Yiddish press was the television columnist for the *Forverts*, Nakhman Zalowitz, who first spotted him in March 1950 and considered him a *landsman*, since their homes—his in Rego Park, Queens, and Caesar's in Forest Hills—were only a few minutes apart. For decades, Zalowitz, who'd been born in Bialystok and come to the United States as a young boy, helped greenhorns negotiate their new homeland: "No area of American life was foreign to him, and in accessible language, he introduced the Jewish immigrant to the varieties of life in the new country," the *Forverts* wrote about him. So, when television became as much a point of entry to America as Ellis Island, it became a key part of his beat. "He wanted people to know what was good, and worthless," the paper explained. And though there were lots of Jews on early TV, from the outset Zalowitz had taken an especial, almost fatherly interest in Caesar, probably because he deemed him the most intriguing and intelligent, and therefore the most exemplary, of the lot. In other words, Sid Caesar was "good for the Jews." For a time that spring, Zalowitz had trouble *not* mentioning him in his column.

"Sid Caesar is what people on Broadway call 'a natural,' a God-given talent," he said in introducing him to his readers. Only two weeks later, he elaborated. "Sid Caesar's humor is not based on cracking jokes. He can make you laugh for 15 minutes straight without saying a single word. His hands speak. His feet speak. His eyes speak." A month later, Zalowitz wrote that all the other comedians on radio and television "can all shine his shoes." And a week after *that*, he furnished a photograph of Caesar for those without TVs. "He looks like a completely 'normal' person," he noted with amazement. "When you pass him on the street, you'd swear he is, let's say, a dentist, or a lawyer, or any sort of serious individual." He then noted the devotion of Caesar's mother, who'd not budge from her TV on Saturday nights "even if you offered her a million dollars."

Kantor, too, wrote of Ida Caesar's devotion to her son: how, on those wintry nights when he was forced to stand outside the Capitol Theatre, she'd come in from Yonkers with her hot soup. While "a balm for the soul," he noted, it also became a bone of contention with Caesar's boss, who considered slurping in front of theatergoers undignified. "My mother came all the way from Yonkers to see me and bring me soup, so what should I do, send her away?" Caesar said he'd replied. "What would you do if in my place? Would you turn away your mother?"

Your Show of Shows generally enjoyed most-favored-nation status with the censor, Helffrich, in part because it policed itself. The only thing "Caesarian" NBC ever actually banned was a broadcast of a live birth on *Medic.* When the censors intervened, gentle kibitzes sufficed. Thus, the writers tweaked a line about Caesar's anthropomorphized slot machine that had become so filled with coins, it couldn't "hold it any longer"; bodily functions were nothing to joke about. The wagging tongue of Caesar's shy boy struggling to ask a girl to dance was also discussed. During a domestic sketch in December 1951, NBC minions hastily inserted a V-shaped piece of black fabric into the guest host Madge Evans's overly revealing gown.* Was it that fleeting bit of cleavage that got *Your Show of Shows* listed among the miscreants by the National Council of Catholic Women? It's hard to imagine it was anything else.

Of greater concern to NBC than all the Mrs. Grundys out there were meddlesome advertisers on guard for anything that might sully their products. "They would all gather in the clients' room to watch the dress rehearsal, pencil and paper in hand to write down their suggestions," Weaver recalled. "After it was over, [the NBC executive George McGarrett] would collect all the notes, agree with every one of the comments, covertly chuck them in the wastebasket, then take the assembled company over to '21' for drinks and dinner." Weaver's approach was similarly hands-off. "He'd come to watch rehearsals, and giggle a lot," Howard Morris recalled.

---

* At least one viewer was upset by that, for a surprising reason. "He said he 'just plain liked low necklines,'" Helffrich reported. "He also said that he didn't give a damn if his kids did see it, [and] said that they would some day anyhow and they might just as well know."

. . .

ENDURING MISCONCEPTIONS TO THE contrary, the writers' room on *Your Show of Shows* never was the storied, chaotic vortex of madness and creativity it was later made out to be. With only three writers on the payroll, it couldn't have been. Liebman liked to quote something he'd once heard Samuel Goldwyn say, in his Yiddish-inflected English: "From a polite conference comes a polite picture." And with Brooks around, no conference would ever be "polite." But the outrageously raucous sessions of lore came later.

Officially, Tolkin was the "chief" writer. But with Caesar and Liebman around, Kallen effectively a peer, and Brooks uncontrollable, the title was mostly ceremonial. Besides, someone whom Brooks likened to "a Jewish Abe Lincoln" and "a stork that dropped a baby and broke it and is coming to explain to the parents," who remained fearful (of red-baiters, Caesar, the other writers, his wife, and life itself), was ill-suited to crack whips. (When an article described an unnamed comedy writer of Caesar's as "a tall, drooping man looking for all the world like an underfed Basset hound," no one had to guess who it was.) But Tolkin *was* influential. For one thing, he was the house intellectual—what Brooks called "our living-in-the-world" teacher. It was from him that all the others learned about literature, and especially Russian novelists like Dostoyevsky and Gogol. He was also their guide to Freud and Freudian analysis, the secular religion to which all of them quickly and eagerly converted. "We coulda had a group rate," said Brooks, who went on to be shrunk by a shrink who'd been shrunk by a shrink who'd been shrunk by Freud himself. Joe Stein, who joined the writers near the end of the show's run, never forgot how, on his first day on the job, he was asked the name of *his* psychiatrist, and when he said he didn't have one, "they looked at me like I was crazy." (Reiner was once asked whether the same thing was wrong with all of them. "Yes," he replied. "Being Jewish.")

The routine in the writers' room, such as it was, was undeviating. "Tolkin and I would arrive at ten o'clock in the morning and start working," Kallen recalled. "And *maybe* around noon, Sid would come in, and *eventually* Brooks would come in—sliding, run in, jump in, or come on a motorcycle in the office. Always an entrance, always a big story about why he was late, some complicated psychiatric reason he couldn't get there. . . . It took them *ages* to get down to work. They never really wanted to." Reiner and Morris would also take part. Coca was also there, but said little. "Dot's a classic," Tolkin would say when they'd put together something promising.

While Liebman was nominally in charge, he deferred to Caesar. And a good thing, too, because his humor was old-fashioned—as Caesar put it, "more in the vein of 'What if Christopher Columbus was an usher at the Roxy Theatre?' or 'What if Babe Ruth sold hot dogs in the stands at Yankee Stadium?'" Besides, he was more concerned with the musical numbers ("the screaming," as Caesar called it) and dances ("the jumping")—as Reiner described them, the "things needed when we changed clothes." And which, for all of those who tuned in the show solely for the comedy, were a chance to go to the refrigerator or talk to their friends. "Guys were coming up with funny things that he did not quite understand because he was an Old World guy," Reiner recalled. "But luckily he had operas to do and ballets to perform. We were very happy when he wasn't around." But Caesar almost always was; the writers energized him. "Sometimes he caught your energy and excitement," Brooks recalled, and that enthused him.

The room was small—roughly fourteen feet by twenty—and its sole window *always shut*, the better to trap the smoke from all the cigars: Liebman smoked them, and since Caesar also did, Tolkin and Reiner smoked them, too. Everyone just tipped their ashes on the floor, then threw the butts out that one window, which was *always open*.* One day Bill Hobin, who began directing the show in its second full season, peered out that window and saw, two floors below, "a pile of cigar butts the size of a small

---

* Yes, according to equally unassailable accounts, that single window was both always closed *and* always open.

haystack"—so formidable, he feared, that the roof below it might collapse.

The room reeked not only of tobacco but of sweat and delicatessen. "Had you been able to see through the cumulus cloud of cigar smoke," Kallen was to write, "you would have discovered, scattered on every horizontal surface, a detritus of soggy paper plates; the remains of pastrami on rye, the nub of a pickle, a puddle of mustard, a tag end of cheese Danish, a sprinkling of Styrofoam cups in whose last inch of cold coffee sat *fasci* of slowly decomposing cigars. On the wall would be a kind of abstract art decoration composed of dangling shreds of coleslaw; on the sofa, a damp spot where a squirt of Pepsi had landed. I learned to wear dark skirts." When the star of the week Arlene Dahl, "a shimmering strawberry blonde with porcelain skin, immaculate in a white linen dress, pale blue shoes, and an exquisite wide-brimmed straw hat," showed up, Kallen remembered, "there was a moment of stunned silence as we all realized there was not one cubic foot of space in that entire room where we could safely deposit" her.

Along with its ambient *schmutz*, the room was claustrophobic. "These men were big, they were loud and they were belligerent," Kallen wrote. "Sid Caesar was large in more than talent. His shoulders alone would crowd a room. Each arm was a tree trunk. His torso invaded the office like an army tank rumbling into a conquered village. Tolkin was not as bulky but there were few doorways he could walk through without ducking. Carl Reiner was hardly puny. Mel Brooks . . . was small but made up in chutzpah what he lacked in height. Max Liebman did not have to be big: he was the boss." The room briefly had a telephone—until it rang once in the middle of a collective case of writer's block, and Caesar, well, it wasn't only sinks he ripped off walls.

One never knew which Caesar—brooding, explosive, businesslike, or remote—would show up. Whichever it was, and encircled by everyone else, he'd gnomically weigh the day's offerings. When he disliked a joke, he'd pull out an imaginary machine gun or howitzer from his phantom arsenal, take aim, then shoot it down. Caesar might formulate an idea himself, or if it came from someone else in what Brooks called "colloidal form," he would tweak it. Never did he *explain* anything. "I don't think I remember any time when he said, 'The thing that's not funny about this is so-and-so,' " recalled Joe Stein. "He'd just say '*Eh!* I dunno. I don't like it.' " And there was no appeal, though Brooks often tried. Once a sketch was on its way, Caesar would leave it with his writers. They'd always change something: Ninth-inning tweaks delighted Caesar and kept him engaged.

The room could be brutal. So tense was the work, Brooks said, that though by now he was making $250 a week, he found himself, as he put it, "vomiting between parked cars." ("*Two hundred and fifty?*" Tolkin supposedly remonstrated. "I started throwing up at *two hundred!*") But for all that, it beat pushing racks along Seventh Avenue. "Every night when I left the writers room, I literally would get in the elevator and thank God," Brooks said. Tolkin suffered more. "The fears, at least in my own mind, were engendered by those empty pages, the unfilled minutes on the air, screaming to be filled," he later wrote. "This particular fear had a German accent: *You vill have five sketches ready by Monday. And they vill be funny. To your typewriters, march—SCHNELL.*" "An ulcer business," Tolkin called his line of work. "You didn't contribute anything for the last ten minutes," Liebman would tell Harold Flender,* who wrote for the show (uncredited), but only for a single season.

As the men shouted, smoked, belched, cussed, and ate, then unbuttoned their pants after eating, Kallen struggled to be heard. She described the scene:

> The decibel count in that room was astronomical. Sid booming, Tolkin intoning, Carl trumpeting and Brooks imitating everything from a rabbinical student to the white whale in Moby Dick thrashing around with six harpoons in his back. To command attention in the midst of this you would have had to be at least Eleanor Roosevelt. This was well before Women's Lib and Imogene and I had grown up to believe that our femininity, maybe even our life,

---

* Grandfather of Timothée Chalamet.

would be threatened if we got into the habit of trying to yell them down. So sometimes we huddled together in a corner and talked about something else, sometimes we just waited until they exhausted themselves, making notes of what we wanted to say so we wouldn't forget, and sometimes I would grab somebody's red scarf or sweater and climb up on the sofa and wave it until somebody noticed me.

It was Kallen's task to get everything down on paper intelligibly and quickly, before it all evaporated. Scribbling furiously on a yellow legal pad sometimes kept her from creating. Years later, Coca marveled to Kallen over how the two of them had survived what she called "this male, mad with power, atmosphere." "We all had success—we all made more money than we'd ever made—but did it have to be that agonizing[?]" she asked. "They had three categories of female" was how Kallen described the men in the room to the historian Jeff Kisseloff. "One was mother. One was whore. And the other one, if she had any brains, had to be lesbian. Mother and wife were the same. Those were good women. Anybody who was sexy had to be a tart. Anybody with brains had to be not female."

Then and forever after, Brooks got disproportionate attention in all discussions of the writers' rooms. He'd arrive not only late, as Kallen noted (the result of insomnia), but hypoglycemic. His entrances could be grand—sliding across the floor as if into third base, or tossing a straw hat across the room and shouting, "Lindy made it!"—all to camouflage his tardiness, which suited his preferred division of labor: Brooks hated the heavy lifting of hatching sketches, preferring to "punch up" what the others had begun. He loved supplying that ineffable something that somehow made something work—"like the great chef who would sprinkle on the parsley and say, 'Now, present it,'" Florence Baum recalled. "All shit!" he might declare after assaying what the others had done. Then, oftentimes, he'd fix it. And then he'd say, "See, you don't have to be on time to be gifted."

Brooks's "writing" rarely involved *writing*, or typing, which was no accident. "The one who typed got tied down," he later explained. "I wanted to be the one who ran around and acted it out." Brooks had what Kallen called "this overpowering need to dominate, to impress." "He was going to prove he was funnier than you, and part of the way to do that was to prove you were less funny than he," recalled Kallen's husband, Herbert Engel. He'd fill every conversational lull, and threaten and insult people, often where it hurt most, which he took care to learn. People feared him, even though he was only a kid. "Suppose you're in a jungle, and you're an antelope, and you come across a very young tiger," Kallen once explained. "It doesn't matter that they're young . . . it's the nature of the beast." Above all, Brooks was relentless. "I would keep going until my joke or my sketch was in the show," he said. "I didn't care if anybody else's was in or out. All of us writers were like a litter of pups, and we all fought for our little tit and struggled and screamed."

Brooks's batting average—the ratio of good jokes to duds—ranged in the various interviews Kallen gave from one in ten to once every generation. But were they honest with themselves, she and Tolkin would have had to credit Brooks with a brilliance both of them lacked. Having been chased by Cossacks and survived, Tolkin once said, "I was ready for Mel Brooks when he came." Only he wasn't and, even later, never was. "Lucille and I worked for days, in the privacy of our room, enclosed by four mute walls, wondering, 'Is it funny? Will the theater audience laugh?'" Tolkin reminisced. "As we slaved over each line, the two of us heard no applause, no laughter. No pat on the back. And here was this short wild-eyed kid getting all this immediate approval, this love by adding an occasional line to what we had worked our butts off [on] for hours. I envied Mel the laughs, applause and approval he was getting. Particularly from Sid, the boss." He wasn't subtle about his angst. Tolkin "seldom, if ever, smiled, and most of the company thought of him as a sourpuss," Bill Hobin wrote of him. As Caesar later put it, Tolkin's customary place in the writers' room was "by the window, contemplating suicide."

"When we wrote sketches for Sid, we wrote with his talent and his persona *in our blood*," Kallen later said. "We knew instinctively that a certain line would evoke a certain look on his face, a certain gesture. We gave and we fed him the things he needed to use his talent." But about Caesar the man, she wasn't so wistful. "When he had a few drinks, a few hundred drinks, Sid would get maudlin and sentimental about us, and other times I think he would have been very happy to have drowned us," she said, "because no actor, no performer, likes to feel dependent for his stardom and his whole persona on things that other people are creating. So he used to throw the script on the floor that we had slaved over and things like that. What he was saying when he did that was 'I don't need you. I'm a big star. I can make it up as I go along.'"

Turning to their families didn't always help. Mel Tolkin liked to describe his mother's visit to the International Theatre one show night and how, after Caesar got a big laugh, he turned to her and said, "I wrote that line, Ma." "Oy, that Sid Caesar. What a funny man," she replied. Then Caesar went into one of his double-talk routines, which Tolkin told her he'd worked on as well.

"What a talent, that Caesar," she said. "And such a good-looking man." After Caesar had sung something in a movie take-off he'd also written, all she'd said was "He sings, too! There's nothing he can't do. What a talent." Once the show had ended, Tolkin went backstage and told Caesar of his mother's comments. "*My* mother was just here," Caesar replied. "I asked her how she liked the show. She said, 'You must have *some* writers.'"

That he did. So natural sounding were the lines Caesar's writers wrote, and so well delivered, that viewers assumed they were improvised. Fed up rather than flattered by this, the team took out an ad in *Variety* to set the record straight. "You mean the show is not AD LIB?" it asked. "No, it's written by MEL TOLKIN LUCILLE KALLEN MEL BROOKS." Caesar, too, found the idea offensive. "I'd like to have seen Edison ad lib the electric light," he said.

The writers' weekly ordeal began on Monday morning, also known as "Bloody Monday" or "bleeding-to-death day." It could just as easily have been called "Starting from Scratch Yet Again

Day." Everyone, looking quite miserable, would discuss how they'd spent their day off and, fishing for an idea, whatever they'd realized about what normal people do. Thanks to his wild week-ends, Brooks came in even later than usual. Tuesdays the writers broke into teams, working on different sketches. On Wednesdays came the first rehearsals. With the writing largely done, scripts could be duplicated, sets built, music scored, costumes made.

On Thursdays, the show went up "on its feet." Ill-conceived routines were scrapped, and new ones conceived. With Friday came the first dry run at the theater; the crew brandished stop-watches and the cameramen worked out angles. For production numbers, the cameras were mobile: No one worried about dis-tracting the audience. But for comedy, where concentration was key, the cameras, and actors, were fixed. After 2:30 or so, Caesar was a free man, at least for a few hours, and might head off with Reiner, Morris, and the writers to watch silent or foreign films at the Museum of Modern Art. Even then, though, they'd be searching for material.

Saturdays were marathons, with four separate run-throughs. Each brought further corrections and refinements. Last-minute cuts inevitably came from the comedy, which was more severable than the production numbers. To conserve his energies, Caesar walked through his parts. Network types sometimes showed up to, as Liebman's public relations man, Dave Tebet, once put it, "see the miracle happen." At seven thirty or so, the cast and crew, seated in the orchestra, heard Liebman's last-minute instructions. Even then, something could fall apart; ninety minutes before one show the guest host, the ventriloquist Paul Winchell, was canned after balking at some last-minute cuts in his routine. Always, there were backup plans for such contingencies.

As nine o'clock approached, Caesar retreated to his dress-ing room for a catnap, or simply to breathe deeply and try to relax. The orders were to leave him alone, but sometimes Brooks would come by, open the door a crack, and lobby for a favorite line. "As soon as I'm lying there, I'd hear Mel Brooks whispering through the keyhole, 'Don't forget to do this. Don't forget to do that,'" Caesar recalled. "I'd yell, 'Would you leave me alone!'

But he'd keep it up. 'Don't forget to do this. Don't forget to do that.'" In her dressing room, Coca washed her hair. At a quarter to nine, the studio audience filed in. "The big theater fills," wrote James Saxon Childers of *The Atlanta Journal*, the only journalist prescient enough to record how it all looked and felt. "Other persons pack the doors and beg for entry." At five to nine, Reiner came out to warm up the crowd. Second by second, Max Liebman's magnificent machine was slipping into gear.

"Announcers take their places before the camera," Childers wrote. "The choral group and dancers move on stage. The second hand begins its final sweep toward 9 o'clock and the theater is still, poised, tense." At one minute to nine, the director started counting off the seconds over the intercom; then he and Liebman took a second to wish each other good luck. "A man at one side of the stage holds up three fingers," Childers went on. "Then two, then one. With a great sweeping gesture, he flings his hand at the announcer." At 8:59:55, Liebman cued the conductor, and the first chords of "Stars over Broadway" sounded.

"*Your Show of Shows!*" the announcer (the longest serving was Dick De Freitas) said calmly, brightly. "An hour and a half of top-notch entertainment." What Liebman called "that ninety-minute chasm" now opened. It was when Coca always wished she were dead, but thanks to the nice vibes always emanating from the audience, the feeling quickly passed. Liebman, too, was finally at peace. "The world could have caved in, and I wouldn't notice," he said. "I was as cold as ice. Nothing touched me because we had done everything we could." The one variable, impossible to predict, was the audience. After the production numbers, a light cued it to clap, but there was no light marked "laugh."

In the control room, Liebman now had a different mission: to bring in each of the show's three half hours on time. The music, sketches, curtain calls, and credits could be stretched, trimmed, or skipped as need be, and still it didn't always happen, especially during the show's scary first few weeks in early 1950; on the second show, the violinist Mischa Elman was cut off mid-note (the stage manager had to yank on his tailcoat) when his piece bumped up against a commercial for Mott's apple juice. "Talk about stupid timing," Walter Winchell complained. "The depths of poor taste," huffed *Variety*, which asked why the ads couldn't have been skipped. Yes, television *was* still young.

Inevitably there were cues missed, lines flubbed, costumes never (or only partially) changed. The guest host John Conte called Sid Caesar "Sid Silver." One time a screwup by Caesar's dresser left Caesar sporting the boots of a Roman gladiator during a bus station sketch. But such slips were surprisingly rare. Brooks likened the performers to great infielders fielding bad hops. Live television offered its own unique high—"like your first sexual experience," said Greg Garrison, the show's second director.

The writers watched it all on a monitor in the greenroom. They'd groan when Caesar muffed some prized line of theirs, but more often, Kallen recalled, "there would be a moment, or two, or five, or six, when Caesar would achieve a pinnacle of performance, and we would sit in silent astonishment, knowing we had just seen genius at work."

Then, thank God, came Sunday. Caesar's always began the same way: For an hour or more, "I used to stand under the shower and shake." Afterward, he'd listen to "Fly Me to the Moon," take his kids to the Central Park merry-go-round, listen to light opera, stare at the fish tank. "Sunday was the one day off, where you could be with your children, your family, see a tree, see the sun," Brooks said. No one savored what they'd just pulled off: There was no time. "As soon as it was over, we just stopped cold, and—next week," Garrison recalled. "We never *thought* about last week's show. It was over and it was great and it worked and this was fine. Erased from the map. Next."

For Tolkin and Kallen, Sundays were spent cooking up the next domestic sketch, often sparked by their latest marital rows. Such sketches dated back to the very beginning of *Your Show of Shows*, before *I Love Lucy*, *The Honeymooners*, and, as Pat Weaver put it, "every other domestic farce in the last forty years of television." While the characters of the couple (he, lumbering, laconic, and boorish, stuck in some anonymous white-collar corporate job; she, socially ambitious, fussy, and snobbish) and

their marriage (disputatious) were fixed, lots of other details—
where they lived, how long they'd been married, whether they
had children—varied from one appearance to the next. So did
their names—Michael or Jack for him, Mildred or Edith for her.

That "Edith" was no accident; it was the name of Tolkin's
wife. Had their own marriage been made in heaven, Tolkin wrote,
topics might have been much harder to come by. ("To Edith, the
inspiration for a host of new material" was how Caesar, in rare
bursts of jocularity and handwriting, once inscribed a picture to
her.) The Tolkins' families back in Canada could gauge the size of
their bank account and the state of their marriage from the show.
After a series of dark solo sketches in which Caesar inveighed
violently against an unseen Edith, Edith Tolkin requested that
the fictional Edith be retired—a request with which Caesar usually, but not always, complied.

By the spring of 1951, three names finally stuck: Charlie for
him, Doris for her, and Hickenlooper for them. The last name
came from Senator Bourke Hickenlooper of Iowa, though politics had nothing to do with it: It was just too good a name. (The
actual Mr. and Mrs. Hickenlooper were not amused.) Judging
from the oval-shaped portraits hanging in their home, the fictional Hickenloopers were of American lineage, going back at
least a few generations. They lived occasionally in the suburbs,
in conventional homes with lawns, but more often in the city, in
an apartment high enough up to throw Doris's terrible cooking
out the window or, if truly horrendous and served at the outset of
their marriage, for Charlie to jump himself.

They were saner than the Ricky Ricardos and richer than
the Ralph Kramdens. Charlie wore a suit to an office, where his
bailiwick was "inventory." While occasionally newlyweds, they
were more often well into mutually irritating middle marriage.
On those (rare) occasions when they were parents, their children
were newborns, stashed somewhere offstage. They had no overt
ethnicity, though when baby Harold had a slight fever, Charlie
was the panicky Jewish mother (calling the doctor, donning mask
and gloves to administer an aspirin) and Doris, the more stoic
Waspy father. ("I never saw such carrying-on in my entire life,"
she says disgustedly.)

Many of the sketches concern what Reiner called "our new-found middle-classity." The Hickenloopers fumble with their freshly secured semi-affluence, in ways large (whether to take a plane or a cruise) and small (what constitutes a proper tip at the posh restaurants to which they can now afford to go). He's crass and, at least when the newly hired maid (for whom he affects British mannerisms, and they adopt a pompous new patois) isn't around, plainspoken; she's fastidious and pretentious, given to calling napkins "serviettes," favoring "pâté de foie gras," dabbling in modern art (purchasing a painting called *Mother and Child Descending the Stairway to Meet Destiny*), teaching Charlie about fine wine (as well as forks and knives), and how to "partake" of fancy foods rather than merely eat them.

But often she overreaches. She says "Merci" to a waiter in an Indian restaurant. Shoving classical music down Charlie's throat, she praises Tchaikovsky's "Pathetic" Symphony and a Beethoven "credenza," and insists Rimsky and Korsakov are separate people. Together, they fumble with the latest gizmos, including movie cameras and tape recorders. "Sometimes," she laments, "I wish electricity had never been invented!" With all their tics, they were sufficiently convincing as a couple that viewers showered them with things for "their" home. "I have more pot holders now than any other woman in America, and I'm in the running for the can-opener record, too," Coca said. "We also get teething rings, booties, bibs and bonnets—for the children." Countless recipes came in for "Mrs. Sid Caesar," along with plenty of unsolicited advice—"Your husband is a very uncertain young man. You should bolster his ego, instead of being so rough on him"—and warnings. "I wonder if Imogene knows about this gorgeous blonde!" Caesar overheard once when he ventured out with Florence.

The women portrayed on the show were often the butt of misogynistic jokes, many with a distinctly Brooksian ring. Caesar the suspicious husband concedes in an early monologue that things have changed: Nowadays, "a woman is considered just like a human being." "Marry a stupid woman, and then you don't have to worry about sharing intellectual interests," counsels Dr. Heinrich von Hartsig, author of *Happy, Though Married,* who advises that every five or six years husbands should tell their wives they love them. (Tell them the truth, though, "and the marriage will be finished in two weeks.") Professor Bicep von Musclebound calls one Hans Schultz the greatest athlete ever: On a javelin he'd thrown from the stadium, he'd impaled his wife back home. "What an eye he had!" he said. "What an eye!" Into this parched soil, Kallen and Coca nonetheless planted some early feminist seeds. "When he yelled at me in a sketch, I think [the audience] knew that it was pure bluff," Coca said. "They also knew I was in no way afraid of him. There was something hysterically funny about this big man with this relatively small woman who was in absolute control of the situation."

Caesar's airport interviews were instantly elevated once Reiner came along. Reiner was on Caesar's wavelength, able to tap right into the Professor's phony expertise and, on occasion, to contribute some erudite nonsense of his own. Somehow he knew exactly when (and how) to laugh at the Professor and when to play it straight, when to prod, to ad lib, to be ridiculous himself. His neatness, crispness, and all-American wholesomeness contrasted perfectly with the Professor's cynicism, fraudulence, and shabbiness. While showcasing Caesar and Reiner, the sketches also marked the first pairing of Reiner and Brooks, the principal author of these routines, presaging by ten years the public debut of the 2000 Year Old Man and affording a bracing draft of embryonic, unadulterated Mel Brooks. "How much you like, or laugh at, the Professor sketches will be in direct correlation to how funny you find Mel Brooks," the historian Karen Harvey has written.

The routine became second nature to viewers of *Your Show of Shows*. On a bare stage simulating a corridor at LaGuardia Airport, Reiner cheerily buttonholes Caesar. He is always described as the world's leading authority on something or other, newly arrived with "a planeload of distinguished visitors." The Professor is a schlump. When, in one sketch, he asks Reiner to describe his outfit, Reiner gets it about right. "Well, you're wearing a battered, dirty, moldy green top hat," he says. "You have a ripped collar with a little dirt on the side from fingers, you have a ripped tie, a dirty tie with food stains on it, and you have a slightly disheveled jacket with frayed cuffs, your vest is missing a few buttons, you have dirty pants that need pressing." The outfit, shabby when sent by the costuming house, was, at Caesar's request, further mussed up upon arrival. "They gave him a kind of loosely-fitting thing and he smashed up the hat and said, 'Let's go all the way with it' and ripped a few things up," Brooks recalled.

As the ads on the show—for ever-improving television sets, frozen orange juice (superior, according to surveys of housewives, to fresh squeezed), and newfangled scouring pads, shoe polish, and pens—attested, it was a time of expertise and discovery, ripe for charlatanism. And no one is more bogus than the Professor, pontificating with what Kenneth Tynan called "the same majestic fraudulence" on all manner of things. "That must be something deep in [the] Jewish psyche, the dump, the undercut: Build, build, build, then [put a] pin in the bubble," said Brooks, for whom the sketches became a handy harbinger, or maybe even the purest and brightest distillation, of his comedy over the next fifty years. In their nonsensical conversations, Caesar and Reiner skewer expertise and certitude of all kinds, ridicule American deference to Europeans and alleged German expertise (and genuine Jewish befuddlement) over technical things and *goyishe naches** generally, like excessive concern for physical fitness or courting unnecessary risk. "Just smashing authority," Brooks said of the sketches, which always came near the beginning of the show, setting up the more ambitious, sophisticated pieces that followed. "We loved that character because he was a windbag," Brooks said. "We loved phony-baloney authorities. He was a perfect character for us."

Actually, *characters.*

He was Professor Jet von Propulsion, an authority on space. (Q: "What's the biggest problem in space?" A: "Closet space . . . parking space.") And Ludwig von Liebestraum, an authority on love and courtship. And Ludwig von Loophole, the eminent legal scholar. And Hocus von Pocus, an authority on legerdemain and magic (as well as the "hippest hypnotist who ever hypnotized a hippopotamus"). And Kurt von Supper, famed expert on food and

---

* What Gentiles care about or take pleasure from.

diet, who advises, "Never—never—eat on an empty stomach." And Ludwig von Heartthrob, an authority on female behavior, who, asked to name the greatest women in history, cites Joan of Arc, Florence Nightingale, Madame Curie, and Hilda Strauss. (Who's Hilda Strauss? a puzzled Reiner asks. "Never mind your own business!" he's told.)

Just about every Professor has recently published a book: *The Human Body and How to Avoid It* (by Hugo von Gesundheit); *I Remember Mama—but I Forget Papa* (Lapsed von Memory); *Don't Be a Slob* (Ludwig von Fingerbowl); *Animals: Their Habits, Habitats, and Haberdashery* (Wolfgang von Complex). On the eve of Queen Elizabeth's coronation came Ludwig von Blueblood, author of *The Prince and His Papa*. Ludwig von Pablum, who wrote *Children Are People, Only Smaller,* was asked at what age kids give their parents the most pleasure. "Twenty-eight," he replies. Ludwig von Fossil, author of *Archeology Made Simple, or Don't Lift Heavy Rocks,* recounts his recent discovery of an ancient cookie jar. What did he find inside it? Ancient cookies. Hans von Bulldozer (*The Dream House or When You Build Castles in the Air, Make Sure the Foundations Are Solid*) offers some important advice: "If you want to build a dam, you gotta watch the beavers, 'cause they're the best dam builders in the world." In choosing a mate, which matters more, intelligence or beauty? Ludwig von Hobflopper (*Love: Its Cure and Prevention*) is asked. "Money," he replies. Filthy von Lucre (*Money Talks, So Listen!*) recounts how ice was the medium of exchange in prehistoric times (why else would it be called the Ice Age?), but how it was replaced by rocks in the Stone Age, until "rockateers" ruined everything. (The rocks were eventually replaced by fish, though after that "nobody wanted to work in the banks.")

"Sleep is wonderful. Sleep is beautiful. But sleep is no good if you're wide awake," explains Sigmund von Sedative, author of *Wake Up and Sleep,* who bids good-night nightly to the various parts of his body, working his way up from his toes. Kurt von Fraidy Katz, an expert on mountain climbing (he wrote *What Do You Need It For?*), advises climbers whose ropes have snapped to scream all the way down, the better to be found once they land. But wasn't there anything else they could do? Reiner asks.

"Yes, there's another thing. When you see your rope break, you immediately extend your arms like this, and you fly. Keep flying! Fly! Fly like crazy!"

"But, Professor, humans *can't* fly!"

"How do you know? You may be the first one, what have you got to lose? You can always go back to screaming."

Coaxing out such foolishness, Reiner remained imperturbable, though, as Bill Hayes recalled, "his eyes were always laughing." The Professor's visits became an easy—and, eventually, too easy—way to fill several minutes of a show. Before too long, the shtick grew as threadbare as the Professor's clothes. "How many crazy German professors can you have?" Tolkin quite rightly asked.

Amid the show's growing predictability, there came a bright spot in April 1951: a last-minute sketch (hastily substituted for a lame routine about two Americans in Paris, searching futilely for a hot dog) in which Doris Hickenlooper, distracted by an Empress Eugénie hat in a store window, totals Charlie's car. Coming home frazzled that night—he's actually lost his appetite, a first and only for a Caesar character—and craving a "nice, relaxing drive," he slowly extracts from Doris what she has done and the wreckage (not just a smashed car, but two smashed storefronts) she has left in her wake. The sketch was principally Kallen's (though she'd yet to learn to drive).

But the show's first full season had only a few such high points. Though better than all the other comedy on TV, the novelty was wearing thin, and the performers and writers were exhausting themselves. As the season's last show drew to a close, Reiner brought out Pat Weaver, who summoned Liebman, who emerged (toupee slightly askew) for a rare bow on camera. Coca and Caesar then threw kisses to everyone. "See you September 8," he promised. Caesar had grown restless, even depressed, in search of newer, more meaningful challenges and outlets. "Caesar Yens Straight Drama Role," *Variety* had reported in January 1951, noting his interest in playing Lenny in a production of *Of Mice and Men*. It never happened, in part because sponsors feared viewers seeing Caesar would look for laughs.

NBC executives feared losing Caesar altogether—to either a

competitor, Hollywood, the army, fate, or changing tastes. "This simply comes down to faith—do we think Sid is going to be a giant for 10 years? I do," one NBC executive wrote in a memo. Others agreed, and Caesar was signed up for the next decade. Given the hefty investment NBC was making in him, the executive urged the company to take out life insurance on Caesar in case, as he put it, "Sid hits the slab." "While we don't have to pay his estate anything," he pointed out, "we would get back some money."

Once again, Caesar unwound during the summer with a weeklong theatrical gig, this time in Chicago, joined by Coca, Reiner, and much of his entourage. Brooks had also tagged along, setting the stage for one of the greatest events, or legends, in the Caesar saga.

Unable to perform on a full stomach, Caesar merely noshed between shows; only when the day was done, and he was back at the hotel, would he have his dinner. He'd just settled down to eat one night when Brooks, having been cooped up all day in the theater, began badgering him to go out. Caesar wouldn't budge; Brooks wouldn't let up. Finally, Caesar exploded. "Do you want to *go out*?" he asked. And with that, he grabbed Brooks by the scruff of the neck, opened the window, and dangled him over the streets of Chicago. "How far do you want to go out?" he then asked, holding him out farther still. "Is that far enough? You want to go out a little farther?" An alarmed Dave Caesar reeled them both back in. As Brooks retold the story over the years, the floor got ever higher, and Caesar's hold on him (whether by the ankles or his shoes or suspenders), more tenuous. Florence Caesar, for one, never bought it. "He didn't *hang him* out the window, he *showed* him the window," she said. It didn't matter: The story really wasn't about Sid Caesar at all, but of, by, for, and about Mel Brooks.

Once the Chicago engagement ended, Sid and Florence were to sail on the *Liberté* to France, proceeding from Paris to Cannes, Rome, Florence, and Venice over the next nine weeks before returning home. For all his cosmopolitan airs, Caesar had never been to Europe, and the papers relished the prospect of his "conversing" with waiters in his various "languages."

Prior to their departure, Joan Crawford threw a supper party for the Caesars, and Pat Weaver brought champagne to the pier. The voyage began promisingly, with bubbly on the table nightly. But Sid was uneasy among the swells, and once in Paris things only got worse: missed connections, dreary weather, the confounding French currency, dim bulbs in their room at the George V. No one stopped him on the streets, or laughed at his jokes. You couldn't get a good cigar, or a bottle of Dr. Brown's Cel-Ray tonic (the celery-flavored drink that was Caesar's favorite, said to aid digestion, especially of pastrami and corned beef), or even a decent glass of tap water. Since real French required real nouns and verbs, Caesar couldn't make himself understood; all those childhood anxieties about speaking came rushing back. Even the *Mona Lisa* was a letdown.

Finally, when they couldn't find their seats at the racetrack, Caesar had had enough. "Mom, let's go home," he said to Florence. She thought that meant "back to the hotel"; in fact, it meant *home* home. So, three days after they'd arrived, back home they went, this time by air. Walter Winchell and Dorothy Kilgallen made light of the fiasco. Caesar quickly retreated to *haimische* Lido Beach, Long Island, a throwback to childhood summers spent in nearby Far Rockaway. While more worldly than the folks from "People's Creek, Nevada," or "Beaver Falls, Iowa," Caesar remained a hick at heart.

A Federal Communications Commission freeze on station licenses dating back to 1948 propped up Caesar in a way, confining television to the big cities where he was appreciated. But television couldn't be contained much longer. "Hundreds of communities from Maine to Oregon are clamoring for TV," the *Chicago Tribune* reported in April 1951.

Liebman wasn't worried; his show, he thought, would play out there as well. Here was someone, as NBC's flacks had it, "who refused to underestimate the American public"; didn't country folk drive fifty miles to watch the program in the nearest general store, then send him thank-you notes afterward? Caesar wasn't concerned, either. Walking with his daughter one day, he found himself surrounded by neighborhood kids demanding his autograph. After they left, his daughter asked for one, too. Visiting

Hollywood that August, he was just as besieged, this time by film producers trying to sign up him and Coca. Hedda Hopper passed up Douglas Fairbanks Jr.'s cocktail party for Anthony Eden to meet Sid. Thanks to the ever-lengthening coaxial cable, viewers in Los Angeles would see Caesar live in the new season. For some, though, having Caesar come on at 6:00 p.m. was a decidedly mixed blessing. "What am I going to do?" one complained. "Fold up my office so I can get home in time? I'd rather see him on a poor kinescope than not catch him at all."

CHAPTER 5

A "JEWISH" SHOW?

A few weeks into the second full season of *Your Show of Shows* in September 1951, viewers were greeted with a new theme song. Also by Tolkin (with Liebman helping on the lyrics), it depicted the same idyllic, carefree, wondrous New York, albeit to a slightly different tune. It began slowly, majestically, almost as a proclamation:

> *Broadway, the big night,*
> *So bright, so shining, so new,*
> *Broadway, the Great White Way tonight,*
> *Is calling to you.*

Then came a pause, and the pace quickened:

> *Stars glow on every Saturday night,*
> *Every Saturday's your night and mine,*
> *You know that every Saturday night,*
> *The town begins to sparkle and shine.*
>
> *Bring your date, or your mate,*
> *Share the fun with the one on your arm,*
> *Take your seat for a treat,*

Here's your invitation,
Don't need a reservation,

Let's meet on every Saturday night,
For an evening that glitters and glows,
It's the sight of sights,
And the night of nights,
It's the Show of Shows!

No doubt it was Liebman's way of freshening things up without changing anything at all. Fans, though, were upset even with that slight tweak, and "Stars over Broadway" quietly returned. And therein lay his conundrum: The show had to evolve, but the people who liked it liked it the way it was.

A more lasting change was hiring as director Bill Hobin, who'd been working on Dave Garroway's show in Chicago. Hobin, who'd developed a more kinetic style of directing and camerawork, had turned down Liebman a year earlier, but after Garroway's show was axed (he would soon anchor the new *Today* show) and Liebman had again come calling, Hobin asked a colleague what to do. "Get your ass on the first goddamn plane to New York" was the reply.

The season premiere, noted *Billboard*, "seemed like something a little too well remembered—nice, but with no quality of the unanticipated or unexpected." Despite the desire of many to leave things as they were, the complaints were becoming as repetitive as the programs: Caesar was still winning, the *New York Journal-American* noted, but his material was "more tired than a night watchman after an all-day binge." Some of the carping was more pointed. "Can we stand another season of Sid Caesar's professor-arriving-at-the-airport? Personally, I doubt it," a television writer in Chicago declared. "I have discovered the way to watch the *Show of Shows*," a viewer wrote. "Once a month."

In addition to hiring Hobin, Liebman had brought on Howard Morris full time. Morris summarized his childhood succinctly: "I was an only-lonely and a teeny-weeny." Born in the Bronx and three years older than Caesar, he'd been the only child of a father who had, as his son put it, died of unemployment.

Shorty and Peanut, they'd called him as a kid. Morris was what Europeans of a certain generation—either Jews trying to hide their identity or Gentiles trying to smoke them out—liked to say was "of Jewish origin": Having gone through "all the bad places where Jews can get hurt badly," his family had become Christian Scientists. "They said, 'Don't be [a] Jew,' and I tried not to be for a long time," he said. His army dog tag had been stamped *P* (for "Protestant") rather than *H* (for "Hebrew").

Ever since sitting spellbound in a Bronx movie palace as a nine-year-old watching the silent film *The Last Command*, he'd known his calling. "Slowly some lights came up," he remembered, "and before I knew it there was a picture on the big screen up above me, and it was a German actor named Emil Jannings whom I've never forgotten, and I looked at it and I watched what they were doing and I remember saying to myself, 'I think I can do that.'" He studied drama at New York University, and once he'd enlisted in the army—only by drinking enough water to get up to 108 pounds—he'd managed to join Maurice Evans's entertainment troupe in Honolulu. That was where he'd run into Reiner, whom he knew from a radio workshop back home. He soon got him into Evans's group, thereby sparing Reiner from having to ship out to Iwo Jima.

Morris's primary role had not changed: He was still the one to rough up, his costumes perforated so they tore more easily. His steady presence further enabled the frequent and sometimes startling violence of *Your Show of Shows*, an inordinate number of whose sketches ended in mayhem and carnage. "Violence was [Caesar's] basic medium and his deepest identifications were with hoodlums, bad men, and giant appetitive oafs who were constantly flying into insane rages and shooting everybody dead, including themselves," Albert Goldman wrote. "The basis of Sid's humor was practically psychotic. If the bit didn't involve a gun or a Mafia character or a screaming German lunatic, it didn't mean a thing to Sid Caesar." Caesar sort of said as much. "There was a time when no matter what kind of a comedy sketch I did, everybody had to get killed," he observed.

Sunday mornings, while Caesar luxuriated in the shower, Morris would inspect himself for bruises and missing clumps of hair. One time, Caesar broke some of Morris's ribs. Caesar, Morris remembered, "was often out of control, part of which made his performance so kind of brilliant, but scary." Morris was in fact very versatile. He was small enough to play either children or old men convincingly. He, too, had a fine ear for languages (unlike Caesar and Reiner, he actually spoke German) and could keep up with the double-talk. But he was less comfortable being Caesar's subordinate than Reiner was, and less comfortable still being Reiner's. It ate at him, and it showed: He came across as angry, edgy, subversive. Throughout his time with Caesar, Morris craved—and felt he deserved—more (and better) roles, more (and better) lines, more respect, more fame. He and Coca bonded over their marginality, he as a third banana and squirt, she as a Gentile, woman, and nonnative New Yorker.

Caesar and Coca returned "in the very best form," but once more undermined by overfamiliarity. "I like my eggs sunny-side up but I even have them scrambled for variety once in a while," a New Jersey reader wrote to Jack O'Brian. In the face of such criticism, Caesar did branch out some: His hayseed "Cousin Ezekiel"—offered a martini at the fancy party he's crashed, he replies, "I guess if you ain't got no liquor that'll have to do"—anticipated *The Beverly Hillbillies* by a decade. But with half-hour sitcoms becoming the norm, some suggested *Your Show of Shows* be similarly streamlined. A Cincinnati station did just that, lopping off the first hour to broadcast *Midwestern Hayride*. Exhaustion of a different sort is what worried John Crosby. "My only fear is that [Caesar will] die young," he wrote. "I think they're working the boy too hard." "Sid Caesar makes you laugh every minute he's on," Jack Benny told *Variety*. "But who cares? He's bound to wear himself out."

Caesar was now making $12,000 a week, with network executives projecting a raise to $30,000 a week within three years. Such paydays were enough for the federal Salary Stabilization Board to hold three days of hearings in New York to determine whether he (along with Dean Martin, Jerry Lewis, Jackie Gleason, and Margaret Truman, among others) should be allowed to make so much. After his brother Abe was arrested for bookmaking, the family candy store in Yonkers was sold, and Caesar put both his brothers on the payroll. Things were much safer that way.

People continued to plumb Caesar's psyche. A handwriting expert said Sid's letters stumbled over one another the way he stumbled over himself in his introductions. Harold Flender recalled how Caesar wore guns at home (and pointed them at people on the street), bought watches just to smash them, and was "pathologically jealous of other comics," especially Jackie Gleason. Even all the money Sid was making upset him somehow, reminding him of how his mother had told him things like "You're not worth the nickel I'm going to give you." "Sid was as jittery, bewildered, compulsive and morose as any *schnook* he ever portrayed," Robert Merrill later wrote. "He worked on his sketches eight days a week, lurching around the rehearsal hall like a Bowery drifter, groaning, sweating, buttoning his jacket up, then down again, as if ready to flee. He smiled only when the skit demanded it." And he talked to his co-workers almost as rarely. "A hello from Sid is a big conversation," a friend of his once said.

But none of this mattered to comedy connoisseurs, for whom Caesar remained in a class by himself. While Jerry Lewis got cheap laughs "crossing his eyes, grimacing and generally acting like a degenerate," Caesar and Coca dug down deep into themselves, Fred Rayfield wrote in *The Daily Compass*. Bob Hope's "sleazy anatomical jokes" couldn't stand up to what Caesar was doing, the *Herald Tribune* observed. While Red Skelton "falls down for every laugh, or gets milk or water squirted in his face," said a Hearst columnist, Caesar had "a light and gentle touch."

But shortly after the birth of Richard Irwin Caesar—his parents designed the name so that young Ricky could lop off the "Caesar" someday should it prove burdensome, but still leave him sounding like a movie star—in February 1952, it was Skelton's program that won the Emmy for best comedy show. (*Your Show of Shows* won for best variety show.) Though the program ducked real-world problems, it had real-world clout: When Caesar, playing a sad sack having a bad day, got zapped while sipping water from beneath an electric blanket, megawatts of fear jolted the electric blanket industry. That April, the FCC authorized 2,053 more TV stations in 1,291 communities. Before a Denverite could say "Sid Caesar," *The Wall Street Journal* reported, the town had gone "stark, raving TV crazy," with sets being sold in barbershops, drugstores, motels, sheet metal factories, jewelry stores, real estate agencies, used-car lots, and even a mortuary. Thanks to the "Cyclops of the living room," as Larry Wolters of the *Chicago Tribune* called it, millions of Americans were mastering a whole new set of rituals: "bolting their meals from trays; shushing people who talk, glaring balefully at the telephone when it rings, and heading for the refrigerator to get away from those repetitious, long-winded commercials." And, he added, acquainting themselves with this new Caesar, "the fellow who is causing sofomores* to forget Julius."

It's hard now to imagine the excitement that the coming of television caused, especially in remote areas hungering for it. "Think of it!" an ad placed by the Television Dealers Association of Ogden, Utah, in the local paper declared in October 1952 as a nearby transmitter became operational. "The view from your living room suddenly and miraculously opens up on the whole world." "Don't figure to wait for a couple of years before getting your set," *The Ogden Standard-Examiner* chimed in. "Sure, there'll be improvements, but TV is plenty good right now. If you want your kids home at night and not over at the neighbor's, you'd better get a set yourself." But viewers in innumerable Ogdens weren't Caesar's constituency; he'd soon have to worry whether, before long, the stix would nix more than hick pix. In fact, some nixing was already under way. "We can stand only so much of the grimaces of Imogene Coca & Caesar, then we switch to something else," Arlene Coon of Goodrich, Michigan, complained to *TV Today*. "May I ask you to discontinue the last half hour of *Your Show of Shows* and give us all of the wrestling show?" a viewer in Bonne Terre, Missouri, asked NBC via the *St. Louis Post-Dispatch*. Even the groundhog found Caesar's shadow dreary: *The Punxsutawney Spirit* in Pennsylvania claimed *Your Show of Shows* actually improved when Caesar and Coca took one of their brief vacations.

But while some saw only sameness, *Your Show of Show*'s ambitions grew, most notably in its willingness to take on Hollywood.

---

* A remnant of the *Chicago Tribune*'s short-lived campaign to rationalize American spelling.

Epic films lent themselves to mockery on an epic scale, giving the program additional gravitas. From the beginning, Caesar had gone after movies—generic movies on wars, gangsters, prize-fights, among others, each with its set of clichés. That both Caesar and Liebman felt spurned by, or unappreciated in, Hollywood would have made it a tempting target. But they had to be mindful of getting taken to court and losing, as Jack Benny had experienced for his parody of *Gaslight*, when MGM had charged him with unfair competition and copyright infringement.

There was no shortage of material: "As long as movies continued to be either silly, or overly romantic, or cliché-ridden, we had plenty of inspiration," Tolkin remembered. It was the very same impulse felt at roughly the same time by another, very similar (young, urban, Jewish) group of satirists a few blocks away, at the fledgling *Mad* magazine. In fact, they'd been doing this sort of thing since high school. "We were a product of our Jewish backgrounds in New York, we were in the same city living in different boroughs, yet we were having the same experiences," recalled Harvey Kurtzman, who'd created *Mad* in 1952 (and was two years Caesar's junior). "We'd pick scenes out of the popular movies . . . all the clichés. And then Danny Kaye and Sid Caesar would do the same scene that we were doing in the lunch room. How they hell did they know?"

In January 1952, Liebman and Caesar burlesqued the film version of *A Streetcar Named Desire*, released the previous September. Caesar played Bill, his version of the brutish, slovenly Stanley Kowalski, played in the film by Marlon Brando; Coca was Magnolia, the straitlaced, genteel sister-in-law and Blanche DuBois doppelgänger visiting from New Orleans. The sketch gave the show a much-needed jolt of adrenaline; Crosby called it "magnificent"—one of the comic highlights of his season, along with Lucille Ball's trying to keep up with a conveyor belt at a bon-bon factory—and wondered whether, one day, it would be more famous than Tennessee Williams's original. There was no lawsuit, so two months later they staged the sketch again.

The following month, at one of those groggy-eyed Monday morning story meetings, Kallen offered up another target: *A Place in the Sun*, the noirish psychodrama (based on Theodore Dreiser's *American Tragedy*) that had come out the previous year. It told the story of an ambitious young man (played by Montgomery Clift) who, eager to run off with a wealthy society girl (Elizabeth Taylor), drowns his pregnant, frowzy, cloying, working-class fiancée (Shelley Winters). Grim and brutal, touching taboos like premarital sex and abortion, it was an unlikely subject for timorous network TV. But something about it—maybe how the earnest and hardworking but dumpy girlfriend is made to look so unappealing next to the beautiful but vapid debutante—had set Kallen off. (It *did* have faint echoes of that story she'd written in grade school, the one in which her beautiful blond rival wound up impaled on a fence.)

Liebman hesitated, but Caesar, who'd play the young man (Montgomery), was all in, in part because it gave Coca (the victim, Mildred) a meaty role. Reiner, off-screen, would play Montgomery's subconscious, and Morris the old man renting out the fateful rowboat. A Greek chorus supplied what Coca called "psycho music" in the background. Between them, and the loons honking ominously overhead, and the fog Liebman had thrown in, Coca felt genuinely menaced by the goings-on. "A Place in the Bottom of the Lake," the mock movie was called. Would anyone find it funny? During rehearsals, there'd not been a single laugh. But the sheer wicked brilliance of the writing and the acting shone through.

"Well, here we are, Mildred," says Montgomery, as their outing begins. "Let's go for a row on the lake."

"You're so good to me, Montgomery!" Mildred whines. "How could I ever have thought you were trying to get rid of me so you could marry that society girl just because she's beautiful and rich and wealthy and gorgeous?"

They board the boat. "Careful, Montgomery . . . I can't swim," says Mildred.

"Good!" he blurts out. As Mildred checks out the oar, he inspects the rope, chain, gun, and knife he's brought aboard. She presses him to get married that very day; marriage would be "real nice." Their apartment, too, would be "real nice." So would the curtains. And the furniture. And the carpets. And the kitchen. And the oranges, and peaches, and pomegranates they'll eat; there won't be anything that's not "real nice." "This girl is an idiot!" Caesar's subconscious exclaims. Mildred lists all of the things she'll do for him once they're married, and how she'll *never* let him out of her sight, and how real nice that, too, will be. "Oh, I *got* to kill this girl!" his conscience repeats. Only he bumbles and fumbles away his chance. Back onshore, Montgomery suggests a sightseeing trip, to the very edge of the very top of the Empire State Building. "I don't like it there," Mildred protests. "I fell off once," she adds, pointing to the scratch behind her ear. "Well, we'll get married tomorrow," Montgomery finally tells her. "It'll be *real nice*." Dot really was a classic, as Tolkin might even have said.

With both Reiner and Morris nimble in double-talk, there were more and better send-ups of foreign films. Homages to classics like *The Bicycle Thief* and *Grand Illusion* bore little resemblance to the originals, but such sketches offered an excuse to see (and study, and honor, and emulate) films they found not only admirable but inspiring—proof that quality *did* matter, and would last. Besides, the need to tune up their foreign accents turned meals out into fieldwork.

Thanks to his wondrous childhood encounters back at the RKO Proctor in Yonkers with Chaplin, Keaton, and other stars of early Hollywood, and his own tortured relationship to the spoken word, Caesar approached silent films even more reverentially. "At heart, Caesar was himself a silent film comedian working in an alien form," the television historian Gerald Nachman wrote. "He was really born to star in Mack Sennett films, with his flickering shadings of joy, sadness, scorn, anger, hatred, or hurt." While placing an enormous strain on the actors, forcing them to move more quickly and jerkily to replicate the originals (and leaving them with blinding headaches afterward), re-creations of silent films became a recurrent feature on the show.

Among the best, from May 1952, was "Sewing Machine Girl," a depiction of the world of sweatshops. which, to many viewers, especially in New York, was not all that remote; it was one sign of Jewish upward mobility that only forty years after the disastrous Triangle Shirtwaist factory fire Jews could find laughs in a world of such pain and heartbreak. The sketch featured Coca as the working waif, Reiner as her malevolent (and lecherous) boss, and Caesar as her noble co-worker, who wields a sewing needle in her defense (most notably by sticking it into Reiner's backside). In these sketches, Caesar's craft was as noteworthy as his wit. "When he did a silent movie, it *looked like* a silent movie," said Woody Allen. "It wasn't some dopey little sketch on a program where you'd know everything was fake."

As eagerly as the show now took on Hollywood, it was slow to go after television, out of either its instinctive caution, or a reluctance to bite the hand feeding it, or an unspoken nonaggression pact among television personalities. When it did, it was more to rib its technical glitches, along with the havoc it was wreaking in American life, than to mock particular shows. In a February 1952 sketch, Caesar and Coca, foiled in their efforts to get a decent picture, stop eating in order to rotate their chairs, adjust the knobs, and find the best spot for the antenna, which winds up on Coca's head. So consumed are they by their efforts that she salts his food, and he tries to eat her hand.

Two other particularly bright spots that season involved classical music. In February 1952, Caesar and Coca pantomimed a pair of impatient percussionists during a performance of Tchaikovsky's *1812 Overture.* The two don't much like each other—here, too, she's a prig and he's a clown, and ham, and boor—but they're stuck together, largely in idleness, passing the time between cymbal clashes and triangle tingles playing gin rummy.* This quickly changes, of course, at the dramatic conclusion to the piece, when the two go into action, frantically loading and shooting off cannons and firing machine guns. As the music comes to a close, the two pin medals on each other, then stand at reverent attention. The sketch was oddly moving—like the famous "Marseillaise" scene in *Casablanca*—American Jews gloriously expressing French patriotism. Years later, one critic still couldn't hear Tchaikovsky's piece without seeing Caesar's "tuxedo-clad percussionist" hurling imaginary grenades.

---

* During comparable lulls Coca's bandleader father had shot craps on the piano—the inspiration for the sketch.

That April, Caesar and Coca portrayed the snooty side of classical music. The setting is a musicale in a fancy private home. The dowager hostess is Coca, playing a sort of diminutive Margaret Dumont, wildly mixing metaphors as she introduces the evening's performer, Miss Rose Weed. As Weed sings Sir Henry Bishop's 1819 coloratura aria "Lo! Hear the Gentle Lark," enter Caesar, in tie and tails. But his every move—sitting down, cracking his knuckles, winding his watch, realigning his nose, writing in his notebook—seems, as Vincent Canby later wrote, "wired for high-fidelity sound." When he catches his finger in his cigarette case, he exits briefly to scream, then sneezes noisily when he returns. Before long, so does everyone else, and the salon is in shambles. "We often worked out twists on dignity or stuffiness," said Reiner. "Rule one: the vulgarization of dignity."

SID CAESAR NEVER EXACTLY advertised his Jewishness, but he didn't hide it, either. In May 1948, he'd participated in a rally at Madison Square Garden sponsored by the Irgun, the militant right-wing group pushing for a Jewish state in all of Mandatory Palestine. Three years later, he appeared with Ralph Bellamy in a radio fundraiser marking Israel's third anniversary, and he returned for the fourth, this time with Robert Montgomery. Hebrew was one language he hadn't had to pick up at the St. Clair Lunch: He'd had Hebrew school for that. But it probably wouldn't have hurt, one Jewish paper complained, if someone had coached Caesar on his Hebrew pronunciation. Caesar also joined John Garfield, Eleanor Roosevelt, and the future Israeli foreign minister Abba Eban, among others, at an Ebbets Field rally marking the anniversary.

Jewish admirers would have seen no explicit nods to anything Jewish on Caesar's show. The Milton Berle era—that anarchic period when television was too desperate for material to worry whether it was "too Jewish"—did not last long. True, *The Goldbergs* (a sitcom that made the transition from radio) held on until 1956, but as it matured, television underwent the same de-Judaization the movies had in the 1930s. This time, there wasn't the (Nazi) German market to worry about, but fears among TV's primarily Jewish brass of standing out too much, plus the broadening demographics of viewers, resistance from largely Gentile ad agencies, and self-censorship from Jewish writers, performers, and directors.

Holocaust references on television, for instance, were scarce. When, in the fall of 1952, the screenwriter Paddy Chayefsky managed to get *Holiday Song* (a drama about two survivors) on the air, it was over the opposition of the Jewish producer of the show, David Susskind. (Chayefsky also felt compelled to change one of the most famous characters in his work—the eponymous Marty—from a Jewish accountant into an Italian butcher.)* Just how little space Jews on television had to be Jews became clear around Christmas 1952, when the playwright and wit George S. Kaufman was yanked off *This Is Show Business* for declaring, "Let's make this one program on which no one sings 'Silent Night.'" Kaufman had actually been *defending* Christian sensibilities, objecting to using Christ to flog toothpaste, but his point was lost. "It's a fear-ridden industry," Kaufman observed. (He was soon reinstated.)

Jewish comics on TV faced additional pressures to lie low. In late February 1951, Abel Green of *Variety* (the man who'd coined the phrase "Borscht Belt") wrote of "some hinterland TV trade and audience opinion that there is too much borscht tinting the TV comedians," though it was matters of taste, rather than Jewishness, to which he seemed to refer. The same was true of the influential right-wing radio commentator Paul Harvey; what he called "that crowded little island"—that is, Manhattan—was "contaminating an awful lot of fresh air," he testified in June 1952 to a House subcommittee investigating "immoral or otherwise offensive matter" on television.

But try as TV might to steer clear of it, the Borscht Belt remained the fount from which most of its comedy sprang; Liebman was proof that, as *Variety* put it, "TV gold can be

---

* Even after Marty switched ethnicities, he continued to watch Caesar on Saturday nights. But as *Marty* progressed from teleplay to Oscar-winning movie, he changed channels, to the lower-brow *Your Hit Parade*.

panned in the mountain camps." So network prospectors went out looking for more. Barely six weeks after Green's plea, in what it dubbed "Operation Lox," *Billboard* reported that NBC planned to scour the Catskills that summer for fresh laughs. "Dozens of Broadway shows, hundreds of movies, thousands of TV and radio programs, have flowered from the seeds that first germinated in the Borscht Circuit," observed the novelist-to-be Herman Wouk, who for a time fashioned jokes in the Mountains. "Perhaps there is a special virtue in beet soup." Of course, the very people mining the Catskills were undermining it, too: Television, along with many other factors, helped do the Catskills in.

Caesar came from that world but steered clear of it, at least on the air. "He never said a Jewish word when he worked for me—not one," Liebman recalled. "They were trying to *get away* from being 'Jew comics'!" But discernibly Jewish tropes did seep in, prompting knowing laughter from Jewish viewers. Yiddish words, for instance, were baked into German double-talk, while "schmo" rhymed with just about everything. Where the words weren't explicitly Jewish, the sentence structure was: Simply by reversing subject and predicate—for example, "A pet he brings to school!"; "A finer girl you couldn't find anywhere"; "From my plate he has to eat!"—they could bond with *landsmen.*

Even when sentence structure wasn't a giveaway, certain sentiments were. The complaint from Caesar's housefly that of his four million offspring not one ever picked up a phone or came to visit anticipated by a decade Elaine May's complaint to her only (NASA scientist) son. "Jack Benny, George Burns, Sid Caesar, Milton Berle, nobody ever said they were Jewish, but the Jews knew they were Jewish," Reiner said. And whenever that synapse led to a laugh, Reiner noted, care was taken to provide an additional something for everyone else to laugh at, too, so that Gentiles wouldn't stew over whatever "those fucking Jews" found "so fucking funny." The explicitly Jewish stuff they did— like Brooks's Yiddish pirate complaining about the high price of sailcloth, or Caesar's Jewish labor leader spouting Yiddishisms on the subway—they did strictly for one another and always off the air.

On the calendar of *Your Show of Shows,* only Christian holidays were marked. Christmas and Easter brought holiday wishes from the stage. Newspapers described Sid's Christmas presents to his kids: the electric train for Ricky, the dollhouse for Shelly. Naturally, there wasn't a menorah, or dreidel, or latke in sight. In one interview, Caesar described his daughter's nightly prayers, and how, one Christmas, "waiting and watching for her reaction to the tree and the presents and Santa, my anticipation was probably even keener than hers!" Later, when Caesar's sketches centered on a trio of suburban couples, publicity photos showed Caesar, Reiner, and Morris caroling even more heartily than their conspicuously Christian wives. Caesar's contribution to a celebrity cookbook was a recipe for cannelloni calling for large helpings of pork, fatback, butter, and cheese.

Caesar's Gentile friends in the press helped him burnish his mainstream bona fides. "J. Moraiarty of the Bronx asks 'The nationality of Sid Caesar and Carl Reiner,' and the answer is 'American,'" Jack O'Brian harrumphed. Around headquarters, Christmas was marked less traditionally. The resident midwestern Gentile, Bill Hayes, would install a scraggly tree in one of the rehearsal rooms, and presents would be placed beneath it. One year Kallen, still single at the time, opened one box to find an ensemble of three gourds, arranged to resemble what Hayes described as "Herculean male genitalia."

Irony, irreverence, insecurity—all were at the program's Jewish core. And there was at least one more element: an absolute fixation with food.

Every culture, of course, cherishes food, and everyone has to eat, but the Jewish relationship to food seems different—more intense, even obsessive, monomaniacal. The distinction that the food writer Mimi Sheraton made between Jews and Italians on the matter applies equally well to Jews and everyone else: Italians care about food every bit as much as Jews do, she observed—only without the panic.

That point, of course, had already been noted. In "Adam and Eve on Delancey Street," a 1949 essay in *Commentary*, Isaac Rosenfeld posited that the nourishment Jews find in food, born of deprivation, dislocation, and vulnerability, goes well beyond calories: "Basic security being unavailable to Jews in a hostile

world, food becomes a source of the satisfactions society with-
holds." Rosenfeld's Lower East Side is teeming with people selling or serving it, leaving little room for, say, haberdasheries. And
understandably so, for clothes offer only superficial security. "Eat,
eat, eat," he wrote. "Not that we are never sated: food is not food
and it cannot satisfy a hunger that is not hunger."

By Caesar's time most American Jews had escaped hunger
per se. But by graduating from mere sustenance to indulgence,
food had somehow become an even greater fixation. In another
food-related piece in *Commentary*, Ruth Glazer argued that as
God worship waned, food worship intensified, and a reader in
New England named Samuel Persky agreed. "Why complain
that delicatessen is vitaminless?" he asked. "Let us, instead, thank
God for it. Vitamins are for drug stores. They should be taken
in pills and capsules exclusively. They have no place in food."
Orson Welles, then in Hollywood, chimed in to say that he'd
hung around enough Jews long enough to connect Jewish cuisine
to Jewish creativity. "Without pastrami sandwiches there could
be no picture-making," he noted.

Reiner, who often went without as a child (only years later
did he realize that the Romanian rice-and-beans dish his mother
served was supposed to include meat), was once asked why so
many sketches on the show revolved around food. "Because we
were Jews!" he replied. Asked another time what difference being
Jewish had made in his life, he listed a "better appreciation" for
food and comedy—in that order. Liebman, too, was a sucker for
a good food joke, including one he remembered from fifty years
earlier, the same one that, he felt, Woody Allen had rendered
imprecisely in retelling it.*

Food had always been central to Caesar: It was, after all, the
family business. Later, dispensing sage advice to patrons about
what kind of sandwich they had time to eat—a function of how

---

* As Allen uses it in *Annie Hall*, one elderly Jewish woman at a Catskills resort complains
to another, "The food at this place is really terrible," to which her friend replies, "Yeah, I
know. And such small portions." "It actually is: 'The food is terrible. *It's just like poison!* And
they give you such small portions,'" Liebman complained to the writer Max Wilk. "That's
what gives it the sock!" he said. "The extra punch!" (Liebman interview, Feb. 1978, Dorot
Jewish Division, New York Public Library)

long it took to prepare, to chew, and to swallow without it sticking to the roof of your mouth—was a key part of his doorman
duties at the Capitol Theatre. The sketch about the "Five Dollar
Date" was all about food, as was the riff on scrambled eggs in *Tars
and Spars*. Food was also a staple of the earliest profiles of Caesar,
especially in the Yiddish press, for which his prodigious appetite,
backed by a limitless budget, was as much a source of pride as his
talent or success.

Nakhman Zalowitz of the *Forverts* described Caesar's typical lunch—"four gigantic corned beef sandwiches at Lindy's
restaurant"—and was in awe of his extravagance as much as of
his appetite. "You would pay $1.50 apiece for such a corned beef
sandwich," he marveled. Interviewing Caesar six months later,
his colleague Jay Grayson stopped en route at the Stage Deli,
where an autographed picture of Caesar hung in the front window. "I'll give you something to take with you, which will open all
doors—I mean, to Sid's heart—for you," the owner of the place,
Max Asnas, told him. And with that, he shouted at his counterman to make a "Sid Caesar Special": corned beef on rye, with a
pepper on the side. "For God's sake, don't forget the pepper!" he
added. Already, Grayson was impressed. "You have to be truly
famous to have a sandwich named after you in a Broadway restaurant," he noted. And when, during a break from rehearsing,
Caesar beheld Asnas's gift, his eyes lit up. Caesar ate his sandwich
not just with mustard but with relish. "It is a pity, I tell you, that it
was not televised," Grayson wrote. "How Sid chewed his corned
beef sandwich and washed it down with soda, it was something
to see!" When he told Caesar's mother of his offering to her boy,
she laughed. He'd become Sidney's best friend, she said.

When he became famous, Caesar cataloged his multicourse
meals to goggle-eyed reporters, like the ones—to "let off steam"—
at Dubiner's on the Lower East Side Tuesdays after work:

> We would start off with a family-style, mixture-plate of
> stuffed cabbage, chopped liver and ptcha.[*] Then we'd

---

[*] Boiled calf's feet, suspended in gelatin, with garlic and hard-boiled eggs.

order a couple of bottles of seltzer, and it had to come in blue bottles. If it came in green bottles, I'd return it. Then we'd have a bottle of wine, and we'd mix the seltzer and the wine. Delicious! Then came soup. Sometimes I'd order three soups mixed. We'd tell them to take the noodles from noodle soup and put them into green pea soup, then add the vegetables from vegetable soup. Then I'd order broiled sweet-breads, with stuffed derma* on the side. Then came the piece de resistance: mashed potatoes, with chicken fat and fried onions. Also, potato pancakes with apple sauce. We'd finish off with a fresh fruit dish, and then the last course was loosening the belt and staring at the ceiling for an hour.

Tales of Caesar's culinary feats abound: how Florence bought him two pounds of cheese every other day for snacks; how he'd leapfrog from breakfast (the juice from four oranges, two eggs with bacon, kippered herring, three slices of stale white bread, and two glasses of yogurt) to a late morning snack (egg salad sandwich with a bottle of Dr. Brown's Cel-Ray tonic, often taken in a single swig, followed by a long belch) to lunch (turkey leg, wing, and neck, more Cel-Ray) to an afternoon nosh (four hot dogs and two cocktails, cream of tomato soup, sirloin steak and fried potatoes, apple pie and more yogurt) to nightly rounds of restaurants, picking up Cantonese soup and dumplings, then a main course at the Italian spot with the best marinara sauce, then dessert at his favorite bakery. "Double Caesar," Liebman called him; "he had to have two lobsters, two spring chickens, two everything."

Days off weren't days off from eating. On Sundays the comedian Fat Jack Leonard might stop by bearing cheesecake, or Dave Caesar would bring a cream cheese pie. The Nova Scotia salmon and sturgeon came from Barney Greengrass, on the Upper West Side, even though sturgeon was going for $5 a pound. Until meeting Caesar, Neil Simon had never seen anyone eat an entire block of halvah. "He once said to me, 'You know, they say wine,

---

* A chopped mixture of flour, fat, and vegetables stuffed in a sausage-like casing.

women, and song, Mel, are the things,'" Brooks remembered. "He said, 'Out of that, I would have to say, *food—then* wine, women, and song.'"

One writer who'd dined with Caesar left his own meal untouched. "Eating with a guy who persists in twisting his features into strange shapes, accompanied by sound effects, is no boon to the appetite," he complained. Janet Kern of the *Chicago Herald-American* once accompanied Caesar, exhausted, grouchy, and hungry, followed by a herd of hangers-on, to his home after a show. "The vivacious Mrs. C. becomes as silent as wallpaper and almost slave-like in her anticipation of his every wish," she wrote. "She sees to it that Sid's bath is ready, and when he's through with that, a huge steak or roast beef dinner is at hand—regardless of the hour."

Greg Garrison, who'd directed *Your Show of Shows* early on, recalled how, every day before noon, while going through a sketch with Caesar and Coca, Liebman would walk in and quietly confer with the two. "We'd start doing the scene again, and there was more punch to it," said Garrison. "I'd say, 'Max is just fantastic!'" He then learned that what they'd been discussing wasn't the show at all, but that day's lunch order from the Stage Delicatessen. (In which Coca wouldn't have said much: "She takes such tiny bites, one sandwich lasts her for days," Caesar once said with amazement. It was just one more reason why she'd never have been one of the boys.)

The noshing in the writers' room was nonstop, and it showed: Tolkin went from the "Jewish Abe Lincoln" Brooks described to a Jewish William Howard Taft. The proprietor of Al and Dick's on West Fifty-Fourth Street would set aside two-pound steaks for Caesar; why, he asked himself, should he save them for someone who wouldn't appreciate them? The eating poured over into the shows themselves. "Why does Sid Caesar always have to eat on his show?" the Hollywood columnist Sidney Skolsky asked. (And, evidently still vexed over the matter, asked again two years later.)

Chinese food was especially important to Caesar and his generation of Jews, probably because it epitomized something even more precious than prosperity: freedom. Tasty, spicy, crunchy, undercooked, and often proscribed, it represented everything their mothers would never have served. So it was often on Caesar's menu when he took his crew out. "Sid would order in 'Chinese,' and the waiter would kind of lean forward and almost get it, beginning to write something down and hesitating, not quite sure he got it right," Joe Stein recalled about an outing to Chinatown Charlie's, near City Center. (Another time, Caesar took umbrage at an uncomprehending Chinese waiter and stormed out of the place, his flock in tow.) The Charlie Hickenlooper character liked Chinese food, too, spurning the steak Doris had prepared for him in favor of some takeout he'd picked up on his way home. When she insists their wedding vows included a pledge to eat whatever she fed him, he suddenly becomes Patrick Henry:

Why? Where is it written? Supposing someday I want to get up at three o'clock in the morning and have a nice lunch? There's nothing wrong with that! Supposing I come home from work at seven o'clock and have a nice midnight snack? There's nothing wrong with that! Someday I'd like to start out the meal with a big piece of strawberry shortcake, and for dessert have a salami sandwich with pickles! How about that?

The two eventually compromise—and go out for Indian food.

To get anything out of Caesar, Brooks advised Maurice Zolotow of *The Saturday Evening Post*, one had to eat and drink with him. So when Caesar downed four huge hot dogs (with mustard and sauerkraut) in a few bites, along with four tall glasses of chocolate milk, Zolotow did his best to keep up, and it worked: For the first time, Caesar actually smiled at him. Then it was off to a Greek restaurant for dinner. How could the man eat so much? Zolotow asked Brooks. "What do you mean *eat*?" Brooks replied. "Up to now he has not eaten. Now he is going home and he's *really* going to eat."

From the very first *Your Show of Shows*, when Coca sang of falling in love over smorgasbord and Caesar's Samson asks Coca's

Delilah, "You got any food in the house? I hungry," there were sketches on eating. A visiting *nudnik* (Reiner) lectures Charlie and Doris on the dangers of drinking water during meals. ("Very, very bad. You see this fatty, greasy food, it doesn't mix with the water, sort of emulsifies and goes to the top and big lumps and globs of fat float around there. It's very unhealthy. A lot of people go before their time! That's digging your grave with your teeth!") What Charlie Hickenlooper fears most when burglars ransack his house is losing his precious stash of Worcestershire sauce.

A miraculous "tutti frutti" tree, one that yields apples, bananas, pears, chicken, and roast beef, is at the center of an Italian film spoof. "What gave them the idea that lions only eat meat?" one lion at the zoo (Caesar) asks another (Coca). "I like a little mixed green salad once in a while." In a courtroom sketch, Judge John Poundcake certifies the marriage of Eleanor Ryebread to John Pumpernickel. Ludwig von Dumpling, author of *A Loaf of Bread, a Jug of Wine, and Wow!*, expounds on food, while Hookline von Sinker recalls his toughest fight as a fisherman, with a tenacious can of sardines. The criminologist Ludwig von Bloodhound describes an innovative new prison, with its very own Chinese restaurant—the first such institution harder to get into than to break out of, especially on holidays. Ludwig von Snowcap might not have been the first to conquer Everest, but he *was* the first to eat corned beef and pastrami atop it. The mayonnaise mogul J. Evans Worcestershire wants to invest a "lot of lettuce" in a Broadway show, but only if his tomato can star. Several sketches highlighted the mysterious rituals of fine dining: The Hickenloopers marvel at the white tablecloths, and recoil at the check. Then there were niceties of tipping: Leave too little and you looked like a tightwad, but leave too much, and you're a sucker. In one sketch a snooty waiter (Reiner) glowers at Charlie as he unloads first his coins, then his bills, then his watch, and finally Doris's mink stole.

Equally challenging are unfamiliar foods. Charlie is confounded by the forbidden *frutta di mare*—shellfish; he bites into an unshucked oyster, and stabs a lobster. Baffled by the offerings at a posh seafood restaurant—they include "spare ribs of swordfish sautéed in seaweed," and "octopus toes smothered in fried minnows"—he pleads for a steak. But for his maiden smorgasbord—all that food! Not just chicken à la king but chicken à la queen! And all for the same price, no matter how high you load your plate—he is suddenly fearless. "You're eating as if there's no tomorrow!" Doris complains. "One never knows!" he says, staggering toward the desserts.

ESPECIALLY ATTUNED TO, AND appreciative of, Caesar's elusive Jewishness was a small new subset of American Jews: Holocaust survivors. To wounded people in an alien culture, Caesar, able to communicate without words and willing to ridicule Germans (even though, for the sake of comedy and good taste, these Germans served the kaiser rather than Hitler), became a balm. And their *Amerikanishe* kids, who watched him with them (translating and offering explanations where needed), were grateful.

"Coming to America with my parents, Polish-born survivors, home life was depressingly subdued," recalled John Thorn, later the longtime official historian of Major League Baseball.

> Having spent four years hiding under a bed except at night, when he ventured into the shrubbery outside the house, my father was an exceedingly reserved, repressed, depressed man. My mother—who had spent the war moving from town to town using false papers—was frequently animated, but with rage, not joy or laughter. I remember watching *Show of Shows* with them in our Bronx apartment as a time of hilarity and joy, evidenced nowhere else in our family history. To see my parents laugh—with their heads thrown back, with tears coming to their eyes—was a tremendous anomaly and a release for me, and a clue to a world outside where people might not be as frightened and downtrodden as they were. I, too, learned how to laugh, not merely smile, in some significant measure from my parents' reaction to Sid Caesar, Imogene Coca, Carl Reiner, and Howie Morris.

The parents of Jacob Edelman, also Polish Jews, who had spent the war in the Soviet Union, had ended up in Los Angeles. His father worked in a brush factory; his mother operated a sewing machine in a factory downtown. "Dad worked six days a week and was pretty exhausted by Saturday night, when Sid's show came on," he remembered.

> He'd relax in his armchair, with a smile on his face and his eyes fixed on the TV, continually rocking with laughter throughout the show. When Sid played the German professor or did one of his mock foreign-language bits, he'd sometimes laugh until tears came to his eyes, and shake his head in pleasure and appreciation. English was still a challenge for my parents, but they seemed to have no problem following the show, with a little help now and then from my sister or me. There was an underlying Jewish flavor to the humor that they instinctively relished.

Jan Winter was a Polish Jew who'd covered the Spanish Civil War as a journalist. He came to the United States to raise money for Spanish refugees. "We got a television set in 1949," said his daughter, Margaret.

> By far its most important use was watching Sid Caesar. Caesar was a genius and a Polish Jew—of course! What else? Watching *Your Show of Shows* was a sacred family tradition.
>
> Caesar seemed to me, eerily, an alter ego of my father. He portrayed dozens of versions of a character I identified with my father: hysterically funny, mercurial, tenderhearted, brilliant, manly, noble, tragic, pretentious, puncturing, easily moved to crazy shouting rages and tears of joy. My father was completely fluent in Russian, German, French, Spanish, Polish, and English, and my mother was multilingual, too. They marveled over the finesse and wit of Caesar's double-talk. Daddy started chortling almost immediately, but tried to stifle it, so

his laugh came out like a cough—like Caesar's own nervous cough, in fact. As the gags piled up, he laughed so violently that he started choking, and the rest of us, also weak with laughter, pounded on his back to make sure he didn't actually die from laughing.

Those Saturday nights with Sid Caesar were cathartic. The secret message I took from it, at age four or five, was this: Rage, craziness, and tragedy are all around us and inescapable, but they coexist with wit, love, and hilarity. Learn to understand the sad and scary stuff along with the sweet.

For at least a few Jewish immigrants, watching Caesar offered a chance not just to laugh but to *shep naches*.* "Zey takeh batsoln far dem? Me makht zikh narish!" Joe Stein's mother exclaimed once while taking in one of the shows her son helped write. "They *pay* you for this? They're making fools of themselves!"

* Take pride or joy, especially in one's children.

CHAPTER 6

RESTLESSNESS

Two months after the program entered its third full season in September 1952, Caesar's hometown threw him a party. "Yonkers Stages Own 'Show of Shows' for Sid Caesar," the local paper, *The Herald Statesman*, blared. The celebration began in Manhattan, where six Yonkers policemen on motorcycles came to fetch the honoree. "I will never forget it," recalled Bill Hobin, then the director of *Your Show of Shows*. "Sitting in a black limousine, running all the red lights over to the West Side Highway and up through the Bronx to Westchester, with a police escort, sirens screaming." A second, separate phalanx of comics, including Jack Carter, Morey Amsterdam, and Jack E. Leonard, followed. At Yonkers City Hall, Caesar accepted a two-foot-long key to the city that only Dwight D. Eisenhower had received before. Then came a ticker-tape parade to the local armory, where, at a dinner for five hundred people, Caesar collected a scroll describing him as a "shining example of the American way of life." Rabbi David Shohet, who'd presided over Caesar's bar mitzvah seventeen years earlier—and lived to see his prophecies of Sid's greatness come to pass—called his humor "a wholesome tonic to jangled nerves." Supplying the music were members of the Sid Caesar Alumni Band, made up of local musicians who'd played with him.

Liebman, Reiner, Morris, Weaver, and Coca joined in the festivities, which were featured on the next morning's *Today*. The picture with the city fathers in *The Herald Statesman* showed Caesar looking haughty and supercilious, but the paper published his thank-you note to everyone involved. "I am still a little dazed by the magnitude of the affair!" he'd written.

Caesar had spent much of the previous summer golfing at the Concord Hotel in the Catskills, where the water hazard on the eighteenth hole bore his name. His duties at the resort were minimal, apart from "refereeing" a celebrity golf tournament featuring Bob Hope and Ben Hogan (with Tony Bennett also on hand). Once Caesar returned to the airwaves, John Crosby saluted him as one of those rare artists (Edith Piaf was another, and Coca a third) with "the great gift of making you glad you're alive, of making you feel the world a fine place to live in." Life was good: The shows on other networks were weak. And once more Liebman had largely stood pat. "When you've got a winning formula going you don't mess with it," said Tolkin. "Look at Jack Benny—the same format for twenty years." But as *Advertising Age* noted, "Even the motor companies, whose basic body designs have changed little over the past few years, add new radiator grilles." Caesar was defying what Albert Goldman called "Lindy's Law," which postulated that an entertainer's life expectancy was inversely proportional to the frequency of his appearances. On that score, said Goldman, the ubiquitous Caesar made showbiz traditionalists "gasp and grab for digitalis."

The new season had more bursts of brilliance, like a splendid parody of *High Noon* in October. The film's point was that anyone risking his life for his principles is a hero; "Dark Noon" countered that such a person is actually a damned fool. As Sheriff Silent Slim (Caesar playing Gary Cooper, though even less audibly) straddles down the deserted street of a godforsaken western town, a cowboy croons, "You're gonna die, you lily-livered coward." Due in on the next train is Frank Killer (Reiner), out to murder Slim. Slim has so cleaned up his town (all the gamblin' and shootin' has vamoosed) that while everyone likes him, they also sort of hope he's killed—everyone, except his new bride, Mary Ellen (Coca).

"How can you wait for a man to come here and kill ya?" she asks. "'Cause I'm stupid," he replies, whereupon she, too, skedaddles. "Gosh, Slim, I sure would like to help you out, but I can't hear a word you're saying," his deputy (Morris) tells him.

Caesar himself displayed stoicism worthy of Cooper's character that night. In the minute or so his dressers had to put on his western wear, gun belt, and boots, they neglected to tape a rubber sponge to his chest, the one into which the pins were supposed to have gone when, one after another, his cowardly subordinates surrender their badges before skipping town. Slim winces with every jab, but somehow carries on. "By the time I got backstage, blood was running down my chest," he said. "Gee, Sid, we knew you did great pain takes, but this was terrific," someone said. Caesar—who'd already played Professor von Sedative that night—still had to portray a housefly in a solo number. (Both Caesar and Coca claimed credit for the idea, inspired by a fly they'd seen crawling over a hunk of feta at their favorite Greek restaurant.) For nine minutes he buzzes around, at one point spotting an ad for an insecticide that "kills flies instantly." "There's a lot of hatred in this world," he laments. The fly eludes a swatter, then finds camouflage atop a raisin cake before a nearly fatal brush with flypaper. His glorious night finally through, Caesar flew off himself for a tetanus shot.

The same month saw the Hickenloopers celebrate Charlie's birthday over dinner—at Doris's insistence, naturally—at an East Indian joint called the Ancient House of the Golden Lamb. Chinese food was too established a part of urban Jewish life to offer comic possibilities—there was nothing mysterious about chop suey or fried rice—but the exotic new cuisines gradually infiltrating American cities were fair game. Here, Caesar and Coca are greeted by a bone-shattering gong; then, with the place too dark to read the menu, the waiter (Reiner at his unctuous best) reads off the entrées: klochomoloppi, lich lock, slop lom, shtocklock, rishkosh, and frocklish.

"Yuch!" Charlie exclaims.

"We have yuch, too," Reiner coos. "Boiled or braised?"

As always, all Charlie wants is his trusty steak. When Reiner brings out a dessert flambé, Caesar exclaims, "The place is on fire!" and throws water at him before fleeing.

By late 1952, the show's "gears began to slip," as Bill Hayes put it. The program "remains an island of engaging literacy in TV's sea of vaudeville mediocrity," wrote Jack Gould, but so closely was Liebman hewing to his formula, Gould said, "that an experienced viewer practically can tell time by which act is on the stage." Larry Wolters of the *Chicago Tribune* suggested slashing the show to half an hour every other week, and urged Chicagoans bored with the program—"and who isn't?"—to watch a church-sponsored soap opera airing at the same time. By November, *Your Show of Shows* had dropped out of the top ten, now led by *I Love Lucy*.

Liebman finally brought in a fresh writer: Tony Webster, who'd written for, among others, the comedy team of Bob and Ray. He stimulated things, in part, by diversifying them. "We needed a Gentile," said Reiner. "If Tony would laugh, the country would laugh." Though Webster wasn't Jewish (his background was Irish and German Catholic), he felt close enough. "He was just as bad as the Jews—you know, guilt," Morris recalled. "He always complained about being at a disadvantage, but there was nothing to it," said Kallen. "We loved him. He had a Jewish soul. An Irish-Jewish soul." Tolkin considered Webster not just a colleague but an insurance policy, the friendly Christian who'd come in handy when the troubles started. For Webster, working with all these smart Jews was the stuff of fantasies: Finally, he said, you could "be as bright as you were capable of being without being hit with a ruler."

Still, Webster did not have an easy time of it. A tortured soul and a drinker, he would regularly call the Tolkins in the middle of the night to announce that he was about to kill himself. ("Promises, promises," Edith Tolkin once told him after the latest of these threats.) His relationship with Caesar was combustible, in the way that ties between drinkers can be. "That's the only thing they had in common," said Morris. "Tony wanted to kill him all the time. *Hated* him." But Caesar appreciated Webster's honesty—his frowns and winces—as others pitched jokes.

The show's difficulties didn't dim Caesar's luster. Caesar's daughter looked on at an amusement park in Queens as people filched French fries off her father's plate as souvenirs. He finally left Forest Hills, but rather than follow Reiner and Morris out of the city, he bought (for $13,000, or around $160,000 today) an eight-room apartment at 940 Park Avenue. Liebman approved the move; he thought it would broaden the horizons of someone who remained a small-town boy at heart. Caesar had a history with Park Avenue: On Sunday morning visits to the Lower East Side when Caesar was a boy, his father would drive down it, past fancy apartment buildings like 940 Park. To young Sidney it was "like being in another world." Now he'd made it there himself. As prestigious as it was, his new home didn't get a clear television signal; for that, Caesar had an illegal antenna installed outside one window.

Caesar's new digs afforded plenty of room for his booty. Along the walls of the den he displayed his growing arsenal of "pistols, revolvers, automatics, .22 caliber rifles, shotguns, guns for doing in deer and guns for annihilating elephants," collectively worth $10,000. "I can't understand it!" his mother confessed to the *Forverts*. "When he was a child he was such a *tsarbaleykhayim-nik.** What is he doing now going out and shooting animals?" In fact, he hadn't changed all that much; after bagging his first and only deer, Caesar was heartsick for weeks. He was similarly tenderhearted with fish. "Please throw me back," he imagined the striped bass he'd just caught pleading with him. "I'm suffocating. What do you need me for? You're rich. You've got everything. I got nothing. Don't be selfish. Throw me back." Creatures and objects still elicited a degree of *rachmones*† from Caesar he didn't always show for humans.

Caesar continued to acquire the folkways, and accoutrements, of the nouveau riche: fancy cigars (Romeo y Julietas from Havana, a dollar apiece), hand-tailored suits, expensive scotch. He collected art, works by Vlaminck, Vuillard, Rouault, Picasso, and

---

* Someone honoring the Jewish command to prevent the suffering of all living creatures.
† Compassion, mercy, or pity.

Bonnard, among others. He said he related to the impressionists (actually, it was more like the postimpressionists), and sought to imbue his comedy with the same vivid, slightly exaggerated view of things they had brought to art. He read and loved *Lust for Life*, Irving Stone's fictionalized portrait of Van Gogh, which Florence had bought for him, and came to identify with him; Van Gogh, too, was violent, clumsy, easily hurt, deeply pained, and driven to put the "essence of life into his art." At the Museum of Modern Art, he'd stare for an hour at Van Gogh's painting of a sidewalk café—imagining himself sitting in such a place, looking at the stars—and it relaxed him.[*]

At the same time, the Caesars made at least a stab at remaining just folks. Rather than trading up for something newer and shinier, Sid held on to his 1949 Cadillac; as he took care to explain, it had only eleven thousand miles on it. When the Caesars entertained—the Jack Carters, the Jack E. Leonards, the Mel Tolkins, the Carl Reiners, and the Irving Mansfields[†] were regulars—it was generally at home. "He just sits there and listens, and laughs his head off," one guest reported. "You'd think he was a bank teller who'd somehow crashed a party of real, live celebrities." Florence complained that were she not always dressed to the nines around Park Avenue, "first thing you know the word gets 'round that Sid's rating is slipping." But she scored proletarian points when, asked during the Easter Parade telecast to name her couturier and milliner, she replied, "Oh, it's just a hat and coat. I went into a store and bought them, that's all."

CAESAR WAS A VICTIM of the smart set's lingering disdain for television. Chevy Chase had to catch Caesar's show at his grandparents' because his parents refused to buy a set. But when such holdouts inevitably relented, it was often Caesar they credited.

[*] Actually, MoMA doesn't have that painting; more likely, it was *The Starry Night*, which it does have.

[†] Mr. Mansfield was the producer of, among other shows, *Arthur Godfrey's Talent Scouts*; his wife was, among other things, the bestselling-author-to-be (*Valley of the Dolls*) Jacqueline Susann.

"The main disadvantage of television, other than the stupidity of some of its shows, is that one must sit and look," one critic wrote. "You can't iron the old man's shirts, change the baby's diapers, scrub the bathroom or even sit in the car and neck with your girl friend. You either look or you don't." But Sid and Imogene, she allowed, were "just about worth" the price.

A taste of Milton Berle had soured Isaac Asimov on TV for a time, but watching *Your Show of Shows* at the home of the famed Harvard astronomer Fred Lawrence Whipple in April 1950 changed everything. "That was different," Asimov remembered. "I felt my snobbish antitelevision attitude evaporate." Though it took him two more years to buy a set, once he did, nothing came between him and Caesar. When the Whipples invited the Asimovs to dinner the following Saturday, "I was adamant in refusing, despite all their blandishments," he wrote. "I think I nearly lost their friendship over that incident." Others also agonized over television-era etiquette. A North Carolina man asked the local paper if he should offer Saturday night dinner guests the option of watching Caesar and Coca, or if that would be considered rude, as his wife maintained? "Move the TV set to another room where it won't disturb the conversationalists," came the Solomonic reply. "If this party can produce repartee and entertaining chatter that beats Caesar and Coca, we'd like to be there. Perhaps NBC can get them a sponsor."

"Mom and Pop maintained that they had bought the set for the Army-McCarthy hearings," wrote Rick Hertzberg, later a writer for *The New Yorker*. "But even at our tender ages my sister (age eight) and I (ten) were perceptive enough to notice that they had grown awfully tired of having to wangle invitations from people as their only access to Sid Caesar and Imogene Coca." Robert Mitchner, a buttoned-up medievalist at Indiana University, initially refused to watch anything on the TV he'd bought for his son Stuart, banishing it to the boy's bedroom, only to discover from peeks at *Your Show of Shows* that this Caesar character disdained blowhards and bores every bit as much as he did. "A lot of time when I was watching, I thought, 'How could people in Nebraska know what this is about?'" recalled Al Jaffee, later a cartoonist for *Mad* magazine. But in Lincoln, Nebraska, beginning with the first notes of "Stars over Broadway," young Dick Cavett watched, enthralled. "I thought, Jesus! There are people who are *there*, watching this in the same room!" he remembered. "How do you *get there*?"

Aspiring young comics including Bill Cosby, Richard Pryor, Jonathan Winters, and Phyllis Diller studied Caesar. Seeing his show in person persuaded Joan Rivers to go into the business. Precocious kids tuned in, too. "There was nothing in there that an intelligent child couldn't appreciate, and yet it was not childish," said the comedian Robert Klein, a nine-year-old in the Bronx when he first saw Caesar. (When the makers of Crosley televisions depicted three generations of a prototypical American family sitting around its 1951 model, it was *Your Show of Shows* they were watching.) When the German ambassador to the United States complimented Al Franken on his fine German accent, Franken credited the bootlegged tapes of Caesar's German professor sketches he'd watched as a teenager.

Early on, *Your Show of Shows* couldn't quite reach Champaign-Urbana, Illinois, but thanks to an uncle with an antenna powerful enough to pull in Peoria (and, on a good night, Indianapolis), a classmate of the future film critic Roger Ebert came to school Monday mornings imitating Caesar. "Without ever having seen Caesar, I knew by hearsay he was the funniest man in America," Ebert wrote. Because the famous apartment building in which nine-year-old Peter Osnos (later a prominent journalist and book publisher) lived on Manhattan's Upper West Side wasn't wired for TV, he could watch only the first and third portions of the show, lest his primitive transformer burn down the building.

Your Show of Shows was on the short list of programs Steven Spielberg was allowed to watch.[*] Culture was scarce in Long Branch, New Jersey, "but once a week a great American artist did his work, *right there in the house*," the poet Robert Pinsky remem-

---

[*] "Television to me was Imogene Coca, Sid Caesar, Soupy Sales, and *The Honeymooners*," Spielberg said in 1978 (Mitch Tuchman, "Close Encounters with Steven Spielberg," *Film Comment*, Jan.–Feb. 1978).

bered. Along with Jackie Robinson stealing home in the 1955 World Series, watching Caesar doing double-talk ("Speaking French and Japanese not / Through knowledge but imagination," as he described it in a poem) was one of his two most indelible images from early television. To Howard Rosenberg (later the television critic for the *Los Angeles Times*), the singers and dancers only delayed the comedy, and he was "impatient for them to scram." But the opera selections let the young Marvin Siegel, later culture editor of *The New York Times*, behold Marguerite Piazza's ample breasts, then discuss them the next day with pals who'd tuned in for the same reasons.

MAURICE ZOLOTOW, WHO'D PROFILED Caesar for *The Saturday Evening Post* in 1953, had never forgotten Caesar's "dietary phantasmagoria" at the time. But only upon revisiting him twenty years later did he clue in his readers to something else on Caesar's bill of fare back then: four double scotches. "You know, if all of us knew how to relax, we'd lead a much better life" was how Caesar began a solo piece in October 1952. And, increasingly, drinking was what he did to do that.

Though it's hard to believe, never would Caesar come into the office under the influence, or hungover. But he'd drink after hours with Tolkin in the Russian Tea Room. He'd drink after the show in his dressing room, then drink in the limousine to the after-party, then drink some more there, then drink on the way home, then drink some more once he got there—"anything," Caesar later said, "to relax, slow down, get rid of some of the heavy physical feeling of depression"—then he'd drink to get to sleep, to turn off the newsreel of mistakes, missed opportunities, and second guesses about his latest show forever looping around in his head, or to calm his anxieties about his next one. He'd drink to help him cope with success of a sort he'd neither anticipated nor trusted: Because he didn't know where his strange powers came from, he never trusted them to last. "When a show came off good, I could hardly believe it," he said. "I was never happy walking around—I was afraid to show that I was happy." All that booze might have exacted a far greater toll had he not vomited it up before it could.*

Inexplicably—and, really, implausibly—Kallen and Coca later said they'd not known of Caesar's alcoholism. Perhaps this, more than anything else, showed what outsiders they were. But Reiner and Morris did know. Years later, Morris scoffed at Caesar's admission that he drank after every show. "What, 'every show'?" he said. "After *each day*!" At some point—precisely when isn't clear—Reiner and Morris developed a routine for dealing with it: Half an hour or so before every show, they'd descend into the catacombs beneath the theater, and between what Morris called "a little intramural vomiting," they'd go over that night's program, and plot how to keep Caesar on track, compensating for the good stuff he mislaid and adjusting to inspiring improvisations he found. "We had to be ready," Morris said. "We knew [Caesar] would wander and we would have to corral him back somehow."

Whether out of recklessness, honesty, defiance, blindness, bravado, self-hatred, or despair—or simply because it was a timeless, reliable source of laughs, offering the blend of comedy and pathos Caesar so prized—Caesar the performer plunged headlong into the issue of alcohol. And, evidently oblivious to Caesar's personal stake in the matter, NBC's house censor, Stockton Helffrich, let him. "The treatment of such a subject by a Coca and a Caesar is deft, sophisticated, and of the highest sort of humour," he opined after complaints from a Milwaukee station over a drinking-related sketch. Such talent, he said, should not be inhibited by "straight-laced provincial standards."

Nor were there recriminations following a silent film parody in early 1951 in which a drunken Caesar succumbs to the vampish Coca, even though a large advertising agency reproached NBC for using "drinking and drunkenness as subjects for humor and farce." Or when, a year later, Doris Hickenlooper gets looped in

---

* And not always in private: En route to the bathroom once at Lindy's, he puked all over Leo "Lindy" Lindemann himself. "And I thought Sid liked me," Lindy lamented (Caesar, *Where Have I Been?*, 126).

front of the boss (Reiner) Charlie needs to impress. ("A disturbed alcoholic, no doubt," Reiner declares, before barring any further drinking at the table. "Speak for yourself, Jim," *his* plastered wife then tells him. "I'll have a double scotch on the rocks.")

Much darker was a Caesar solo from May 1952, in which he plays a postwar American Everyman who, imaginary brief-case under his arm, steps into an imaginary saloon to unwind. He greets the bartender and his fellow patrons, then asks for "the usual," gagging over the first sip. His second drink goes down more easily, though his body convulses briefly as it does. With his third, his head shakes, his voice thickens, and his face creases into an aggressive mask. "You're all a bunch of bums!" he shouts. Why are they in a bar instead of with their families, as he'd just been? He then turns maudlin, gushing about the "li'l woman" back home faithfully cooking his supper.

With his fourth drink, he takes stock. "Life passed me by," he laments, noting how he'd once dreamed of becoming a pilot. "*Time* passed me by: Tick tock tick tock tick tock. I'm all tocked out." Following his fifth drink, he impersonates a plane landing. After his sixth, he's shaking wildly. "You know what's wrong with this world?" he asks. "The trouble with this world is whiskey! That's right, whiskey! There's not enough of it! I want more!" He slobbers over another patron, only to conclude he's a "dirty rat." He staggers through his seventh, then butts into someone else's fight. Some swigs of hot black coffee snap him back to sobriety, and respectability. "Thanks, George," he declares in his original voice. "I'll see you in the morning."

A year later, with another year's worth of booze under his own belt, Caesar went through the whole routine again, virtually word for word. Whatever else it was doing to him, alcohol hadn't impaired his memory. This time, though, the sketch brought multiple complaints and a plea from the censor to "light-pedal" such routines going forward. Then, in December 1953, came "A Drunkard's Fate," a silent film in which a pal (Morris) prevails upon the teetotaling Caesar, a devoted family man, to join him for just one drink, which of course is all it takes for his world to come apart. "Flippancy about drinking goes badly during the Christmas season," said Helffrich.

That Caesar kept delving into so fraught a topic with such seeming nonchalance was astonishing. "My analyst told me that I can drink as much as I want so long as I don't feel guilty," Caesar told Liebman. But if a retrospective (it appeared five years after the fact) story in one of the scandal sheets of the day is to be believed, Caesar's problem had been apparent as early as October 1952. Out of sorts and maybe having had "a few too many," the account went, Caesar, the emcee at a champagne-soaked party for the famously flamboyant actress Tallulah Bankhead, started trashing Bankhead's showbiz crowd. Bankhead promptly yanked him off the dais, using "a lot of words that even H. L. Mencken wouldn't put in the Dictionary of the American Language." Friendly columnists wrote nothing about the episode, which, according to the report, jarred Caesar "out of his private mixed-up world in which he hated almost everybody" and led him to heed Liebman's suggestion that he seek professional help. In fact, he already had: One of the reasons the Caesars opted for their new Park Avenue apartment was its proximity to the office of Sid's shrink.

Caesar's treatment was well known enough by January 1952 for the *New York Post*'s Broadway columnist, Leonard Lyons, to write about it. At Lindy's one night, he'd asked Caesar the name of his shrink, and Caesar wouldn't say. But one of their table-mates that evening, the famously neurotic pianist, raconteur, and film actor Oscar Levant, wouldn't let up. Man or woman? he asked Caesar. East Side or West Side? North or south of Sixtieth Street? Levant then took a guess—wrong, as it turned out. "What's his name?" he finally asked. And Caesar told him. By late 1953 Caesar was declaring publicly that analysis had not only helped him grow up and make friends but saved his life.

HOSTING THE SHOW IN January 1953, Robert Preston told Caesar he'd "like to make it a yearly thing for the next 150 years that you'll be on." In fact, the show soon fell out of Nielsen's top twenty-five. While Liebman and Caesar professed not to care, NBC did. Deep down, Caesar's colleagues knew their lease was running out. "We were entertaining ourselves," Reiner said. "We had to be brought to reality by somebody saying, 'Hey, fellas, you think they'll get this in Peoria?' We didn't care."

Your Show of Shows pulled in $7 million in gross returns for the 1952–53 season, as much as *Oklahoma!* did on Broadway over four years. But Lucille Ball, Groucho Marx, Jack Benny, and Jackie Gleason, along with programs like *Dragnet* and *What's My Line?*, had more viewers than Caesar's show, and cost far less to produce. Extravaganzas like *Your Show of Shows*, *The New York Times* noted in February 1953, were "pricing themselves right off the television screen." And the tenor of programming continued to change, with more emollient fare like *The Adventures of Ozzie and Harriet* gaining among viewers and, therefore, advertisers. Edgier comics were being put out to pasture, which led *TV Guide* to wonder whether Caesar would soon join the "geldings." Increasingly, it warned, television wouldn't let people be funny: "Creeping censorship from every conceivable direction has descended on comedian and comedy writer like a dank fog."

In March, George McGarrett sent off an SOS to other NBC executives, Pat Weaver among them. "The Show of Shows Problem," he titled the memo. The program, he charged, was "so lacking in vitality that it is allowing small-time competition to cut deep inroads into its popularity." Even hit Broadway shows eventually close, he noted ominously; he urged that Liebman be hauled in to Rockefeller Center for a "hair-down straight-out discussion" about the situation.

McGarrett didn't blame Caesar or Coca, who he felt were better than ever, displaying "a maturity, polish and flexibility" they'd previously lacked. "We have made a colossal investment in them, and cannot even consider the thought of losing them," he said. Reiner and Morris, too, had "grown to great heights." If the show lacked its old zest, he theorized, maybe its writers were at fault. And NBC would also do well, he suggested, "to practically wipe out" all the secondary acts (like the Billy Williams Quartet and Marguerite Piazza), if only to "create the illusion of a complete face-lifting job." That would also help cover the raises Caesar and the others were demanding. The time had finally come, he said, "to give up the idea that in *Show of Shows* we have the greatest thing since Sen-Sen." *Variety* picked up on the turmoil, reporting that the show was being "subjected to some drastic 'rethinking.' " "Lotsa Problems Beset Liebman, NBC on 'Shows,' " it added a couple of weeks later. And there was one more they probably didn't know about.

By now, Caesar's periodic dalliances with Hollywood had become a joke, even to the people reporting about them. It wasn't a question of his appeal: "His box-office potential is equal to that of any Hollywood star," Ed Sullivan wrote. But every winter Caesar would talk about making a movie there the next summer, and every summer he'd go there and talk about it some more, but nothing ever happened. Brooks, though, feeling hemmed in by television and craving something more substantial and permanent, had fastened on the idea. His vision was simple: Caesar would star in the pictures that Brooks would write for him. He urged Caesar to scrap TV altogether and go with him to Hollywood, where they would live happily ever after.

His plea to him, recounted often in later years, can be reconstituted as follows:

Don't sign, Sidney. ("Sidney" was what he called Caesar whenever he was serious. It was also how intimates like Dave Caesar always addressed Sid, and Brooks liked the sound of it, anyway.) You're better than Danny Kaye, and better looking, and funnier. You're funnier than Hope and Skelton and anybody else in Hollywood. Movies are on *film*—in *Technicolor*. Film has value: the people who work with it respect it, and preserve it, and put it in a vault. If you make movies, you'll live forever, like Chaplin and Harold Lloyd. I don't know what the fuck we're on in television. It's cellophane, or *something*, and in black and white. Thirty-nine shows a year, an hour and a half each, and you'll be gone before too much longer, and nobody will have ever heard of you; in fifty years, no one will even know who Sid Caesar was. Sidney, you're Golden Boy. You're an artist. You're Matisse. Even if the money isn't as good, we'll do better stuff. You'll be the funniest leading man who ever lived. We'll take our time and do a movie a year and get rich and meet beautiful women and live under a palm tree. You'll broaden your reach and be a revelation to the world. They'll love you in *Sweden*, for God's sake.

Brooks convinced Caesar, or thought he had; Caesar pledged to quit TV at the end of the season. They hugged and kissed each other. But then Caesar suddenly went silent on the idea, and it soon became came clear why: NBC was doubling down on him, offering him $25,000 a week—the most in television. This was probably when Sarnoff—sitting behind a desk "about half a mile away"—complained to Caesar that he'd be making more in a week than NBC's best engineer made in a year, and when Caesar told Sarnoff that the greatest tank in the world was just a hunk of iron without the right man inside it. Sarnoff caved. Caesar broke the news to Brooks: In a few years, he promised, he'd go with him to Hollywood, but not now. Brooks had his doubts: By that point, Sidney might well be exhausted, and how much more of him would be left?[*]

NBC promised anxious affiliates "a bright new format" for the show the following season, including guest stars "so big and important that we cannot for competitive reasons mention them now." "We're conscious of the ravages of television," Liebman conceded. "We're not smug or complacent about the show's suc-

---

[*] Brooks didn't abandon the idea of working in Hollywood, taking a short-term writing gig at Columbia Pictures in the summer of 1953. "I'm a natural for this town," he reported to his wife. "Everybody's an actor. The directors act like they think directors should act. The Producers all smoke big expensive cigars and wear white flannel jackets and in general everybody is a complete out and out phony, so you see—I should do well.

"There's really only one hitch in it—I HATE IT. Never before has there been such a desperate place— never before has there been such a caste system. Everyone is scared shitless of losing his job. Everybody kisses everybody's ass, everyone scrapes and bows at the slightest provocation (Letter, Mel Brooks to Florence Brooks, July 1, 1953).

"I have become sick and tired of playing the young fair haired writer from T.V. land," he wrote two weeks later. "I don't like it here—I don't like the climate (it's beautiful but I hate it). I don't like the people (beautiful but empty)" (Letter, Mel Brooks to Florence Brooks, July 15, 1953). He soon retreated to New York, and Caesar.

cess. We get new ideas and we do them. We'll never stand still." Looking to the fall, he pledged to put out something so unpredictable even *he* wouldn't be sure what was coming, with longer sketches and more film satires, including stars spoofing their own pictures. He dangled some names: Groucho Marx, Dinah Shore, Dean Martin, Jerry Lewis, Phil Silvers, Judy Garland, Betty Hutton, Cary Grant, Barbara Stanwyck, Ginger Rogers, Charles Boyer. Maybe Danny Kaye could kick things off. He signed up Nat King Cole for eight guest appearances in the new season, news that *Jet* magazine trumpeted in its weekly listing of Blacks appearing on radio and television.

The purge was, as Arthur Gelb of the *Times* put it, "a ruthless step," one that had made Liebman very unhappy. But all the famous visitors would take some of the pressure off Caesar and Coca, Liebman said, and let them appear more often as themselves in a more informal, "low key" fashion, though of course that would only add to Caesar's woes. And having the show on only three weeks in four in the new season, he added, would "give our blood the plasma to keep going."

DURING THE CURTAIN CALL on May 16, 1953, Reiner told the audience about Maurice Zolotow's newly published profile of Caesar in *The Saturday Evening Post*, one of the most ambitious and acute to date. "After reading it, I think you'll get an idea of what makes Sid Caesar tick so inimitably," he said, no doubt grateful for the additional clues himself. Titled "TV Gives Him Nightmares," it began by describing a recurring dream Caesar had, in which he'd awaken just before nine on a Saturday night, realize he was still at home, and then race to the depot, only to get there as his train pulled out. It was an image that neatly encapsulated "the terror and the tension that beset the hardest-working performer in television today." Jack Gould described Caesar similarly, but added, "And the strain is showing."

As the season wound down, Liebman cast about for ideas. "Why don't Sid, Carl, Howie, and I just stare at the audience for four minutes and not say *anything*?" Coca suggested. (Or, in another version of the story, Reiner said to Liebman, "Let's just tell the audience 'There is no more comedy. That's it.'") Liebman went along with the idea of such a sketch, but insisted that *something* had to happen in it. In two programs in late May, the four principals played four stuffy, superannuated English blue bloods who mumble greetings to one another, then sit together, silently and stoically, as they're soaked during a garden party, or get splattered with mud at Ascot. Such a send-up of "British parasites" won plaudits from *The Daily Worker*'s television critic, who called it "one of the best things I have seen on TV since I got my set," but for less political types it was as if *Your Show of Shows* had suddenly run out of words.

"On Monday morning, I ask myself, 'Is it possible we'll really do a show this Saturday?'" Caesar told Zolotow. "'No, it's not possible. This is the week we're dead.'" He paced nervously as he spoke, weaving from side to side like a caged polar bear, buttoning and unbuttoning his coat. "Caesar is no happy-go-lucky jester, full of sound and gaiety," Zolotow wrote. "His forehead is etched by deep frowns, his large liquid brown eyes are as morose as a cocker spaniel's, his chin drags and he constantly exhales mournful sighs."

Liebman decreed that Caesar and Coca spend their summer in Hollywood with him brainstorming about the program, only to take off for Europe himself. Caesar, at least as Coca remembered it, "spent the summer with his therapist" back east, though now on a four-and-a-half-acre estate in tony, Waspy Westport, Connecticut, rather than on Lido Beach. Come August, he was sleeping in until nearly 11:00 in the morning, then taking a dip in the pool, then moseying over to the Longshore Beach and Country Club, returning home for croquet, then spending quiet evenings watching TV. "He sits next to remote controls which enable him to change programs without getting up," the local paper marveled. So congenial was the place that he'd extended his lease until the following May.

Caesar did get to Hollywood that summer, staying at the Beverly Hills Hotel, dining at Dinah Shore's, eyeing beautiful women at the Marquis. ("Don't even look in her direction," Tolkin warned him. "That's Ava Gardner. You want to get in trouble with Frank Sinatra?") He also tried to sell a movie to Harry Cohn at Columbia, but as Tolkin later related, was "totally unprepared" for his pitch and "incoherent" making it. At a farewell dinner at Romanoff's, Sid rose to speak, only to find himself speechless. Tolkin prompted him—unobtrusively, he thought. "You must be his writer," Groucho Marx said to Tolkin afterward.

Facing obsolescence *and* exhaustion, *Your Show of Shows* limped toward its fourth full season, its greatest.

CHAPTER 7

THAT CHAMPIONSHIP SEASON

Hail to balding trees and burning leaves, Indian summer, sports jackets, football, quilts at night, threats of snow, Broadway shows, oyster months, mufflers and Argyles, ski wax, roast turkey, days left to Christmas, chilly feet, colds and antidotes, brown grass, top coats, Sid Caesar and Imogene Coca, homework help, early sunsets and late dawns," *The New York Times* editorialized on the first day of fall 1953. Eleven days earlier, Sid and Imogene launched *their* new season, in a new place, and with a new look.

With the International Theatre set for demolition, *Your Show of Shows* had moved ten blocks south to the Center Theatre, at Sixth Avenue and Forty-Ninth Street in Rockefeller Center. Twenty years earlier, the place had been born in great splendor as the RKO Roxy, with five thousand seats, luxurious lounges, and an enormous crystal chandelier. But overshadowed by the nearby and still more opulent Radio City Music Hall, it had struggled to find itself, bouncing from film epics to theatrical productions to concerts and ice shows.

Now it was a TV studio that, even with space set aside for cameras and orchestra, still seated thirty-two hundred. Convinced the place was too massive and impersonal for acts like theirs, Berle and Martin and Lewis, among others, had refused to work there.

Caesar, too, had misgivings: How could he do something intimate, like a pantomime, in a place that, as Jack Gould put it,
was "a couple of sizes larger than Grand Central Station"? To
Coca, transplanting the show from its enchanted birthplace to
this cavernous, gloomy barn was like "putting a painting in the
wrong frame." With the camera crews and technicians hovering
around, it was almost impossible to see the action, even from the
orchestra seats; from the mezzanine and the balcony the view was
unobstructed, but everything was too far off. So all eyes focused on
the giant (fifteen by twenty feet) monitor over the stage. Thus, for
all the trappings of a theatrical experience, everyone in the theater
saw what viewers saw at home.

But Caesar found at least one silver lining in the place.
Show after show, the old theater was filled with the same admen
and network types who had first dibs on tickets, for whom the
novelty had long since worn off. Now there'd always be fresh,
appreciative people on hand. Liebman appreciated something
else. In the old, smaller setting, the audience rendered a single,
instantaneous verdict, up or down. And if it was down, there'd
be silence. But now, he explained, "we had *five* responses. If one
section didn't think it was funny, or another section didn't think
it was funny, some section up in the third balcony thought it was
funny, and started the laughter. You almost couldn't miss." So the
Center Theatre was its own comic ecosystem, in which, when
conditions were right, laughter could spread, reverberate, *cascade*.
And outside, with its majestic Art Deco facade and wraparound
marquee—"MAX LIEBMAN'S YOUR SHOW OF SHOWS
STARRING SID CAESAR & IMOGENE COCA SATURDAY
9 PM," it proclaimed, again and again and again—the theater
finally lent to the enterprise the stateliness and dignity it had
always deserved. The fix was strictly short-term; at season's end,
this building, too, would be torn down to make room for a more
lucrative office tower.

To rally the troops, NBC staged a closed-circuit dress rehearsal.
The season to come, the announcer declared, had viewers and
critics alike salivating in anticipation. Ominously, though, some
advertising spots remained unsold, prompting a panicky ad—

"$1,356,000 buys *Your Show of Shows* for the full '53–'54 season"—
in the *Times*. The writing team got additional fresh blood with
Joe Stein, who'd written for Zero Mostel and Henry Morgan.
"Well, Joe, so you've finally hit the big time," Tolkin told him on
his first day. ("If that's your idea of a joke, no wonder they called
me," replied Stein.) Also joining the staff, but only until Kallen
returned from maternity leave, were two Tamiment alums, Danny
Simon and his kid brother, Neil, known as Doc. Shy and barely
audible in the writers' room, Doc Simon whispered his witticisms
to Reiner rather than shout them out, which didn't spare him
from the usual hazing. "Mel Tolkin and Mel Brooks had a bit of
a sadistic streak," Stein recalled.

The premiere began not with the usual dancers and choris-
ters but with the veteran newsman John Cameron Swayze seated
behind a desk and a microphone, a Teletype machine clack-
ing noisily behind him. "The television news of the moment
is the opening of *Your Show of Shows*, for the fifth season," he
announced. The scene then shifted to the Center Theatre, where
a voice off-screen directed Reiner and Morris to their respective
dressing rooms, followed by the guest star, Nat King Cole, followed by Caesar and Coca. Caesar looked older, trimmer, more
respectable. His painfully awkward remarks to Coca (protesting
that all the encouraging telegrams had gone to *her*) showcased his
familiar shortcomings. The jokes to come had better be better.

Within a few minutes, once Cole and the opera star Lily Pons
had sung their songs, they were. The opening sketch, a spoof
called "From Here to Obscurity," came less than two weeks after
the film *From Here to Eternity* had opened. Caesar is a dopey boxer
turned musician turned GI named Montgomery Bugle who, like
Montgomery Clift's Robert E. Lee Prewitt in the film, refuses to
placate his martinet sergeant (Reiner) by returning to the ring
for a tournament on the base. Worse, he steals Reiner's girl, the
Duchess (Coca). Caesar and Coca wind up lying together on the
beach just as Burt Lancaster and Deborah Kerr had in the film
(though Lancaster wasn't wearing black socks left over from a
previous routine)—a notion that, half a century later, still made
Tolkin, always the show's arbiter of cinematic verisimilitude,

splutter. "What kind of a lay is that?" he asked. "You'd get sand up your ass!"

But the water washing over Lancaster and Kerr had at least been *warm*. Caesar had instructed the stagehands to let the water they'd hurl down at them from their ladders sit at room temperature for a while, as well as to space their dousings so that he and Coca could breathe between them. The stagehands did neither: The "surf" was freezing and came in torrents. Coca caught a mouthful, and feared she'd drown on national television. To Tolkin, the old lefty, it was a case of alienated labor. "They were people who were getting very little money, and Sid and Coca were getting thousands a week, and they just had a little fun," he said.

In Sid Caesar's list of thespian sins, breaking up on camera was a close second to cue cards: It destroyed a performance's spell and was self-indulgent to boot. But in this case, even Caesar couldn't resist. "Kinda rough tonight, ain't it?" he said after a "wave" hit him squarely in the face. Already suppressing a smile, Coca buried her face in his shoulder, but only briefly: Within seconds, she'd regained control. By sketch's end "the entire stage was like a swamp," Hobin recalled, with water running in every direction; during the commercial, nearly everyone in the crew was onstage, frantically manning their mops.

It was probably the greatest film spoof to date, the extra layers of wit and polish demonstrating that talented reinforcements had arrived. But not everyone found it funny. "A famous producer watched the show . . . and was laughing," Tolkin recalled. "His wife said, 'You fool, they're making you an idiot . . . you did a serious movie and they're making fun of it! Sue them!' He did." "He" was Harry Cohn, head of Columbia Pictures, who accused NBC of copyright infringement and unfair competition. Caesar had ripped off his movie, he charged, and on the cheap; the script's three authors—Tolkin, Brooks, and Tony Webster—were paid a grand total of $4,000 to plagiarize a film he'd shelled out $2 million to make. NBC claimed First Amendment protection and denied any meaningful resemblance between the two stories. While Prewitt was a "hard-head," it argued, Caesar's Bugle was a "knuckle-head." The judge agreed.

The second show included another splendid movie takeoff. This one, called "Strange," skewered *Shane*, the classic Western about homesteaders and ranchers fighting turf wars in Wyoming Territory. Once again, Tolkin put things pithily: What kind of schmuck would risk his life to protect a family of total strangers? Caesar, mirroring Alan Ladd in the original, is said schmuck, riding in one day (on his wonder horse, Nathan) and befriending some yeoman sodbusters. ("You seem kind of thirsty, stranger. You had yourself a long, dry ride?" he's asked after guzzling ladle after ladle of water. "Nope," he replies. "I ate a herring for breakfast.") "Folks call me Strange," he tells them; his first name is Very. Morris is the farmer, Coca their adorable, towheaded son. Reiner is Barton, the black-hatted gunslinger imported from Cheyenne by the ranchers, modeled after Jack Palance. (Also listed in the credits are two "dead men," three "murderers," and twelve "cowards.") Strange goes into town to confront Barton, and to get the adorable boy a lemon-and-lime lollipop.

"You know what you are, stranger?" one of the black hats at the saloon asks him. "You're a lemon-and-lime-lollipop-licking sodbuster."

"You called me a lemon-and-lime-lollipop-licking sodbuster?" Strange replies.

"That's right! You're a lily-livered, lemon-and-lime-lollipop-licking sodbuster!"

"You called me a lily-livered, lemon-and-lime-lollipop-licking sodbuster?"

"You're a low-down, lop-haired, lily-livered, lemon-and-lime-lollipop-licking sodbuster."

Though he's forgotten his gun, Strange still single-handedly vanquishes the lot of them with what turns out to be the only seven-shooter in the West. (A shame it hadn't been an eight-shooter, Strange complains, or he'd have dispatched the annoying, besotted boy as well.) Then, like Shane, he rides off to places unknown, despite the boy's pleas to stay. The noble gunslinger's parting words to him echo throughout the valley: "Go home, ya rotten kid! Go home, ya rotten kid! Go home, ya rotten kid. Go home, ya rotten kid!" "Sid says he works best when he's mad at something," one interviewer observed. "He doesn't like the way villains are all bad and heroes are all good."

The sketch was really high art. (Morris always chafed whenever people called such sketches "skits." "Skits," he said, were what "you do at Camp Tonawanda.") Some thin-skinned Hollywood loyalists thought it impudent. "Imogene Coca made no friends with her parody on 'Shane,'" the columnist Sheilah Graham groused. But George Stevens, who directed *Shane*, wasn't complaining. "It was great publicity for the picture," he said. "I hope it happens to all my films."

Continuing one of the program's most extraordinary stretches, the next show featured another classic: a pantomime about the clock, one with human-sized, mechanical figurines, that for centuries has marked time in a Bavarian village. The idea was Caesar's; he credited both a visit to St. Mark's Square in Venice and *The Stranger*, a film in which a former Nazi (played by Orson Welles) meets his end in a clock tower, as inspirations. The Simon brothers spun out the story, wordless but for the narrator.

The clock's stone figures mark the hour in an elaborate dance: Caesar presents an anvil, Reiner hammers it, Morris squeezes the bellows, and Coca ladles water over it before Caesar rings in the hour. They move, and look, like marionettes. But the mechanism speeds up and out of control, and the four start abusing one another. And Teutonic technical know-how can't fix it. "Anyone want to buy a ten-ton clock?" the narrator finally asks. The segment helped spring the Simons out of the purgatory of a stairwell, but only temporarily; when Kallen returned, Liebman let the Simons go. "Didn't throw off any sparks for me," he later explained. Caesar felt differently. Encountering the younger Simon afterward, Caesar pulled him aside, tapped his head, and declared, "I want that brain." And before too long, he'd get it back.

On the same show, the Hickenloopers launched their most acrimonious season yet. "That's all! No more looking! It's over!" Charlie shouts to the neighbors after a particularly vicious spat. "Tune in again tomorrow night, the same window!" In succeeding weeks, Doris ridicules Charlie's dining habits ("Why don't you eat in a stall with a bag around your neck?"), and Charlie declares, "You're no wife for me . . . you're a sparring partner." The show's humor darkened. "You're not the only one," an operator tells a panicked Coca, who's called to say someone's about to kill her. "Other people are being murdered too." There were also fleeting signs of topicality: One sketch ridiculed Soviet culture, including claims to have invented the telegraph, television, and Arthur Godfrey.

Despite its reinvigoration, the perception that *Your Show of Shows* was tapped out proved hard to shake. Jack Gould still thought it lacked "any real pep or imaginative verve." Dan Jenkins of *TV Guide* urged Liebman to drop the ninety-minute format before the audience did, and put Caesar, Coca, Reiner, and Morris—"perhaps the four most talented damn people working together in the world"—on a no-frills half-hour show the following season. Liebman sort of agreed, while pointing out that given its dependence on ad revenue, NBC could never recoup what it was paying Caesar and Coca in thirty measly minutes. "That's why the show is beginning to resemble a supermarket with the products shouting 'buy me,' 'use me,' 'I'm only $1.49,'" Liebman wrote. "Somewhere in the plethora of merchandise are actors and music and jokes. Sometimes people see them."

"COMEDY ALMOST REQUIRES PARTICIPATION on the part of the audience," Coca once observed. "That's why people get violent about comics. An actor they can take or leave alone. Comics are very controversial. If you don't like them you want to kill them." And many people beyond the cities' limits loathed Caesar. They smelled what they sensed was his condescension, and he only aggravated things by making no effort whatever to win them over; he didn't say "May God bless" in cloying baby talk at the end of his shows, the way Red Skelton did. With the resentment Coca had described, some viewers relished Caesar's falling fortunes, which only accelerated as more and more of them tuned in.

Mrs. Lois McGill was agitated enough to vent to Eddie Jones, TV columnist of the *Nashville Banner*. "Why does WSM-TV have so much of 'Show of Shows'?" she asked. "Thirty minutes of Sid Caesar is about all anyone can endure." Intrigued, Jones opened up the floor to his readers, and got an earful: "If anyone wants ulcers or to have a nervous breakdown just make them sit through the hour and a half of *Your Show of Shows*" (Mrs. Iro Rickert); "If it were only 30 minutes that would still be 29 too long" (Mrs. Owen Hunt); "I don't like 'Your Show of Shows' either and don't know anyone who does" (Mrs. Gladys Miller); "If all of TV was like 'Your Show of Shows,' there would be no market for TV sets" (Mrs. R. E. Farris).

A small minority—the scattered few in and around Nashville who presumably spent their Sunday afternoons listening to Metropolitan Opera broadcasts or reading *The New Yorker* in the privacy of their homes—defended the show. Perhaps, one of them suggested, Mrs. McGill should listen to *Tennessee Jamboree* instead. "The Grand Ole Opry is in town that night," another, calling himself "the president of Sid's great club," told Mrs. McGill. "Why not pick you-uns up a couple of bags of popcorn and go live it up?" But judging from Jones's mailbag, up Nashville way and places like it, Caesar boosters were scarce. Caesar had appreciated how, on Bishop Sheen's own enormously popular show, *Life Is Worth Living*, he'd said nice things about him. But at this point Sheen's prayers might have helped more than his praise.

Caesar's own chronic insomnia probably explained a charming Hickenloopers routine from mid-November, when a sleep-deprived Charlie mistakenly takes "Zippos" instead of "Sleepos" to knock himself out. (It was a sketch Leonard Bernstein liked so much that he reenacted it for his kids.) One week later came a hilarious sketch set in the Vitality Health Food Kitchen, the severely vegetarian establishment to which Doris takes carnivorous Charlie. The very premise of the place—that eating means short-term suffering for long-term health, rather than instant gratification, regardless of the consequences—galls Charlie; why live longer if it's only to eat more such dreck? "I don't want to feel *better* after a meal. . . . I want to feel *full*," he says. He longs for his favorite Italian place, Pepito's, home of spiced snails, hot tamales, pickles with hot mustard, and spiced sausages—to the newly emancipated Jews of Caesar's generation, a trifecta of the exotic, the flavorful, and the *treyf.** "After all," he asks, "why take chances with your stomach?"

The blissed-out waiter (Reiner, of course) brings a vase filled with flowers: the appetizers. Caesar tries one, and spits it out in horror. "Look, Doris, the next time we go out, we'll eat separately," he protests. "I'll eat at Pepito's and you can eat at the Botanical Garden." Reiner soon returns with two flower boxes filled with plants and a pair of watering cans: the salad dressings. Twenty-five years before Alvy Singer suffers through alfalfa sprouts and mashed yeast with Annie Hall, Charlie Hickenlooper eats fake veal and flowers with pussy willow dressing out of a planter—with a trowel.

Food deprivation of a different sort was the theme of another memorable sketch, from December 1953. It's set around a table in a boardroom, at the head of which Caesar the imperious executive presides over a group of sycophantic subordinates. There is something snooty—vaguely British—about him; no wonder his secretary is named Devonshire. He listens distractedly as two of his deputies, Bagsby and Bixby (Morris and Reiner), debate the wisdom of a proposed merger, then cuts them both off. "*Gentlemen!*" he thunders. "You are forgetting one very important thing: *Lunch!*" He quickly makes sure the sandwich order has been placed, and when it arrives—and as Bagsby and Bixby drone on—Caesar drops his Westminster mien and becomes the Jewish businessman, hectoring the hapless delivery boy for dunking the tea bag into the hot water rather than letting him do it himself (and thereby conserving it sufficiently to coax out a second cup). But quickly, a more serious problem arises: *His* sandwich isn't in the box!

He is crestfallen—*stricken*. He looks on forlornly, lips trembling, as everyone else stuffs their faces, brandishing their slabs of bread and meat for emphasis as they make their points. (An ear for languages wasn't the only tool Caesar picked up at the St.

---

* Nonkosher food.

Clair Lunch. "You could get a person's character from the way they eat," he said. And *what* they eat: The scene gains an extra measure of wit, at least for some Jewish viewers, from the types of sandwiches, either pedestrian, skimpy, or grotesque, the men have selected, including a ham and cheese, Caesar's own bacon and raisin, and Reiner's ham hock, something utterly foreign to many Jews, who would know only that it wasn't anything for them. There wasn't a pastrami, corned beef, or even a tuna salad in the bunch.) His agony peaks when Morris, rising once again to defend the deal, punctuates his points by wagging and waving a pickle directly under Caesar's nose.

Obscure and underemployed when he'd shown up in Liebman's office, Morris had become a vital part of the show, less third banana than co-second. But he continued to feel underutilized and underappreciated, relegated to the "schlepping stuff"— that is, whatever was left once the "two behemoths," Caesar and Reiner, were done. No matter what he did, he'd always be the guy to pick up and toss around. "It was like a Jewish family, where you're either the oldest and the strongest, or you're the youngest and the most pitiable," he said. "I was the youngest and most pitiable. And I made do with it. I was making the same impact they were. They didn't know that. I didn't know it, either."

As a performer, Morris allowed, Caesar was "fucking brilliant, a ge-ne-ius," but as a human being he was clueless. "He never used to listen to anybody," he said. "He was on his own track. Looped. Going 'round and 'round and 'round." In one sketch he'd shot off a toy gun in the milk can Morris was wearing over his head, either oblivious of or indifferent to Morris's eardrums. There were, he said, "big gaps" in Caesar's brain, but given his gifts you made allowances. He was less forgiving toward Reiner, who, he felt, was a brownnose. "Carl has an air-conditioned three-bedroom apartment up Sid's ass," he liked to say, "and next year he's putting in wall-to-wall carpeting." "Howard was a malcontent," Reiner recalled. "He was always figuring he didn't have enough to do. And he was right!" Morris was perhaps angriest at himself, for staying in his gilded cage rather than flying to some place more risky but worthier of his talents.

As an actor, Morris had been told to respect what was on the printed page. But he was also, as he put it, "young and resilient," "pissed off and a fighter." So he had launched his own guerrilla war with the show, fighting to squeeze more out of his meager roles. And in that pickle of his in the boardroom sketch lay such an opportunity.

Of all the edibles on a show obsessed with food, pickles make the most appearances: Simultaneously superfluous and essential, complementing so much that we savor, there's something endearing and comical about them. So, the pickle bearers are the first to board the subway on the pantomimed outing to Coney Island; in one of Caesar's solos, a man changing jobs must choose between being head taster for a sweet-and-sour pickle company and being head differentiater between red and white horseradish; Charlie Hickenlooper dreams of meals beginning with strawberry shortcake and ending with a salami sandwich and pickles, and, while wrestling with the potted plants at the Vitality Health Food Kitchen, he covets the pickles with hot mustard at Pepito's. Until now, pickles, like Morris himself, were strictly side dishes, and hadn't starred at anything; suddenly both do. Up and down Morris waves his dill, up and down, up and down, smack dab beneath Caesar's snout. Caesar follows, and mimics, its every move; twice, he snaps at it. The faster Morris waves it, the faster Caesar's head shakes in sync. And since they couldn't have anticipated the scene's blatant sexual suggestiveness, the censors, like everyone else, had to sit and watch. "As close to the perfect comedy performance as we get," the comedian Robert Klein later said of the sketch.

DESPITE ALL THE CRITICISM of the show and its falling ratings, Leonard Lyons of the *New York Post*, for one, had noticed how Caesar had upped his game. "NBC-TV pays Sid Caesar $25,000 a week, just for himself, and he's worth every penny of it," he wrote in December 1953. But it was taking a toll. Even during his weeks off, Caesar's hands started to sweat around 8:30 on Saturday nights. A television magazine disclosed how he'd spent one of his hiatuses that fall: "With nerves all a-tingle and stomach askew, Sid vacationed at Mt. Sinai Hospital!" The piece described Caesar reviewing kinescopes of the show from his hospital bed. That he was probably drying out went unmentioned. "The press must have known, because I was in the hospital many times," Caesar later said. "Maybe they were too kind to me."

The forgettable programs up against *Your Show of Shows* closed in on it, and friction with Liebman grew. "Sid's relationship with Max Liebman was like every boy's relationship with his father," Brooks said. "He's afraid to surpass him, but he knows he must." One time Liebman, irked by Caesar's inattentiveness, kicked him in the groin, forcing an assistant to rush down to the nearest drugstore for smelling salts. Another time, accompanying Max to the *shvitz*, Caesar absconded with his toupee—and peed on it. But Caesar never could forget who was boss. On top of the printed programs prepared for every show were the same three words: "Max Liebman Presents." Liebman's name was also the first thing viewers saw when the show came on.

Caesar, however, certainly acted boss-like, enough to put off the newsman from Atlanta examining how the show was put together. "Caesar, his Cuban cigar jutted toward the ceiling, was talking fast out of the unoccupied corner of his mouth," the reporter, James Saxon Childers, wrote. "Light flickered back from his watch chain, a zoot loop halfway to his knees. He was telling 'em, all right." Given a draft of the piece to review (a prime example of the extraordinary deference then accorded celebrities), an NBC flack attempted a defense. "Sid is a guy with great heart and warmth," he pleaded. "That cigar routine is just a front that is really meaningless." But more than ever, Caesar craved his own candy store.

Caesar felt sufficiently secure about things in the fall of 1953 to attend (with Brooks) a performance of *The World of Sholem Aleichem*, whose creators and stars had all been blacklisted. While not exactly a bold gesture (large numbers of people attended), heading there wasn't without risk: Ed Sullivan, for one, denounced the principals' "pinko leanings." But as inseparable as Brooks and Caesar seemed, when Brooks and Florence Baum married that November, they didn't invite Sid to their wedding. "It never—not even for a second—entered either of our minds," she recalled. It was, she said, partly a matter of caste, and partly one of character: Caesar was "in a class by himself, rich, famous, and nuts," and not much fun to have around. "Without a character to play," said Baum, "he was sort of blah—as relatable as a jellyfish." That said, she also thought Caesar was decent in a way the other stars she'd encountered weren't. "Sid was a very classy guy," she said. "The way he dressed, his manners when dealing with the cast, the crew, servers in restaurants, at the beach, wherever. Not at all like the piece of trash Gleason, who used to fuck one of the dancers in his dressing room and had his Jewish writers toss their work to him through the transom. Sid never had ugly, outrageous tantrums and instead was always courteous (but shy and awkward and restrained)."

Harry MacArthur of the Washington *Star* found the Sid Caesar of October 1953 little changed from the earnest, humble guy he'd met seven years earlier, except for a tinge of bitterness. "Over in Europe, a man writes a fine book fifteen years ago and seven flops since and he's still a great man," Caesar told him. "Here, you do a terrific show, a sensational show. Then at the end you say, 'Good night, ladies and h-k-k-k gentlemen,' and you're dead. You ask somebody later, 'How was the show?' and he says, 'Ya sure loused up the ending. Whatsa matter, ya stutter? You can't even say good night?'"

Coca, too, was unhappy, pushing for better material and greater creative freedom, including the right to appear on other programs. (Her agent seems to have been encouraging her to push for a show of her own.) Brooks was also pestering Caesar, and for something a lot more important than a few prized jokes.

On Thanksgiving Day 1953, a seemingly carefree Caesar rode shotgun aboard a float in Macy's parade. A week or so later came a dress rehearsal of *Your Show of Shows* broadcast in early, primitive color. "The beginning of the rainbow," NBC called it; the figures on the Bavarian clock now appeared in red, pink, green, and turquoise.* There were disturbing reports about Caesar's

---

* Jockeying for scarce color sets—barely eight thousand of them were made in the first six months of 1954—was intense; the publisher of *The New York Times*, Arthur Hays

health, including one about "an alarming loss of weight, now reaching a dangerous low." By New Year's 1954, he was telling Pat Weaver he wanted a new ten-year contract, providing him with his own one-hour show, with billing as producer, director, and writer. "Sid also wants an offer, in writing, that shows 'what we think of him,'" Weaver told his colleagues.

The press picked up whiffs of change. "Rumors persist that Sid Caesar and Imogene Coca will break up their partnership," Ed Sullivan reported in late January 1954. Under a banner headline, *Variety* predicted that the program's current season would be its last, with Caesar and Coca getting their own shows in the fall. A gala fourth-anniversary party for *Your Show of Shows* set for February was quietly shelved. "It's now reached the point where everybody in the Trade knows, or thinks he knows, about what's going to happen. Everybody, that is, but the Press Department," an NBC publicist complained. "We are now beginning to look foolish. Isn't it better to admit that there will be changes than to play dumb?"

Caesar, wrote Harriet Van Horne, was "a man of surpassing talents," but she bristled over reports he felt underpaid. "Gallant, much-abused artists they may be in their own little hand mirrors, but the public is more apt to call them greedy pigs," she wrote of him and others like him. "Any man earning $25,000 a week and enjoying rapturous acclaim at the same time ought to feel that the gods have been good to him," she went on. "When such a man announces that he wants more money he is betraying a secret of his inner soul. It's not money he needs. It's wisdom." Van Horne had another beef: the $15,000 gap between what Caesar and Coca made per show. "If Mr. Caesar is worth $25,000 a week, so is Miss Coca," she wrote.

For now, though, NBC was concerned only with locking Caesar down, which began with some sweet talk from Pat Weaver.

Sulzberger, tried wangling one from NBC through Jack Gould. "It is not clear whether he wishes to have a set on loan or to purchase one," an NBC executive wrote to General Sarnoff. "However, in view of Mr. Sulzberger's importance, I am bringing this to your attention to see what can be done" (Sid Eiges to Sarnoff, n.d., box 166, folder 48, NBC Records).

"Almost from the day I became associated with NBC I have had a vital interest in your show business career," he wrote to Caesar in mid-February. "I have watched you develop and progress, as television itself has grown during the time you have been in it." "We have only scratched the surface in television," he went on. "We have not even started to realize its impact. We are already over the threshold of color, which is adding an entirely new scope to the medium. Before long we will have tape to work with too. I want to have you in our long-range planning, Sid."

Weaver proposed a new ten-year deal, with the network guaranteeing Caesar $100,000 against his earnings in any particular year, a shorter-term but more lucrative version of the arrangement with which they'd tied up Milton Berle. Just how he'd be deployed during that time—the frequency with which he'd appear, and how—might vary, but the following season there'd be thirty one-hour episodes of a new Sid Caesar show, airing on Monday (or possibly Sunday) nights. Coca would get a weekly half-hour show of her own, while Liebman would produce a revamped, Caesar-less *Your Show of Shows* (which quickly shed the name and morphed into a series of freestanding "spectaculars").

With word that the *New York World-Telegram* would soon break the story, on February 25 the network scrambled to make an announcement. Coca, who'd been told nothing about developments despite promises from Liebman and Caesar to keep her apprised, was rehearsing a dance number when Liebman's publicist, Dave Tebet, entered the room ashen-faced, and asked her to come with him to Liebman's office upstairs. "It was like a Marx Brothers movie: I'd never seen so many people in a room that small in my life," she said of the scene when she got there. "And all the cameras, 'psh psh psh psh.' And they're all yelling, 'How do you feel about the show going off the air?' Like an idiot, I broke into tears." And not garden-variety tears but "big, bitter, reluctant crocodile blobs."

She and Caesar took their positions, flanking Liebman, on a couch. Arrayed in front of them was a sampling of the trophies the show had amassed. While Caesar looked "pale, glum, and a little sick to his stomach," Theo Wilson wrote in the *Daily*

News, Coca "cried, blew her nose, hid her head behind Liebman's shoulder, apologized, and cried some more." (She also clenched Liebman's hand and "nervously clung to him like a child seeking protection.") Liebman reminded everyone that it was a happy occasion. Caesar and Coca said little to each other, but that was nothing new. When the photographers asked them to kiss, they obliged.

"It's really a heartbreaking thing," Caesar said, acting like the passive bystander before acknowledging he wasn't. "*Show of Shows* has been the cradle of great talent. But when a star starts to grow there comes a time when he has to go on his own." It was only fair, he added, that he and Coca should get shows of their own. "Oh, I suppose that's quite true," Coca replied when asked if she agreed. That afternoon, the *World-Telegram* put the story on its front page, above the fold. Accompanying it was a picture of Caesar and Weaver signing their new ten-year pact.

"The truth is that Max, Coca and myself have to split up because there just isn't time for three of us to express ourselves on one show any longer," Caesar explained a few days later. "In other words, we've grown up, and if we hope to continue grow-ing we must get out on our own. I know Coca is capable of doing more, and so is Max." In other words, he was doing them both a favor. He had "certain things I want to say and do," he told John Crosby. "It's like the old days when the Paul Whiteman band had the Dorseys and Benny Goodman in it. They had to break away, too." Despite her agent's agitations, Coca had hoped to better her lot on Caesar's show rather than break away. A show of her own, she later said, she'd wanted "like a hole in the head." She did not say so publicly, but privately she seethed.

"Sid wanted his own show," Morris later told the writer Jeff Kisseloff. "He's a *chazer*.* You know what a *chazer* is? He's a fuck-ing animal. Coca was thrilled with what was going on. She'd had five careers already and this was all a whole new thing for her. He just was a pig. He didn't like that lady up his ass." Morris

---

* A pig, or piggish person.

reprised the story in *King of the Hill*, a play à clef he co-wrote* a few years later. "A star must be king. King!" the Caesar character, Eddie Romaine, declares. "And I can't be great king when I got half-assed queen. Too old! Too grumbling! Too unhappy! Too much showing me fanmail [*sic*]! Too much ambitious! Too much co-star!" In the play, too, it's only at the press conference that the Coca character learns Caesar is scrapping their show and going off on his own. "What kind of a man are you?" she asks him. "Have you no respect for another human being?" And then she answers her own question. "You're a great star, Eddie, a very great star, but you're a lousy human being. Lousy! Lousy! Lousy!" In an interview with *The Boston Globe* later that year, Caesar was surprisingly candid on his feelings about the real Coca. "I don't prefer working again with anyone as closely as I did with Imogene," he said.

To Jack Gould, the breakup, though sad, was inevitable: The program "simply had run its course." The Caesar-Coca "divorce" was "Topic A" at Cerutti's, Walter Winchell's watering hole on Madison Avenue. "Coca without Caesar will be like Ham without Eggs, Burns without Allen and Rodgers without Hammerstein!" a teary-eyed fan told him. Already looking toward the history books, John Crosby said some Caesar sketches belonged in the Museum of Modern Art. "These are terrible times," a paper in North Carolina declared. "Europe won't unite to defend itself, H-bombs are getting bigger and bigger, Indo-China goes from bad to worse, Senator McCarthy is about to take over the U.S. Army, and Imogene Coca and Sid Caesar are going to split up." One columnist likened the move to an operation dividing Siamese twins, with similarly dire prospects.

"The program will not be comedy or variety or review—it will be a blend of all three and more," related an internal NBC memo about Caesar's new show from early March. Its comedy would be "based on pathos and real life," with sketches of up to twenty-two minutes—long enough to "give Sid an opportunity to demonstrate his tremendous gift for characterization." And some of the material would be serious. "It is not generally known,

* With Daniel S. Broun.

but Sid is an accomplished dramatic artist," it noted. There'd also be nods to Pat Weaver's "frontal lobes," though nothing too heavy; while such musical eminences as Jascha Heifetz, Vladimir Horowitz, and Gregor Piatigorsky might periodically appear, they'd forgo "heavy classical music" for "more middlebrow material." ("In this way Sid hopes to be able to advance the tastes of the public without being branded long hair or pretentious," the memo explained.) Above all, the new show would be, unlike *Your Show of Shows*, unpredictable. "You will not be able to set your watch by the Sid Caesar show," it promised.

Unsurprisingly, Reiner was sticking with Caesar. "Right now, I'm making wonderful dough," said Reiner, proud owner of a $30,000 house in New Rochelle. "It's the kind of financial rut I'd like to wallow in for the rest of my life."* Morris, too, was staying put. "Why should I want to be a sandlot player when I'm in the big leagues?" he asked. Joining them down the road would be a new female co-star, though Caesar was in no rush. "Caesar is never going to run out of ideas so long as there are animals and people on the planet," wrote Crosby, noting how Sid and his brothers were hanging out at the Bronx Zoo, inventing dialogue for the animals. "But he's a born worrier and, between now and fall, he's not going to sleep much."

Caesar was warmly applauded when he took the stage the Saturday following the announcement. There were more repeats in the coming weeks, including the first two sketches on the show of April 3, 1954. But letting go also meant letting loose, a luxury Caesar had never allowed himself or his colleagues. And there now emerged what many consider the program's, and television comedy's, crowning sketch. With its bursts of inspired improvisation, it was also the show's most atypical, something that could have happened only when the show was winding down and the usual restraints cast aside.

The sketch took on TV, and specifically *This Is Your Life*, a

---

* Reiner could have afforded something more rarefied, he later explained, but he'd wanted his children to mix with other kids, and it had worked out well, especially for his son. "Robby is naturally a shy and retiring boy, and he's flourishing in the warmth of suburbia," one reporter noted (*Akron Beacon Journal*, April 22, 1957).

show that had been around (on radio before television) since 1948; everyone knew it, and how it worked. Though sometimes offering up celebrities, more often it revolved around ordinary people who, lured to the theater by subterfuge, were plucked from the audience and brought up onstage. Once there, they were confronted by an array of long-lost, far-flung friends and relatives rounded up and smuggled in for the occasion, and made to relive their painful pasts and hard-won triumphs before a voyeuristic nation. Presiding over the proceedings was the oleaginous Ralph Edwards, who'd periodically consult an oversized "Red Book" for the highlights and lowlights of the subject's life. To some, it was touching and inspirational, to others, hokey and manipulative: "that lachrymose invasion of privacy," Crosby called it. New York City's welfare commissioner claimed it amounted to abuse.

Though satires on TV about TV remained rare, *This Is Your Life* presented too tempting a target. Several other satirists had already gone after it. But it was especially appealing to Jewish wits, with their more jaundiced view of how the world really works. The show's treacly optimism and naivete, its conviction that the universe is ultimately just, that virtue is rewarded, that righteousness triumphs, that God is good and endings generally happy, was infuriating to Caesar's crowd, almost a personal affront to a people who knew better. The idea, according to Tolkin, was his—his latest sally against fairy tales. "What person in his right mind, told that his entire private life was about to be revealed in front of millions, would agree to step on that stage?" he asked. And what about all the others up there who, the moment they're on camera, become overwrought on cue? What, Caesar and the others must have thought, was there to lose? With any luck, with their own show on the way out, they'd catch the suits and prudes and admen, and maybe even Max Liebman and Stockton Helffrich, napping.

For all the lumps it took, the Edwards show was among the first to acknowledge the Holocaust, and that made a peculiar kind of sense, for who knew better the lives of disruption and tragedy the show feasted upon than the Jews? And what better way for TV to approach so ghastly a topic than obliquely, upliftingly, and commercially? The same survivors who appreciated Caesar could see stories of themselves on the program; a year earlier, it had featured an Auschwitz survivor named Hanna Bloch Kohner, and she wasn't the last. Had Tolkin been watching just that past February, when Gregor Shelkan, a Latvian-born cantor from Roxbury, Massachusetts, was lured into the theater and then, to his astonishment and horror, hauled onto the stage, where he was confronted with a photograph of his murdered parents and siblings? Had he been outraged by the spectacle, or by the juxtaposition of genocide and Hazel Bishop no-smear lipstick? Or, alternatively, had he been mortified to see Jews flaunting their suffering before all the Gentiles rather than just sucking it up? Had he squirmed as a Jew when Shelkan's two surviving sisters (flown in from Israel), whom Shelkan hadn't seen since before the war, couldn't keep their hands off their baby brother, then wouldn't let him go?

The sketch was allotted eleven minutes, longer even than the movie spoofs. It was scripted, but with more than the usual wiggle room for improvisation. Given its physicality, it couldn't be rehearsed with the usual rigor, something Caesar opposed anyway; "I don't want to entertain empty seats," he'd say. It begins when, buoyed by a harp glissando, a smiling, bow-tied Reiner—"Ralph Baxter"—bounds through the curtains and onto the stage. "Welcome, America, and hi there, everybody!" he chirps. "Once again, we present 'This Is Your Story.'"

Then, elephantine cameras and lights in tow—an extraordinary display of nimbleness for TV of the time—Reiner steps down from the stage and into the seats. Even then, the sketch is an important historical document, a precious snapshot of a place, era, and culture: For the first and only time, Caesar's audience, or at least the part in Reiner's aureole, comes momentarily into view. The people in it are white, and mostly middle-aged, though back then "young" looked middle-aged, too. They're wearing their Sunday best, in the style of Broadway theatergoers of the day. They look like sophisticated New Yorkers rather than out-of-towners. They are in fine spirits and understandably so, having landed coveted seats to their favorite show, and in the nick of time.

The sketch was listed in the printed program. But unusually, viewers at home, too, had been alerted to it in a way that wasn't customarily done, as if something unusual and possibly unsettling were about to happen. "We're all about to have a perfectly wonderful evening of, well, just about everything—lots of comedy and songs, and dances," the evening's guest host, the actress Phyllis Kirk, told them innocently enough. "Oh, and I think you'll probably be particularly interested in our own version of that wonderful television show called *This Is Your Life*." Four routines in, during a commercial for Griffin Microsheen Boot Polish, Caesar slipped out into the audience and took his place about ten rows back on the right. Next to him, on the aisle, was Dave Tebet; Caesar had refused to venture into the audience without having him there.

"As you know, each week we give you the intimate, inside story of some person's life," Reiner declares as he makes his way into the audience. And after a couple of feints to other people— "Now, could it possibly be *your* life, sir?"—he descends on Caesar, who points smugly toward Tebet: Surely he's the guy they want. But Reiner sticks with him. "Yes, sir! This is *your* story—Al Duncey!" he shouts. The woman directly behind Caesar bursts out laughing. So does everyone else in the enormous theater, or so it sounds.

"Aw, he must be kiddin'," Caesar was supposed to say. Instead, his comic instincts kicked in: It wasn't a time for words. "He had the courage to find something that was funny and stay with it until it became funny for the audience," Morris later said. So he *says* nothing, blacking out momentarily instead. Then, when Reiner brings him to, and tries dragging him up onstage, Caesar fights him off: America wasn't about to have *his* life. He tries smothering Reiner with his raincoat, then knocks him over, then bolts toward the exit. The massive audience erupted in laughter of a lustiness never heard before on the show, ricocheting—just as Liebman had anticipated—throughout the hangar-like hall. And, as Caesar tries to make his escape, it kept coming. "I was used to the peaks and valleys of laughter," Brooks remembered. But here was laughter that was "literally nonstop."

Caesar runs toward the exit behind him. But blocked by the ushers, he turns around, dashes down the aisle and up onto the stage and across it, then runs back up the other aisle, where three more ushers finally subdue him, haul him back up on the stage, and deposit him—panting, disheveled, soaked in sweat—on the couch. The cameramen had somehow caught it all, and the director, Bill Hobin, had gotten it on the screen. As Caesar catches his breath, Reiner effortlessly regains his customary control. It was time for him to bring out the first emissary from Al Duncey's past, dating back to his boyhood in Darling Falls, Montana.

"Can you remember way back, when you were a little boy, there was a man—a very *kind* man—who encouraged you," he asks him. "It was his encouragement and his kindness that helped to mold your life, and make you the person you are today. Do you recognize this voice, Al?" Only Al can't, at least without hearing it a second time. "Arggh!" he exclaims. "Uncle Goopy!" Then a small man, his mouth and arms wide open, his eyes crinkled from crying, rushes in. The script called for only limited slobbering: The two would embrace a bit before Reiner pries them apart. But watching from the wings as Caesar ignited the sketch with his brilliant embellishments, Uncle Goopy—Howard Morris— resolved to outdo him, to go for broke. "Use your funny lenses— *please*," he'd always tell the cameramen before going out onstage. This time, he wouldn't need their help.

Morris not only grabs Caesar, but won't let go. He hugs him, fondles him, jumps into his arms. Reiner keeps pulling them apart and dumping Morris somewhere else—on a chair, on the couch, under the couch, on the floor—only to watch Morris repeatedly muscle, slither, crawl, claw, and climb his way back. Uncle Goopy won't let go, and Morris, outdoing anything even Harpo Marx ever tried, wouldn't stop. Years after, Morris could still summon the thrill—the "release from Jewish tension," he called it—he'd felt that night.

"We broke every—*I* broke every, never mind 'we,' fuck you!— *I* broke every comedy rule there is, including, you do something three times, that's it," he continued. "We did it *forty-three* times. I kept coming back, 'cause it was getting huge, *huge* laughter. That takes balls, 'cause I'm working with the boss. Am I overstepping my bounds? 'Fuck you, boss! It's getting laughs!'" It was "the first time really in my theatrical history where I was allowed to take over and do whatever the hell I wanted in a sketch," he said. "I think I matured comedically in those twenty minutes."

In fact, they were entirely in sync. Duncey loves Goopy back every bit as much; far from feeling upstaged, Caesar eggs Morris on, continually throwing him come-hither looks. "If *he's* getting laughs, *I'm* going to get laughs," he explained. Caesar had always thrived on the unpredictable—"Mistakes were always good for him, because he'd always overcompensate and come up with some burst of insanity," Brooks said—and Morris's improvising only inspired him more. "We related like I have never related to another actor in my life," Morris said.

Things peak when Morris attaches himself to Caesar's thigh; Reiner later likened it to "a dog humping a lamp post." "I watched every Tarzan picture available" was how Morris explained the maneuver. "I was doing Cheeta." And Caesar takes it, literally, in stride. Because all of Morris was hanging from him, that meant *lifting*, rather than *dragging*, him around. "You get a lot of strength when you know that millions of people are watching," Caesar remembered.[*] Reiner, imperturbable as always, lets Morris do his thing. "Carl always pretended that nothing unusual was happening," said Joe Stein; it's what made him "the best straight man in the history of television." "The audience couldn't get enough of it," Reiner recalled. "The audience told us what to do. Told *them* what to do. I just had to stay there, and watch." And, of course, keep watching the clock: Several other "guests" were still to come.

There was Aunt Mildred, flown in all the way from Johannesburg. And Mr. Torch, the fireman who'd once saved Duncey from a burning building (played by the comedian Louis Nye, an

---

[*] One was six-year-old Billy Crystal, who henceforth made his father lug him to bed the way Caesar had lugged Morris. Decades later, in his film *Mr. Saturday Night*, the embittered comedian Crystal portrays glowers while his family enjoys the sketch because, as Crystal explained, he knows he'll never be *that* good.

army pal of Reiner's). Then came, as the script described her, "an extremely beautiful girl dressed in a stunning gown," played by an Eileen Ford model and actress named Vikki Dougan. She hasn't a name, not that it mattered. "Hello," she says to Duncey seductively. "Don't you remember me?" "Oh, honey baby!" declares Caesar, who throws his arms around her, bends her way back, and kisses her, repeatedly and ravenously. (In doing this, Caesar sprained Dougan's back, an injury she felt for decades to come.)

"Yes, after all these years," Reiner coos. "I guess you're very happy to see her, aren't you, Al Duncey?" He then asks him to tell everyone who she is. "I dunno who she is, but it's OK wid me!" replies Duncey, who stiff-arms Reiner as he tries to break *them* apart. (It's all a mistake, Reiner then confesses sheepishly: She was meant for *next* week's program.) The drum-and-bugle corps to which Duncey once belonged then marches in—an old vaudeville trick for ending a sketch with no satisfactory ending in sight. Miraculously, the sketch came in on the button—Reiner's doing, of course. Caesar floated off the stage "on a cloud of euphoria."

Ethel Daccardo of the *Chicago Daily News* called it "the funniest sketch we have ever seen on television." Jerry Lewis said he'd laughed more during it than he had in fifteen years, and ten times more than he would have watching *I Love Lucy;* to him, it highlighted live TV's glorious, spontaneous superiority over the staged and spliced sitcoms supplanting it. But "This Is Your Story" generated surprisingly little comment at the time; television was still too young and disparaged for superlatives. Kallen dismissed it as just another "beating up Howie Morris sketch" and "a great opportunity for Sid to carry on," a reminder of how humorless some humorists can sometimes be.

A few days later, Caesar experienced a very different kind of high when he was among the honorees at a gala marking opening day of the baseball season thrown by B'nai B'rith's Sports Lodge in Boston. While celebrating Red Sox greats of the past—the occasion marked the twenty-fifth anniversary of Tom Yawkey's purchase of the team—the Jewish organization also saluted Caesar; one local columnist wondered whether he'd create even more of a stir than Ted Williams, the Red Sox star outfielder, just back from two years of duty in Korea. "The No. 1 Ted Williams fan," Caesar called himself, and given their shared perfectionism— "Caesar's eye for human foibles is as sharp as Ted Williams' was for a fastball," *Newsweek* once observed—the bond between them wasn't that much of a stretch. Smiling at the Hall of Famers (Jimmie Foxx, Joe Cronin, and Lefty Grove) sitting to his left in the photograph in the next day's *Boston Globe*, Caesar looked far more comfortable than he had with Berle and the other comics at the Friars Club a couple of years before.

After the cancellation had been announced, Caesar's fan mail tripled, and the tributes multiplied, too. "Sometimes I think Sid Caesar is the greatest living comedian, with nobody a close second," the normally persnickety Dorothy Kilgallen wrote. Meanwhile, Caesar was laying out his future, resolutely and confidently. In early May, he rented two floors and the penthouse above Milgrim's, a swanky women's specialty shop on Fifty-Seventh Street just west of Fifth Avenue, for his new offices. He was moving uptown, and up.

Then came the last of the show's landmark sketches, a duet in German double-talk, with Caesar playing an imperious German general (or so it seemed) and Morris his loyal valet. Most of the piece reprised a scarcely noted segment from the previous season; like anything involving Germans, and particularly the German military, it had been presented gingerly, with Bill Hayes coming out beforehand to suggest in so many words it was okay to laugh at *these* Germans because they dated from World War I. The occasional ads for Adolph's meat tenderizer marked *Your Show of Shows'* closest brush with the Third Reich.

Caesar's bemedaled German general first appeared, in February 1952, as Baron von Schmutzendangle, performing the Germanized version of "The Whiffenpoof Song" he'd first sung as a student in Heidelberg. When he reappeared in January 1953, it was in a robe, barking orders to the dutiful, attentive Morris, who undresses, then re-dresses, him. The sketch, inspired by the classic 1937 French film *Grand Illusion*, was something Morris said he and Caesar had cooked up by themselves, with none of the writers around; it ended with the usual mayhem and carnage.

Revisiting it in May 1954—by which point it had been dubbed "Man Muss Sich Aufputzen," or "All Slicked Up"—it was given a very different ending. Finally in full regalia, the General exits his dressing room, struts through an elegant affair in the salon next door, then steps outside and strikes a proud, proprietary pose. But when he pulls out a whistle as a well-dressed couple approaches and hails them a carriage, for which he is duly tipped, we learn who this imperious fellow really is. Everything he'd embodied— pretense, pomposity, hierarchy, authority, vanity—turns out to be its own grand illusion. Brooks took credit for the new ending, saying he stole it from *The Last Laugh*, F. W. Murnau's German expressionist film from 1924, in which a proud hotel porter (played by Emil Jannings) is stripped of his uniform following a mishap and banished to duty in the men's room.

For its last few episodes, the show ran recycled material. As it did, some already grasped that an epoch, television's first, was coming to a close; for the first time, a medium built on evanescence had something lasting long enough to commemorate, and mourn. As Dwight Newton of the *San Francisco Examiner* put it, "The show is ending—and the legend is about to begin." The finale came on June 5, and in television news that week only the ongoing Army-McCarthy hearings got more ink. *Life* came to the last rehearsal, where Coca "sniffled every 10 minutes and wept in the arms of the old-timers, dance and music directors and chorus girls" and Caesar "said he felt numb and morosely chewed his cigar." "Last Time Together for a Great Pair," its cover story was called. Two years before publishing *The Last Hurrah*, the novelist Edwin O'Connor described for the *Boston Post* another last hurrah.

"This is the last one, Imogene," Caesar told Coca at the beginning of the show. "Five wonderful years," she replied. "You can say that again," he said. "Come on, Imogene, let's have some fun." Then, once again, Doris Hickenlooper served the first meal of their marriage to Charlie. And then a fickle Coca once more toggled between two French soldiers, played by Caesar and Reiner, heading off to the front. Caesar and Coca took another turn as those clashing percussionists, Coca the consumptive sewing machine girl once more flew off into eternity, and those four English blue bloods once more sat stoically in the rain. (The only original sketch to emerge from the show's demise came not on the show itself but at a cast party, in which, unable to summon the right euphemism for "pregnant," Coca shouts, "You knocked me up!" at Caesar as he walks in the door. "We were five years ahead of the theater," Tolkin joked.)

"It's the finale of a great adventure," the last guest host, the actress Faye Emerson, said as the program drew to a close. The chorus broke into "Stars over Broadway" one last time, though they'd tweaked the tense. "We're happy you took in *Your Show of Shows, Show of Shows, Show of Shows*!" they sang. The entire company of more than two hundred people then assembled onstage. One by one, the Billy Williams Quartet, Reiner and Morris, Hayes and other principals of the show, and finally Caesar and Coca, took their curtain calls.

As the applause swelled, Caesar steeled himself, went up and down on his tiptoes, cleared his throat. To one observer, he resembled "a funeral-parlor visitor who doesn't quite know how to say what he feels." To his credit, he didn't pretend to be sad. "Thank you very much, ladies and gentlemen," he said. "This is . . . this was it. Imogene, this was our last show, on the *Show of Shows*. It's been a wonderful five years and I just want to say, 'I love you, baby.'" He kissed and hugged her, then fobbed the emotional buck off on her. A trouper to the last, Coca took it, smiling and breathing deeply, no longer biting her lip. Someone had told her that spelling her name backward would keep her from crying; she did, but it didn't. "We'd like to thank the wonderful audience that we have, the audience that's been so really terrific to us through all these years, and tell you how *all of us* are so *deeply* grateful to you," she said quietly, sneaking peeks at the floor as she did. "All hands looked as if they wanted to break out in tears," *Variety* said.

In the control booth, Bill Hobin tried to capture it all for the folks at home. "I panned close-ups of Max, the stars, the singers, the dancers—everyone—to show the millions of viewers throughout America the true depth of our love for the show," he wrote. "I must confess that my eyes weren't completely dry, either." Caesar threw out a kiss. Then, at twenty-nine minutes and thirty seconds past ten, Hobin gave one last signal. "We're off the air!" he said. "And with that," he remembered, "*Your Show of Shows*—a brilliant gem set in the Golden Age of Television—passed into history."

As the audience filed out, the cast made its way to the Rainbow Room, atop the RCA Building, for an informal farewell party, featuring a buffet dinner and dancing to a Dixieland band. At the right time, Pat Weaver and General Sarnoff would summon Liebman, Caesar, and Coca, to thank them and wish them well. But still smarting over how the show had been canceled behind her back, Coca had to be leaned on to come; network muckety-mucks suggested to her how awkward and awful it would look if she didn't. "I knew I damn well better," she later said.

At one point, Caesar picked up his saxophone and played. At another, surely only by popular demand, he and Coca took a solo turn on the dance floor. As Caesar twirled Coca around, he engaged in another, very different kind of spin, suggesting what would become a trope for him in the years to come, becoming more persuasive as memories faded: that the death of the show had been someone else's doing. "He said to me, 'It's terrible what they've done to us,'" she recalled. "And I wanted to say, 'You simple son of a bitch, *you* did it. Nobody else, you're the one that broke the whole thing.' But I didn't say that. I simply said, 'Sid, I can't dance with you much longer, 'cause I promised—what's his name?—a lot of dances.'" Maybe it was a reference to Pat Weaver, who'd oversee her new show. Caesar persisted with his ruse. "And he said, 'Well, what are we going to do?'" Coca went on. "I said, 'You're going to have a wonderful career, and every-thing will be just fine for you, and—bye.' That was our farewell. He was ready to really make a dramatic thing about it, and I knew he didn't feel it for two minutes. He broke the show up.

"I'll never understand Sid's attitude," she added, "'cause he would never, never admit that he did it. And Max apparently let him."

There now followed the postmortems. *Variety* compared its

closing to the last nights of *Oklahoma!* and *South Pacific.* "They quit while they were ahead," one of the show's great champions, Donald Kirkley of the Baltimore *Sun,* wrote of Caesar and Coca. "Their place in show business history will be secure, as two of the new set of household deities who are displacing the senescent idols of Hollywood." While representing the best of television's formative years, Philip Minoff reflected in *Cue,* "there is a limit to human resourcefulness." With *Your Show of Shows* gone, abandoned rituals could now be revived. "Saturday night will revert to noisy parties," went one prediction. "Youth will seek the forgotten pleasures of the corner ice cream parlor and old folks will reinstate the regular Saturday night card game."

Caesar's hand would now be freer, but he'd have a hard time replicating the novelty, energy, and intimacy of *Your Show of Shows,* especially since he'd grown more arrogant and remote, less hungry, and even less relatable. And while he'd developed as an artist, he'd also, thanks to his drinking and the pills he had started to take, mostly to sleep, grown more impaired. When audiences heard him slur his lines—something that dated as far back as the sketch in the health food restaurant—in the insomnia sketch, those Zippos and Sleepos suddenly seemed real.

What Paddy Chayefsky wrote about his own kitchen-sink dramas was just as true about comedy. "Very few television writers can seriously hope to keep up a high-level output for more than five years," he said. "Television is an endless, almost monstrous drain." "TV's Overexposed Comics Running for Cover; Fewer Shows, Less Time," declared *Variety.* Martin and Lewis would appear no more than five times in the coming season, and Bob Hope "will make himself extremely scarce." But far from rationing himself, Caesar would be nearly as omnipresent as ever.

Just what he'd be doing when, as *Variety* put it, it came time for him to "don his toga as a solo" was "one of the major trade secrets of the '54–'55 semester." Fearing leaks or theft, Caesar wouldn't even tell the NBC brass; network flacks touted Caesar's "own new laugh-a-minute show," but had no idea what they were peddling. Caesar *did* say he was not about to fall back into what he called the "format trap"—that "slow form of strangulation" that had made *Your Show of Shows* so predictable. He'd also hold off on a female co-star, because, he explained, she'd inevitably, and unfairly, be compared with Coca. He vowed "to be more of a human being" on the new program, maybe even talking to the audience at the start of every episode. The new show would be called *Caesar's Hour*, which marked a compromise: NBC had wanted *The Sid Caesar Show*, and he'd wanted to leave his name off it entirely, or so he said.

With so much in the offing, Caesar passed up relatively remote Westport for something tried and true and closer to home; the man from the *Los Angeles Times* found him back among his *landsleit** at good old gemütlich Lido Beach. "They know what I like here," he explained. Spotting his suite in the hotel was easy, even from half a mile away: It was the one with the air conditioner poking out the window. Even in August, Caesar liked sleeping under the covers. When he wasn't reading (biographies of Freud and Napoleon), he'd sit in the sun, keeping an eye on young Ricky and sneaking peeks at a ball game on a portable TV. He didn't let his kids watch him on the air—"Why disillusion them?" he asked—but was sticking with the medium. "He says his six years on TV seem to him 'like 60 years of something else,' but he loves it," wrote James Kilgallen, a reporter for the Hearst papers and Dorothy's father.

"People nowadays are too tightened up," he told Kilgallen. "We haven't been relaxed since 1939. Every time you pick up a newspaper, or listen to a radio news commentator, there's a new crisis. Human beings are pushing too fast in this atomic age. Let's brush off these crises. Let's step back and laugh at ourselves once in a while. Let's enjoy life. We're here for only a little while." It was good advice, which he seemed extremely unlikely to follow himself. And if, now that he was on his own, he didn't enjoy life, he'd have only himself to blame.

---

* People from the same town or district.

CHAPTER 8

CAESAR'S HOURS

On a Friday night in early October 1954, live on national television, Edward R. Murrow talked "person to person" for fifteen minutes with Sid Caesar. This was the amiable Murrow, not the grim chronicler of the London Blitz and the scourge of Senator Joseph McCarthy. But even in this largely forgotten guise, Murrow was consequential: Appearing with him attested to one's influence and respectability. And after a couple of years of trying, he'd finally landed Sid, who was to be interviewed sitting nervously in his Park Avenue apartment.

"If everything had gone according to plan, Sid Caesar would probably still be playing the saxophone for a living," Murrow began. "Caesar has come a long way in show business, and he's still very much on the move." Caesar then appeared on-screen with two-year-old Ricky, who was in his pajamas. Caesar wound him up like a toy soldier. Then he introduced Murrow to Shelly, aged seven, and bade them both good night before making his way to the living room, where Florence awaited him on a couch.

"Sid, do the kids ever make you work at home?" Murrow asked. "I'm not a comedian at home, actually," Caesar replied as he sat alongside Florence, whose name Murrow momentarily misplaced. "Tell me, is Sid funny at home?" he asked her. "Well, everyone asks me that," she replied, a bit testily. (As one reporter was to note, Florence Caesar was "not one to burble with false ecstasy.") "People think that I keep laughing *constantly*. And it's not true." She caught herself and quickly reversed course. "Because Sid takes his work very seriously," she went on. "I think most comedians do. And they worry a lot. And he does." Caesar's associates weren't accustomed to such volubility from her: In Kallen's six years with Caesar, she said, Florence "never said two words."

Murrow asked Sid what he did to relax. With that, Caesar stood up, kissed (and patted) Florence's hand—"she's beautiful, and you have to pay attention," he explained—and walked into the next room. Three rifles hung from the wall, and another seven or eight leaned against it. Caesar inventoried his collection, which included a double-barreled Browning, a .375 Magnum, and a "220 Swift with a six-power scope." It was with that last one, he said, that he'd "killed this baby right here," tapping the head of the deer peering out from the wall hard enough to loosen it from its moorings. "Now tell me about that," said Murrow. "Well, it's a heartbreaking story," said Caesar, launching into his short, unhappy life as a hunter. But he loved the poor creature, he said, kissing it more enthusiastically than he'd just kissed his wife.

"This is my famous—not my famous, my *favorite*—painting," he said back in the living room, pointing to his Vlaminck and noting his "kinsmanship" with certain great painters, like Van Gogh. He also pointed out a piece by the Italian sculptor Marino Marini—a gift from Coca, he noted. And if he weren't Sid Caesar the comedian, Murrow asked, who would he like to be? "Albert Einstein," he replied instantly. "I'd like to actually contribute one one-thousandth as much as he's contributed to the world," Caesar said, "and what he will give to the world will not be known for another few hundred years." "And I'd be Mrs. Einstein," Florence added. After it was over, the television columnists Tom O'Malley and Bob Cunniff revealed how Caesar had downed a couple of scotches beforehand for courage.

Caesar had sweated copiously—"you got a lot of lights here, Ed," he complained—but no more than those colleagues of his who'd tuned in. "We were writhing on the floor out of embarrassment," recalled Stein, who'd watched with Reiner. Another eyewitness, described as "one of Caesar's closest friends," recalled watching him "from behind a potted plant in my living room." A columnist in Los Angeles said Caesar had been almost as funny unintentionally on Murrow's show as he was intentionally on his own. "Sid Caesar was what you would call in English 'tongue-tied,'" Nakhman Zalowitz of the *Forverts* wrote. "It was actually painful to watch."

Pat Weaver and the NBC brass were surely just as apprehensive. They were gambling on Caesar. They knew he was prickly, that his head was swelling, that he was increasingly unstable. They also knew, surely, about his drinking. They knew, too, how some viewers had tired of him, while others in television's less sophisticated second generation of viewers were spurning him from the get-go. And there were a lot more of them: By one calculation, American homes now had more televisions in them than bathtubs. But the network was betting that pure, unchained, unadulterated Sid Caesar would reach new heights of wit, and find enough of an audience.

To Caesar, it was a good bet. Finally, as he later put it, "all the toys were mine." The problem was a familiar one: Once again, there was no hand, whether Dave Caesar's or Max Liebman's or Florence's, on the rope. "There was nobody there to say no," he recalled. "And that was when I started to go crazy." "Sid was like a racehorse out of the barn," Reiner recalled.

Caesar, who had his pick of writers, had kept Tolkin, Stein, and Webster from the old show, and added Aaron Ruben, who'd written for Milton Berle. Kallen was gone: Coca needed her and, besides, she'd tired of the testosterone, cigars, and Brooks and wanted to run something herself. More surprisingly, Brooks was also gone. The two had grown exhausted with each other: Caesar with Brooks's hectoring, Brooks with watching his material ignored or run into the ground. "Every day he came home and bitched about Sid," Florence Baum recalled. "He was despondent, beside himself, tired of having his best ideas thrown in the garbage. He was creating masterpieces, and Sid was addicted to drugs and booze and, at the last minute, throwing his gems away. It drove him insane." There'd been fourteen or fifteen occasions, Brooks later told Kenneth Tynan, that he'd contemplated suicide; he'd even had the pills. Baum recalled standing alongside her husband on a pedestrian bridge near Columbia University, begging him not to jump into the traffic below. Instead, he jumped ship. For a time, he toyed with writing a play. For a few hours, he took a job with Red Buttons. And then, as Coca's show foundered, he went to work for her, which meant working *under* Kallen—a superstar-crossed collaboration if ever there was one.

Back at the Milgrim Building, Caesar now oversaw his own mini-empire, including twenty-six staff people, ten dancers, eight singers, an orchestra of thirty, a conductor, three arrangers, three copyists, and a choral director. "At the beginning, Sid Caesar became a big star and he was kind of trying to catch up with the name and *be* 'Sid Caesar,'" Brooks recalled. "Later, when he segued into *Caesar's Hour*, he *was* 'Sid Caesar.'" He grew more surly and difficult and, as the business of business impinged on him, more distant from the business of comedy, much to his big brother's chagrin. Dave Caesar had things about right. "Funny is money," he said. "Exec is *drek*."

Other titans of comedy, like Jackie Gleason and Steve Allen, had fancy digs of their own. But Caesar's, which had cost him more than $1 million to set up, were the most imperial. Floors ten and eleven were utilitarian, for rehearsals and underlings. It was floor twelve—the penthouse, Caesar's personal aerie—that got all the oohs and aahs. "On the sybaritic side," one visitor called the space. It was where Caesar conducted serious business, mostly in person, for he disliked the telephone; how could he tell if someone was smiling or making faces at the other end of the line? It was also where he found peace and/or hid out.

The place was accessible only by a carpeted indoor fire escape lined with paintings, making it what one reporter called "perhaps the only Picasso-Rouault-Rodin-adorned fire escape in the world." "Like something out of *Citizen Kane*" was how Aaron Ruben described the approach. Once you reached the office, the first thing you saw was a teakwood desk, "large enough to accommodate the Ice Capades." It rested on a raised platform, the better for looking down at supplicants. Overhead was a skylight, through which glories from heaven afar streamed down upon him. On the nearby bookshelves were assorted trophies, along with volumes of Shakespeare and Eugene O'Neill, and a bronze bust of George Bernard Shaw. On the mantelpiece was a photograph of Caesar with Carl Sandburg, another of his fans.

Part of the renovation had gone into a kitchen and bar, which came with a white-jacketed butler named Homer whose "nearly full-time function," *Redbook* related, was "to keep Caesar supplied with celery tonic and corned-beef sandwiches." "His valet would bring in a tray of celery and salami, and Sid would eat and never offer you a thing," Charlie Andrews (referred to during his brief time in the writers' room as "the tamed Gentile") remembered. In the fridge were ice cube trays filled with *ptcha*—those jellied calves' hooves, with slices of egg and garlic, that Caesar liked so much.

The lighting in the place was all indirect; flicking the system on and off, "Sid looks like a little boy with a new train for Christmas," one visitor recalled. The floor was "carpeted with expensive broadloom, across which a houseboy occasionally treads discreetly," while "the luxurious drapes at its windows" were "tightly closed against the outside world." Other distractions included a "garrulous parakeet," a futuristic twenty-one-inch color television set, and a tankful of exotic tropical fish; staring at them, Caesar found, was soothing. Should he grow restless and the weather cooperated, he could go out through the French doors to a terrace with chaise longues. It was here that Caesar ate his lunch when the weather allowed, and from which, armed with binoculars, the boys could watch beautiful women streaming into Bergdorf's or strolling along Fifth Avenue.

For trips to the office and back, Caesar treated himself to a limousine with a white top, the better to differentiate it from everyone else's. A rotating red light on the roof signaled arrivals and departures. Pulling away, Caesar would wave a hankie out the window, "like the mayor of a small town in Italy," Florence Baum recalled. "He was sitting in the back seat of his Cadillac, which was the longest one ever made, wearing the biggest pearl-gray hat ever made, and wearing a suit with shoulders so wide there wasn't room for anybody else on the back seat," recalled a friend who'd cadged a ride. "He was sipping a martini as the chauffeur drove him along, except that he wasn't just sipping; he would take a drink and then make about a dozen faces . . . real Sid Caesar comedy, coughing, smacking his lips, blinking, wrinkling his nose, everything exaggerated." With the air conditioner always in overdrive, the temperature inside, noted Jack O'Brian, would "do justice to frozen beef."

Even while devising new directions for his comedy, Caesar itched for more. "Sid Caesar is casting his genius-type eye on a dramatic script by Paddy Chayefsky," Dorothy Kilgallen reported in June 1954. He gave Chayefsky an office in his offices. "Paddy is downstairs right now working," he told a reporter in July 1955. "A guy has to feel kind of grateful when he can get someone like that to write for him."* Though their collaboration never materialized, Chayefsky's *Marty* very clearly inspired the much-anticipated debut of *Caesar's Hour* on September 27, 1954. It featured twenty-seven-year-old Gina Lollobrigida—the "Italian Marilyn Monroe," the network flacks called her—who happened to be in New York. She'd never heard of Caesar, who'd enticed her onto the show in Italian double-talk. "Eef his name is Caesar, he got to be a nice fella," she explained.

No complete version of the premiere survives: Caesar proved a less conscientious curator of his work than Liebman had been. But in every respect, beginning with its name, *Caesar's Hour* struck a far more modest tone than *Your Show of Shows*. Those dancers and singers reaching heavenward yielded to peculiar rubberized puppets setting up lights and cameras, and "Stars over Broadway" to sprightly, wordless, generic music. All references to New York in the introduction were gone. "Hey, Sid! You're on!" the announcer, Don Pardo, cheerily announced. And then Caesar, dressed in a business suit, emerged.

Caesar was feeding on the "tiresome old casserole" of situ-

---

* For a time, Caesar also provided space to the song parodist Allan Sherman.

ation comedy, Van Horne wrote afterward. He played a grease monkey named Charlie who, like Marty, is a loser, with little to do on Saturday nights except hang out with his fellow numb-skulls, played overenthusiastically by Reiner and Morris. They prod him to go on a quiz show whose grand prize is a date with Lollobrigida. He does and, somehow, wins. On the big date, he is predictably flustered. But an old friend of hers shows up and hijacks the evening, reducing Charlie to a hapless bystander. He rejoins his friends and resumes his old, humdrum existence. That was pretty much it.

Caesar, it turned out, was as starstruck by Lollobrigida as Charlie—whose tongue, one critic noted, "was hanging out all evening"—and it clouded his judgment. While his most deter-mined admirers praised his debut, to clearer-eyed viewers the show laid a gigantic *uovo*. "A whole hour of Caesar goggling over the charms of Miss Lollobrigida, extensive as they are, made for pretty thin and intermittent merriment," Crosby wrote. Newfangled Cold War idioms best captured the disaster. A bomb "of the thermo-nuclear variety," *The Detroit News* called the show. Assorted Cassandras quickly concluded that Caesar without Coca was doomed, and calls for a reunion intensified as her show also sputtered. But Caesar was indifferent to her and her difficulties. He "sort of" missed her, he said, but couldn't imagine them reuniting. Maybe, he allowed, he'd have her on his show sometime as a guest. Nor did he extend her a helping hand. When Liebman "saved my ass" by sending over an old sketch for reuse on her show, Coca recalled, Caesar's lawyers threatened to sue. Caesar also squelched Berle's attempts to sign her up for some appearances. The debut sketch also used Reiner and Morris poorly, reducing them to goofy giggling. Resenting Coca's suc-cess was one thing, but did Caesar want to bring *them* down, too?

The show suffered from what Crosby diagnosed to be a larger problem. "Caesar is one of those rare animals—a thinking comedian," he wrote. But this "thinking comedian" was thinking about thinking more than about comedy; better he "get back to the drugstore and watch someone wrestle with a banana split." Caesar counseled patience. "I'll be conventional at first; around the sixth or seventh show I'll get revolutionary," he said. And the program rebounded decisively the following week with "On the Docks," a first-rate send-up of *On the Waterfront* done, Caesar later claimed, despite threats of legal action from the film's producer, Sam Spiegel.* It opens with Caesar, playing Marlon Brando's tormented dockworker, walking toward the camera, the Brooklyn Bridge behind him, as the credits roll. (Listed were the actors playing "good longshoreman," "bad longshore-man," "indifferent longshoreman," "nice longshoreman," and "dead longshoreman"; the supplier of Caesar's chewing gum, "Mike's Candy Store," and the flavors of the gum—in order of appearance, Clove, Wild Cherry, Tutti Frutti, Grape, Black Jack, Pepsin, Cinnamon, and Peppermint.) Speaking in what Walter Winchell called "Method mumbling," Caesar describes his hard-scrabble childhood. "Do you know how poor I was?" he asks. "Never tasted a tangerine . . . never had fruit in the house! It's a miracle I didn't wind up with scoivy!"

"Brando called me up after and said, 'I really enjoyed that. Thank you.' Very nice," Caesar remembered. The sketch "left Humphrey Bogart howling," a Hearst reporter wrote, "but will Bogie howl when Sid does a similar treatment of Captain Queeg in *The Caine Mutiny*?" To Sid Shalit of the *Daily News*, it was "one of the greatest bits of comedy ever to hit the TV tube." But no one was happier than Spiegel, who promptly offered to send over the script for the forthcoming *Bridge on the River Kwai* for Caesar's review, and ridicule. When the *Waterfront* sketch was redone the following April, Spiegel came on the show to praise it.[†]

A few months later, Caesar sat down with Brando—along with Tennessee Williams and Marilyn Monroe—at the Astor

---

* For all of Caesar's ex post facto tough talk, the spoof went ahead "only after careful arrangements" had been made between Caesar's lawyers and Columbia Pictures (Unprocessed CART report, Oct. 5, 1954, box 1, folder 7, NBC Records).

† One dissenter was Joan Martin of the communist *Daily Worker*, who knocked Caesar for endorsing "the Kazan-Brando school of acting," which portrayed the workingman as a "near-brute" and "sub-human" (*Daily Worker*, Oct. 17, 1954). That approach, she charged, appealed both to women ("based on grossness and physique") and (through "sign language in facial expression, stance, and gesture understandable to those in the know") to gay men.

Hotel in Manhattan for an interview with Tex McCrary and Jinx Falkenburg. "I never saw you looking so very young and handsome," Brando told Caesar. ("Thank you very much and . . . same to you!" Caesar replied with a laugh.) But when Monroe said that as part of her work at the Actors Studio she'd been imitating a cat, Caesar cut her off. "I'm working on a tree," he said dismissively. "I think it's an elm." Then, when Monroe mentioned Stanislavski, Caesar riffed on how a man named "Bowlerslavski" had studied how ten pins went down. "Acting is just what you are," he finally said. "It just comes out. That's what it is."

Falkenburg prompted Brando to say he'd "roared with laughter" over Caesar's version of Stanley Kowalski. Caesar then volunteered that he was thinking of doing *On the Waterfront* in French.

"Listen, did you ever think of playing a serious part, a straight part?" Brando asked him.

"Well, I've talked a lot about it but I'm not an actor," Caesar replied. "I'm a . . ."

"No, listen," Brando said. "I think it's *because* you *are* an actor that you *are* as good as you are, because I think that all of your performances, really, have a basis in reality." Then, his awkward mix of deference and defiance yielding to the primitive eloquence he could sometimes summon, Caesar told one of the greatest actors of his generation what *he* thought acting, or at least comic acting, should be:

> Even in comedy people know if you believe in what you're doing. As soon as they sense . . . bang! like that! [that] they don't believe you any more, you can stand on your head, with your eyes folded and your nose crossed, and you'll not get a laugh. But if they believe that *you* believe in what you're doing, no matter how silly it is . . . if it's a half-truth even, if they know you believe it, they'll respect your belief in it, and they'll go along with you. But once they sense it . . . there's a sense, between an audience and a performer, that once that feeling, that rapport, that, I can't explain it, but once they find out . . . it's like an

animal almost, an animal knows when you're afraid of him, an animal knows you're not afraid of him, but as soon as they feel it, an audience is not with you any more, and there's nothing you can do to get them back. But as long as they believe that you believe in what you're doing, they'll give you the respect, and watch you. And they'll go along with you. Then it's up to you how good you are.

Florence had been waiting for her husband in the wings, but Caesar, busy flirting with Monroe, seemed in no rush to leave.

Having his own show had perks. On the third episode of *Caesar's Hour*, devoted entirely to the adventures of three commuters (played by him, Reiner, and Morris), Caesar got to horse around with the singer Peggy Lee. Then, the following month, he sort of reenacted Benny Goodman's opening at the New York Paramount twenty years earlier with Goodman himself, jamming with him and his band and playing a short solo in "Sing, Sing, Sing." But the contrivance in which the music came wrapped— Caesar, Reiner, and Morris pretending to be goofy teenage groupies—upset jazz buffs. "They jumped and screamed and rolled their eyes in a frenzy of asininity that would shame African voodoo dancers," groused Jack Mabley of *Down Beat*. "So 10 or 20 million Americans were exposed to good, sound jazz for once, and at the same time were as much as told by Caesar and his fellow goons that the freaks who listen to this stuff are at best idiots." An erstwhile Caesar fan, Tom Scanlan of *Army Times*, gave him "a fat F" for the sketch. "If Caesar or his production staff want to prostitute music," he complained, "they could hire Guy Lombardo or Liberace."

But the King of Swing himself was delighted, sporting what the jazz historian Will Friedwald called "among the biggest smiles I've ever seen Goodman give on camera" after Caesar's solo. "You're the world's greatest," a tuckered-out Caesar told Goodman at the curtain. "Thank you very much," Goodman replied. "You blew up a storm yourself." Herman Talmadge couldn't have been pleased: Featuring Goodman's trumpeter, Charlie Shavers, the segment marked one of the few times a racially integrated ensemble had appeared on TV. It also showed a side of Caesar—awestruck, ecstatic, at home, at ease—viewers had never seen before, nor ever would again. Four shows later came "Dragnyet," the Russian version of the popular police show starring "Sgt. Joe Borscht." And two months after Edward R. Murrow had interrogated Caesar on *Person to Person*, Ted Burrows (Reiner) interviewed Professor Ludwig von Kleinmacher, a noted authority on travel, on "Man to Man." The Professor handled Burrows better than Caesar had Murrow, but the sketch (and the show, for that matter) clearly missed Mel Brooks.

Russell Baker, a young newspaperman about to join *The New York Times*, returned to Baltimore after a sojourn abroad to find all his highbrow friends watching Caesar—even during the welcome home party they'd thrown for him—with a fealty once reserved for FDR's fireside chats. Down from Yale on Thanksgiving 1954, Dick Cavett got to see his hero atop that float in Macy's parade. "My mind swirled," he recalled. "Does it sound stupid to say that I think every cell in my body buzzed? I was in the same *area* of the world with Sid Caesar. . . . No jolt has ever equaled it."

Caesar labored to find the right formula for his show. Without good writing, "longer" wasn't "better." The new show's stumbles, plus nostalgia for the old one, helped explain why, in a survey of a thousand New Yorkers that fall, *Caesar's Hour* and *The Imogene Coca Show* were the two most unpopular programs of the new season, and *Your Show of Shows*, the most missed. *The Hollywood Reporter* was already pronouncing *Caesar's Hour* "through." With many people tuning out midway, *Caesar's Hour* was really Caesar's half hour. Lower than expected ratings brought complaints from the very top. "I should have thot [*sic*] that Sid Caesar was funnier than Burns and Allen," David Sarnoff complained. To create some buzz for the show, NBC's press department hatched plans to send Caesar out to promote in Chicago, Detroit, Cleveland, Philadelphia, and Atlanta. It suggested that at each stop (1) Caesar play a "French" chef on local cooking shows; (2) local restaurants offer specials on Caesar salad; (3) Caesar meet with the rod and gun editors of local newspapers; and (4) local disc jockeys hold contests for "Cleopatras" to greet him when he got to town.

NBC was promoting him even more than Groucho Marx, but Caesar wanted still more. "Sid is taking off like a skyrocket on the question of newspaper advertising," an anxious NBC executive told Weaver. "It takes a little time," Caesar pleaded. Some of the problems he attributed to the very different Monday night audience. "You can't powerhouse them too much," he explained. "Monday is more of a stay-at-home night and the people want to relax." To some, Caesar himself seemed different—*off.* "What's happened to Sid?" asked Dwight Newton of the *San Francisco Examiner,* who'd confessed he'd "wept in print" when *Your Show of Shows* was canceled. "Where is the sharp delivery of lines? The superb timing? And the marvelous pantomiming? Can this really be the man who brought such merriment to 'Show of Shows' for so long?" Caesar's already-inadequate writing staff thinned out: Joe Stein departed mid-season to prepare his new musical, *Plain and Fancy,* for Broadway, and the explosive Tony Webster was fired when, characteristically in his cups, he'd mouthed off to the boss. Neither of their replacements, Charlie Andrews and Sheldon Keller, made much of a mark.

One of Caesar's principal problems was his three commuters. Rather than go lightly on a dubious proposition—the hilarity of suburban life—he'd doubled down on it: Entire programs highlighted the hijinks of Bob Victor (Caesar), George Hanson (Reiner), and Fred Brewster (Morris). All were as white-bread as their names,[*] lived in the generic bedroom community of Springdale, were married to generic suburban wives, took generic trains to generic white-collar jobs in generic offices in a generic city, then returned nightly to their generic houses or pursued generic frolics at their generic country club. To stand Lenny Bruce on his head, if everyone in New York City, even the Irish and Puerto Ricans, were Jewish, everyone in the suburbs, even the Jews, were Gentile. Inexplicably exiled from the city's infinite comic possibilities, the

---

[*] Reiner said Caesar had wanted to give Sid's character a Jewish-sounding name, and that "Victor" was as close as he thought he could get. Things were less uptight on *The Honeymooners,* where the Grand High Exalted Mystic Ruler of the Raccoon Lodge was Morris Fink, and Ed Norton worked alongside Nat Birnbaum in the sewer.

segments marked a perplexing leap backward before the first lines for them were written.

The twenty-four-year-old Philip Roth, a Caesar fan, then apprenticing as television critic for *The New Republic*, said one *could* "rake suburban life over the barbecue coals." But Caesar was hardly up for that. Instead, he served up a pallid version of wackier, wittier sitcoms—"'The Honeymooners' with a station wagon," Harry Harris of *The Philadelphia Inquirer* called it. The Kramdens and Nortons went roller-skating (with predictably disastrous results); the Commuters played Scrabble. While Bob Victor, like Ralph Kramden, was a boor and blowhard, he had none of Kramden's shambolic grandeur, absurdity, or poignancy; when it came right down to it, he was just an ass—a pipsqueak next to the people and things Caesar had always played. "Caesar's best characters always had an immense and substantial dignity about them," John Fink wrote in the *Chicago Tribune*. "His Professor, his Waiter, even his Slot Machine are, in their special ways, Great Men."

Albert Goldman speculated that Caesar, panicked over losing all those well-educated viewers now fleeing to the suburbs, had followed them there, no matter how anodyne their concerns. "The vast majority of American viewers do not live in Victor's income-class suburbia, commute, or consider the issue of wall-to-wall carpeting vs. bound rugs a major crisis in family life," wrote Sid Shalit of the New York *Daily News*. If, as Reiner had said, Caesar always felt Christians were "better" than Jews, here was his most conspicuous attempt to step up to their level. It was not just comedic suicide, an instance in which his insecurities trumped his customarily faultless instincts, but a form of self-mutilation, one made possible by Caesar's new autonomy. A Max Liebman would surely have kept Caesar's character from moving out of town.

Philip Roth quarreled with another of its premises: that "there is something uproariously funny about a husband and wife when they don't love every cubic inch of each other." That became an issue only after Caesar finally broke down and got himself a new wife: Nanette Fabray, who'd twice guest-hosted *Your Show of Shows.* Fabray, who debuted as Nan Victor in November 1954, couldn't save the sketches but probably saved *Caesar's Hour,* which, as she later recalled, was "really going down the tubes" when she got there.

Once an extra in the *Our Gang* juvenile comedy shorts who'd later trained with Max Reinhardt, Fabray, like Coca, was multi-talented. She had a superb singing voice, and starred in Broadway musicals like *High Button Shoes.* She was nimble, able to antici-pate, and accommodate, Caesar's moods and moves. And she, like Coca, had taken her lumps: When Caesar approached her, she'd just checked out of the institution to which she'd gone after being told she was going deaf from a degenerative disease. Though that never happened, she warned Caesar that she couldn't memorize even the first two lines of a song. But Caesar felt he'd never find anyone as pretty, funny, versatile, and composed, someone who'd remain upright when he "fumfered." When she'd agreed, she said, Caesar teared up, took her hands, and promised to take care of her. "There was a madness in her that Sid seemed to unlock, and she was wonderful when she was crazy," said Larry Gelbart.

But Fabray was less intrinsically funny than Coca, and her emotional range much narrower. She lacked Coca's imagination, nuance, pathos, depth, and elfin charm. It was difficult to care, let alone worry, about her, let alone love her as viewers loved Coca. "She can dance and sing very nicely," wrote Harriet Van Horne. "She has lovely legs and a pretty face. But her work is one-dimensional. She misses a lot of the fun." Nor did she have the authority and stature to coax out Caesar's best. "Caesar seemed broader and more raucous than ever before now that Coca's slyly provocative stylization was no longer available to relieve him of some of the comic responsibility," Andrew Sarris wrote.

But Fabray—dark, sunny, and fresher-looking—was beautiful and, unlike the unmistakably ethnic and older-fashioned Coca, had an all-Americanness that made her easier for some to swallow, along with the modernity and confidence of an emerging femi-nism. Though the Victors, like the Hickenloopers, slept in twin beds, one could actually imagine Bob, unlike Charlie, hopping from one to the other once the lights were out. As Caesar's wife, she represented the same sort of upgrade as his new television home, an A-frame pseudo ski chalet of the sort oppressed apartment dwellers supposedly coveted, only to discover how much they missed the old neighborhood once they moved in. Freed from Liebman's hang-ups, the new show could have become at least nominally "more Jewish" than *Your Show of Shows*, but Fabray nudged it further in the other direction.

Fabray got off to a bad start with Tolkin after telling one reporter that "nine-tenths" of *Caesar's Hour* was improvised; his chewing out made her vomit. But she quickly silenced some of the pleas for a second coming of Coca. Even some erstwhile Coca loyalists were won over, guilty though they felt for thinking it. To Joseph Purcell of the *Boston Record*, Fabray was "the tiny capsule of Benzedrine which sent *Caesar's Hour* aloft." *Variety* had its own word for her: "peacherino." Mary Tyler Moore, Carol Burnett, and Gilda Radner all in time acknowledged their debt to her. By the summer of 1955, when Coca said the split was a mistake for both her and Caesar, her comment was met with "royal indifference" in Caesar's camp.

Publicists for *Caesar's Hour* tried to milk the suburbanite theme, arranging in May 1955 for the New Haven Railroad to bring a trainload of commuters from Connecticut and Rhode Island—actually, most of those they rounded up were women married to them—to New York for the show. (Two bar cars assured the program one of its most receptive audiences ever.) Morris liked the Commuter sketches because viewers could see him as himself, rather than disguised as some bratty kid or bearded geezer. Brooks liked them because they made his work sparkle by comparison. But eventually these sorry segments were completely and quite rightly forgotten, except as a source of ridicule.

Thanks largely to Earl Wild, the concert pianist Caesar had brought in to bulk up the classical offerings (and, often, to squeeze laughs out of them), music became a bright spot on the new show. There was an ingenious pantomime of a domestic quarrel between Caesar and Fabray, set to the first movement of Beethoven's Fifth Symphony. By suggesting that arias be replaced with popular songs—singing something in fake Italian to the tune of "I've Been Working on the Railroad" was not only funnier but easier than performing a Puccini original—Wild inspired a spate of sophisticated opera spoofs. He also became Caesar's surrogate shrink. Off camera, when stressed or depressed, Caesar would have him play something—Rachmaninoff, Chopin, Debussy, Ravel—and felt better, and grateful, for it. "Sid wasn't gay, but he had a thing for me," said Wild, who *was* gay. "He used to kiss me right on the mouth. And hold it there. And I used to be so embarrassed in front of these people because it led to great jealousy. One night at a party he did that in front of his wife and I thought I'd die."

The show took another musical turn in April 1955, when Caesar, Reiner, and Morris debuted as the Three Haircuts, their version of one of the pomaded pop trios then in vogue. Despite their hokey getups, gravity-defying pompadours, moronic songs, and numbing repetitiveness—*Variety* called them "unfunny after the first chorus"—they were, quite literally, a hit: A recording of one of their songs ("You Are So Rare to Me") sold a hundred thousand copies. The segments were also blessedly easy: maybe five minutes to write the music and ten minutes to rehearse.

Reports had Sid either taking an additional floor in the Milgrim Building or buying it outright. If, as the comedian Jerry Lester said, Caesar was "a nervous wreck at the age of 32," maybe the *shvitz* he was said to be installing in the place would calm him down. Caesar also bought his first house, one fit for a sub-urbanized superstar, in the Kings Point section of Great Neck, on Long Island. It cost $90,000, had sixteen (or eighteen) rooms, sat on three acres, and took seventy men two months to alter to his specifications. Staking his claim, on the day they'd moved in—July 1, 1955—Caesar planted a sapling on the property. "I hope to live to watch it become a shade tree, under which we can see our grandchildren cavorting," he explained. It was an apt sentiment for the "Television Father of the Year," which was what the National Father's Day Committee crowned Caesar during his closing show that June, pinning a medal featuring George Washington on his jacket. Caesar shuffled, sweated, and gulped as he accepted the honor. "Ah, if you talk to my children, I don't think they'd say I deserve it," he said with a nervous laugh.

The press described Caesar's new manse—Walter Winchell called it a "Study in Succe$$"—even more minutely than it had his new office, pondering how it reflected, and affected, his psyche. To the *New York Post*, then the great chronicler of American Jewish upward mobility (it ran separate "His" and "Her" profiles of Mr. and Mrs. Sid Caesar), the place was "a discreet realization of a Hollywood fantasy." In *Holiday*, Alfred Bester called it "a magnificent show place decorated in gold, ebony and white, with Empire, Chinese and modern furniture, a fine collection of modern paintings, a kidney-shaped swimming pool, a mini-golf course, a small yacht, a full-sized pool table, enough rifles to arm a *Panzer* division, a juke box, a soda fountain, a projection room and wall-to-wall air conditioning."

The house included floor-to-ceiling windows in the living room, offering sweeping views of Manhasset Bay; seven televisions, including one with a primitive remote control (the wire ran under the carpet), and another on which you could watch *The Wizard of Oz* or *Peter Pan* in living color; a pagoda for Caesar's skeet shooting; a kiddie-sized pool table for young Ricky; and an instant, imported lawn. Also on the premises was a ten-kilowatt generator, a two-hundred-pound Great Dane named Julius, a maid, cook, nurse, and butler, and a gardener named Eddie Wisz, a deaf man with whom Sid, between the sign language he'd picked up (enhanced by his own inventive gestures) and his empathy for the speechless, claimed to have conversations more satisfying than many of those he had with hearing people. Wisz strengthened the kinship Caesar already felt with the deaf, who appreciated Caesar's pantomimes, along with the sign language he'd sometimes insert into sketches to highlight gags they'd otherwise have missed. Watching Caesar, the wife of one deaf man wrote to Jack O'Brian, "my husband is the happiest man alive." A sculpted pair of hands making the sign for "help"—a gift from the Pennsylvania Society for the Advancement of the Deaf—had a cherished place near Caesar's desk.

The veteran journalist Richard Gehman wrote of "a kind of baronial air about Caesar," an "aura of awe" that even Florence

Caesar honored. ("Shh," she cautioned one visitor. "Sid is watching television.") Arriving there one night, the young Kenneth Turan, later film critic of the *Los Angeles Times,* recalled feeling "like I was entering the palace of a Jewish king." "See that building over there?" Caesar asked one visitor as they gazed across the bay. "That's the yacht club. Then comes the Vanderbilt estate. And the Morgans and the Whitneys. Very nice neighbors around here!" "Sid often sits on his front lawn peering through binoculars at Long Island Sound, muttering resentfully when a boat larger than his own appears," *Redbook* noted. Competitive though he was, he also felt contentment. Reiner recalled how, floating on his back in Caesar's pool one day, he'd heard his boss, a man never known for his eloquence, come out with four words that perfectly encapsulated how far he thought he'd come. "Eh?" he'd asked his company as he surveyed the scene. "Isn't this better?"

In what was no doubt a ghostwritten paean to suburbia, Caesar said he felt closer to the folks down the road than he ever had to the people across the hall on Park Avenue, and described how his daily ride into Manhattan gave him time to relax, dream, and create. "If any of you like the show more now than you did last year, you can blame it on my new house," he wrote during *Caesar's Hour*'s second season. But one of Ricky Caesar's pals remembered a different domestic Caesar—the one who, when he wasn't entertaining guests, lurked in the background, "tempestuous, mercurial, capricious." "He basically had two speeds: 'coma' and 'frenzy,'" the friend remembered, "and was always in a borderline rage."

Wide-eyed journalists savored every snippet about Caesar's lush life. They noted how pretty much everything he wore was monogrammed and how his closets bulged with handmade suits. They observed that his Havana cigars, said to be Churchill's favorites, were "the approximate size of a Louisville Slugger." "He pulled up in a limousine at least seven feet longer than Milton Berle's the other night," Dorothy Kilgallen wrote, "stepped out with a cigar that made Berle's stock model look like a cigarette, and surveyed the passing throngs as if he were an Emperor on his way to the baths."

A gold chain hung from one of his belt loops, holding a solid-gold Dunhill lighter and cigar clipper. His cuff links were "big, knobby-looking pieces" that "average an inch across, weigh up to a quarter of a pound and are studded with multicolored stones." (One set featured images of the "other" Caesar.) "Not even Jackie Gleason is more resplendent," one reporter wrote. The truck driver who'd stumbled over Caesar's $4,000 diamond and blue star sapphire pinkie ring in the gutter outside the Milgrim Building hadn't turned it in right away, because, he explained, it "was so big he thought it must be worthless." Tiffany, Caesar later said, had become his candy store: He could go in, pick out whatever he damn well pleased, and then just walk out with it—no questions asked, no signatures, no nothing. He'd become the macher he'd once have ridiculed. One story had him ordering a flunky to unwrap the stick of gum he was to chew in a sketch to wash off the sugar coating before he deigned to use it.

While the Sid Caesar *TV Guide* saw in early 1955 could be endearing, he could also be cruel. "Go ahead, eat the cake," he'd tell Florence. "You really need those 600 calories. They'll look good on your hips." As for his drinking, the press either was clueless or covered for him. "In liquids, his tastes run to chocolate milk and celery tonic," the *Daily News* declared. Don Ross of the *Herald Tribune* insisted the bar in Caesar's office was strictly for visitors. "Mr. Caesar is an abstentious man himself, but some of his guests are not," he explained. People described his pill popping and guzzling as washing down fistfuls of vitamins with gallons of ginger ale.

With the loss of Brooks, the late arrival of a female lead, a persistently subpar collection of writers, his peculiar fixation on boring suburbanites, a surprising timidity, and a tendency to strut and preen, the first season had been a rocky debut for the liberated Caesar. "I had to be the big shot, making big decisions, trying to act the role of big producer," he explained. "I was up here in the office waiting for the writers to bring in a script instead of being down there working with them." Later, studying the first batch of kinescopes of the new show, he winced. "The critics were right," he said. "I was playing too much in a high key, forgetting about the little subtleties." But out of loyalty, wishful thinking, habit, and the lowly state of the competition, Caesar's fans had stuck with him.

IN THE FIRST EXTENDED sketch of *Caesar's Hour*'s second season—it was called "Bullets over Broadway," a title he later bequeathed to Woody Allen—Caesar is a tough-talking, cigar-chomping mob boss named Moose who moves around with his entourage, as Caesar did with his, in a pack. He's smitten with Moxie Hart, the cigarette girl at a local speakeasy (Fabray). "Cigars . . . cigarettes . . . bullets," she chants seductively. No one spurns Moose, but *she* does. He's "uncouth," she tells him.

"What's that, 'uncouth'?" Moose asks his most proximate henchman, played by Morris.

"Uncouth, boss?" he replies. "That means you ain't got no couth."

"So I ran short on couth! What's that? I can fix that!" Moose reaches into his jacket and hands Morris a wad of bills. "Look. You go right out in town and you buy every drop of couth there is. Every drop of couth in town! Take the truck!"

"But, boss! You don't get couth like that! That ain't the way it comes! You gotta go to a school and loin it."

"All right! I'll loin it. We'll go to the biggest college, and I'll get the biggest couth teacher there is!" That turns out to be the bookish Bernard Cyrano (Reiner), who schools Moose in Napoleonic history and Shakespeare's sonnets. The trouble is, Moxie falls for Cyrano. Though riddled with lead following a shoot-out with a rival, the dying Moose blesses the two. As did *Variety:* "With the preem as criterion, Caesar is feeding on Grade-A meat."

Suddenly things began to gel. Caesar was in top form. The cast had solidified. And backing it now, for the first time, were the writers Caesar deserved, and needed—just as Liebman had recognized a decade earlier. The most important addition was Larry Gelbart, a comic prodigy; while still in high school, he'd written jokes for Danny Thomas, then worked for Red Buttons and Bob Hope. Many people, Caesar among them, considered him the

most gifted of all of his writers, able to produce lapidary lines in
an instant. Born in Chicago and raised in Los Angeles, Gelbart
had a surface ease and tranquility that his more conspicuously
neurotic New York counterparts lacked. As Gelbart himself put
it, he was the most Gentile of Caesar's Jews.

During Gelbart's first couple of weeks on the job, Caesar
barely acknowledged him. But one night, as the two stood by
Caesar's limo outside Danny's Hide-A-Way, the midtown celebrity steak joint where Caesar had his after-parties, Caesar put
his arms around him, told him he was too young to be smashed,
then bent over him as John Gilbert had bent over Greta Garbo
in *Flesh and the Devil* and kissed him on the lips. He soon won
the dubious honor of going over last-minute tweaks with Caesar
while everyone else—Gelbart called them his "eight comradely
cowards"—looked on.

Also joining the team was Selma Diamond, the raucous successor to Lucille Kallen as spokesperson for the "women's point
of view"; Gary Belkin, who later wrote for Carol Burnett (and
did some of Muhammad Ali's lesser doggerel); and Mike Stewart
(born Myron Stuart Rubin, and briefly "Stuart Robinson"), who
assumed Kallen's role as scribe, along with organizer and filterer
of material. Stewart, who'd go on to write the books to *Bye Bye
Birdie* and *Hello, Dolly!*, was unusually pedigreed for Caesar: He
had earned a master's degree in fine arts from Yale. "We had a
lot of writers, but only one or two could actually spell or write,"
said Reiner. Stewart "didn't come up with a lot of jokes, but knew
what the good ones were." Morris described his duties more colloquially. "Whatever the shit was going on, somehow he typed
it," he said.

But the most significant development was the repatriation
of Mel Brooks. As frustrated with Caesar as he'd become, he'd
been desperate to rejoin him—discovering, he later said, "that I
couldn't produce without the Pavlovian stimuli of *Your Show of
Shows:* noise and cigar smoke." For a time he'd been too proud,
or scared, to ask, and hadn't until his wife pressed him. "I said,
'Sid loves you—he'll take you back, I promise,'" she recalled.
"He gave me the phone number and when it rang I handed Mel

the phone." "Sid, I want to come back," Brooks then told Caesar. And "Sid said, 'Ten o'clock Monday,'" Baum recalled, "and they both hung up. It was the shortest telephone conversation I ever heard."

Universally ignored, by Semites, philo-Semites, and anti-Semites alike, was a cultural milestone of sorts: All seven of Caesar's writers were Jews. "A pastiche of Jewish minds mashed together" was how Brooks described this writers' room. "A roomful of screaming Jews," Morris called them.* The revamped show would still have more misses than hits, partly because, as Jack Gould noted, Caesar remained "addicted" to those woeful Commuters. But with the brilliant new team in place, promising premises not only popped up far more often but could be massaged into greatness.

Shortly into the new season, Caesar and Fabray moonlighted in *1976*, a pet one-off of Pat Weaver's depicting American life twenty years hence. It had Caesar commuting to Saipan (a twenty-minute trip by rocket) and thirteen hundred push buttons lightening Fabray's housework. The host, Dave Garroway, pledged that at the nation's bicentennial in twenty-one years NBC would check how those predictions panned out. But the very next night, the newly improved *Caesar's Hour* featured a sketch that would be remembered long past 1976.

It came in a send-up—by the "Caesaro Opera Company"—of Leoncavallo's *Pagliacci*, the classic one-act Italian opera about a cuckolded clown. "Gallipacci," as the sketch was called, had all the sophistication that Earl Wild had brought to the show's classical music numbers, but what immortalized it was something entirely unscripted, or at least it looked that way.

Things begin with a festive chorus singing out a welcome—to the tune of "Santa Claus Is Coming to Town." Gallipacci (Caesar) then pokes his grease-painted face through the curtains and, in musical double-talk, describes the show to come. He introduces

---

* It was also the first and only collection of comedy writers to take a mail-order course, the Great Books of the Western World, a Tolkin initiative in all likelihood that helped make up for the college education most of them had never had.

his wife and co-star, Rosa (Fabray), and declares his great love for her. But it turns out she's entangled with another member of the troupe, the dashing Emilio (Reiner). They sing of *their* great love (to "Take Me Out to the Ball Game"), then embrace. Gallipacci's pal Vesuvio (Morris) spots the couple in flagrante and informs Gallipacci that Rosa and Emilio are "making a deal-eo." The heartbroken Gallipacci repairs to his dressing room, and as he croons mournfully in operatic gibberish, he starts to draw a tear by his right eye, only to have the tip of his pencil break. More attentive audience members laughed: It looks planned. In the greenroom, Caesar's writers looked on, petrified, wondering what he was going to do next. As Caesar later explained it,

> The pencil broke. Now I got to keep it going and I see some paint with a brush so I dip it in. I had already made a mark so I continue the mark and I make another and another, I went this way, then this way, then this way, then this way. I played Tic-tac-toe on my face. And that was just from nothing. I always ad-libbed but this is the best I ever done.

"That was a spark," Caesar said on another occasion. "It happens."

That Caesar was poised enough not just to surmount the slipup but to fashion an elaborate joke, one requiring physical and even optical dexterity (doing it in a mirror, with everything backward), was remarkable enough. Even more amazing, as Caesar marks his face with *X*s and *O*s, is that he's singing bilingually, mixing Italian double-talk and New York vaudeville, concluding each verse staring into the camera and crooning, "Just one of those things." (According to Caesar, Cole Porter, who'd written the original, had given him carte blanche to use any of his songs.) What Caesar pulled off that night, Brooks said, moved him to tears. The memory of it, said Gelbart, he'd take with him "to the grave."

Afterward, at Danny's, Caesar felt someone's gentle hand on his shoulder—Marilyn Monroe's. "I just came over to congratulate you," she told him. "I never saw anything like that. When you started to play tic-tac-toe on your face, I screamed. I almost wet my pants." The public appreciation came later. Long afterward, Brooks and Tolkin hinted that Caesar's feat that night wasn't all improvisation. "There was some previous work done on it," Brooks remembered. "It's hard to believe that he didn't think of it before," Tolkin allowed in one hemming-and-hawing interview. "That's just an opinion. I couldn't say." Of course he, more than anyone else, could have.

That same month, dressed in tails and sitting before an imaginary keyboard, Caesar pantomimed a rookie pianist performing Grieg's Piano Concerto on a phantom piano. He hams it up, hits some wrong keys (or misses all eighty-eight of them), and plays with the backs of his hands, all while Wild, monitoring him from backstage, hit the actual notes, true and false. It was some feat, not just because the two were perfectly synchronized, but because it showed how intimately Caesar knew the piece. He'd even gone over the fingering with Wild beforehand, so his hands weren't just moving willy-nilly.

Caesar's cool was tested again in late November, when, near the end of a show, a seventy-five-pound pipe fell on Fabray's head backstage. The television audience in New York could hear her scream; as Caesar went out to do the night's closing sketch, he was told Fabray had been killed. Performing under such circumstances, he said, was the toughest thing he'd ever done on a stage. The accident was front-page news; NBC hired four extra operators to handle all the calls about Fabray, including a hundred from women claiming to be her mother. (One actually was.) In her week in the hospital, Fabray received ten thousand letters.

On the day after Christmas 1955 came one of the grandest and most ambitious of Caesar's film sketches. "Aggravation Boulevard" depicted the travails of a silent film star named Rex Handsome (Caesar), modeled after John Gilbert, whose career had been upended by the talkies. The piece was long, running over twenty-five minutes, and of a different order of ambition and complexity than anything ever on *Your Show of Shows; Caesar's Hour* had been created, among other reasons, for such efforts.

The idea was Belkin's, coming during what he called a rare microsecond of silence in the writers' room. Before proceeding, Caesar later remembered, he got permission from Clara Bow, a leading silent film star who'd been close to Gilbert.

For fifteen years, Handsome has been one of Hollywood's biggest stars. When he'd married the beautiful Mara Bara (Fabray), fifty thousand women had gone on a hunger strike. His daily arrivals at the Vita-Cash Studio, beginning when the front part of his limousine passed through the gate (and ending a few minutes later when the rest of it did), were much-anticipated events. They're mid-shoot on a film called "The Sheik of Oxford" when someone rushes in with the day's *Variety*. "Movies Talk," it declares.

Handsome's director, the elegant (and, inevitably, faintly British) Flo Florenz (Reiner), is thrilled. "We'll hear the sound of hoof beats!" he exults. "We'll hear cannon roar! We'll hear birds singing! Rex! My boy! Rex! Do you realize what talking movies will mean for you?" "At last!" Handsome shouts in a high-pitched, grating, shrill, effeminate squawk. "The world will hear Rex Handsome talk! And talk. And talk and talk and talk and talk and talk and talk." And when it does, he is laughed off the screen. The calls from the studio stop coming. "Sir, you've been sitting by this telephone for four years," Handsome's loyal valet (Morris) pleads. "At least have a little something to eat." He's given another chance, but his squawk is still there. A disconsolate Handsome walks out into the rain and promptly catches a cold, one that lowers his voice back to the mellifluous baritone it had been. Once more he is a star—so long as he's doused with ice water before every shoot. Like much of Caesar's best work, it's both funny and poignant. One writer accused him of heartlessness: Some of Hollywood's silent stars were still around. But to Hedda Hopper it was "one of Sid's greatest."

As 1956 got under way, Caesar was quite literally flying high, commuting to Manhattan daily by helicopter. "Sid Caesar is the only comic who becomes funnier and funnier," *Look* magazine wrote that March. The sportswriter Jimmy Cannon facetiously blamed him for the recent demise of baseball's Piedmont League.

"Are you going to pay money to see Class B baseball when you can get Caesar and Nanette Fabray for nothing?" he asked. Some, though, couldn't stand Caesar's success, suggesting it wasn't even his doing. "Sid Caesar's 10 writers are in a hilarious groove," Jack O'Brian wrote.

Caesar's comedian pal Jan Murray was now hosting a game show, while Jackie Gleason was doing a sitcom, *The Honeymooners* having become a half-hour show in October. But despite the perils of live sketch comedy, including high costs, acts of God (floods in Connecticut forced the scuttling of a spoof of *Singin' in the Rain*), and the toll it was taking on him, Caesar was sticking with it.

By now, there'd been enough of *Caesar's Hour* to stack it up against *Your Show of Shows*. Caesar's viewers, and even his writers and co-stars, disagreed on which was better. To Brooks, *Your Show of Shows* had a freshness and authenticity, an edge and fizz, that *Caesar's Hour* lacked, reflecting both the charming anarchy of early television and the creative abandon of young minds unencumbered by traditions and expectations, children and mortgages. And Caesar, too, had changed. "At the beginning there was nobody funnier than Sid, naturally funny," Brooks said. But repetition, exhaustion, and the higher expectations he now faced had sapped him of some of his initial enthusiasm. Caesar "didn't have the appetite of doing the shows like when he was a kid," Brooks said. "It became a very big, tough job instead of a thrill. The electricity was gone." For the audience, too, Brooks ventured: All that much-derided "screaming" and "jumping" on *Your Show of Shows* had given everyone a break from Caesar, making his every appearance a treat; "everyone was happy when Sid got on," he said. On *Caesar's Hour*, on the other hand, there was too much uninterrupted time with him.

Reiner preferred *Caesar's Hour*. So, too, strictly as a fan, did Woody Allen. To him, the humor on *Your Show of Shows*—the Professor, for instance, and even Uncle Goopy—was "too broad." But with *Caesar's Hour*, Caesar "just sort of blossomed," largely because the writing was so much more sophisticated. Morris seemed to favor the second, too. So did Caesar, unsurprisingly:

After all, his name was on it. But to his great irritation, in the court of historic memory, *Caesar's Hour* always got short shrift—that is, when it didn't vanish altogether into what effectively became the glorious eight-year-long run of *Your Show of Shows.*

Connoisseurs of comedy in the mid-1950s appreciated Caesar all the more as the competition plummeted, something Jack Gould noted with rare asperity in January 1956. "All too often, comedy on television sinks to the level of a prefabricated commodity intended only for the toothless moron who sits transfixed in front of the hypnotic watching box," he wrote. "Bright kids and educated people"—that was how Pauline Kael of *The New Yorker* described Caesar's constituency. Gelbart compared its viewers to a cult. For them, and for Caesar, he and his colleagues could paint on a blank canvas. As Gelbart said,

> There were no footprints in the snow. When we did something, we could be pretty sure that no one else had done it yet. And we were able to be urbane. We were able to be very smart. We were able to be very hip. And a lot of the people connected to that show were different [from] the original writers in radio and television. This was probably the first generation of writer[s] ever to be psychoanalyzed. They knew about themselves. They knew about their families. They knew more about their wives. They knew more about relationships than anybody had ever brought before to the art of television comedy. When I say "urbane," between us we read every book. Between us we saw every movie. Between us we saw every play on Broadway. You could make jokes about Kafka or Tennessee Williams. Nobody said, "Let's dumb this down" or "Who the hell is that?" We always felt if we said something that was a little esoteric, well, "what's wrong with going to the dictionary and looking the word up?"

"It went beyond street smarts," he said. "We zeroed in on the rough spots in life—there's no fun in happiness. Bliss is boring. Fortunately, none of us had that in abundance."

The show's braininess, along with its zaniness, explained the call Caesar got one day in April 1955, when someone interrupted a rehearsal to tell him that Albert Einstein's office was on the phone. "I looked at my writers and I said, 'Now you're making jokes? We got two days to finish the show. What the hell's the matter with you?'" But Einstein's secretary, Helen Dukas, *was* on the line, inviting Caesar to come see the great man in Princeton. Caesar quickly agreed—it would have been like talking to Copernicus, he said—but Einstein died before it could come to pass. The story sounded apocryphal. But a reporter interviewing Caesar in 1959 recalled Caesar pulling out and showing her a piece of paper, "worn and often handled," memorializing Einstein's call. A year or two after receiving it, Caesar said, he ran into J. Robert Oppenheimer, who explained to him why Einstein had sought him out: Einstein had "figured out the physical equation," but wanted Caesar to tell him about "the human equation."[*]

Caesar had been in far better shape—more robust and energetic, more confident and facile—in the earlier going. Over time, wild fluctuations in his weight became less a matter of aesthetics than a barometer of his well-being. In his newer, trimmer state, he looked and sounded more fragile and frazzled. It wasn't a constant thing: From week to week, his performances, and even his appearance, varied. But the trend line was clearly downward. Early on, Caesar fought to keep his talent under control; he held plenty in reserve. Now, increasingly, he was giving it everything he had, and still fell short. At the start, he elevated whatever his writers gave him. Now, when the material was better than ever, he wasn't always up to it.

Caesar hired the veteran comedian Milt Kamen to be his stand-in during rehearsals, helping him save his energy for the main event. Kamen also allowed him to step back and fine-tune the show—for instance, the camerawork. "Comedy is very hard to shoot, unless you really know it," Caesar explained. "Comedy is not with the man who says the line; most of the time it's [in]

---

[*] In other interviews, Caesar said it was Oppenheimer who posed the question on his own behalf.

the reaction." So while Kamen played Caesar, Caesar did some directing. "I'd say, 'No, no, no, no. Here's the shot,'" he said. "'The laugh is over here.'"

Only in *Caesar's Hour*'s sophomore season, with the full complement of writers in place, was the writers' room of lore complete. Its weekly rhythms were basically the same as on *Your Show of Shows*, but with more skilled hands on deck and Max no longer around, everything was intensified. "*Your Show of Shows* was a little more reasonable, more right, less *mishugas*, less craziness," said Tolkin, now presiding over a far more rambunctious crew. "We were a family, you were our father and Tolkin was our mother," Neil Simon, who soon rejoined the group, later wrote to Caesar. Tolkin "kept the house clean, made sure we did our homework, and that our hands were clean when we sat down to dinner." At least that was how it was supposed to be. In fact, said Simon, "the kids took over."

The room, unofficially called "the cell," was one flight down from Caesar's office. One entered it through two swinging doors; the place could be divided in two, but with seven writers, four performers, and one brother (Dave Caesar) usually inhabiting it, it rarely was. Chairs and sofas were arranged, horseshoe-style, around two desks. Simon likened it to Jewish Indians on a bluff, surrounding a wagon train. Because Caesar stuck (literally, from his sweat) to leather or Naugahyde, one Christmas, Gelbart had bought him a gold upholstered chair, which, appropriately enough, resembled a throne.

Every day, it started out neat. "Each morning the playroom is brushed and garnished," one of the few reporters to penetrate the place, Alfred Bester of *Holiday*, wrote. "By six o'clock at night it's a pigsty of coffee containers, bent paper clips, cigar butts, pieces of pastrami, the corpses of jokes, and snowdrifts of torn papers." One time, Tolkin claimed, he counted forty-one pencils, thrown up in frustration, that hung like stalactites from the acoustical panels in the ceiling.

While Gleason's writers subsisted on Maalox, "we were on some kind of high between coffee and cigarettes," said Gelbart, who at one time smoked four packs a day. But there was also lots to eat. Along with playing bit parts in various sketches, Dave Caesar did some catering; he'd lay out spreads of delicatessen and Danish, along with boxes of Mars, Hershey's, and Oh Henry! bars, stacked vertically, just as in New York's corner candy stores. One time, after eating some exotic bread Dave had brought in, Gelbart declared, "I think we just ate the Dead Sea Scrolls." Another time, Dave handed someone a slice of Swiss cheese. "My card," he declared. Brooks, still referred to around the room (if nowhere else) by his original name, Kaminsky, preferred to refuel on chocolate bars or bagels. The lumbering, genial Dave also served as the comedic Everyman, arbiter of proposed jokes (whenever someone threw out a line, all eyes would turn to him for a reaction), and his kid brother's favorite whipping boy. "Sid would say, 'Dave, I'm going to take the brother away from you, you're not going to be brother any more if you keep bugging me,'" Morris recalled. "It was so fucking mean."

Other comics avoided their writers. Gleason, Neil Simon once said, was an "abusive, unappreciative shit." By contrast, when the writers were in Caesar's writers' room, Caesar left it only rarely, principally to eat. His entrances were grand. "Suddenly the double doors would *fly open*," Aaron Ruben remembered, "and he'd stand there with his broad shoulders, and these coats that he'd patterned after something that George Raft must have worn in a gangster movie,[*] and a hat right in the middle of his head, and a cigar, clamped." He'd then stand there, expectantly, warily, as if he knew everyone in the room was robbing him blind. And then, Morris recalled, "a hand would reach out and give him an Alka-Seltzer. Bubbling still."

When humid weather flattened creases, Caesar would take off his pants, send them off to be pressed, and work in a raincoat and underwear. Anything awry anywhere annoyed him; before Caesar got there, Ruben would deliberately throw a slat in the

---

[*] Caesar once earned a place among the "Ten Worst-Dressed Men in Television." He also favored footwear in oddball styles he could slip into because he hated tying laces. "Another pair from the Weirdo Shoe Company," Brooks would say upon beholding his latest selection (Sheldon Keller interview, Jan. 10, 2000, John and Susan Edwards Harvith Interview Collection, Syracuse University).

venetian blinds out of whack, just to watch him spot it, ponder it, then get up and fix it. Caesar would shoot the breeze briefly, then light a cigar—his signal it was time to work, and that it was okay for everyone else to light up, too, which, of course, everyone else did, giving the room the air of London during the Great Smog a few years earlier. "You don't see who you're talking to, you just follow the sound," Selma Diamond said. "Everybody goofin' off again, eh? All right, let's hear the brilliance," Caesar might say. Everyone would then talk at once.

"He functions on two extreme levels," Bester wrote of Caesar at the time—before everything got mythologized. "Either he's quiet, subdued, patient; or he's galvanized into frenetic action. He will sit for half an hour murmuring, hardly moving; then a word or a gesture will electrify him and he'll be on his feet, improvising action and dialogue, developing the idea." Brooks's Caesar was more violent, lifting and dropping the corner of his metal desk to punctuate his unhappiness with a given gag. "Sid, we're not married to it," Tolkin might murmur. "There'll be another."

Caesar generally kept his anger in check. "Sid was very quiet when he would lose his temper," Fabray recalled. "He would say 'excuse me' and walk over and put his fist through a wall or a door." "Sid sarcasted you to death," Simon said. But there were periodic eruptions. The writers "came to accept his explosiveness as Neapolitans accept Vesuvius," one writer noted.

Soon the ideas would be flying, with everyone but Brooks (who favored long comic riffs) spewing them out. As each was pitched, Mike Stewart would glance at Caesar; if he nodded, Stewart would write it down. When Paddy Chayefsky sat in once, he marveled how a plot point he'd have agonized over for two weeks was resolved in a couple of minutes. When Caesar liked the state of things, he would wet a finger and flick an imaginary piece of dust off his shoe: That meant—to everyone's immense relief—he felt good enough about things to leave.

Harry Harris of *The Philadelphia Inquirer* got to see one show in utero. As Caesar munched on dried apricots, various ideas—on Lindbergh's flight, or the novel *Arrowsmith*, or Alexander the Great—were bruited about. "Let's do a take-off on 'Mr. Wonderful': 'Mr. Mediocre,'" someone suggested. Out of the smoke, a premise eventually emerged: a bank heist master-minded by an intellectual, though by the time the sketch aired, all that survived of that premise was the bank robber's name, Harry Mozart ("Thanks to me, the name of Mozart will go down in history," he declares), who twists the law enough to rob a bank legally. "The discarded idea was much funnier," Harris wrote a few days later. Disagreeing with Caesar was hard because, as Joe Stein explained, "you can't argue with 'Naaah,'" and because, deep down, you knew he was right. "I think all of us got to feel that way," said Stein. "No matter how wonderful it sounded, he would not do something he would not believe in or could not make his own. I cannot hear Sid say, 'If all you guys think it's wonderful, I'll try it.'"

For all the time he spent with them, Caesar was as maladroit with his writers as he was with everyone else. "I never realized these guys were working for a living," he said many years later. "I didn't realize that they had children and wives. I never went into thinking about human things." "Aside from his brilliance as a comedian, as a person I'd have nothing to do with him," said Stein. One morning Simon suddenly realized to his horror that he was all alone with Caesar. For the next twelve minutes, they said nothing to each other. "After that," Simon later wrote to Caesar, "I would peek in the office and if you were there alone, I would rush off to the bathroom and pee."

Caesar's writers' room has been caramelized into a madcap but fundamentally congenial place, populated by cute, book-ish, wisecracking young men in schlumpy sports jackets or the sleeveless sweaters, brush cuts, and black-rimmed glasses that, at least in Hollywood, betokened the earnestness and innocence of Jews in the 1950s. And no doubt there was an ebullience that came with being young, witty, and working together for the most original and talented television comic there was. Even at the time, Alfred Bester wrote that Caesar's show was "produced with the abandon of a bunch of bright kids playing with unlimited amounts of money." But Bester also captured the other, darker side of things. "They play interminably . . . word games, spelling games, anagrams, cross-word puzzles, guessing games," he wrote. "The games are played angrily and rudely. For the writers, cut off from the world and living too incestuously together, hate each other like blood relations."

"Inevitably, the writers clashed as they competed for Caesar's attention," stated an account by Richard Gehman in *TV Guide* from a few years later, when the Caesar show was history but not yet revisionist history. "Loud arguments, laced with profanity, were common. Savage feuds developed," Gehman wrote. "Anger, bitterness, and tension lingered among the writers long after the show went off the air. Two once met in the street; the first knew the second hated him, and tried to make a gesture of atonement. 'Why don't you and your wife come for dinner some night?' he said. 'We can't—we don't eat anymore,' said the second coldly."

"This isn't a job, it's one great big dirty tenement family," Tolkin remembered. "You had fourteen Jews yelling and screaming at one another all day long," Morris recalled. "And then you had to go home and be a father and a husband. It sometimes didn't work out at all." (Morris was married five times.)

"How did you do it for *six years*?" Selma Diamond asked Lucille Kallen after she'd been there six weeks. Before Caesar fired her—"I told him I didn't think certain things were funny," an anonymous writer, surely Diamond, recalled—her writing colleagues "butchered her," remembered Sheldon Keller, who was nearly as far down on the totem pole as she. "It was madness, the screaming and the yelling and calling each other babies and children," said Simon. "And there were the petty jealousies among the writers: who was getting more money, who was getting higher credit, who was invited to go on the European junket that Sid was taking." Traumatized over being wiped out repeatedly in mid-sentence by some kid with a better line, Tolkin took years to stop interrupting people in mid-thought.

And once they stopped worrying about one another, there was Caesar to consider: What was *he* thinking about them? Tony Webster grew convinced that whenever a joke of his bombed, Caesar would glare reproachfully at him through the screen. Caesar didn't forget the duds. A line Caesar had used only after

Brooks's browbeating—about a snake begging to be sprung from the snake house in a zoo because, he explained, "this place is full of snakes!"—became the paradigmatic flop joke; whenever Brooks would attempt another long shot, Caesar would ask, "You wanna do the snake joke again?" Asked at the time what working for Caesar was like, all the chatterboxes in the writers' room clammed up. "Their statements about him are a sycophantic combination of honest adulation and dishonest fear for their jobs," Gehman observed. Occasionally Keller would emit an unprovoked, all-purpose cri de coeur. "Just a little anxiety attack, folks," he'd explain. "You have to understand: we were all in there fighting for our lives," said Keller, only two years removed from the corset business himself.

But most tormented of them all—and more tormented than ever—was Mel Tolkin.

He might have been with Caesar the longest, and Caesar's best drinking buddy, but that was cold comfort: The sheer firepower of the group he nominally led only revived all his old insecurities. "He would tell Sid, 'This is gold, this will kill them,' and Sid would say, 'No, it wouldn't work,' and Mel would immediately turn around and say, 'I knew it wouldn't work,'" Stein recalled. "I would say, 'What the fuck is it with you, Mel? Haven't you got any spine at all?'" Tolkin was a beat slower than the room. To his credit, he was honest enough later to admit it. As others sentimentalized the place, he became its most candid, and most unpublished, chronicler. Had he written what he knew, it might have been a classic. But right to the end, he was too frightened to.

"After having felt in charge of my destiny working in a show I had a share in conceiving, I found myself in a high-voltage roomful of immensely talented, immensely ambitious kids," he wrote. "There was anger at oneself that one didn't come up with a line that someone else came up [with] and say. There was fear, that if you didn't get too many jokes accepted, you'd have a problem"—less one of losing your job than of "losing your position as a brilliant young man." And there was envy, of whoever happened to have the hottest hand. For a time—he wasn't sure how long, maybe for a few weeks—he simply shut up. "It was all creative anger, terrible competitiveness, trying to please Daddy," he recalled. "Sid of course was Daddy."

As for who was "Daddy's Pet," that, too, was no contest. "It's almost as though Caesar finds through Brooks an outlet for his own hostilities which he can't release," Bester wrote. "He feels that Brooks is a part of himself." Caesar grabbed Brooks's head at a party, too, not to covet it as he had Simon's, but to celebrate that it was already his. "Isn't he great?" he asked. "And I own him." Brooks was smart enough to let Caesar feel proprietary. "Caesar's one groupie," Joe Stein called him; the two, he said, had "a love-hate or sado-masochistic" relationship. Through sheer brazenness, loquaciousness, and longevity, Brooks came to dominate all historical accounts of the room. It's his exploits—leafing through *The Wall Street Journal* while the others worked; spontaneously belting out "All of Me" to break a collective case of writer's block; struggling to find, for a limerick he was writing, a word rhyming with "rocksucker"—everyone wanted to hear.

He was less amusing at the time. According to Earl Wild, Brooks was obnoxious enough to repel Fabray, Diamond, Chayefsky, and Wild himself: "Between hearing about his psychiatrist and the man who was handling his stock investments, it was so depressing I can't tell you." At regular intervals, Wild said, Brooks's antics sent Caesar fleeing to his penthouse; it fell to Wild to try to coax him back downstairs. Brooks insisted that it was his radical material, and not his personality, that sent Caesar running. "I was going to places in comedy that no one was going, so Sid was scared and confused," he explained. "He once said to me, 'Look, I know the stuff is good, I just don't understand it.'"

But in the end, working for Sid Caesar was worth all the angst. To Joe Stein it was "without question the best learning experience for a young comedy writer in the history of the world." "What he taught me in that turbulent and happy time I have never forgotten," Mike Stewart wrote afterward. "I hate that guy, but I got to hand it to him—he's a comic genius," said Selma Diamond. "We knew it was special, and we knew it with the kind of brashness that New York inspires and encourages," Gelbart said. "It was as though we all had a piece of a heavyweight champ," he said another time.

The admiration, Gelbart said, went both ways. "Sid was an appreciator," he said. "He didn't pull any, what I call 'star drek.'" But on the personal front, he and his colleagues always kept their distance, just as Caesar, by his very nature, kept his. "Sid did not drink until after 6:00," said Gelbart. "So we all used to try to get out of there about five minutes to." But with the exceptions of Reiner and Tolkin—who clung to Caesar, respectively, for as long as it was beneficial and for as long as he could—Caesar's associates bided their time. Each longed for, then looked for, something saner, less tied to Caesar's vicissitudes, as well as something they could call their own: "You were one of many," Gelbart recalled, "and nothing was yours." "Don't let any second banana kid you," Reiner told one reporter. "We'd all like our own show." Shortly into his stay, Gelbart was already writing what would become *A Funny Thing Happened on the Way to the Forum*. Or, as he later put it, "I was sort of building my raft to get out of Alcatraz."

CHAPTER 9

'S WUNNERFUL

C aesar's propman, Al Levy, had been a cook in the army, and a good thing, too, because, now that Caesar was master of his own universe, *Caesar's Hour* revolved around food even more than *Your Show of Shows*. Everyone else, the writers and actors, pitched in.

When a sketch called for hot dogs, it was Levy who manned the cart. But it was Caesar who'd shanghaied the cart off the streets of New York, then had it stocked not with *schweinerei* from midtown Manhattan but genuine all-beef kosher franks from the Lower East Side; on one occasion the crew went through four hundred of them. Show days featured a steady stream of eats. "I've seen tons of lobster Newburg consumed, acres of Chinese Sub Gum Wan Ton [*sic*], miles of spaghetti," an eyewitness related. The food was not just good but genuine: If the script called for Chinese or Italian, Chinese or Italian was what it was. Anything else would have been dishonest. And food was always accorded proper respect. Food was for eating, not throwing; no cream pies were ever hurled on *Caesar's Hour*. If the actors had to speak with their mouths full, so be it; they were used to it, and good at it, and it was more realistic, anyway. "We'd cater the sketch from the Stage Delicatessen or something," Brooks recalled, "and we'd all sit around and eat, during the sketch, after the sketch . . . we'd always order too much food and the production company would always pay for it, and we'd live like kings."

Caesar set the pace; Winchell reported his downing four steaks "at a time" at Al & Dick's. And whatever was on the menu tasted even better with Shellric Corporation (Caesar's company, named for his two children) picking up the tab. Caesar, Reiner, and Morris, along with the writers, had their lunches together, sometimes in the office and often out; the dancer Bambi Linn recalled the entourage—Caesar in the middle, enveloped by the others, "taking mincing little steps" down West Fifty-Sixth Street toward the Stage Deli.

Caesar's drinking intensified. At work, he'd drink quickly and furtively. Joe Stein was startled once to see him down nearly a bottle of gin before a show (and then go on to perform brilliantly). "I didn't think he was a drunk," he said. "I just thought he was a guy who drank a lot and it didn't affect him." Asked whether *he'd* known Caesar was an alcoholic, Reiner replied, "Oh, sure! Are you kidding? I went through nine years with him." When he came on as the show's announcer, Hugh Downs quickly discerned the differences between the wild Caesar drunk and the shy Caesar sober. "On rare occasions when I spoke to him in his dressing room, I would knock softly," Downs later wrote. "He would invite me in, jumping up and shaking my hand as if I were the king of Persia instead of just his announcer."

Even before the limousine ride home, Caesar got a head start upstairs. Decades later, Frank Milgrim, whose family owned the women's shop below, remembered all the cases of liquor going up to the penthouse. Milgrim, who'd been in Alcoholics Anonymous since the 1930s, said that "within ten seconds" of meeting Caesar, he'd pegged him as a drunk—"a quiet one, but a big one."

The aftermath of every show was its own boozy ritual, one that was intensifying. "His assault on the Chivas Regal was becoming more and more aggressive," Tolkin wrote. And, he noted, "the greater the applause, the larger the drink." Caesar "did not feel he deserved his audience's approval, did not trust the love offered him. If they loved him, why did he have to prove himself to them, week after week?" When, the show over, an exhausted Caesar returned to his dressing room, "he would have a tumbler waiting for him—a large glass, *totally* filled with Scotch—no ice cubes, no twists of anything," Gelbart recalled. It was, he said, Caesar's way of declaring, "This is for *me*. I did all this for *you*. Now this is for me." "And he would down that drink," Gelbart went on. "And there would be a sandwich waiting for him, but I mean *a sandwich:* there was a Sherpa on top." "He would eat that, wash it down with this slug—and then vomit," Gelbart continued. "He put out so much, he took so much in, he let go of so much. It was incredible—the expenditure of all sorts of energy." Caesar would then hop in his limousine (in which he'd have a couple more snorts) and head to Danny's Hide-A-Way to unwind.

Located on East Forty-Fifth Street, it was rightly called "the most inappropriately named place in town." It was where folks like Robert Mitchum, Jane Russell, and Barbara Stanwyck liked to go, where Ava Gardner ate during New York layovers, where Mickey Mantle, Yogi Berra, Whitey Ford, and Hank Bauer celebrated Billy Martin's twenty-ninth birthday before their famous fracas at the Copacabana, where Joe DiMaggio liked the manicotti. The Caesar party always assembled around an oval table in a private room upstairs, groaning under the noshes until the main courses came. A lobster awaited Caesar, and maybe a "crisscross" dinner: layers of prime rib and sirloin piled atop each other. "Bacchanalian" was the word for it, though minus the sex. "From where all of us came from, the whole thing was one vast miracle," Edith Tolkin later remembered. "Basically, we couldn't believe our good fortune. Sid was on top of the world, and we were being carried along." Groupies came by, too. "Manhattanites are learning where to ogle Sid Caesar," one gossip column noted.

Newspaper people like Ed Sullivan were there, too, and celebrities like Sammy Davis Jr., stretching his legs to reach the floor to stomp wildly whenever someone said something funny. Fellow comics basked in Caesar's blinding glow. Marilyn Monroe danced once to his saxophone. An unwitting Jacqueline Susann flashed an indigo grin after blueberry pie. Sometimes Caesar and his pals improvised sketches. "Sid would assume a role," Steve

Allen's head writer, Leonard Stern, recalled. "He would decide who he was on that given evening, or what he was." Once, Caesar spontaneously ordained himself a rabbi who'd been sent to Alaska to kosherize blubber, and the others became his disciples. When offering stock tips or discoursing on current events, he became the Professor. For stretches of time (estimates later ranged from a week to a year), he became a Polish janitor, in casual conversations and even when ordering his meals. "Tolkin would say, 'Bring him a steak, baked potato,' and Sid would nod, '*Dobja. Dobja,*'" Brooks recalled.

When, coming in from Great Neck, Florence Caesar arrived at Danny's, she'd be aghast at how far gone her husband already was. "My heart would be in my mouth," she recalled. "I never could relax and have fun." "Stolichnaya was his drink. He would pour, no ice, no soda, no quinine water. And he could kill a whole bottle during that party." "Sid always got bombed," Gelbart's wife, the actress Pat Marshall, recalled, and acted tired and gloomy, or so it seemed. "One night he sat at the table staring into space from 10:30 p.m. to about 3:30 a.m.," said one of his writers. "Everybody else was laughing and carousing. At about 3:34 a.m. his wife said, 'Sid, come on, let's go home.' He looked at her angrily. 'Whaddya mean, "home"? I'm havin' a good time,'" he declared.

Caesar's post-show high was brief. "After the show was over, it was two hours of absolute Cloud 9 heaven," he remembered. "Then, we were sitting in Danny's Hide-A-Way, and everyone's saying, 'Good night,' 'Good night,' 'Good night,' and then I'd realize we have to do this all over again Monday. That was tough." If the show had been good, things were even worse: The question then became, "How are we going to top *that*?" "A manic depressive type of existence," he called it. Before leaving Danny's, he'd throw up again, and then he'd be driven home.

NBC knew of his drinking, Caesar would write, but initially did nothing about it. "No one came to me . . . and said, 'Sid, look what you're doing to yourself. Why don't you take time off and go somewhere where you can relax and get better?' When you're on that kind of merry-go-round, somebody has to help you get off." Fearing scandal—as Tolkin put it, "It was not easy for a

celebrity to maintain the 'Anonymous' part"—NBC had refused
to put him in Alcoholics Anonymous, and he wouldn't do it himself. "I was afraid to go in," Caesar said. "People would find out,
'Sid Caesar's a drunk.'" "So," he recalled, "my drinking became
one of the best-kept secrets in New York."

The network eventually persuaded Caesar's doctor to give
him chloral hydrate to wean him off the booze, a plan he thwarted
by taking them together. When that didn't work, he switched to
sodium amytal. To help him sleep, his psychiatrist put him on
Miltown, a tranquilizer. Meanwhile, remarkably, sketches involving drinking and drunkenness remained constants in Caesar's
shows. Had Caesar's fans known about his addiction, they'd have
found these performances still more gut-wrenching than they
already were.

The program of January 16, 1956, attracted two unusual visitors: Dick Cavett, who'd come down again from Yale to watch
from the audience, and Charles Berlitz, who gave Caesar a special plaque ("for promoting, through humor, interest in foreign
languages") at the end of the show. The program that night
included another silent movie spoof, inspired by both the original (1925 silent) version of *Stella Dallas*, which Caesar had seen at
the Museum of Modern Art, and his own guilty memories from
that snowy night when his mother had waited for him outside the
Waldorf. "A Drunk There Was: The Story of a Father's Failure,"
the sketch was called. Caesar must have sensed he was reentering
sensitive territory, for, once again, he took pains to prepare the
audience. "We're doing this in the spirit of fun but we do hope
you get something out of the *moral* of this story," Don Pardo
advised everyone beforehand. "A mea culpa was needed: it was
important that we were clear that we weren't making fun of alcoholics," Caesar wrote.

To Wild's piano score—alternately stately, sentimental, and
foreboding—the dramatis personae are presented: the Father,
Randolph (Caesar), "Torn Between Two Great Loves, Scotch
and Rye"; the Mother, Alice (Fabray), "Who Didn't Order a
Marriage on the Rocks"; the Villain, Demon Rum (Demon
Rum). The story opens on a happy note: It's Randolph's birthday

and Alice's, too, as well as their anniversary; she's expecting, the cat has just had kittens, and the canary has just laid some eggs; Randolph has just gotten a raise. He is a teetotaler, but to celebrate, his boss (Morris) insists he have just one drink. "Little did he know that this would be the shot heard around the world," the title card reads. He's jolted by his first nip, but within seconds he's swigging from the bottle.

"Five years and 6,522 bottles later," according to another card, Randolph is a widowed father and a drunk. He neglects his job as a stamp licker, and has secreted liquor in every niche and crevice in his office. As he uncovers and empties every stash, the audience howls. When his boss learns what's up, he fires him, only to relent for the sake of Randolph's motherless young daughter. And for the next fifteen years, he stays sober. But fearing that his past will surface and thwart his daughter's engagement to a handsome high school graduate (Reiner), and convinced that only by sullying himself can he persuade his boss to adopt the girl, give her his good name, and save the union, he goes on a bender at her engagement party. That does the trick, but sends him to ruin.

In the final scene, Randolph stands in a downpour outside the mansion where the wedding is taking place, watching the ceremony through a window (until the shade is pulled down). Having secured her daughter's future, Stella Dallas walked away triumphantly; in Caesar's darker tale, Randolph is disconsolate. The laughter at the Century Theatre died down; a mournful violin joins the piano, and then the entire orchestra joins in. "An Ounce of Love Is Worth More Than a Case of Scotch," the final card declares.

Way back when they first met in Palm Beach, Liebman had surmised that Caesar would need good writers, and it was true. But in this instance, the only writing was on the cards; the rest was him. It was the purest possible display of his own gifts—of his judgment, his heart, his knowledge of film history and respect for the power of film, his imagination, his musicality, his generosity, his courage, and his acting skills, which in this instance he summoned in spite of his impairments; indeed, by affording Randolph extra helpings of credibility and passion, his own plight surely enhanced his performance. No one could sneer about "Sid Caesar's 10 writers" this time around.

The archaic format even gave him a measure of protection; in a silent film, you can't forget your lines or slur your speech. That said, for a split second mid-sketch, with the camera on a card, Caesar's mind went completely blank, sparking a panic in him unlike anything he'd ever experienced. "Sidney, this is *insane!*" he said aloud, another luxury a silent movie routine afforded. That got him back on track. Still drenched, still standing behind the iron fence, Caesar reappeared for the curtain call. He thanked the audience and then, just to make sure everyone was okay with what they'd just seen, he repeated Pardo's admonition. The sketch was one of the pinnacles—maybe *the* pinnacle—of Caesar's career, eighteen minutes of astonishing power and virtuosity. It was also, Caesar later said, a cry for help. And maybe, self-help: If Randolph could stop drinking, so too, maybe, could he.

In 1950s Manhattan, "help" usually meant psychoanalysis, which of course was nothing new for Caesar. Several shrinks had tried to help him stop drinking.[*] Far from being secretive or ashamed about his treatment, midway through the run of *Caesar's Hour,* Caesar began evangelizing for it, becoming a prime example of what Walter Winchell called a strange new willingness among celebrities to "publicly expose the dark corners of their subconscious." Early on, before his boyhood memories turned Dickensian, Caesar had depicted life in Yonkers as one big howl, in which he and his brothers vied to "out-gag" one another. "And I didn't always win either," he said. Now everything was in a minor key. So impressed was Paddy Chayefsky by the sheer volume of Caesar's problems that were Caesar less famous, he said, he'd have been a perfect subject for his forthcoming TV show on the psychiatric histories of the emotionally disturbed. But Caesar was doing something about it, and the benefits were clear, at least to him.

---

* One was Lawrence Kubie, a well-known practitioner whose celebrity patients included Tennessee Williams, Vladimir Horowitz, Moss Hart, and Kurt Weill. But Caesar's description of Kubie in his memoir is so far off—he gives him, a man born in Boston, a thick German accent—that one has to wonder about the rest of his account.

"He is voluble about the benefits of psychotherapy, and, characteristically, thinks that everyone ought to have some!" said *Redbook*, in a Caesar profile headlined I GREW UP ANGRY. In 1954, Caesar said he'd "reached the end of his rope" two years earlier, and that only psychoanalysis had kept him going. But then he was being interviewed by an obscure arts magazine; now he was shouting it from the terrace atop the Milgrim Building. "Everyone should have analysis," he told *Look*. "It's like turning on the light before you go into a room."

In September 1956, in an ad for that story, *Look* offered a preview. "A man who has made tens of millions of people laugh—Sid Caesar—until a few years ago was beset by emotional troubles," it read. "He was almost constantly in a state of deep depression. Finally, he started going to a psychoanalyst. He tells the absorbing details in 'What Psychoanalysis Did for Me.'" Two weeks later, there was the Professor on the cover of the magazine. As Caesar saw it, in describing how treatment had helped him surmount childhood neglect and abandonment, then cope with middle-aged angst and unimaginable success, he was performing a public service; at his request, whatever he was paid for the piece would go to a school for delinquent and disturbed Jewish children.

His ghostwriter, Richard Gehman—who'd wept as Caesar told him his tale—soon repurposed and expanded the story into a seven-part series in the Hearst papers titled "TV's Tortured Clown." Psychiatry had made him more productive, Caesar said, and efficient; freed from his neuroses, he found that tasks formerly requiring a day now took him only a few hours. He had become both a better and a more humane comic, with "a deeper feeling for the idiosyncrasies and foibles on which so much humor is predicated." It made his introductions at the beginning of his shows less agonizing, and improved relations with his co-stars. It made him a better husband and father. It helped rid him of all manner of *mishugas:* No longer, for instance, was he afraid of haircuts, a superstition dating back to reading about Samson and Delilah as a boy. Thanks to such treatment, Gehman (who'd raised the issue of Caesar's drinking, only to say it was under control) was bullish on Caesar's future. "Seven years ago he seldom, if ever, derived any enjoyment from his life," he wrote. "Today he lives like a truly secure, contented, and happy man." The brilliant future once prophesied for Caesar "has come brilliantly true—and gives every indication of continuing to be brilliant for a long time."

But a few months later, Nakhman Zalowitz of the *Forverts*, who'd followed Caesar far longer and more perceptively than Gehman, offered a less optimistic assessment. "It's been six years already that Sid Caesar has been searching to find out 'who' he is, and what he is," he wrote in March 1957. And after five sessions a week at $35 a pop, he wrote, Caesar still wasn't happy, but only "less unhappy than before." "Instead of feeling 75 percent unhappy, as he did four, five, or six years ago, he feels only, let's say, 40 percent unhappy, and some days not more than 30 percent," Zalowitz observed. But still, "there isn't a day in the week, not a week in the year, when Caesar can say: 'I am currently 100 percent happy and satisfied.'" Among Caesar's current concerns, he noted, was a curiosity about three aspects of his family's history: (1) What was his true family name? (2) Which of his parents did he take after more? (3) Did his parents actually love him? "He would give and do a lot to know the answers," Zalowitz wrote. Caesar, he concluded, "is not yet finished with psychoanalysis—or, perhaps I should say, psychoanalysis isn't finished with Sid Caesar."

Around the same time, in a tell-all interview with the *New York Post*, Florence Caesar weighed in. ("The new trend is to bare everything," she explained. "I've just had to make up my mind that Sid is a public figure. And all the revelations don't seem to hurt career-wise. Look at what's been printed about Marilyn Monroe.") Her marriage had been "vastly improved" since they'd begun treatment, she said, he six years ago (he was "not quite finished") and she, two. (But no longer, she admitted, did he seek out her thoughts on his work. "What do *you* know?" he'd sneer when she'd venture anything negative.)

His colleagues weren't convinced. They'd reportedly "hooted" at his claims to newfound happiness; Tolkin called Caesar's hosannas to psychiatry "damned foolishness." "I don't think Sid has really changed so much," he said a few years later. A "perceptive man who knows him well" (probably Tolkin) agreed. "Sid Caesar can never be happy," he told Marie Torre of the *Herald Tribune*. (Her diagnosis of Caesar: "emotionally muscle-bound.") "He was not very nice to anyone—not to himself, not to his wife, not to his children," Edith Tolkin recalled. "He was very talented, very brilliant, but a very sad, mixed-up guy." Not that this surprised her: "Every Jewish boy we ever knew was totally screwed up," she said. "It was not a unique experience. We were just a vast family of screw-ups. The writers anyway."

Others found all of Caesar's public gut spilling either a joke (his "pathos-ridden" boyhood, one writer sniped, "would make 'Uncle Tom's Cabin' look like a two-reel comedy"), a "thumping bore," or just plain icky. Already criticized for putting too much of himself on TV, he was now faulted for a different sort of overexposure. Comedians, the thinking went, should stick to jokes. All this "inside dope," John Crosby complained, was turning Caesar and other confessional types into wet blankets. Jack Gould agreed, though without mentioning Caesar by name. "Surely, over the years Mr. Hope, Mr. Benny and Mr. Burns, for example, have had their share of problems," he wrote. "But how often does any one see them in public wringing their hands or revealing their doubts[?]" he asked. Caesar's treatment "sounded good in print," one scandal sheet declared, but by living his strange double life—"America's funniest clown for one hour every Saturday night, and America's most miserable man the rest of the week"—he remained "a pretty sick cookie."

Even Caesar's brothers felt Sidney was embroidering a bit. "Papa wasn't that bad," one of them insisted, and Mama protected him: "He [Sidney] was such a pretty boy that when my father wanted to hit him, my mother would say, 'Don't hit him in the face, hit him [on] the *tuchis*,'" Dave Caesar remembered. But as of late 1957, according to Zalowitz, Sid Caesar remained an orthodox Freudian; all the rest were "treyf." "In Sid Caesar's presence one should not say anything positive about Carl Jung, or Alfred Adler, or Otto Rank, or Karen Horney, or Erich Fromm, or Harry Stack Sullivan, or any other dissenter from Sigmund Freud's original teachings," he reported. "Freud is his 'rebbe.'"

Surprisingly, it wasn't in some jaw-breaking multipart series by a seasoned journalist but to a high school girl who'd lugged her giant tape recorder from Brooklyn that Caesar came closest to revealing his "Rosebud." It happened when the girl, fifteen-year-old Barbara Ashpes, interviewing him for a student project, asked him about his childhood pets. "A long time ago I had a canary," he told her, in what she described as "a low and infinitely sad voice" she'd never heard from him on TV, his eyes tearing up as he spoke. "I had him for about a year before he died," he said. "He paused and was silent," she went on, "then, as if remembering that he was a comedian, he jerked his head up, and in an attemptedly [sic] gay voice he said, 'We called him "Dr. Padoodle."'" It wasn't much, but it was more than he'd shared with anyone else. And it was important enough for him to preserve her article (from the Prospect Heights High School newspaper) in his scrapbook.

Caesar found new, more innocuous outlets for his angst. Parts of his weeks off he'd spend with a couple of new pals: Harry Radutzky, head of the Joyva Halvah Company, and a contractor named Milt Chasin. The two would fetch him after the show and drive up to Avon Lodge in a four-wheel arsenal of revolvers, rifles, and elephant guns. Evenings they'd eat steaks and discuss ordnance; mornings, they'd rise early, don yellow hunting gear, and head for a hillside they'd dubbed "Lead Mountain," where they'd line up cans of shaving cream and halvah tins vacuum-packed with water and then, from 150 feet away—after shouting out the names of people they hated—blow them to bits. "The tins go up like Old Faithful. I love it," Caesar enthused.

Out of deference to Sid, the one thing these hunters never did on their hunting trips was hunt: The guilt he felt looking into the blue eyes of that poor deer he'd bagged and then—for some masochistic reason—mounted on his wall was still too fresh. Instead, they'd sit down in the woods and light their cigars, as if to warn off any animals nearby. Evenings, Caesar headed into town to play pinochle with three other new friends, a mechanic, a gunsmith, and a farmer, with whom he'd talk about "guns, carburetors, and crops." "It relaxed him quite a bit," Radutzky remembered. "Then he came back and got crazy again."

These Catskill safaris were among Caesar's few forays into the real world, a paradox for someone whose comedy was said to be rooted in reality. In fact, his orbit was shrinking. "If he occasionally leaves his office penthouse and walks, not rides, to a restaurant, it's a big deal with him," Bester wrote. "He feels exalted because he's mingled with the people." Caesar's overzealous handlers kept him "in awful seclusion, like a baby in an incubator," Bester noted. But he was more relaxed at home, tossing cigar butts into the flower boxes as he talked. (In the summer of 1956, Sid and Florence welcomed a third child, Karen—induced, family lore had it, on a Friday so that Caesar's usual Saturday golf game could go on as usual. In her honor, "Shellric Corporation" became "Shellrick." Or, at times, "ShellricK.")

Around the Milgrim Building, Caesar seemed ever more robotic, especially on interminable elevator rides with him. "He just never had anything to say," recalled one of his dancers, Frances Rainer. "He walked around like a zombie in jewelry." And at times, he made the leap from "troubled" and "eccentric" to "positively off the wall." All of Caesar's deep dives into military history—an interest said to date from childhood, when he "felt unloved at home and wanted to lose himself in other people's troubles"—and especially into World War II, fed his fears. He grew convinced that Otto Skorzeny, the Waffen SS colonel who'd led several Nazi undercover operations (including the one springing Mussolini from his Italian captors in 1943), was out to kill him. Among what Brooks called the "ribbons of paranoia always flapping in the wind" for Caesar was, he said, a broader fear of Gentiles:

> I think Larry [Gelbart] just talked him out of Skorzeny parachuting down onto his building and getting him. He said it would be very hard for him to get to America, to get a cab, to find his way up the East River Drive. . . . Sid had a nice, wide brushstroke of paranoia, and every once in a while when you're a paranoiac, you have to coalesce it into some kind of fantasy. That year, I think Sid had some fantasies that there were a lot of unknown

people out there and that a lot of stuff that he'd done might offend them, and that one of them might come after him. He was always thinking of "What could have offended them?" Was it the movie sketch where he was fired because of his voice? Maybe people with very high voices would be very angry that he made fun of them and, late at night, might think of rubbing him out. So he always had paranoid fantasies. But the Skorzeny one— that one took the cake.

Milton Berle had once described television as "the only medium in the world where you can reach millions of people who luckily can't reach you." But Caesar wasn't so sure about that. "He said, 'Who are they? Where are they? How are they listening? Are they grouped around the TV set?'" Brooks recalled. "I said, 'Sid, there's no way they can climb into that set and find their way to the studio and kill you. There's no way. You're safe.'"

At times, Caesar could be pretty menacing himself. Mel and Florence Brooks visited Sid and Florence Caesar in Kings Point shortly after they'd moved in. Such occasions were never easy. "You didn't connect with Sid," Florence Baum recalled. "Women made him nervous. People made him uncomfortable." During a trip to Caesar's beach club, Baum remembered, Caesar acted "as if he were responsible for the day, the weather, the sun, the ocean, the beach, the sky—it was all his doing." And then, when they got back to the house, Caesar ushered them into his garage, where he kept his guns. He took one out, pointed it at his wife, and, with slurred speech, threatened to "blow your fucking head off." The Brookses beat a hasty retreat.

A friend recalled asking Caesar to remove the bullets from the gun he'd brought to a New Year's party. And Caesar himself remembered how, returning from the country, he'd come to work with a loaded .357 Magnum on his hip and started waving it around. "They were pretty scared," he said of the writers. "'Cause I was pretty nuts. To say the least." In the end, for Caesar as for so many others, psychiatry proved another god that failed; his very public love affair with it proved "a little premature." Brooks, though, thought that while psychiatry hadn't *cured* Caesar, it might have saved him. "He may not have been able to function and he might have killed himself," he said. "I think it freed him from compulsions and fears and anxieties that were detrimental to the happy state."

COMING UP WITH NEW material remained a challenge for Caesar and his writers. There was the "Somerset Winterset Playhouse," in which Caesar played a fusty British host (invariably napping or nodding off) when introducing sketches. In a faintly amusing sketch from late 1955 (surely just a chance for them to hang out with some jocks), the Commuters play basketball against a team of real-life New York Knicks (Harry Gallatin and Kenny Sears) and Boston Celtics ("Easy" Ed Macauley and Jack Nichols). There were more film parodies, of both domestic films (for example, *Bad Day at Black Rock*) and foreign ones, especially from Japan, then the rage in Caesar's circles.

In several such sketches, Caesar's writers uncovered a heretofore hidden aural link between Japanese and Yiddish. The hero of the first—titled "U-bet-U" (an homage to Kenji Mizoguchi's *Ugetsu*), and telling the story of the love between a samurai warrior and a young maiden—is Shtaka Yamagura. In "Tea and Samurai," Reiner plays Baron Kasha*-Moto, who presumes he'll win the hand of the emperor's daughter, and Caesar is Taka-Metzieh,[†] the humble houseboy who does. Another sketch, "The Brave and the Bamboo," features the great warrior Gantze Mishpocha;[‡] his bride, Princess Schmatta;[§] and the villain, Chazerai.[¶] This small and uncharacteristic burst of Yiddish went uncommented upon at the time but was overanalyzed afterward; the novelist Wallace Markfield crowned Caesar "perhaps the boldest, most compulsive user and misuser of Yiddish," while Irving Howe considered

---

* Buckwheat.
† "Truly a bargain."
‡ The whole family.
§ A rag; torn or old clothing.
¶ Junk food.

Caesar a guerrilla warrior for the language, "*shpritzing* one-liners with a willed abandon." What was really most significant about it was how aberrational it was.

Even as his ratings slipped, Caesar remained a favorite of television peers, cineastes, and highbrows. Asked to name the greatest comics by category, Buster Keaton listed Caesar under "television." Groucho Marx said that *Caesar's Hour, You'll Never Get Rich* (Sergeant Bilko), and *Meet the Press* were among the only shows he watched, and called Caesar "the greatest comedy actor in television." Around the "comedians' roundtable" at the largely Jewish Hillcrest Country Club in Los Angeles, George Burns said Caesar was "one of the greatest mimes of the time." Writing in *The American Scholar*, Morris Freedman included *Caesar's Hour* among the shows approved by orthodox nonconformists—the same folks who favored Adlai Stevenson over Richard Nixon, espresso over instant coffee, foreign films over American ones (unless they were cheap and badly lit), and Leonard Bernstein and Mozart over Tchaikovsky and Irving Berlin.

To Sid Shalit of the *Daily News*, Caesar remained "TV's brightest ornament," but he warned that satire was losing out to "folksy, low-key comedy," which bypassed Weaver's "frontal lobes" for the "involuntary nerve centers." To him, Caesar was partly to blame: While Jackie Gleason now concentrated on Ralph Kramden, Caesar roamed all over the place. Increasingly, sitcoms were where it was at: Not a line from *Caesar's Hour* made the 1955–56 edition of *Best Television Humor of the Year*, but bits from *The Life of Riley* and *The Adventures of Ozzie and Harriet* did. Meanwhile, Westerns—relaxing, digestible, durable—multiplied like jackrabbits on the prairie. For all of Caesar's talk about food, America craved something he wasn't serving: pork and beans. Ratings, good or bad, didn't interest Caesar. "People walk up to me on the street and say, 'That was a great show,'" he said. "That means more to me than any other rating."

In March 1956, Fabray announced she'd not be returning the following season. Bob Hope quipped that Caesar now had "a used-wife lot." There was the usual speculation over Fabray's move, and what—Ego? Money? Control? Competitiveness?—

accounted for it; Fabray later blamed an overzealous agent. Like Coca, she insisted she'd have stuck with Caesar forever. A couple of weeks later, Caesar got to watch Fabray collect two Emmys for *Caesar's Hour*, which was two more than he got.

Restaurateurs looked on with consternation as Caesar grew thinner. "Now when Sid walks along Broadway, restaurant proprietors see him and shake their heads sadly," one magazine reported. "I just don't know what's happened to Sid," lamented the owner of Blair House, the celebrity hangout on West Fifty-Sixth Street that Caesar frequented. "He could have been the greatest celebrity eater since Diamond Jim Brady." But even eating looked different to Caesar in the light of his analysis. "Sometimes you eat because you're mad," he said. "You take it out on a chicken."

NBC decreed that come September, when the show launched its third season, Caesar would move back to Saturday nights. The terrain was familiar to him, the thinking went, and strong shows before and after his—hosted by Perry Como and George Gobel—would prop him up. There was just one hitch, something all those cosmopolitan nonconformists with their hi-fis and espressos might have missed. He'd be going up against Lawrence Welk.

ON THE SUNDAY ARTS page of *The Dallas Morning News* on October 29, 1944, two items appeared a few inches apart. In one, the paper reported that *Tars and Spars*, starring one Sid Caesar among others, was about to open at a local movie house. In the other, listed under "Dining and Dancing," came word that the bandleader Lawrence Welk was looking for a new "girl vocalist," someone with what he called a "champagne voice." The lucky winner, the paper prophesied, would have "pretty close to a permanent job."

And that was so: In the ensuing decade, Welk's popularity steadily grew, to the point where, one Saturday night in July 1955, when *Caesar's Hour* was on summer hiatus, Welk's own TV show, until then airing only in Los Angeles, had gone national.

"Thank you, Lawrence," said Myron Floren, an earnest young accordionist from South Dakota, after Welk introduced him. "It's really wonderful to be able to go coast-to-coast and see all of our friends way back in the Midwest and the East, and we hope we can do it for a long, long time."

"The small town this generation has known has ceased to exist," NBC's press department had boasted around that time. "Television has created similar tastes in all sizes of communities. Sectionalism and regionalism are vanishing as people sit in their living rooms, looking into the magic window of television at their 'neighbors' thousands of geographic miles away." It was hard to abandon Weaver's starry-eyed notion that folks outside big eastern cities would be thrilled to have sophisticated entertainment dumped on their doorstep. But in what one advertising executive derisively called "East Cupcake, Iowa," this wasn't necessarily so. Far from binding together two different Americas, television only highlighted—and, maybe, even widened—the chasm. And the more televisions there were, and the more dispersed, the more apparent that chasm became. Helen Dearborn, a dentist from Iowa, complained to the *Chicago Tribune* in January 1955 that NBC was trying to "ram" Caesar "down our vision." "In some magazine I noted that Sid Caesar was rated the wit of the year," she complained. "Should that be so, I'm Samuel L. Clemens' twin sister."*

Within the industry, and along Madison Avenue, calls intensified for television to broaden its appeal, to "cross the Hudson River and the Sierras more often," as *TV Guide* put it. Some of what these critics might have had in mind originated several nights a week west of the Sierras, in the Aragon Ballroom in Santa Monica, California. That was where, since 1951, Welk (born in a German-speaking home in Strasburg, North Dakota, to devout Alsatian Catholic parents) and his orchestra offered their bouncy

---

* Caesar had a better chance with Grace Keillor of Anoka, Minnesota, who—overcoming both her husband's opposition and her own fundamentalist upbringing—finally got a TV in late 1954, largely to watch all the Jewish comedians from New York. But according to her son Garrison, she found Caesar too angry for her taste.

"Champagne Music." In case anyone missed the symbolism, bubbles rose perpetually on the wall behind the bandstand. The imagery was odd, since Welk himself never drank anything stronger than milk. "I play the kind of music mother likes," Welk liked to say. America "is not made up of wise guys or slick sophisticates but of people who enjoy the real and simple values of life."

Welk avoided anything newfangled—"I've never been much for coming up with an original idea," he confessed—or unsettling, like, say, jazz. Women performing for him couldn't wear anything revealing, and his musicians had to look contented. There was a religious undertone to the program, appealing to what one Catholic newspaper called "the still Christian soul of America." Even at then-lowly, desperate ABC, habitual also-ran to mighty NBC and CBS, executives had balked at making this "North Dakota cornball" a summer replacement. But when that went well, it signed him up for the full 1955–56 season, during which Welk promptly clobbered Jimmy Durante and threatened Arthur Godfrey. People watched, and discussed, and wrote about him; adolescent boys developed their first crushes on Janet Lennon, the youngest of the four very wholesome singing Lennon Sisters. Paul Cotton of *The Des Moines Register,* who'd welcomed *Your Show of Shows* to Iowa with such fanfare only a few years earlier, now got way more mail about Welk than about Caesar or anyone else.

Like Caesar, at least in this one respect, Welk was awkward onstage. He stammered a bit, and had a strange accent no one could quite place. "That accent may be one of his greatest assets," the *Chicago Tribune*'s Larry Wolters wrote. "It pegs him as an ordinary, average guy." Taking potshots at Welk and his "shy, clodhopper charm" became a favorite urban sport. To John Crosby, Welk was "a toothsome man with a rather elusive personality" who played "the sort of thing we all used to dance to back in the early '30s, in places called the Tick Tock Room in the Coronado Hotel in East Elbow, Nebraska."

But a musical militia, armed with accordions, was marching on network television. "Welk may have discovered a secret which has evaded more talented show-wise performers—that there are viewers who prefer not to have their entertainment thrust at them; who like to keep one eye on the set and still chat with friends, browse through the evening paper and nibble at sandwiches," the television writer Steven Scheuer noted in 1956. Welk, he predicted, was "in for a long spin of the wheel."

Caesar had made a business out of mocking musicians—divas, percussionists, concert pianists, pop singers, and, in January 1956, hip jazz musicians. That was when, inspired by a visit to Birdland, he introduced a new character on *Caesar's Hour:* a bop saxophonist, "accoutered in padded shoulders, a hair-do like Madame Pompadour's and eyeglasses as thick as the Whitney telescope," named Cool Cees. Caesar could handle additional criticism from Jack Mabley of *Down Beat*, who surmised that the character was designed "to demonstrate (a) Sid Caesar can play the saxophone, and (b) he'd never do it in public because people who play jazz are queer." But after a school for the blind in Maryland complained that Cees shamed the sightless, Caesar quickly retired the character because, he explained, he liked to sleep nights. Caesar prided himself on his fairness; "anything I take off on has to be in a position to hit back at me," he'd explained.

To Caesar and his crowd, Welk hadn't even been worth noticing, let alone ridiculing; he was on a different network on a different night of the week, catering to different folks in a different part of the country with entirely different demands.

BUT ONCE NBC PUT him up against Welk, all bets were off: Caesar's fairness doctrine didn't apply to existential threats, which is what Welk was. "He *was* the real enemy," Brooks said. "He was going to do us in." Caesar must have known that milquetoast Welk wouldn't fight back even if Caesar concerned him, which he didn't. "I don't think he'll give us much trouble," Welk predicted. Maybe not exactly trouble, but Sid was about to bare his fangs.

Caesar's first attack came in late May 1956, four months before the shows would go head-to-head. Out came Don Pardo, talking about the growing popularity of television shows with "danceable, singable music." "And so," he said, "in keeping with this trend, *Caesar's Hour* presents a new feature: The Lonnie Bilk Show!" The curtain opens on Caesar, seen from the rear in a white dinner jacket, with a wig worse than Liebman's perched lopsidedly on his head. He turns and greets everyone with a big smile and an accent of uncertain provenance and accuracy: North Dakotan Alsatians hadn't had a table at the St. Clair Lunch.

"This is Lonnie Bilk and his smooth-as-milk orchestra, played by contented musicians," he declares, before introducing "a special arrangement of 'Love Is a Many Splendor-ed Thing.'" He flounces around as the band plays. Then he summons the Bilktones—Sonny (Reiner) on his "$25,000 accordion," and Chuck (Morris) on guitar—"who ask the musical question, 'Jeepers, Creepers?'" Their smiles, like everyone else's on the show, are frozen in place, forcing them to produce consonants without the benefit of lips, tongues, or teeth. The band then heads "south of the border, down to sunny Spain," with Sonny performing on his back, feet kicking in the air. Out then comes "Candy Cutie, America's Kid Sister of Song" (Fabray), who—with the glazed look of a cultist—sings "Ma, He's Making Eyes at Me."

"Candy, that was wonderful," Bilk gushes when she's done. "Candy, that was wonderful. Just wonderful. Just wonderfully wonderful. Wonderful. Wonderful." She goes offstage momentarily; then Bilk brings her back for another bow. "Candy, that was wonderful," he says. "Wasn't that wonderful? That was wonderful! Oh, that's wonderful. Yes, wasn't that wonderful?" She mechanically resumes her song. "Oh, that's wonderful," Bilk tells her, before muttering, "That's enough!," then covering up her grin and shoving her off the stage. "Wasn't that wonderful?" he then asks. "Wonderful. That was just wonderful. Wasn't it wonderful?" He then brings her out one last time. "Candy, that was wonderful," he says. A smiling Reiner then sidles his way over. "May I say something?" he asks Bilk. "That was wonderful."

And so was the sketch, a hint of what the show could be were it to take off the gloves more often. More than just about anything else Caesar ever did, it revealed the anger underlying so much comedy, including his. And, predictably, it angered conservative commentators. While phrasing it carefully, Jack O'Brian accused Caesar of depicting Welk as a homosexual. "The touch of lavender suggested in Caesar's blond and bewigged burlesque character certainly was totally misleading and thoroughly unnecessary," he fumed. "Strictly desperation stuff." Welk's aggrieved admirers also pounced. "If I were Welk, I'd sue," "North Side fan, completely intoxicated by Champagne Music" wrote to the *Columbus State Journal.* "Fan" savored the prospect of Welk and Caesar going head-to-head in the fall, when, he or she predicted, "the so-called comedian will find out that he isn't half as funny as he thinks he is." Anthony La Camera of the *Boston American* was agog. "Satirizing a TV opponent before the competition even begins must be some sort of TV first," he wrote. Welk, of course, was a perfectly good sport about it. "Your skit was wonderful, wonderful, wonderful," he reportedly telegrammed Caesar.

Three weeks later, supposedly by popular demand, Caesar took on Welk again. The wig was gone and Lonny Bilk was now Ricky Tick, but the permafrost smiles remained as the Rick Tones (formerly Sonny and Chuck) did their frantic take on "Nagasaki." "That was really swinging. Really swinging, indeed," Tick tells them as he shoves them, too, to the side. Another soloist, played by Milt Kamen, comes out to play what Tick calls his "$25,000 Stradivarius violin," only to have Tick smash it accidentally as he flaps his wings conducting. "Well, that's show business," he says. Candy Cutie then reappears to sing "Button Up Your Overcoat," grinning even as Tick crushes the microphone in her face. ("She takes pain wonderfully," he notes.) Then comes "novelty time," featuring "Shorty Sims and his magic head." After tapping out a scale on his cranium, Shorty (Morris) becomes so addled that he, too, has to be carted away. "Folks, would you believe that Shorty was six foot seven when he came on the show?" Tick asks. Then comes Val Kyrie (Reiner), "going south of the border to play 'Donkey Serenade.'" After holding the last note for nearly a minute, he finally blurts out, "I think I'm going to be sick." "Get him an ice bag," Tick says as the credits roll. Brooks thought the sketches a mistake. "I said to everybody in the room, 'We're not helping ourselves! We're making him more popular!'" But

Welk remained—what else?—cheerful. "I laughed myself sick," he said, adding that he was grateful for the "plugs." He resisted calls from his fans to impersonate Caesar. "You have to be an actor to do those things," he explained.

By midsummer 1956, a third of the commercial spots for *Caesar's Hour*'s new season remained unsold. The network put together an elaborate booklet filled with more of those tired Roman metaphors—"Caesar Reigns," it was called—to entice skeptical advertisers, assuring them that like so many of their products Caesar's show, and Caesar himself, were new and improved.

There was Caesar's latest TV wife, Janet Blair, who'd won the bake-off (against Gisele MacKenzie, Edie Adams, and Polly Bergen) for what the *Boston Herald* called "the most coveted job since Scarlett O'Hara." Caesar said chemistry had dictated his choice, but Morris offered a baser motive: "'Cause she was the lead in a movie called *Tars and Spars* and he wanted her to realize that he was now a big star." (Blair was diplomatic about their roles being reversed. "He was just a tall, skinny kid then, and I can still see the small boy in him in spite of his wonderful success," she said. "I like him.") There would also be two lively new female co-stars—the comedienne Pat Carroll (another Tamiment alum) and Shirl Conway, who would be married off, respectively, to Morris and Reiner in the Commuter sketches. "Now with three strong female stars in the cast, [Caesar's] domestic sketches will highlight the woman's point of view, making an ideal atmosphere for Wesson Oil Products," the network pitched one advertiser.

NBC insisted that Caesar just kept getting funnier: *TV Guide*, *Look*, and *Motion Picture Daily* all described him as the "Best Comedian on TV." "Other 'name' comics have gone down against TV's insatiable appetite for new material," the pitch claimed. "But not Sid Caesar. He gets bigger and better." Madison Avenue could not be blamed for wondering why, if things were really so peachy with Caesar, the network had to push him so aggressively.

The new season loomed, and with it, one big question: Would the maestro of Champagne Music be the one who'd finally burst Caesar's bubble?

CHAPTER 10

THE (NEARLY) FATAL
BOWL OF COLESLAW

*C*aesar's Hour! Caesar's Hour! Caesar's Hour!* Welcome to . . .
Caesar's Hour!" The chorus sang the words brightly. And
then the camera swiveled right, and there was Caesar himself.
"Good evening, and welcome to our show," he declared: no frills,
nothing to stumble over. And with that, he yielded to a new
announcer for the 1956–57 season: Hugh Downs, hired specifically to spare Caesar from having to say much more than what he
just had. Easygoing and amiable, Downs lent a gentle, reassuring
tone to what promised to be a turbulent, make-or-break season
for the program.

Though, as the Wesson Oil folks had learned, the show
had been newly feminized, no women would be writing for it.
Replacing Selma Diamond was Neil Simon, now minus his big
brother, and with his arrival the mightiest combination of writers
in the history of television, before or since, was finally complete.
As Albert Goldman put it, Caesar's operation had become "a big,
fucking 12-reel locomotive," with "all the manic crazy firemen,"
Brooks and Gelbart and Simon and the others, "shoveling it on,
trying to get up the speed." Caesar described the newly enhanced
writers' room more scientifically. "It was like, really, a cyclotron
in there," he recalled.

Before the new season got under way, Caesar's loyal supporter, Pat Weaver, was gone. Only in the Wild West of early television could a Pat Weaver have prospered, but his lease had finally run out. As two men with strong ideas and egos, Weaver and David Sarnoff inevitably butted heads; it hadn't exactly helped Weaver when *The New Yorker* had done a two-part profile of *him* rather than of the General. As their competition intensified, Weaver's idealistic ethos—that the bottom line wasn't always the bottom line—had fallen out of favor. "Nobody ever called Pat a business or financial genius," one anonymous "TV man" told *The Wall Street Journal*. And Weaver hadn't exactly helped himself by admitting he hated most of what he put on TV and watched little of it himself. (How else, he asked one reporter, "would I have time for all the other things I like to do?")

While Sarnoff groomed his son Bobby to succeed him, somehow Weaver had continued to thrive. In December 1955, as *Caesar's Hour* was hitting its stride, he'd been named chairman of NBC's board and signed a seven-year contract. Emboldened, he urged station managers gathered in Chicago to focus less on short-term ratings and more on elevating programming. "From the beginning, we have been against the know-nothings, the primitives, because we do not believe that television should be run merely to give the people what they already want," he said. "Television is far too great an instrument to be degraded into a home jukebox to keep the kids quiet," he went on, but should be, instead, "one more weapon in the fight against bigotry, stupidity, intolerance and prejudice." For that, Weaver got a standing ovation from the managers and a pat on the back from Sarnoff. But within nine months, he was out. It was, as *Variety* put it, "an omen of sterility and dullness, of sameness and smugness." The *Daily News* expressed doubt that another programmer would ever run a network; "that post," it predicted, "will be filled by the expert in finance or sales."

Out of work, destined to become better known as Sigourney's father, Weaver repaired to his home in Sands Point, New York, just a stone's throw from Caesar's place. Had Caesar picked up his binoculars and surveyed the waterfront, he'd have seen that he and Weaver were in the same boat: Their lofty aspirations for television were passé. The first Saturday night of the new season marked a television first, and last: Viewers could watch the real Lawrence Welk on ABC or Caesar's version of him on NBC. Welk was curdling into an obsession for Sid. When Caesar all but gave him the finger that night, he was extending it to his bosses, television, and the evolving TV audience as well.

"Hi there, nice Americans," said Ricky Tick, promising what he called "another program of toe tapping, tip tapping, toe tipping, tap topping, toe tipping tempo tunes" from his "all musician orchestra." Out again come Sonny and Chuck, followed by Candy Cutie, now played by Blair. "This is a fun show, and I always say, if you can't have fun, then don't," Tick declares when she's done. Shorty Cupcake (Morris) then returns and, while attempting to sing "Deep Purple," electrocutes himself with his "245,000-volt electric guitar."

While Caesar seemed fixated and Welk remained magnanimous, the critics were either annoyed or bored. "Caesar had himself a ball—and then came the dawn," reported the *Newark Star-Ledger*, noting that when the ratings came out, Welk "had clobbered Caesar to a fare-thee-well." Caesar could take off on Welk all he wanted, but couldn't take him out. The premiere featured yet another dreary Commuters sketch but picked up with a takeoff on *The King and I*, with Caesar playing Yul Brynner playing the King of Siam. Young Billy Crystal never forgot the barefoot Caesar shouting, "Who's smoking in the palace?" after stepping on a lit cigarette someone had discarded on the set; years later, he always greeted Caesar with that line.

Critics and admirers alike warned that the show was on thin ice. Caesar was still first-rate, wrote Crosby, but his audience had gotten "too hep to his tricks." And Janet Blair turned out to be a bust, a pale imitation not only of Coca and Fabray but also of her two new co-stars, Carroll and Conway. Of all the Commuters, Bob Victor had got himself the dullest spouse. Worse, Blair proved a prima donna: When, in a rehearsal early on, Caesar directed her to lie down on the floor for one sketch, she insisted that papers be spread out first. "That was it," Earl Wild recalled.

"Sid went upstairs and he didn't come down for a long time. We knew then that [the show] was dead."

But it soldiered on, spoofing old Hollywood on the "Blast Video Theatre" and taking off after Westerns. The excommunicated Cool Cees was reborn as Progress Hornsby, equally hip and abstruse, but with 20/20 vision. Professor Wolfgang von Forever, a geriatrician and author of *Try Not to Die*, described a man still going strong at 210. (His secret? Giving up spicy foods at 175.) In a page out of *Mad* magazine, there were mock commercials for "Blast" toothpaste, made with hexaglobolobolin found in elephant tusks; "His Majesty's TV Dinners," cooked by plugging them into the backs of TVs (the chicken legs doubled as antennas); and the "1957 Fiasco"—"the newest, the biggest Fiasco on the road," with filter-tipped pistons and stickball suspension. An energy supplement called Poop-a-Trol (secret ingredient: the tears of thousands of unhappy girls crying into giant vats in Passaic, New Jersey) was recommended by four out of five actors playing doctors on television.

Caesar's show still inspired some. The young Carol Burnett, new to New York, became a big fan, and when Milt Kamen offered to sneak her into a dress rehearsal, she gave away two precious tickets for *My Fair Lady* to go. But the trend was clear. Caesar retained the coasts, while Welk was cleaning up in the no-man's-land in between—what Caesar liked to call "the Midwest." Dwight Eisenhower's reelection in November 1956 was an ominous sign: Mamie Eisenhower and her mother were great fans of Welk's show, and this go-round it was Welk rather than Caesar who was asked to perform at Ike's inauguration.

Caesar's Hour for November 17 was standard stuff: The Commuters spot featured a movie star in a pizza parlor; Blair sang a white-bread version of "Take the 'A' Train"; and on "Ominous," a spoof on Alistair Cooke's ruminative weekly *Omnibus*, Ludwig von Zebramacher, author of *Tigers I Have Hunted and Hospitals I Have Known*, traced the evolution of amoebas from paramecium to pari-mutuels (the seahorses that the amoebas bet on), and described how monkeys had evolved from man. But wasn't it the other way around? Aristotle Cookie (Reiner) asks him. "Did you ever see a monkey stand onstage and sing 'I Ain't Nothin' but a Hound Dog'?" the Professor replies. Cookie also contested von Zebramacher's claim to live with a man-eating chicken. "My wife's brother," the Professor explained. "You want to see a man eating chicken, come down to my house and see a man eat chicken!"

Ordinarily the kinescope of that show would have gone on a shelf, to be watered periodically. But alarmed by Caesar's falling ratings, NBC gave it to William J. Millard Jr., PhD, of Jerome Barnum Associates, management consultants, whom it had commissioned to diagnose what ailed *Caesar's Hour* and propose some cures. Millard devised a set of questions for the 230 or so people he'd assembled in a movie theater in New Rochelle one night in mid-December 1956. They watched the show, pushing the buttons on their "Televac audience response boxes" every few seconds to register whether the entertainment held their attention "very much," "fairly much," "a little," or "not at all."

The results, presented to the network five weeks later in a confidential report, were sobering: The show's "Program Satisfaction Coefficient" was a paltry 29 percent—"one of the lowest scores registered to date"—and its "holding power" weak. To most of those surveyed, *Caesar's Hour* marked a steep drop-off from *Your Show of Shows:* "Needs Imogene Coca" was the most common complaint. "Janet Blair doesn't seem to be his type," one viewer complained. Many who'd once admired Caesar no longer did. He was especially unpopular among women with a high school education or less, a group that, Millard noted, "expects more enjoyment from Welk." Yes, Welk was making inroads in Caesar's very backyard. Viewers had liked the much-put-upon Charlie Hickenlooper a lot more than surly Bob Victor; when Bob picked on Nan, "they do not see this as satire, but literally as man beating wife," a trait "not likely to win the favorable attention of the great American housewife." (Maybe, he mused, reminders that Sid Caesar wasn't really Bob Victor were warranted.) Most considered Caesar's material "old, repetitious, boring, worn out"; nearly two-thirds felt he was "on the way down." Whether NBC shared the report with Caesar is unclear; what he'd have done with it wasn't.

Annoyance, fatigue, and incomprehension blinded many viewers to the show's brightest spots. Thanks to its superlative writers, Caesar's show was often sharper, more sophisticated, and more original than it had been. And, as its precariousness became clearer, also angrier—angrier, even, than in the Welk sketches— as a takeoff in early December proved. The target was *What's My Line?*, the durable program in which a panel of New York sophisticates tried to divine the obscure occupations of various contestants and, blindfolds in place, the identity of a celebrity "mystery guest." With its clubby air of snobs at play, the show was ripe for satire; hence, "What's My Business?," the "award-winning panel show with its award-winning moderator," Ron Bailey, played by Reiner.

As the knowing laughter attested, Reiner's impersonation of the program's real host, the former newsman John Charles Daly—right down to fumbling around on his fake desk, fidgeting with his face, and speaking in a vaguely British accent—hit home, though his takedown was gentle, as was Reiner's wont. Not so Morris's skewering of Bennett Cerf, the co-founder and head of Random House as well as a fixture on the show, presented here as "the Academy Award columnist and social climber, Mr. Clifton Gelding." He is insufferable and priggish, has Locust Valley lockjaw, and even wears Cerf's signature round glasses. "Thank you for a delightful description of a delightful person—me," Gelding says when introduced.

Caesar plays a peculiarly lecherous Professor, also on the panel, more interested in necklines than lines of work, hitting on both women panelists—Conway and Carroll, presumably playing the show's two other regulars, Dorothy Kilgallen and Arlene Francis—when he wasn't attacking the hoity-toity Gelding. "You're fooling with that voice, aren't you?" he asks him. "You talking with kumquats in your mouth or something? You're a phony!"

"Ron, I have a hunch," Gelding, blindfolded like the others, declares when the mystery guest, a glamorous starlet named Kim Shane (Janet Blair), appears. "Are you possibly Slapsie Maxie Rosenbloom? No, you couldn't possibly be with that voice.

Therefore you must be Joe DiMaggio. Well, then Sir Laurence Olivier or Tony Gallentio [sic]?" When it dawns on him that she is a she, the Professor starts flirting with her, too. "I imagined for a moment that I saw blood dripping from the TV set. It was brutal," one critic wrote afterward. But the sketch, and program, come to a screeching halt before anything is resolved, the most ragged ending of any Caesar sketch since Mischa Elman was cut off mid-note for an apple juice commercial. Caesar's usual iron-clad discipline was beginning to break down.

Writing in *The New Republic*, Philip Roth praised Caesar for standing by his bile rather than backtracking into the usual "just kidding" bromides. "One feels of his satire that he believes in it," Roth wrote. "One can hardly imagine him coming out after the *What's My Line?* parody and saying, as I think Mr. [Jerry] Lewis or Mr. [Fred] Allen might, 'John Daly is really doing a great, great job over there, and so is the rest of the gang, all great, great human beings, etc.'"

The following show rebounded with one of Caesar's most ambitious, and wonderful, sketches, also with autobiographical overtones—a mock Hollywood musical called "The Dancing Towers." Taking up the entire show, it tells the saga of Tony Towers (Caesar) and his rise from the humblest of beginnings (painting "Hello, New York" on the backs of turtles) to star dancer in his own troupe. Tony has devised a catchy dance step (it actually happened when he tripped) that sweeps the nation and becomes known as the "Towers Trot," named for the veteran vaudeville dance family (a couple, played by Morris and Carroll, and their daughter, Nola—Blair) with whom he's joined forces. He wins over Nola, but Tony shares what had been Caesar's *other* addiction: to food. The sketch is a *Lost Weekend* about gluttony.

Tony eats, compulsively and prodigiously, ballooning into roundness. Food literally comes between him and Nola when she hugs him and, it turns out, the lunch he'd squirreled away in his coat pocket. "Don't you ever do that again!" he shouts at her. "You crushed my egg salad sandwich!" "He can't say he loves me," she laments, "because his mouth is always full of food." By the time Florian Ziegfried (Paul Reed) enlists the Towers for his famous Follies, Tony is too fat to dance; when he tries, he's laughed off the stage. He finds solace in the usual place. "Where's the candy?" he asks. "Where's the food? Something! Run out and get me a corned beef sandwich! All fat!" When Ziegfried kicks him out, Tony needs a hatchet to squeeze through the exit. He winds up as a gigolo at a dance hall.* But a year later, miraculously slimmed down, Tony returns to Nola's loving arms, which she can finally get around him. The "Towers Trot" became a record, and soon every episode of *Caesar's Hour* closed to its romping theme.

The following show was also sensational, and topical. The subject was quiz shows, then at their peak, just before scandal felled them. The mock show is called "Break Your Brains," and its genial but frenetic host is Jimmy Popular (Reiner). The contestants include an eight-year-old atomic scientist (who's also an expert on comic books), a ninety-three-year-old grandmother (whose category is pole-vaulting), and a baker from Wayzata, Minnesota (whose category is bakeries in Wayzata, Minnesota). But the action centers on one Harry Hempstead (Caesar). Throughout his twenty-five weeks on the program the folks on "Break Your Brains" have been trying to break Hempstead's brain, and though he's won a fortune, he's a wreck, crying uncontrollably, unable to walk under his own power, begging for mercy.

In head-spinning fashion (it was the only time Reiner ever read from cards), Popular rattles off Hempstead's options—to go home with his loot, or to give it up and start all over again, or to take all his winnings in embossed luggage, among other choices. Then, after great exertions (actually, an assembly-line scene from *Things to Come*, a futurist movie from 1936 written by H. G. Wells), the "Selectatron" machine spits out Hempstead's next question. It seems simple enough: He must identify an aria. But after that, he must name the opera from which it came, five

---

* One of his dance partners is a sassy sailor played by Bea Arthur, who had several bit parts on *Caesar's Hour*. Caesar, she later said, taught her "to be outrageous." "Such courage!" she marveled. "He would do things nobody else had the nerve to do" (New York *Daily News*, May 23, 1989; *Chicago Tribune*, Dec. 25, 2001).

leading tenors who sang it before 1930 (and for which opera companies), four of the leading ladies in those productions, the composer who wrote it, five unpublished operas of his, and the names of his wife and children—all in a few seconds.

From Hempstead's mouth comes a gallimaufry of names: *Rigoletto*, Caruso, Jan Peerce, Tony Galento, the Metropolitan Opera Company, Sal Maglie, Dolores Del Río, Bess Myerson, the *Niña*, *Pinta*, and *Santa Maria*, and, after a riff of Italian double-talk, *The Girl of the Golden West*. "Ladies and Gentlemen, this is absolutely phenomenal!" shouts Popular. "It's amazing! *Every answer was wrong!*" Harry collects the $250,000 anyway, only to put it all on the line against a contestant who's been on the show 103 weeks. Off they go to their respective "Humiliation Booths"; Hempstead nearly suffocates when someone forgets to switch on the air in his. When his rival can't name the capitals of Abyssinia, Uruguay, Bolivia, Paraguay, New Zealand, Newfoundland, Belgium, and Pakistan in fifteen seconds, Hempstead wins, but only after identifying ten different paintings and, after tasting each with his tongue, separating the real ones from the fakes. "Stay tuned for the next five quiz shows, which follow on this station immediately!" shouts Popular as the show ends.

To Reiner, who put in a virtuoso performance, it was as good a sketch as they'd ever done, one of the reasons he considered *Caesar's Hour* the superior of Caesar's shows. And to Harriet Van Horne, Caesar was "responsible for the most wonderful, wicked subversion TV has yet seen." But what no one seemed to notice, or at least comment upon, was Sid Caesar's extraordinary physical transformation. Poor Hempstead had been on TV only twenty-five weeks; Caesar had now been performing for eight years and, thin and haggard, wore every week of it. It was astonishing to behold how dramatically he'd deteriorated from the beefy, robust figure who'd jammed with Benny Goodman barely two years before. It had happened in spurts rather than in increments, and there'd been ladders along with the chutes: At times, he looked like his old self. But the general trajectory was down. Hilarious as the quiz show sketch was, to anyone watching closely, it should have been alarming, too.

Young Sid and his saxophone. A good thing it was, Caesar later said, that when a delinquent boarder fled the flophouse upstairs from the St. Clair Lunch, he left behind a musical instrument instead of a gun.

Florence Levy and Sid Caesar in the Catskills, 1942. She thought it was just a summer romance; he knew it was for keeps.

Pretty much every comic and comedy writer (including those who wound up working for him) first saw, and were dazzled by, Caesar in *Tars and Spars*.

Camp Tamiment, summer 1948. That only three years after the Holocaust two young Jews, Mel Tolkin (left) and Lucille Kallen (fourth from right), had so much to be happy about showed how capricious history could be.

Imogene Coca meshed seamlessly with these guys, further evidence of how protean a performer she was.

Mel Brooks auditioned for and seized the roles of Caesar's sidekick, gofer, and groupie.

Rarely comfortable with peers or anyone else, Caesar looked vaguely ill at ease among his fellow comics at Milton Berle's bachelor party in December 1953.

Sid and Florence (to his left) on the town, October 1953.

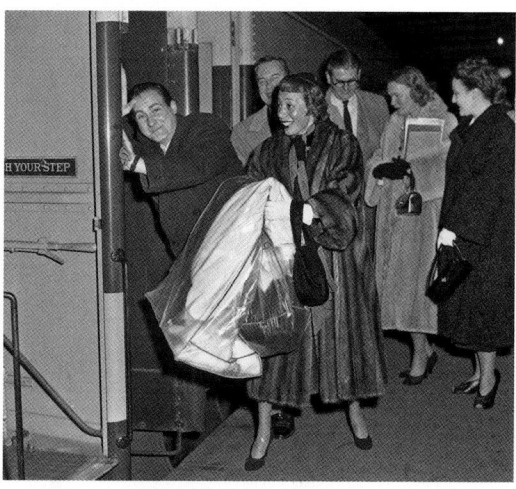

Sid and Imogene en route to perform at Ike's first inauguration, January 1953.

Yonkers Welcomes
SID CAESAR

Yonkers' Own Star of "Your Show of Shows"

AT CITY HALL, TUESDAY NOV. 18th AT 5:00 P.M.

YONKERS TAKES PRIDE IN WELCOMING A NATIVE SON. EVERYONE IS INVITED TO ATTEND.
MAYOR KRISTEN KRISTENSEN WILL PRESENT SID CAESAR A KEY TO THE CITY.

A Testimonial Dinner for Mr. Caesar will be held at the State Armory at 7:30 P.M.
Sponsored by the Yonkers Chamber of Commerce, Citizens of Yonkers and the Dinner Committee

This Advertisement Sponsored by:
The Members of The Yonkers Chamber of Commerce
The Yonkers Railroad Co., Leroy Frantz, President

In November 1952, two months after *Your Show of Shows* entered its third full season, Caesar's hometown honored him.

Your Show of Shows, September 1953. A dousing by frisky stagehands in a spoof of *From Here to Eternity* led both Sid and Imogene to stray uncharacteristically—and only momentarily—from the script.

Caesar was in awe of the Red Sox Hall of Famers seated to his left, including Jimmie Foxx, Joe Cronin, and Lefty Grove, at a banquet thrown by the Boston chapter of B'nai B'rith in 1954. But he identified with Ted Williams (rear, second from right).

Ever the trouper, Imogene Coca played nice for the cameras in Max Liebman's office that day in February 1954 when the end of *Your Show of Shows* was announced.

top left: By playing a very different kind of wife, Nanette Fabray developed her own following, but she never prompted the laughs, or tugged at the heart-strings, as Coca had.

top right: Caesar enjoying an unidentified sandwich (probably corned beef), accompanied by his customary bottle of Dr. Brown's Cel-Ray tonic. Throughout Caesar's glory years, on and off the screen, food was another of his co-stars.

left: The Caesar of *Caesar's Hour* retreated to his fancy penthouse office to feel like a *macher*, eat jellied calves' hooves, and flee Mel Brooks.

Caesar's writers, 1956–57: (front row from left) Gary Belkin, Sheldon Keller, Mike Stewart, Mel Brooks; (back row) Neil Simon, Mel Tolkin, Larry Gelbart. Little noted either by anti- or philo-Semites, all seven writers that season were Jews.

Guilt-ridden over shooting a deer, Caesar substituted cans of shaving cream and halvah tins vacuum-packed with water for more customary prey on his Catskills hunting expeditions.

For a time, Caesar evangelized tirelessly for psychoanalysis, which he said had cured him of many ills. But not everyone was convinced, or even interested.

For the women who danced on *Caesar's Hour* (from left to right, Frances Rainer, Greb Lober, Ina Kurland, and Florence Brooks), such lighthearted moments with the boss were rare, and elevator rides with him were torture.

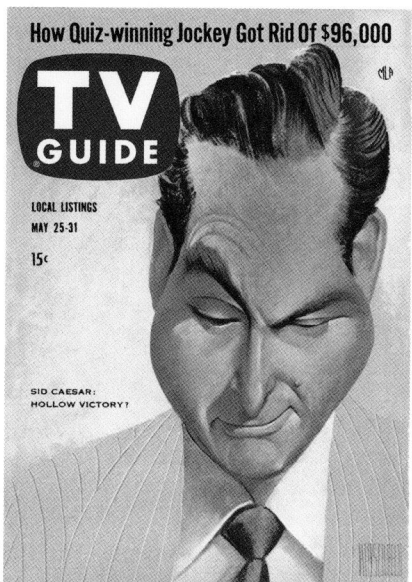

As his career sputtered, Caesar had the considerable consolation of an Al Hirschfeld portrait on the cover of *TV Guide*.

Like many, Jack Davis of *Humbug* blamed hayseeds in the hinterlands for the shellacking Lawrence Welk gave Sid Caesar in the television ratings.

Mel Brooks and Woody Allen teamed up for a Caesar special airing in May 1959. As if the reactions from the live audience somehow weren't enough, the program marked the first Caesar show with a laugh track.

Given Caesar's manic state at the time, playing a crazed dentist in *It's a Mad, Mad, Mad, Mad World* (1963) wasn't such a stretch.

The great love people felt for *Grease* (1978) spilled over onto Caesar, who played Coach Calhoun to John Travolta's Danny Zuko in the film.

Received rapturously when he guest-hosted *Saturday Night Live* in February 1983, Caesar (here with cast members Julia Louis-Dreyfus and Eddie Murphy) was difficult on the set and critical off it, alienating even those in awe of him.

Caesar was an inspiration to younger comedians like Billy Crystal, who presented him with TV Land's Pioneer Award in March 2006.

For Caesar, playing Hempstead wasn't acting so much as autobiography. He appeared frazzled. His lifelong struggles with language returned, but in a new and different form: He now man-handled his lines, spoke frantically, slurred his words, repeated himself. A man who only a few years earlier could discharge torrents of verbiage effortlessly now fumbled rudimentary phrases. Muffs once confined to his introductions leached into the rest of the show. Formerly able to toss off long passages from memory, he now displayed desperation in his delivery. He got a laugh during an amusement park sketch when he ordered both a hot dog *and* a frankfurter, but it's unlikely any joke was intended. "Let's keep a sharp lookout for Indians and Apaches," he warned during a stagecoach sketch, one in which the contrast between the sparkling writing and his own faltering performance was especially glaring. No longer did characters offer refuge: It was painful, and especially unfunny, to hear Bob Victor stumble his way through a speech at the Springdale Country Club. Even the Professor stammered. Caesar stopped doing pantomimes, which required greater concentration than he could manage. Double-talk became his best camouflage, his refuge of first resort.

Caesar recognized his problems; they were clear from the kinescopes. "I could see the timing wasn't there, and it just wasn't right, it wasn't *clean*, it was wrong," he said years afterward. "I overstated myself, I kept on repeating, it was just a little bit off. People were still saying, 'Oh, he's all right,' but I knew it." No one said anything explicit, but the veteran comic Jimmy Durante might have come closest. "Poor, poor Sid Caesar!" he declared in late December 1956. "Week in and week out, he's knocking his brains out on TV." Caesar's decline was all the more stark next to the ageless, imperturbable Reiner, who remained as fresh and sure-footed as ever. Reiner revealed years later that he'd turned down a good role in a movie starring Ernie Kovacs and Jack Lemmon because he felt an increasingly unsteady Caesar needed him. Caesar's impairment hadn't tempered his ambitions: The pieces he somehow pulled off were among his best. But Reiner came to realize that, as he put it, "Sid wasn't going to go on much longer."

"For the first time in my life, the booze and pills were overlapping into my working days," Caesar was to write. "My big strong body wasn't metabolizing the stuff so efficiently anymore." "He was literally—*literally*—wearing his brain out," Brooks remembered. "By the time it was nearly over, you could see the angst. You could see it in his performance, the anxiety. There was a worried look when he was thinking of the next line, thinking of the next beat. And that never happened in the early days. A lot of the moist gray little cells were drying up, and he kind of told you, with stuttering. Sometimes he would completely forget something. But Carl was always there."

Occasionally, usually at the last minute, when a sketch had fallen through, Caesar and his team worked after dinner. "I have to stay. They threw the script out the window," Tolkin would often say when he called home, conjuring up for his young son an image of his father, on hands and knees, picking up pages off the sidewalk. But sometimes Caesar just got clingy. "He didn't want to go home. He just wanted to play with the guys," said Morris. (How, Gelbart was once asked, could someone who loved his wife enough to punch out a horse for her not want to go home to her? "A horse is one thing; marriage is another," Gelbart explained.)

On one such night, needing a new movie sketch, the group headed to Blair House, where the plan was to have a few drinks, then eat, then work. The problem was that Caesar had just been prescribed a new sedative, Placidyl. Still unsure of the proper dose, he had taken more than he needed. At some point, in the middle of some pronouncement or complaint, he blacked out and fell face-first into some food, either brook trout (according to Morris), soup (Simon), or a bowl of coleslaw (Reiner). Or, as Brooks contended, all of the above. "There was coleslaw, brook trout, *and* mashed potatoes," he said. "I think he hit them all. He had a big face."

His dinnermates initially assumed Caesar was just horsing around, only he *stayed* down. "I was worried he'd drown in the coleslaw, but he was breathing OK," Reiner recalled. "And there's Sid Caesar, who was the biggest star in the world at that point, face down in the brook trout," said Morris. And surrounded by other diners, every one of them a potential mole for the gossip columns. "We're all sitting there like schmucks," Morris added. "What do we do?" So they pretended they were either rehearsing a crime caper—"So, Inspector, this undoubtedly is the murder weapon," said one of them, standing above Caesar, steak knife in hand—or holding a séance, or in prayer. After a while—the consensus is forty-five minutes or so—Caesar "rose out of the fish, covered with gravy and all kinds of shit," said Morris, and picked up precisely where he'd left off, either ordering shoestring potatoes or complaining about Janet Blair. The episode popped up regularly in recollections of Life with Sid. "It's funny," the reporter Dick Schaap, putting together a story on Caesar twenty-five years later for the television show 20/20, told Morris after hearing his version of events. "Everybody tells this story, but it's always a different dish!" As for Caesar, he didn't remember any of it. He was too "zonked out," he later wrote.

AS THE NEW YEAR got under way, Welk continued to clobber Caesar in the ratings. For a quarter or less of what Caesar's show cost, he was delivering one and a half times as many viewers, including some in Caesar's backyard, as Shirl Conway discovered visiting her hometown of Franklinville, New York. "Why doesn't Sid Caesar do his show at a different hour?" a local asked her. "We just love Lawrence Welk." The Chicago Tribune predicted Caesar's show would be "changed, rechanneled—or canceled." A report that NBC might move Caesar off Saturday night sparked a war of words in TV Guide. Alice Martin of Los Angeles thought the switch unnecessary because Caesar and Welk weren't really competing. "Anyone who can endure the Welk com-pa-pa could scarcely have the intelligence to understand what the Caesar show is all about," she argued. How good of Martin to enlighten everyone, countered J. B. Van Noy of Hollywood: "I know now that my failure to appreciate the Caesar show was due to my lack of intelligence. However, along with 35 or 40,000,000 other morons, I shall continue watching Welk shows."

In late February, Marie Torre of the Herald Tribune discerned "a distinct ray of hope for all television": NBC had resolved to save Caesar, ratings be damned. But according to *Variety*, Caesar was poised to either lose half his airtime or be relegated to specials. He was about to be washed away "by the champagne music of Lawrence Welk," reported *Newsweek*, "and just where he might bob to the surface again was a matter of dismal conjecture." On March 16, *Caesar's Hour* won five more Emmys, including best one-hour show and best comedian in a regular series (with Caesar beating out Jack Benny, Phil Silvers, and Ernie Kovacs). "May I say one thing: one man does not do it alone," Caesar said stiffly when collecting his first statuette. "It takes a lot of people, and it takes their patience with me," he added just as stiffly when collecting the second. Also winning that evening were Reiner, Pat Carroll, and Fabray, even though she'd left the show six months earlier. (Blair soon gave notice she'd not be back next season— assuming there was one.)

Crosby couldn't resist. " 'We didn't come to bury Caesar; we came to praise him' might well have been the refrain" for the evening, he wrote. The five Emmys were five more than Welk won for what Caesar's great loyalist on the Yiddish *Forverts*, Nakhman Zalowitz, called his "hillbilly band." "There was no category for inoffensive sweet band leaders with Alsatian accents," one newspaper editorialized. One NBC executive saw in the statuettes a stay of execution, but nothing had really changed. A "hollow victory," *TV Guide* called the awards. *Caesar's Hour* was doomed by its originality, wrote Jack O'Brian—proof of Robert Benchley's aphorism that "what's trite is right." What Jack Gould called "the inexorable law of overexposure" had caught up with Gleason, Caesar, and other TV comics.

The show ground on. On April 6, it took off after *Tonight! America After Dark*, a Weaveresque program catering to voyeurism by sending out reporters to parties, premieres, and nightclubs. In Washington, the hostess with the mostest Mrs. John Meddler (Carroll) had laid out for her guests (including the Maharajah of Fluoristan) the Treasury Department in chopped liver, the State Department in baked halibut, and Congress as "one long egg roll." Two shows later, Caesar demonstrated that

even in his diminished state he remained nimble. Cast as a sham-
bling, decrepit country lawyer, he argued so persuasively on
behalf of a nebbishy client accused of murder (Morris) that the
extra playing the jury foreman declared him *not* guilty rather than
the other way around, as the script called for. "Sid was in a panic,
but of course ad-libbed and ad-libbed and ad-libbed, and saved
the day for us," Gelbart recalled.[*]

Publicly, Caesar remained confident, and uncompromising.
He wasn't interested in a half-hour show; "I have nothing to say
in 24 minutes," he explained. Nor would he do ten hour-long
shows on alternating Sunday nights. While Welk couldn't last,
he predicted, with "a new breed of writers to supply the jokes,
and a new breed of people to enjoy them," he would. Whatever
concerns they had privately about Caesar's well-being, his trusty
sidekicks were sticking with him. "I have no fears about the future
with Sid," said Reiner. "He has to go on. He's only thirty-four."
"Sid's a giant, and you don't cut a giant's cloak to fit the times,"
Morris said.

A meeting Caesar had with Bobby Sarnoff and Robert
Kintner, the former ABC honcho who'd just joined NBC,
"got exactly nowhere," *Variety* reported. "Audience-wise, SID
CAESAR is a losing proposition on all counts," an NBC executive declared in an internal memo that month. Caesar's audience
share, he reported, had tumbled from 62 percent five years earlier to 26 percent; of 130 shows on evening TV, *Caesar's Hour*
ranked 94th. Small wonder NBC couldn't find him sponsors for
the next season. "I think Caesar is the greatest, but I wouldn't
buy him if I was a businessman," Phil Silvers noted. "His humor
is too esoteric."

Once more, Caesar felt unloved: No matter how much NBC

---

[*] Though repurposed from earlier sketches, Morris's stirring plea for mercy was another
of his finest performances, as it was for Caesar's writers. "I never had a break," he testifies.
"I never had the nice things. I never had fresh fruit in the house. I never ate Chinese food
in the rain. I never had my teeth fixed in the summertime—no, I never had no advantages. I
used to think that the bottom of my bare feet were shoes. I never saw a crocus or a rosebud
nor a robin on the wing" (*Caesar's Hour*, April 20, 1957). Like Brooks in the Mountains, he
ends up, à la Al Jolson, in song.

was paying him, it was less than what *he* was giving *them*. Morris remembered Caesar looking out from his office window at the RCA Building and declaring, "Jesus Christ, wouldn't you think the fucking building would bend over and give me a kiss?" "NBC said, 'Listen, don't do a show every week. Do one show a month,' but Sid wouldn't have it," Morris remembered. "He said, 'No, my audience would not stand for me not being on every week.' He was full of shit. They said, 'Oh, is that how you feel? OK, good-bye. We'll call ya.' And he kept waiting for them to call."

On April 27, the program targeted Mike Wallace, then still establishing himself as television's Grand Inquisitor on *Night-Beat*, a program shown only on a small station in New York but which, thanks in part to Caesar's attention, was about to go national. Reiner's Wallace reduces Professor Ludwig von Integrity to a sweaty mess, revealing that while claiming to hold a chair in Heidelberg, the Professor was actually fixing fights in Salzburg. The slow death of a show so "excruciatingly funny" was, said *Variety*, "a sad commentary on American viewing habits and social mores."

In fact, the divorce was already a done deal. Under their contract, NBC owed Caesar $100,000 a year for the next seven years, but on the advice of his lawyer, convinced another network would snap him up, Caesar didn't hold the network to it. "That's how nuts I was," he later said. No doubt the brass was delighted; they'd paid Weaver $300,000 to walk away. "They didn't put up any kind of a fight," Caesar wrote. "In fact, they looked relieved. . . . I knew what they were saying to themselves: 'He's a drunk. He won't accept help. Let's dump him.'"

The program of May 4, 1957, turned out to be the last with original material. It featured a takeoff on the NBC program *Wide Wide World* (which featured live dispatches from around the globe), in which the keeper of the San Francisco Municipal Menagerie, Wilbur Burkee (Reiner), makes his assistant (Caesar) hold a "South American finger eater" in his hands, then place a poisonous snake around his neck. "You people with color sets are lucky, because [Caesar] is a *lovely* shade of lavender now," he says. "The most they can bring is temporary death." In the same sketch, Morris, playing a baby gorilla named Howie, gets to tweak Caesar's nose, stuff a banana down his throat, and wrestle him to the ground, rather than the usual other way around. It was a long time coming for Morris, and must have been fun.

Then came the show's last movie send-up, a lame piece about a hayseed musician named Lipscott Fitzgerald, played by Caesar. "Young man, do you know there's a whole new craze sweeping over this country?" he's asked. "It's called corny music." And so it was. "The Man Who Killed Caesar," Larry Wolters called Welk the next day. The network brass had another nickname for him: "The Meatgrinder." "Only recently," *Look* later reported, "the favorite comedian of the intellectuals, Sid Caesar, went through the chopper."

Speaking to *Time* in mid-May, Caesar was alternately defiant, rambling, and abstract. "They would like to control me and I cannot be controlled," he told the reporter. And he continued:

> I'm 34 years old. I like to work. I'll not retire with four or five shows a year and spend the rest of the time reading a bunch of pseudo-intellectual books. Right now I'm working six days a week. I work till 7, 8, 9, 10 p.m., maybe 2 a.m. You can't turn creativity on and off. I get up early to read. Have you read *Oedipus Rex*? I could never do a satire on *Oedipus Rex*. I'd never read it before and it's opened up a whole new world. Now I'm reading through history. From Alexander the Great through World War II. You know that before going into battle the waiting is almost intolerable. In war, either your plan works or it doesn't. The thing between NBC and myself, it's a war of attrition. There's something [*sic*] up there that does not like me.

"Caesar in real life is like a Caesar imitation of a professor off his rocker," a stringer for the magazine wrote in a memo afterward. "He has the most intensely loyal fans of anyone on TV," one NBC executive told *Time*. "It's almost a cult and I'm proud to be a member of it." But "there must be something wrong in what

Sid is doing," he went on. "If somebody could tell us maybe even Sid's analyst would be delighted to hear it."

Reporting on Caesar for *TV Guide*—a story that secured for him the immortality of an Al Hirschfeld caricature on the cover—Frank DeBlois found an angry, defiant Sid sipping Cel-Ray tonic behind his gargantuan teakwood desk, his office drapes drawn tight. "Sure, my show is expensive," Caesar told him. "We use the best of everything. And maybe another guy's show doesn't cost as much as mine, but gets higher ratings. Well, does that mean that *nobody* wants to look at Caesar? . . . Television is my business and I love it. I'd hate to leave TV. But there are areas where I won't make any compromises." He walked over to the window, pulled open the curtains, and gazed out at New York City. "Great town," he said. And then he drew them shut.

On May 16, the divorce was official. The final show would be on May 25—at the request of disgruntled sponsors, two weeks ahead of schedule. Bobby Sarnoff expressed regret, and wished Caesar well. But Caesar's prospects were unclear. Much as an ABC executive said he admired him, he also said they had no interest in hiring him. CBS said the same thing. In a statement, Caesar pledged to "continue to try to bring entertainment to the American people." After nine years in the business, he added, he hadn't "even begun to scratch the surface" of television; time would vindicate his focus on ordinary people rather than on "things like guitars and long sideburns and cowboys and private eyes." Caesar was buried "by the men in the charcoal grey togas," quipped the *Daily News*. "CAESAR: MCMXLIX–MCMLVII," *Variety* pronounced.

Letters of protest swamped Caesar's office. The folks atop the RCA Building got mail, too. "Sid Caesar's fans continue to plague us," one internal memo went, noting 257 letters in April and another 1,074 in May. "In the somewhat hysterical search for ratings, ratings, ratings, you ignore the salient fact that a smaller, loyal, appreciative audience can do more for a show's sponsors than a larger, indifferent mob who just watch a program out of a lack of anything better to do," went one. When Caesar asked viewers which segments he should repeat in his last two shows, more than ten thousand of them weighed in. On May 18, he redid a Japanese movie and "Break Your Brains"*—two exhausting sketches that showed he wasn't just going through the motions. "Like a ball player coming to bat for the last or next-to-the-last time, he swung for the fences," one commentator noted.

Then came the final telecast. While the Lennon Sisters sang "Zip-a-Dee-Doo-Dah" for Welk, Caesar replayed his bit on Grieg's Piano Concerto. And then, to conclude the show—was it an admission, or simply his determination to reprise his very best work?—he brought back "A Drunk There Was." Drenched just as he had been the first time around, Caesar summoned everyone for a final curtain call. He heaped praise on his team. "Until we meet again, good night and God bless you," he told his audience, in the theater and beyond. As the credits rolled, viewers could see Howard Morris, in a tone-deaf burst of gallows humor, jumping up and down on the stage. The orchestra then broke into one final round of the "Towers Trot."

The tributes, and eulogies, followed. "Caesar may have been too clever, too intellectual for a mass comedian," Ben Gross wrote in the *Daily News*. "To appreciate him requires not only a knowledge of books, plays, movies, psychological and social trends but also a willingness to use one's mental processes. In other words, to think." "If you laughed your sides off during the farewell performance of *Caesar's Hour* last Saturday night, I hope you had a few tears to shed as well," Philip Minoff wrote in *Cue*. "Not so much for Caesar, but for television." Within a few days Caesar had signed on with Weaver for various unspecified projects, including several movies in which he'd star.† It was all so vague that around Caesar's offices their joint enterprise was referred to simply as "The Thing." Just about the only sure thing about the thing was that Tolkin would be doing it with him. "Everything

---

* This time it came, courtesy of Brooks, with a Yiddish twist: Unable to name the composer of the opera *Faust*, a frustrated Hempstead declares, "Go know!"—the Anglicized version of "Gey veys!" a Yiddish declaration of befuddlement. "That's right! Gounod!" Reiner shouts. It was one of Brooks's pet jokes.

† The two had bought first refusal rights to the next novel by Sloan Wilson, author of *The Man in the Gray Flannel Suit*. Like so many of Caesar's movie projects, nothing came of it.

will be all right," Ed Wynn reassured Caesar. "Art endures when all else passes."

While showcasing some of Caesar's most dazzling work, *Caesar's Hour* never took hold the way *Your Show of Shows* had, or generated the same passion and affection. But in the history of television, its death is the real milestone—the moment when TV showed its cards. "The cost-per-thousand boys and the ratings rajahs and the sponsors' wives and the demographic samplers had taken over television, and the noble experiment with live, sophisticated entertainers was terminated," Andrew Sarris wrote. Its end marked the death of the delusion that merit mattered. Finally, one of those hackneyed Roman images was apt: Television really had crossed a Rubicon.

Sure, it was a business. And sure, Pat Weaver's nostrums about television's responsibilities sounded quaint even when he said them. But as late as the spring of 1957, otherwise sane commentators still believed TV could, should, and maybe even would protect its brightest gems from the ravages of the marketplace. When, a few days after Caesar's cancellation, Harriet Van Horne asked whether ratings had to rule, it was still a legitimate question. "There is something vicious in this kind of thinking," she marveled. "It penalizes talent—not to mention wit, audacity, and charm. It grovels to mediocrity. Worse, it orders the gifted men among us, 'Go thou and be mediocre, too!'"

Caesar's champions were humbled by his fall. Earl Wilson of the *New York Post* was agog that nobodies on couches in the boondocks hooked up to Trendex or Nielsen boxes, and not people like him, were determining what the American public got to see. "You sit around in your pajama bottoms," he wrote. "With one twist of the little dial, you can put Sid Caesar out of work." "A negative landmark in the young history of the medium," *Variety* called Caesar's demise; surely, some way could have been found to make his show pay, and even if it couldn't, why couldn't NBC carry him the way it had Toscanini?* "Any

---

* NBC had created a symphony orchestra for the great conductor in 1937, which he led until his retirement in 1954. It disbanded shortly thereafter.

rating that puts Sid Caesar out of business is no good," Paddy Chayefsky told the *Herald Tribune*. "The last remnants of talent are leaving TV." "That Lawrence Welk, a tenth-class musician, should defeat Sid Caesar, a first-class comic—that is not just a heartache, but a shame," the *Forverts* lamented. During his glory years, Caesar had subscribed to the notion that *"di shtime fun folk iz di shtime fun got"*—that "the voice of the people is the voice of God," Zalowitz later wrote. Now he was ready to swear that *"der oylem iz a goylem"*—that "people are blockheads."

The public had had its fill of Caesar, Crosby conceded, and much as he'd miss him, so had he. But for such a "social thinker" and "cultural force" to lose to a Lawrence Welk portended programming of "pure mildness, pure torpor, pure opiate." Gould was less apocalyptic. Sure, Caesar was principled, he wrote, but good things, too, must come to an end. Just the same, viewers still believed they could make a difference. For the next couple of months, pro-Caesar letters accounted for three-quarters of *TV Guide*'s mail. The satirical magazine *Humbug*, which *Mad*'s founder Harvey Kurtzman had recently launched, gave its "Humbug Hero of the Month" award to "He Who Didn't Watch Sid Caesar," depicted by the artist Jack Davis as *two* people: the famous pair from *American Gothic*, though in this version the man held a telephone receiver and the woman sported a "We Love Lawrence" cameo pin. "Trendex Informants," Davis called the couple.

In a mock interview with *Variety*, the world's leading authority on Sid Caesar, Professor Hugo von Opinion, said Caesar's problem was that he was too talented for television. "Dot's vy he's now kaput," he said. A blame game also ensued—television's version of "Who Lost China?" "During the final months of the Sid Caesar program . . . how many times did YOU look at it?" a columnist in Philadelphia asked his readers. "If the public is so indignant, why didn't it watch him and buy the sponsor's products?" Jack Benny asked. Jerry Lewis said Caesar had put himself out there too much. "By the time you got to the hundred and fiftieth show, they'd know which way your eyebrows slanted, the profile you like best, every pore in your skin," he said.

Jo Coppola of *Newsday* asked Caesar if he'd been too highbrow. "I never played down to the audience," he replied. "I gave them credit for intelligence." Most of his fan mail came from small towns, he insisted, conjuring up images of all those mute, inglorious Milton Berles tuning in when they weren't reading books banned from the local library. As for being overexposed, Caesar told her, "the only thing that's overexposed is Strontium-90." Mass audiences had always preferred the sweet to the satirical, Coppola noted, yet Caesar had still pulled in more than sixteen million people. "He accomplished the impossible," she wrote. "But the impossible wasn't enough." For its part, NBC had no second thoughts. "If we listened to the eggheads we'd be out of business in six months," Bobby Sarnoff said.

Caesar's fans dug in. The most tenacious, and resourceful, of them was Harry J. Macklis, a lawyer in Queens and founder, chairman, and one-fifth of the membership of what he called the "Committee for Caesar's Longevity." Hoping to inspire a populist revolt, in early July he sent out a lengthy manifesto to newspapers throughout the country. It began with something about the other Caesar—in this case, a snippet from Mark Antony in Shakespeare's play:

> *O mighty Caesar! dost thou lie so low?*
> *Are all thy conquests, glories, triumphs, spoils,*
> *Shrunk to this little measure?*

Adopting Antony's sardonic tone, Macklis declared that everyone responsible for Sid Caesar's demise—the network executives, advertisers, the people determining the ratings—were, like Julius's assassins, all honorable. But collectively they'd toppled "an inspired, unadulterated genius," leaving Macklis and countless others with the bleak specter of a Caesarless season. He urged the newsmen to whom he'd reached out to urge their readers to urge NBC to reconsider. "I have the feeling that Mr. Macklis represents that part of the TV audience describable loosely as the 'Intelligentsia,'" one columnist observed. "This group watches TV more than it pretends it does."

Florence Caesar wouldn't have signed up with Macklis. For

her, nine years in television was quite enough. But her husband felt he still had lots to say, and as his longtime producer, Hal Janis, later put it, Caesar "went literally crazy sitting on his can." So, playing his trump card, Caesar called Coca, the only one of his "wives" who'd "ever really operated on my wave length," proposing a reunion. She quickly agreed: As distastefully as her "marriage" with Caesar had ended, she needed him more than the other way around. Then he called NBC, offering them a half-hour show with the two of them. Suddenly he *could* say something in twenty-four minutes after all.

Caesar leaked word of their reconciliation to his favorite reporters, who splashed it over their front pages in July 1957. "Sid and Imogene May Walk Up TV Aisle Again in Fall," the *New York World-Telegram* proclaimed. But talk of a new Caesar-Coca program was way premature; nothing about it—the format, timing, budget, sponsors, cast—was nailed down, including whether NBC even wanted it or had room for it if it did. One reporter detected "an air of desperation about this reunion-from-the-blue bit."

With nothing cooking by early September, Harry Macklis sprang back into action, taking out small ads—tucked inside black borders usually reserved for death notices—in the nether regions of *The New York Times* and *New York Herald Tribune*. "DON'T BURY CAESAR!" pleaded one on the very last page of the *Times*, which set Macklis back $33. "Do we get Sid Caesar Back or Do We have to throw away our T.V. Sets? Bring Back Caesar (And we don't mean Julius)." And, miraculously, his prayers were soon answered. On September 20, still-lowly ABC announced it had signed up Caesar and Coca for a half-hour show, to begin in January 1958. The show would run for only half a season, at least for now, but the network envisioned Caesar and Coca being with ABC for years to come. Sponsoring the show would be Helena Rubinstein, now eighty-four years old. She'd never advertised on TV before, and had watched Caesar and Coca only once. But she'd always trusted her whims (in this case, over the objections of some of her executives), and they'd served her well.

The restoration was celebrated at a jam-packed press conference at "21" in September. Caesar and Coca smiled at each other for the cameras, held hands, rubbed noses. How long, he was asked, would the two stay together this time? "I hope for eternity," he replied. "Now I can relax," Caesar declared. "Television is where I belong." At one point Mme Rubinstein reached out to Caesar. "Shake my hand," she whispered to him. "When I shake hands, it brings that person good luck." When Caesar was about to describe the new show to someone, she shushed him. "Don't tell him all the new ideas," she said. Harry Macklis was pleased, but wary. "We plan to assume a watchful, waiting attitude," he said.

SID CAESAR INVITES YOU, as the new show was to be called, would air on Sunday nights. Reiner signed up for it, but Morris did not, figuring he'd be even more marginalized in the shorter format and still craving more for himself than playing "a commuting nebbish, a Japanese nebbish and a Nazi nebbish for Sid," as someone had described his repertoire. As for the writing staff, Tolkin returned from a short exile with Jerry Lewis, joined by Brooks and the Simons, with Mike Stewart back behind the typewriter.

Thanks to his latest diet—high on protein and tomatoes, low on fat and starch—Caesar was in fighting shape. (He'd also cut back on the cigars, from ten or fifteen a day to three—and smaller ones at that—one after each meal. He was thinking ahead; "I want to be able to smoke at 70, so I cut down now," he explained.) "Why did Sid Caesar knock off twenty-five pounds," asked Zalowitz. "What's the matter—was he unseemingly fat, like, God forbid, Jackie Gleason?" In fact, he explained, it reflected Caesar's determination to unveil a man renovated physically, spiritually, and comedically on his new show. People would now see someone wiser and more humble, able to poke fun at himself. It would remind people they were not alone, that their foibles were his foibles, too. Zalowitz, at least, felt betrayed by Caesar's new approach: By abandoning satire, he said, Caesar was deserting his audience and forsaking what he did best. "The group who delight in *The Lawrence Welk Show* or in *I Love Lucy* or in *The Honeymooners* or in *Wagon Train*—those tens of millions do not like satire," he complained. "Sid Caesar, it seems, decided to give the *oylem-goylem* what it wants."

Caesar said ABC had promised him creative carte blanche, and the shorter show meant fewer cooks with less broth to spoil. Still, he tamped down expectations. "I'm not gonna bust no sound barriers," he said. But to the consternation of his handlers, Caesar seemed more eager to discuss his latest obsession—the Civil War—than the new show. Rather than reading *Variety*, *Billboard*, and Mickey Spillane stories like everyone else in his world, Van Horne wrote, Caesar's head was back in Chancellorsville in 1863. "I think there's a Civil War raging in every man," he told her. "Each of us is a battleground." Listening to Caesar, Zalowitz picked up a surprising sympathy for the Old South; one might have thought, he wrote, that Caesar's mother was in the Daughters of the Confederacy, and that his father had fought for Robert E. Lee. But this wasn't a matter of politics—"Sid Caesar is not in favor of slavery," Zalovitz assured his readers—but lifestyle: as a certified millionaire and member of the Great Neck squirearchy, he'd developed a taste for antebellum-style elegance. "Gracious living," Caesar called it, and he couldn't stop talking about it.

NOT SINCE THE BIRTH of Little Ricky Ricardo on *I Love Lucy* five years earlier was a television debut so highly anticipated. *TV Guide* put Caesar and Coca, gently caressing each other, on its cover. Tickets were precious enough for the New York *Daily News* to request its readers to please not write in asking for them. "It isn't too corny to speculate on how many throats will tighten nostalgically tonight when Sid and Imogene square off once again," the *Herald Tribune* declared the morning of the premiere. Macklis was giddy. "RATINGS, SHMATINGS!! CAESAR'S BACK, AND COCA'S GOT HIM," went an ad he placed in the *New York Post*, in which he compared Caesar to Coca to Reiner to Tinker to Evers to Chance, the great baseball double-play combination. But ABC's leash was short: The pair would thrive, a network executive said, "so long as they don't get egghead."

Then there was what Zalowitz ominously called "The Sid Caesar Problem." How often, he asked *Forverts* readers, had they seen Tomashefsky, or Caruso, or Kreisler, or Paderewski, or Chaplin? Maybe fifty times, tops. But after seven seasons of him, they'd now seen Sid Caesar a *couple of hundred*. How much more of his shtick and *mishugas* could, and would, they take?

"For the first time since 1953—live from New York—Sid Caesar and Imogene Coca!" Reiner shouted at the beginning of the show on Sunday night, January 26, 1958. Reiner, uncharacteristically, was off by a year, but it hardly mattered. "With that, one of the great comedy teams of television's history strolled out from opposite wings of the stage, heads ducked, shy, pretending they were meeting again for the first time since they parted," wrote Terry Turner of the *Chicago Daily News*. "'Sid, Sid, Sid,' said Imogene of the wonderfully flexible face. 'Sid, Sid, Sid, Sid. Oh, Sid, Sid, Sid.' Sid ducked his head, shuffled his feet, looked up and said: 'Imogene, Imogene—that's hard to say—Imogene, Imogene, Imogene.'"

"You know, you look like yourself," Coca gushed.

"Who else have I got to look like?" Caesar replied.

"Not a particularly amusing line," Turner noted. "The audience roared." On this night, he noted, "nothing that Sid or Imogene could do would be wrong."

Ratings-wise, the show beat out Ronald Reagan and *General Electric Theater* on CBS and Dinah Shore on NBC, even with Frank Sinatra on her show. In fact, playing what *The Philadelphia Inquirer* called "a hat-wearing, open-collared, cigarette-puffing, finger-snapping crooner named Johnny Hat," singing "Love Is a Gasser" from his latest album (*Songs to Make Money By*), Caesar had gone right after him.

More than thirty million people tuned in to the broadcast, which was marred by the same overzealous Caesar friend alongside a microphone who'd cackled at many of Caesar's shows in recent years. Hundreds of people jammed ABC's phone lines to complain. But neither that nor Caesar's look—"drawn, almost anemic"—nor his evident tenseness dampened the occasion. "There was hardly a dry eye in the house," wrote Crosby. "That's television for you. These fabulous personalities burst out of nowhere in a shower of sparks. Then in very short order the public tires of them. They disappear altogether. Then suddenly they are welcomed home like Ulysses. And all this in so short a time. Sid Caesar is only thirty-five years old for heaven's sake. Yet he's being treated like an elder statesman. It must be disconcerting."

Mindful of Caesar's fragile psyche and physique, and his role as standard-bearer for quality television, the critics were kind. "Even drizzle is welcome in a drought," declared *Time*. More than kind, in fact: They were positively *protective*. "This must have been an ordeal for Mr. Caesar, a sensitive man, and a shy one, in private life, who knows very well that he is at an important turning-point in his career," wrote Donald Kirkley of the Baltimore *Sun*. He importuned readers to send Caesar letters of support, even providing his address. ("Letters mean a lot to him," he explained.) To John Lardner of *The New Yorker*, criticizing Caesar only aided and abetted the corporate cretins. "It seems to me unwise, to put it mildly, to contribute in any way to their folly and thus to make television unsafe for one of the few original spirits, and the finest comedian, in its history," he wrote. All this TLC galled Caesar's detractors. "Why is Sid such a pet with the New York critics, anyway?" asked "Sally" in the *Akron Beacon Journal*. "Before, he was just conceited. Now he's humbly conceited, having been psychoanalyzed or something."

Caesar's second show got better reviews than the first, though Caesar himself did not. So troubled by Caesar's appearance was one critic that he couldn't enjoy him. "Here's hoping his health improves," he wrote. But the third show produced one of the last great Caesar sketches, abounding with all the old sparkle and obsessions. Caesar is Luis Flamingo, an aged bullfighter who'd abandoned the bullring for the rag trade (and, specifically, children's ready-to-wear—an inside Seventh Avenue joke they once would have shunned). On a dare from a jealous rival matador (Reiner) he attempts one last match. He is mortally wounded, prompting a long and lachrymose bedside vigil, during which he makes one dying request: for an American cheese sandwich.

"An American cheese sandwich," Coca, playing an American

dowager who's just ditched her husband for him, orders a flunky (Kamen) to fetch.

"An American cheese sandwich. All right. I'll get it," Kamen replies somberly.

"No, I had cheese for lunch," Flamingo suddenly interjects. "Make it roast beef. On rye."

"I'll cancel the American . . . I'll get the roast beef," says Kamen.

"*I'll* have the American cheese," says Reiner. "I didn't eat before the fight."

"Make it *two* American cheese sandwiches," Coca directs. "And don't put mustard on mine because I'm allergic to it."

As everyone reviews their sandwich orders, then specifies just how they take their coffees, the dying Flamingo sits up indignantly. "Wait a minute! Wait!" he shouts. "Let's have an assortment of cold cuts. And drink some sodas. And don't forget a bottle opener. I always . . . forget . . . the . . . bottle . . . opener."

Death is imminent. The ululating intensifies. But Flamingo isn't done. "And don't forget to wake me when the food comes," he blurts out before expiring.

More than fifty years later, even thinking about the sketch made Mike Nichols's eyes water with joy. And sixty years later, it still captured for Brooks how Caesar and he were sending comedy in a startling new direction. "It didn't end up with 'you were the greatest and I love you,' it ended up with 'what did you order? A cheese sandwich? I want pastrami,'" Brooks recalled. In other words, shorn of the sentimentality they both "*abhorred.*"

Since Caesar was no longer saving his work, few episodes of *Sid Caesar Invites You* survive. (Among the losses was his long-delayed spoof of *The Bridge on the River Kwai*, the bridge in question dental.) But people knew a retread when they saw it. One jaded network type compared the program to "the thrashing about of a dinosaur in the marshes of evolution." The ratings sagged; when the show went head-to-head in March with Bob Hope's, the final tally was Hope 33, Caesar 9. At the Emmys that month, only Reiner won an award. Ever loyal, he bent over and kissed Caesar before bounding up onstage. "This was easy for me to do because I'm supporting one of the greatest comedians in the whole wide world," he said once he got there. (A photograph taken that night—the one on the cover of this book—was misleading, or at least dated: It showed Caesar at peak *macherdom* [smiling smugly, a cigar between two fingers and a pinkie ring on a third] and Reiner still playing the courtier. Though their positions were rapidly reversing, that night each still stuck to his customary role.) "I'm also being written for by the greatest comedy writers in that same world," Reiner took care to add.[*]

Sid Caesar Invites You expired nearly as fast as poor Señor Flamingo. By now, the demise of a Caesar show had become a rite of spring; this time, even Harry J. Macklis let it pass. To Caesar, the loss of what turned out to be his last weekly show was momentous. "It was like the earth opened up and swallowed me, because I had nothing to fall back on," he said.

Berle or Gleason got little sympathy when they fell off the air, Ed Sullivan noted; "about the only one who was cheered, win or lose, has been Sid Caesar." Caesar was in a professional death spiral, Mike Nichols and Elaine May told *Variety*, "at the mercy of dial-twirling philistines." Caesar was simultaneously more esteemed—"almost everyone mentions him nowadays in the hushed tones usually reserved for Albert Schweitzer, Stan Musial, science and motherhood," said a story from May 1958—and less sought after than ever. "Sid Caesar, probably the greatest clown produced by teevee, now represents one of the tragedies of the medium," Walter Winchell wrote. And movies were no longer an option, either. "Hollywood wasn't that interested," said Brooks.

The BBC signed up Caesar and Coca for a summer television series, which got very mixed reviews. "What a strange genius this man Caesar has!" wrote Philip Purser in the *News Chronicle*. "In himself, he is faceless, without identity. He becomes real only

---

[*] The writers needed some salve: For the third straight year, they'd been beaten out by Sergeant Bilko's. This annual snub, Brooks later claimed, prompted him to hop atop a table during the ceremony and scream, "Nietzsche was right! There *is* no God!" (Caesar, *Caesar's Hours*, 137) In fact, Brooks uttered his cri de coeur eight years later, when he and Buck Henry (then co-writing *Get Smart*) lost out to Bill Persky and Sam Denoff of *The Dick Van Dyke Show* for the Emmy for best comedy writing.

when he does a guise." But to *The Times*, Caesar "gave no impression of the qualities which are said to have held American audiences in thrall," and the critic for the *Evening Standard* found Caesar's Grieg Piano Concerto unimpressive coming only two weeks after an entire evening spent with Victor Borge.

Back stateside, Caesar rented out a chunk of his space in the Milgrim Building to Pat Boone. Instead of taking a sabbatical, as some urged, he tossed aside another taboo and signed up for two specials for Chevrolet the following season. "Television is his vocation, hobby and therapy all rolled into one," Marie Torre wrote in the *Herald Tribune*. "That he chooses to remain in it even in troubled times is no more astonishing than the shoemaker who sticks to his last."

For the first of the Chevy shows, Gelbart agreed to reunite with Caesar, but on one condition. "Without everybody, Sid," he insisted. "I can't do the room anymore." But joining Gelbart would be one other writer, someone he described as a "tadpole in horn-rims": Woody Allen, then twenty-two years old. ("You. You're hired" was how Caesar informed Allen that he had the job. "That was typical of the kind of grand personality that he had," Allen recalled.) Getting to work for a man he'd long admired was "mind-blowing," Allen said. But he soon got to observe some trademark Caesar eccentricities, like watching him wave a loaded gun around the office ("a harrowing experience") and being asked to work with him naked in Caesar's Kings Point *shvitz*. While Gelbart was game, Allen refused. "My sense of panic was too great," he explained.*

The show they wrote, which co-starred Art Carney and Shirley MacLaine, aired in early November 1958. In a rare (for Caesar) foray into politics, it poked fun at the emerging breed of political consultants, who counseled clients on whether they should smoke pipes, cigars, or cigarettes and what neckties they should wear. It also included a takeoff—eviscerated, Gelbart later complained, by squeamish sponsors afraid of offending teenagers who might steal a lot of Chevys—on *American Bandstand*,

---

* Gelbart remembered things a bit differently. "Nobody's funny when they're naked," he said Allen had protested. "That's when we're funniest," Gelbart countered.

with Caesar playing an addled groupie from "Sal Mineo High School." John Crosby welcomed Caesar back; the program, he wrote, "had all the hallmarks of his unique genius." "A scarce Caesar," declared *Variety*, "is infinitely better than a weekly Caesar." The program marked Caesar's tenth anniversary in television, but instead of ripening, said Harriet Van Horne, Caesar had ossified into self-parody. "What, one wonders, went awry with this clever young man?" she asked.

"This was undoubtedly a key show for Sid, about whom there have been many vague and disquieting rumors," wrote Bernie Harrison of the Washington *Star*, probably a rare and very veiled allusion to his drinking. (Working with Art Carney, Caesar later said, he'd found a kindred spirit. "Art knew I was a drunk, and I knew he was a drunk, and we had kind of psychedelic conversations in which we tap-danced around the subject," he said.) One prominent entertainment reporter speculated whether, at thirty-six, Caesar was already "washed up."

A second Chevy show, also written by Gelbart and Allen and co-starring Audrey Meadows, aired a month later. Featuring a spaceship spoof—having been bitten by a termite in the nose cone, the scientist Caesar began gorging on wood himself—and a takedown of cookie-cutter television Westerns, it got poor reviews. Forced "to shy away from anything that smacks of egg-headism," one television writer observed, Caesar had become "a semi-Caesar"—occasionally funny, but lacking his former bite. Caesar blamed timid TV types, playing it safe. "If it keeps up," he said, "you'll have disk jockeys on TV just the way we've got them on radio."

Meadows and Carney reappeared with Caesar in another hour-long special in May 1959, the first and only time Mel Brooks and Woody Allen joined forces for him. (Tolkin was on hand, too.) The show's featured sketch had Caesar (as Anthony Stunning) leaping from silent-era extra to a Valentino-type star based on his stupendous patent-leather-like mane. But Stunning is fired for refusing a role in a Western and goes on a bender that leaves him bald. This story of alcohol abuse, though, has a happy ending: He comes back, gloriously, as Yul Stunning.

The sketch was widely praised; in twenty years, one critic

predicted, scholars at the Museum of Modern Art would be "laughing so hard they'll drop their notebooks and pencils." But it offended hard-nosed types who still thought Caesar pampered and effete. Caesar, snapped Robert Sylvester of the *Daily News*, should have no trouble making a comeback; "all he needs is six writers, a director, a producer, a manager, and a few more show-men none of whom are named Sid Caesar." The show marked the end of Allen's brief apprenticeship with Caesar. "He believed that I had a contribution to make and that I was talented, but I wasn't the same extroverted *tummler* that Mel [Brooks] was, nor the same drinking sophisticate that Larry Gelbart was," Allen explained. "I came up with jokes, and they were good jokes, so he tolerated me. But he found my persona eccentric or strange, or that I didn't fit in with his boys' club mentality or something. I was not the guy who would get into the steam room with him."

Another of Caesar's red lines—that his shows be aired live— had now been crossed: The program had been taped (before a live audience at New York's Ziegfeld Theatre) the previous February. But that wasn't the reddest one. Though the seven hundred peo-ple on hand supplied plenty of "yoks" (as *Variety* called them), the honest mirth was sweetened by a laugh track—something Caesar had once likened to artificial insemination. The machine had been imported from Hollywood in a suitcase, hovered over by its handler, Allen recalled, like a precious object; by pushing a but-ton or two, the man inserted belly laughs, snickers, or titters of varying lengths at will. Opinions differed on whether Caesar was in on the arrangement, but either way it was ominous: If two of mid-century America's greatest comic writers working in tandem on behalf of one of television's greatest comics couldn't make Sid Caesar sufficiently funny, who could?

Mad magazine ran a number of illustrated sketches credited to Caesar, but surely written by someone else. It was a good deal for both parties, conferring some of Caesar's residual prestige on *Mad* and giving Caesar a younger audience and an appear-ance of productivity. It also honored him—for "Best Cough in Television"—at a mock awards program at Danny's Hide-A-Way. Lenny Bruce, too, remained a fan. In the summer of 1959, he divided comics into two categories: funny and not funny. Milton

Berle: not truly funny. Red Buttons: not funny at all. George
Gobel: not funny. Jerry Lewis: doesn't make it at all. Laurel
and Hardy: great comedians. W. C. Fields: a great genius, great
comedian. Lou Costello: not funny (and the fact that he'd just
died didn't make him any funnier). Sid Caesar: a creative comedian and very funny.

In the 1959–60 season, Caesar did two specials sponsored by
U.S. Steel. In the first, on an automotive theme, he was in fine
form, good enough to keep up with the young Tony Randall. But
the second, focusing on marriage and shown in December, was
less successful. Its portrayal of a mock bridal show, in which couples (Caesar was half of one) were coerced into marrying "in front
of millions of strangers," was a rancid knockoff of "This Is Your
Story," suggesting yet again that as often as he said he still had
something to say, with disconcerting frequency he didn't. But in
May 1960 came a sketch that entered the canon in which Caesar
played Progress Hornsby playing Leonard Bernstein playing
pedagogue. "What is *jazz*?" the semi-stoned Hornsby asks.

> Jazz is the feeling in emotional upheaval, of the cat-
> aclysmic creation of the inner dynamic of reverberating
> vibration. . . . Jazz is the sound of the wind in a storm,
> jazz is a wild wave beating against the shore! Jazz is a
> mountain, jazz is a swinging desert, jazz is a purple bird
> flying into the morphosis! Jazz is a pencil sharpener, jazz
> is a frying pan, jazz is a handball court, jazz . . . jazz is
> a beautiful woman whose older brother is a police*man*.
> What is jazz? I don't know!

But even this seemed tired to some. "Watching Sid Caesar's
outing last night I had the feeling I'd seen it all before. Ever so
many times," Dave Reque wrote in the *Washington News*. Hornsby
had gotten old, he complained, and as for the Professor (who'd
also put in an appearance), "Sid ought to put that one away in
the trunk for keeps." Even friendly critics were getting fed up:
Anticipating sensitivities to come, Jack Gould called Caesar's latest foreign film spoof "a stereotyped and cheap jest at the expense
of the Japanese, their language and their customs." "I want to

move into realer, deeper parts of human satire," Caesar told a friendly reporter. "I want to cut sharper, right to the core." But it was just talk. His last special, in June 1960, was built around Gene Barry, a.k.a. Bat Masterson. With Westerns riding high, Caesar was given—or, worse, gave himself—the degrading task of acting awestruck in Barry's presence. "Such an important man! To come and visit a *plech* like me!" he tells him. "Sid has slipped from a groove into a rut," Jack O'Brian wrote. Even the ever-loyal Tolkin was equivocating. "Caesar had a lot to give," he told David Susskind in 1960, before catching himself: ". . . and I hate to speak in the past tense, because I think he still has a lot to give." Already, the critic Robert Brustein was talking about Caesar's successors; Mike Nichols and Elaine May, he wrote, had picked up where Caesar—their "less sophisticated mentor," he called him—had left off.

Caesar was philosophical. People took water for granted once they no longer had to fetch it from a pump outside, and the same was true of TV comedy: "too easy to come by—just as easy to reject." But in a no-confidence vote against himself, he stopped keeping the scrapbooks of clippings he'd maintained since 1946, and gave up his quarters in the Milgrim Building. Meanwhile, the diaspora of his old associates intensified. Brooks went off to work, briefly and unhappily, for Jerry Lewis. Then, with Reiner, Brooks released the first of the hugely successful *2000 Year Old Man* albums.

Meanwhile, Reiner's semi-autobiographical novel, *Enter Laughing*, became a play and then a movie. And while the sitcom he'd pitched, built around the antics of a TV writer whom he'd play, hadn't been picked up—"too Jewish," the (Jewish) gods of television decreed—once "Protestantized" (as Frank Rich put it) with a different leading man, it emerged as *The Dick Van Dyke Show*. Caesar assumed that Van Dyke's boss on the program, Alan Brady, was modeled after him; Reiner said the character was a composite of Phil Silvers, Milton Berle, and Shelley Berman. Churning out scripts for the new show, Reiner blossomed as Caesar continued to wilt. As Reiner later put it, the generation of TV comics following Caesar had an easier time of it than he'd had; they'd all had the chance to grow more slowly.

Howard Morris wasn't so lucky. Like Coca, he had learned that while working for Caesar was no picnic, neither was leaving him. "When you walk in the clouds, it's tough to come down in the valley again," he said. "It was a bad period" was how he described his life after Caesar. "I spent some of the time starving, some of the time moving to California, and a lot of the time learning about me." For a while, Caesar's principal role in Morris's life was as a character in his angry play à clef about a thinly veiled Caesar-like character with a Caesar-like show named Eddie Romaine. While publicly insisting Romaine was "a composite," he, too, dresses like a gangster, smokes expensive cigars, eats two pounds of raw steak for lunch, washes down deli with Cel-Ray tonic (and belches afterward), pukes before performances, speaks like Gon-Gon (when he's not lapsing into "Polish"), forgets the names of colleagues, ignores his own children, and stays late at work because he doesn't want to go home. Morris's Romaine is also boorish, stupid, bigoted, and cruel. The play's real composite character is the show's head writer, Woody Green, a bit of Brooks (his background and his shtick, including his Jolson-like song of introduction), but mostly Morris, including his full panoply of feelings—admiration, resentment, contempt, bitterness—for Caesar. "You're a lousy human being, but you're the greatest creative nut genius on the stage," he tells Romaine, not to his face, but in a mock prayer scene, rocking back and forth like an Orthodox Jew as he does. "Morris won't admit it's based on Sid Caesar," Hedda Hopper wrote. It hardly mattered; the play was never staged.

The Dick Van Dyke Show set an ignoble precedent in the Caesar saga. Whether fearful of debasing him, or eager to get out from under his shadow, or still bearing old resentments, or not wanting him around, or worrying he wasn't up to it (or wouldn't or couldn't take orders from them), or would think himself too mighty for bit parts, or *was* too mighty for them—too "majestic," as Woody Allen put it—or might show them up, Caesar's former subordinates left him out of nearly all of the wildly successful things they collectively went on to do. Reiner never threw Caesar work, in part for fear, Brooks theorized, that Caesar would upstage him. (To Persky, on the other hand, Reiner was being merciful: for him to have hired Caesar would have been to degrade him even more.) Early on, Brooks said he'd love to do a movie with Caesar but didn't "have the vehicle"—a role that would take advantage of his unique powers. "If anybody else could do the part, it's not for Sid," he said. But more indebted to Caesar than any of the others, he was also kinder to him, and cast him where he could.

Publicly at least, Caesar blamed the industry for his problems. "In ten years TV reached the point it took Hollywood fifty years to reach—the point of playing everything safe," he complained in 1960. Now it was all just "pleasant shows about pleasant people with pleasant problems." But he acknowledged that in his own TV viewing, he'd become as undiscriminating as everyone else. "Yes, because I don't have to think," he explained. "I can sit there and go to sleep. It is good therapy, and it is good for married couples with no maid on Sunday. They can turn on the set, and the kids will sit there hypnotized." In September 1960, Sid Caesar turned thirty-eight. So many years lay before him. What would he now do with them all? And with himself?

CHAPTER 11

BOTTOMING OUT

Were Sid Caesar, rather than Al Duncey, ever to have appeared on *This Is Your Life*, by 1960 most of the pages of Ralph Edwards's oversized scrapbook would have already been turned. With at least some overstatement—it made for a better story when the reckoning came—Caesar later described his next couple of decades as "a twenty-year lost weekend."

He'd been squeezed off—or had squeezed himself off—the comedic spectrum: too sophisticated for mainstream comedy, too retro and prudish to adopt newer and darker material, too apolitical to be topical, too stubborn to change (and too impaired to have done so even were he willing), too tattered and difficult to be rescued by admirers and disciples. But because his star had blazed so brightly, and because enough people gave him additional chances to shine, it took some time to dim, then for people to notice that it had.

He did little television, spending most of his time in Kings Point. Old colleagues rarely visited. "I can't blame them," Caesar wrote. "I wasn't easy to take in my constant state of semistupor and/or belligerence." Jack Carter called him "the golem," referring to the monster, fashioned from mud or clay, in Jewish folklore. By January 1961 one friendly newspaper columnist described his "virtual unemployment." But later that month the National Press Club in Washington invited him to reprise the German General sketch there; newly inaugurated President Kennedy was in the audience, and delighted Caesar by saying "Hello, Sid" to him. He played opposite Ronald Reagan on an episode of *General Electric Theater.* He boasted about all the lucrative offers he was fending off while telling friends he was "at the end of the line." The German Professor was repatriated that October, when, along with an entourage including Louis Armstrong, Caesar accompanied Ed Sullivan and his show to West Berlin. "He worked hard, but it was a losing proposition," *Variety* noted. On the CBS series *Checkmate*, he played a psychotic, drug-addled disc jockey terrified that a rival was about to kill him on the air; even admirers thought his performance overwrought.

In early 1962 the producer and director Stanley Kramer invited Caesar to join an all-star cast of comedians—Berle, Silvers, Buddy Hackett, and Buster Keaton among them—in his frantic, overstuffed comedy *It's a Mad, Mad, Mad, Mad World*, then filming in Southern California. Kramer had long wanted to work with Caesar, despite being "warned by everybody, and I mean everybody, that Sid Caesar had strange ways. I heard he even carried a gun wherever he went." Playing a henpecked dentist, Caesar was jittery and aggressive, far more menacing than funny. Off camera, while the others exchanged jokes, Caesar kept largely to himself. His drinking brought a reproach from another member of the cast, William Demarest. "People look up to you," he told him. "You should have more respect for yourself." His behavior may explain why, when Kramer cast about for people to reprise key roles in his films for a retrospective on his career, he asked Caesar to play *The Caine Mutiny's* paranoid Captain Queeg, immortalized by Humphrey Bogart. "You don't have to copy him," he assured Caesar. "I'm looking for something better." He'd come to the right man.

As *Mad, Mad World* was shooting, Caesar filmed the first three episodes of *As Caesar Sees It*, a monthly half-hour series for ABC in which he performed with members of the Chicago-based comedy troupe Second City. More important, perhaps the most personally devoted of his former writers, Neil Simon, threw him a lifeline, casting him in *Little Me*, a Broadway musical for which he'd written the book. The show called for Caesar to play the various husbands and lovers of a theatrical diva—*eight* different characters in all. So plum a role for someone so on the skids was "like an oxygen tent to a patient with an advanced case of double pneumonia," the syndicated columnist Margaret McManus wrote. With the television series also in the works, Caesar worried whether he could handle it. "You're a *shtarker*,"* Simon assured him. So did Claude Rains. "My dear fellow, you do a beautiful job," he told him backstage during tryouts in Philadelphia. Caesar nearly choked on the compliment.

As Caesar Sees It debuted in October 1962. "There is insecurity and perhaps a touch of fear in his eyes," one critic wrote. "If only Caesar would do what he knows is right. But maybe after the incredible triumphs and dismal slumps he had experienced on television . . . maybe he doesn't know any longer. It is a sad thing to see." To Harriet Van Horne, Caesar had become a "stunted plant," one that "seems to blight its own green shoots by some malign inner chemistry." Somehow, a past master of subtlety and taste had become exaggerated, vulgar, and unfunny; his witty pitches for Dutch Masters cigars (yes, he'd become a huckster, something else he'd once vowed never to do) were funnier than his routines. "Maybe he should shorten the sketches and pad out the commercials," Van Horne cruelly suggested, exposing the sense of betrayal some Caesar fans, ignorant, perhaps, of his dire circumstances, felt. "Somewhere in all this, there's a sad story," she concluded.

When *Little Me* opened in November 1962, *Life* and *Newsweek* put Caesar on their covers. But saddled by his addictions, unable or unwilling to stick to his lines, and resistant to criticism, he turned in uneven performances. "When you saw that show on a *good* night, you saw a performance that would just absolutely blow you away," said the director Greg Garrison. "But unfortunately, there were only about two good nights a week." One night

---

* An extremely tough guy.

he fainted, ostensibly from exhaustion. "It was a bad night for the Caesars on Broadway," went one report. "Julius got stabbed at the Rivoli, and Sid collapsed on stage at the Lunt-Fontanne." "He wasn't always coherent," Simon recalled. "Yet when you needed it, the brilliance was there. Sid was, as far as I know, sober whenever the curtain went up. When the curtain went down, I don't know." "The Last Hurrah of My Glory Days" Caesar later called the show, which had run for 257 performances by the time it closed in June 1963.

Throughout the show's run, *As Caesar Sees It* appeared monthly. Abrogating yet another of his taboos, the program's spoof on *Candid Camera* in March featured a "pie-throwing free-for-all." No longer, then, was Caesar's food only for eating. Interacting with the audience at season's end, two weeks before *Little Me* also finished up, Caesar was almost importunate. "We're all looking forward to seeing you in the fall," he said. "Please consult your local newspapers for the date and the time. If you can't find it there, call your local station. If nobody answers, give me a ring at home. If we're not at home, we'll be at my mother-in-law's, and call me there. If you can't get her there, call me again at my mother-in-law's because she likes to talk on the telephone. Oh, look, I tell you what, if the whole thing is too much trouble, just leave your set on for the whole summer, and we'll be back."

ACCORDING TO THE DIARIST John Malcolm Brinnin, "the decline of Sid Caesar and St. Tropez" were among the topics discussed at a dinner party Gloria Vanderbilt threw in New York in the spring of 1963. Around the same time, revisiting Caesar in Kings Point, Richard Gehman found him "stalking through the split-level corridors of his own Elba, alternately waiting like an itchy, oversized Napoleon for the telephone call that would tell him his subjects wanted him back" or cleaning his guns "in mummified silence." "Although he uses these weapons only for target practice," said Gehman, "it may have occurred to him, occasionally, to turn one or another toward the [television] set and pull the trigger."

Gehman, who'd ghostwritten "What Psychoanalysis Did for Me," reported that Caesar was now off the couch; his doctor had fired him four years earlier. His furniture of choice was now the contoured chair; he'd worn out five of them staring at the tube. Young Ricky Caesar had taken to hiding his father's liquor bottles and tossing his pills. Periodically, Florence had to summon Caesar's pals to get him off the floor. In an appearance in Las Vegas, Caesar was chagrined that the "doll-like Korean girls" opening for him got as much applause as he did. What one Hollywood columnist took away from the experience was "you can't get away in a night club with using old television material that everyone has seen."

"Sid Caesar's good-luck charm, Mel Brooks, won't be with him next season," went a story from May 1963, which noted that Brooks would be writing, producing, and directing a film called "Springtime for Hitler" instead. Brooks's explanations for not casting Caesar in what became *The Producers*—a film with plenty of parts for the ersatz Germans Caesar personified—varied: The studio wouldn't let him, or Caesar was out of commission, or Brooks's mind was somewhere else. "I was too busy blazing a new trail for myself," as he put it. On that, at least, his former wife agreed. "He was moving on to a whole new Hollywood life and Sid was Fifty-Seventh Street and New York City," said Florence Baum. (The two had divorced in 1962.) "I don't think that Sid at that moment registered in his life."

A week after that story appeared, and six years after he'd trashed *What's My Line?*, Caesar tried stumping the blindfolded panelists as a mystery guest. With all of his accents, he should have been one of the most mysterious, but he was quickly found out (and, for anyone paying close attention, had given himself away by clearing his throat as he signed in). "Are you by any chance one of the *finest* entertainers in America, Mr. Sid Caesar?" Arlene Francis asked. Bennett Cerf—"Clifford Gelding" in Caesar's brutal spoof—was equally cordial, while the program's courtly host, John Daly, was awkward, wistful, and compassionate. "Of course, golly, I guess television will *always* owe you a tremendous debt," he told Caesar. "You brought a great talent, and a great deal of integrity and quality, to television." "You used to work so hard," Daly then added, as if to explain Caesar's current, sorry state. "I hope you're not working that hard any more." "Well, we'll see," Caesar replied. "You do us much honor to give us some time," Daly said gently as Caesar prepared to run off.

As Caesar Sees It gave way to *The Sid Caesar Show*, a half-hour program airing alternate Thursdays on ABC. He took off the night of November 17, 1963, to attend the New York premiere of *Mad, Mad World*, which doubled as a fundraising gala for two Kennedy family charities. Rose, Bobby, Ethel, Teddy, Joan, and Eunice were all on hand; Caesar got to mix with them and other New Frontier luminaries like Arthur Schlesinger Jr., Ted Sorensen, and Robert McNamara. "One for the books— the Social Register, the Celebrity Register, Who's Who and you name it," the gossip columnist Suzy Knickerbocker said of the festivities, not knowing it would be one for the history books as well, the last festive occasion before John F. Kennedy's assassination a week later; opening night for Kramer's comedy turned out to be closing night for Camelot. The film got only modest reviews, and the scant references to Caesar weren't kind. "Caesar, whose nervousness and poor memory were always a hindrance to him on TV, now seems to have that nervous blurriness ingrained in his technique," went one. At an awards ceremony afterward, when a giant white spotlight shined on him in the audience, he was falling asleep.

Caesar's television show quietly expired in March 1964. "The most insecure man in the business," its chief writer, Goodman Ace, called him afterward.

Reiner's success with *The Dick Van Dyke Show* hadn't lessened Caesar's scorn for sitcoms, which he still viewed as soap operas with jokes, a format certain to obliterate his edge and wit. But in the summer of 1965, Caesar, more beggar than chooser, signed up for a sitcom based on the movie *The Mouse That Roared*, playing the same three characters in a fictional European principality that Peter Sellers had portrayed in the film. The pilot, written by the blacklisted (and Oscar-winning) writer Frank Tarloff, was charming (and Caesar, adroit), suggesting that something well scripted and run by others was just what he needed. But CBS wanted only one Caesar, not three, and when he wouldn't pare things back, the project died. Television "would have turned Chaplin into sausage," Brooks told *The New York Times* around this time. "Laurel and Hardy could never have gotten past the first 26 weeks." And now, he said, it had "chewed [up] Sid Caesar."

One project in which Caesar had to be cast was a *Show of Shows* reunion, clunkily called (because Liebman wouldn't let them use the original) *The Sid Caesar, Imogene Coca, Carl Reiner, Howard Morris Special* and filmed in Los Angeles in December 1966. Bill Hobin, who was to direct it, recognized everyone on the set except for one tall, thin man. "Aren't you going to say hello?" that man—Sid Caesar—asked him when they met. In addition to his streamlined self, Caesar had gone native, taking on "the protective coloration and sartorial splendor of the Hollywoodian—wild plaid sports jacket, open-neck sports shirt with polka dotted neckerchief and long, always-just-washed hair," one reporter wrote. Caesar hyped the reunion show beforehand, including in a return visit (this time with Coca) to *What's My Line?* (Bennett Cerf called his absence from television "simply disgraceful.") He also gave some interviews, discussing comedy "the way Ralph Nader discusses automobile safety," one of his interlocutors wrote.

"Sid Caesar!" Coca exclaimed at the start of the reunion program, which aired in April 1967. "Where?" Caesar replied, and it was a good question. "Oh, same old Sid!" she said. Only it wasn't: The guy who, as Brooks once had it, "could kill a Buick" now looked as if he couldn't dent a Volkswagen. The show's main sketch, a takeoff of *Who's Afraid of Virginia Woolf?*, was coarse and unfunny, and the characters so alcohol soaked that American Motors, fearful of any association with drunken driving, nearly pulled its ads. The rest was a rehash. "It was wonderful and it was somehow all wrong," the *Times* lamented. Zalowitz compared the program to the *Tkhies-Hameysim* (the resurrection from the dead in the Hebrew prayer), and prayed to the Almighty to make it happen. (He also prayed that Caesar regain forty-one and two-thirds of the pounds he'd lost.) The happiest event for many that night wasn't the show, but the announcement after it: "*The Beverly*

Hillbillies and *Green Acres* will return next Wednesday on most of these same stations." The four principals had signed up for possible return engagements; there were no takers.[*] But whatever this latest incarnation of Caesar looked like, Morris for one found it an improvement in at least one sense. "He's more in touch with reality than when we all worked with him in New York," he said.

With the entertainment business moving west, Caesar had little choice but to follow. Besides, having landed a role in a movie called *The Busy Body*, he'd suddenly fallen for film; on live TV, he explained, "you didn't have time to think." And he'd soured on 1960s New York City, which had degenerated, he said, into "an office building with slums." The Caesars sold the Kings Point house and, in July 1967, decamped to Los Angeles. So hasty was their departure—they left clothes in the closets, food in the freezer, and family pictures (some with BB holes in them) on the walls—that the new owners assumed he'd been institutionalized.

He returned to New York that fall for a three-week run at the Latin Quarter, a once-proud venue that was also showing its age. Though people thought he looked sick, he defended his changed appearance. "Maybe it was the psychoanalysis," he mused. "Maybe it's the way I always wanted to look. Maybe it's just because I got tired of being a compulsive eater who had to order what the other guy was eating even before I finished my meal," he told the *Daily News*. "I don't know answers any more." The *Daily News* noted his "Robert Kennedy–style hairpiece"; COMEDIAN LETS HIS TOUPEE DOWN IN A REVEALING INTERVIEW, the headline read. The rug gave Caesar an artificially youthful, even spooky, appearance; Larry Gelbart later said it made Caesar look like his own son. Caesar, one critic observed, resembled a young imposter who'd

---

[*] The show *did* win two Emmys (not the ten Caesar repeatedly said it had). One was for best writing, beating out Jackie Gleason; *The Honeymooners* never did win an Emmy. "Ironically, the same people who used to belittle us while applauding more sophisticated efforts like Sid Caesar or Ernie Kovacs now tell me they watch our reruns on local stations every week and love them," said Gleason's chief writer, Marvin Marx (*Allentown [Pa.] Morning Call*, June 2, 1967). But Gleason's writers achieved a kind of immortality Caesar's never did: Thanks to endless reruns of their work, people can rattle off vast swaths of their words by heart.

cribbed Sid Caesar's material. What struck Walter Winchell even more than Caesar's look was his moldy material. Caesar, he said, had gone cheap and passed up on the writers, "a not very bright thing to do, pal," he advised.

Around this time an English instructor at Columbia University, Albert Goldman, set out to write the first book on Sid Caesar. He felt personally indebted to Caesar, who was only a few years older than he; *Your Show of Shows*—"the most brilliant comedy playhouse in the history of television," he called it—had helped him survive a desolate time in his life during which all he had to do during the week was look forward to watching Sid Caesar on Saturday night. He'd feared none of the programs had been saved, only to learn from Max Liebman, whom he'd tracked down in his old office on West Fifty-Sixth Street, that he had them all, stacked from floor to ceiling in khaki-colored cardboard boxes in his closet. To Goldman, it was "like walking into Aladdin's Cave." Liebman then unpacked one of them and threaded a wagon wheel of film into an ancient projector. "And there it was, exactly as I had remembered it," Goldman recalled. "Rather brownish and sort of old-fashioned Sunday rotogroveur [*sic*] pictures—brown sepia. Perfectly clear and with sound distinct. Sid Caesar roaring along in full cry." But in the hands of a diminished Caesar and transplanted to the down-at-the-heels Latin Quarter a decade later, those sketches didn't work. "That after all these years he still uses this old stuff doesn't speak well for his vaunted creative abilities," Goldman noted. "Sid is definitely passé."

In the summer of 1968, the Caesars had moved into their new home on Loma Vista Drive in Beverly Hills. It lacked the panoramas of downtown Los Angeles Florence had wanted, but the sweeping views west to Coldwater Canyon, Mulholland Drive, and the San Fernando Valley were nearly as spectacular. Nestled just north of Sunset Boulevard, the location supplied a ready-made (and oft-invoked) metaphor for what his life there was to become: Like Norma Desmond, the elderly character (played by Gloria Swanson) in Billy Wilder's 1950 film, *Sunset Boulevard*, Caesar, though only forty-six, was a faded and reclusive former star, dreaming of past glories. Interviewing him there, Goldman found Caesar, a man with only a high school diploma, "very uptight about meeting someone, especially a college professor," throwing him "weird disassociative star[e]s." Caesar was bitter, too, complaining that in this country, "they" can't wait to kill you, so "they" put you on a pedestal, only to stone you when you screwed up on something silly, like those introductions. He was disinclined to help Goldman. "He feels that if anybody writes a book about him, that's the same thing as putting a headstone over him," Goldman said.

In a shed by the pool, Goldman spotted another set of kinescopes, "lined up in military procession" on a shelf. It was Caesar's private collection, which, unlike Liebman's, also included *Caesar's Hour*. With NBC having jettisoned them, it was the *only* set of those; "One flash fire and they'd all be wiped out." Caesar also showed Goldman his guns, one after another, describing the historic significance of each. "I thought, 'I'm talking to the world's greatest comedian so I'll make a little joke,'" said Goldman. "So the next gun he hands me I say, 'Gee, Sid, all these rifles, and not one machine gun!' And he looks at me *real serious* and he says, 'Oh! I didn't know you were interested in automatic weapons, too. Those are in the next room.'"

People still remembered, and honored, the Caesar of old. Carol Burnett modeled her new television show on *Your Show of Shows* and *Caesar's Hour*, and quickly invited Caesar on. Thanks to Greg Garrison, now directing Dean Martin as he once had *Your Show of Shows*, Caesar also appeared annually on Martin's various programs, despite grumbling from Martin's underlings that Caesar no longer had it. Caesar spent the late 1960s riding the circuit of lousy sitcoms, in one instance portraying a sloshed has-been comedian for laugh-track laughs on *That Girl*, starring Marlo Thomas. He spent much of 1968 appearing in theaters and tent shows in a dozen cities with Coca; by now the old routines, in some of which Coca reprised parts originally played by Fabray, seemed dated even to those who'd loved them. On *Playboy After Dark*, Hugh Hefner welcomed him to the Playboy Mansion, and told a pair of wide-eyed Bunnies how big Caesar had once been. Though not known for his magnanimity, Jackie Gleason gave over substantial chunks of a couple of his Saturday-night shows to Caesar (though the contrast between Caesar reprising his tired acts and the Great One in full Miami Beach swagger only accentuated their very different trajectories). Bob Hope was less generous. "Have you ever played Gaithersburg, Bob?" Johnny Carson asked Hope when Caesar, fresh from performing with Coca in the Maryland town, appeared with him on *The Tonight Show*. "No, I play the *big* places," Hope replied.

Caesar began working cruise ships out of Miami. In January 1970, travelers could choose between him (departing on the seventeenth) and Myron Cohen (on the thirty-first). He played a hungover philanderer on *Love, American Style*, and paid a halting visit to *The Hollywood Palace*. "Once upon a time I would have been mildly excited to report that Sid Caesar opens April 17 at Bimbo's,* but times and mighty Caesar have changed," Herb Caen wrote in the *San Francisco Chronicle* in 1969, less than a decade after he'd called Caesar "the best comedian on TV even when he's off TV." Dick Cavett had heard Caesar was "in trouble," and fan that he had always been, when Caesar appeared (with Carol Channing) on Broadway in a short-lived production of a play called *Four on a Garden* in March 1971, he invited him on his show. Caesar's hair and eyebrows looked lacquered and his conversation was fragmentary—"It's strange to see a man who's made me laugh so much be serious," Cavett confessed to him—but Cavett carried him when he faltered. "Totally aloof and totally preoccupied" was how Joe Bologna described the Caesar he'd encountered when play-doctoring the show. "He was so spacey, it was like he wasn't in the room." That November Caesar opened in Neil Simon's *Last of the Red Hot Lovers*—in Paramus, New Jersey.

So spectacular and inexplicable (at least to those unaware of his situation) was Caesar's transformation that some believed something nefarious had to be afoot—that Caesar had been blacklisted, or blackballed, or black-somethinged. That's what *Esquire* suggested in May 1972, when it put Caesar—actually, *two* Caesars, the contemporary one (in living color) with his arm

---

* A popular San Francisco nightclub.

around the thicker, crazier original (in black and white)—on its cover. "Great Caesar's Ghost," it proclaimed. "Why isn't the funniest man in America on television?" Rather than dig for an answer, the magazine put together a twelve-page "Sid Caesar Festival," featuring interviews, snatches of double-talk, a conversation with the Professor, and photographs of classic sketches. To Brooks, it all resembled an obituary. "Sid was a terrific person," he told the magazine. "When did he die, by the way?"

There were skeptics. "A species of nervous wreck with some hair but little timing left," Stanley Kauffmann of *The New Republic* called Sid. "Given a few years of unemployment, an untimely death or perhaps a self-imposed exile, your comedian has a way of mutating into a 'comic genius,'" observed *The Atlanta Constitution*'s amusements editor, Howell Raines, later executive editor of *The New York Times*, in effect questioning whether Caesar had ever been great.

Esquire feted Caesar in the Rainbow Room nonetheless, an event Lucille Kallen reluctantly attended, then described in a lengthy dispatch to Mel Tolkin. Kallen had fashioned a post-Caesar life as a successful mystery writer, but suffered from the same fate many veterans of *Your Show of Shows* endured: It was all anyone ever asked her about. Worse, whenever the honor roll of Caesar's alumni was read, including by Caesar himself, her name was invariably left off the list. It was something she regularly commiserated about with Tolkin, who, for all *his* subsequent successes—first as "house liberal for Bob Hope," and later with *All in the Family*—suffered all the same slings and slights. "The predilection of interviewers to sprinkle their articles with the Niels [*sic*] and the Mels and the Larrys" was how he described their plight. He might have thrown the "Carls" on his list; equally irritating to him was how Reiner had held himself out as "a seminal mind behind YSOS, a pose which he has carefully worked on over the years." That resentment had only intensified during the making of the reunion special, during which Tolkin had felt shoved aside by Reiner and his two principal writers on *The Dick Van Dyke Show*, Bill Persky and Sam Denoff, whom Tolkin dismissed as "the white hopes of TV."

While nursing his own grievances, Tolkin savored—and, on

occasion, stoked—those of others, including from one of those Larrys: Gelbart, irked over a separate disagreement with Reiner. "If he were a larger talent I might feel a larger anger," he told Tolkin in 1966. "As it is, he annoys me in the way a housefly might." "I find that the pap on which his reputation and esteem is founded (and I must include Doc, as well) is too much—really too little—to swallow," Gelbart told Tolkin a year later.

But to Tolkin and Kallen, Brooks was the worst offender. He hadn't exactly endeared himself with them by telling *The New York Times* that after disbanding, Caesar's other writers had "wandered off like atrophied little Jewish spores . . . waiting for a wetness and a sunniness to make them blossom again." Tolkin dismissed Brooks as both "a talented *tummler*" and, noting how he name-dropped Dostoyevsky and Tolstoy, "a termite feeding off the Taj Mahal." Even an apology for leaving him off the roster of Caesar's writers didn't spare Howard Rosenberg of the *Los Angeles Times* from Tolkin's wrath. It was, said Rosenberg, "as if he were Michelangelo and I'd credited another painter for the Sistine Chapel ceiling."

Kallen hadn't really wanted to go to Caesar's soiree, she told Tolkin; "only the certainty that if I didn't show up the myth would be reinforced that Brooks and Reiner between them had ad-libbed the entire six years of the show forced me to walk with clenched jaw into the N.B.C. elevator." Also, Liebman had evidently told her the party was meant to help revive Caesar's career and maybe even to relaunch his old show. She'd quickly spotted Caesar—"looking like Michael Caine in a quietly psychotic mood"—and Neil Simon, both being interviewed. " 'Ha!' I thought," she wrote. " 'Tell 'em, Doc. Tell 'em all about *Show of Shows*, how it was in the beginning, working in the boys' dressing room at the Malin Studios with the sweaty jock straps. . . . Tell them about all those years. Oh, I forgot, you weren't there. Well, it doesn't matter, it's you they want to hear from, even if you didn't have much to do with it.' "

When she reached Caesar, he embraced her so effusively she thought he thought she was someone else. "I expected to hear the Romeo and Juliet overture swelling to crescendo like we used to do in those movie takeoffs," she recalled. "His eyes were welling (that's the only word for it, welling) and they continued to well throughout the next two hours. I said (because Max had told me this was what the party was all about), 'well, when do we start the new season?'" And Caesar, at least, was taking that possibility seriously. "Listen, yes, who knows, it could be," he'd replied. "I asked Doc, 'Would you do it' and he said sure and I asked Carl and he said sure." "And I thought to myself my god what are they building this man up for?" Kallen related. "Does he really think Neil Simon and Mel Brooks and Carl Reiner are going to step down and play 'you're the boss oh great one'?"

Then parts of the kinescopes were shown: a Professor sketch, Coca about to jump off the Empire State Building, Caesar pantomiming a woman getting dressed. "We howled," Kallen wrote. "It was brilliant. One forgets." "If this gets Sid back on the air, good luck to everybody," she concluded. "But watching that lean, suntanned, haunted face (Oh, I forgot, Sid also spoke, raising inarticulation to new heights) I had a terrible feeling that the juice was gone for good." All the old hatreds and rivalries were still there, but so, too, was everything that had brought them all together; Kallen wondered why everyone wasted their time pretending to like one another when, regardless of how they really felt, they shared something far more profound. "The one thing we all seemed to be saying," she told Tolkin, "was that *Show of Shows* was the best time of our lives, and that, if nothing else, was the truth." Kallen's obituary in *The New York Times* in 1999 restored her to the usual roll call of Caesar's writers, but only fleetingly.

The *Esquire* article led David Frost and Johnny Carson to book Caesar on their television shows, as well as to persuade Cavett to give him another shot. The kindly Cavett gently steered Caesar into the safe harbor of double-talk: What did they think of the *Esquire* article in Germany? he asked him. In France? In Italy? Dining with Caesar in his hotel room before escorting him to the studio, *Esquire*'s Lee Eisenberg recalled how, at one point, Caesar accidentally knocked over a trash can. "He promptly bent over, set it right, said he was sorry (to IT)," he recalled. "And not as a joke. Just popped out. Seemed a bit strange." Not really:

While Caesar might have stopped *portraying* inanimate objects, he'd never stopped believing that they had feelings, too.

The story also helped inspire Julian Schlossberg of the Walter Reade Organization, owners of a chain of movie houses, to try to assemble a package of Caesar's best sketches from *Your Show of Shows* for theatrical release, for which he went to see Caesar. Their encounter proved disconcerting: During it, Caesar disclosed that because of his expertise on the Civil War the White House consulted him on military matters. "You think they make a move in Vietnam without me?" he'd asked. He wasn't smiling.

Schlossberg, along with his friend and co-producer Milly Sherman, made the selections. Most of the candidates were easily culled, because they were either redundant, mediocre, or dated. They chose ten, including a Professor number, the Bavarian clock, Coca's stuffy musicale, the German General, the boardroom scene, "From Here to Obscurity," and "The Sewing Machine Girl." Things would start, as the show had, with a Hickenloopers sketch—Doris's car crash—and conclude with "This Is Your Story": There'd be no topping that. Caesar, cast as the Professor, taped introductions to each segment, but everyone, Caesar included, realized they were terrible, and that he *looked* terrible, too. "Get rid of the old guy," he instructed. Caesar and Liebman also screened the old shows together—"with great anxiety," Liebman confessed. "After all those years, we felt as though we were watching strangers," he said. "And, believe me, we laughed until we cried. There were times when we had to tell the projectionist to stop the machine because our eyes were blurred with tears of laughter, and we couldn't see the screen." Morris found the exhumation unsettling. He'd not expected the time capsule to be exhumed so soon; here they were, all still alive, and already people were treating them like the very late Laurel and Hardy.

Ten from "Your Show of Shows" opened in February 1973. Old fans greeted the sketches like long-lost friends, while at least to some younger viewers they came as revelations. In the former camp was Johnny Carson, who'd ripped off "Wings over Bombinschissel" for his act at the University of Nebraska; three times, he invited Caesar on *The Tonight Show* to flog the film, and showed snippets from it. "Sid was starting to tell me what they were," Carson said as the lights went back up, "and I said, 'You don't have to tell me, I saw every one of your shows, I know *every* one of those bits.' And they hold up so beautifully."

Reiner was watching the film in the Tiffany Theater in Hollywood when he heard a woman sitting very close to him shriek with delight—laughter of a kind, and intensity, he'd never heard before. "That woman screaming," he said, "was me!" "I was viewing it through the eyes of a sixteen-year-old who had been hearing all her life about the 'only great comedy show ever done on television,'" Kallen, who'd gone with her daughter, told Tolkin. "What could live up to that?" But it did. Thomas O'Brien took his ten-year-old son, Conan, to see the film when it played in Brookline, Massachusetts, and it—actually, "This Is Your Story"—persuaded the boy to become a comic.

After a screening in New York, Caesar was mobbed by students from the Lexington School for the Deaf. The version of Caesar sitting near the columnist Bob Greene at a screening in Chicago seemed six inches shorter than the man on the screen, who "moved through the sketches as if he had invented television." Pauline Kael of *The New Yorker* was struck by how he'd shrunk. "It's as if what his ten years on TV did to him were symbolized by his loss of flesh," she wrote. Caesar's heft, unlike Gleason's, had always conjured up superiority and power, but with the disappearance of his "funny man's fat moon face" he'd become ordinary and unfunny: Sid Caesar was no longer *Sid Caesar*. Publicizing the picture, Caesar could be sullen, kvetchy, testy, paranoid. "Americans today have forgotten how to laugh," he told a reporter in Boston. "It's too bad, because the country could use a little laughter." ("And, actually, so could Caesar," that reporter observed.)

The film found only modest commercial success. (Caesar was furious that *The Poseidon Adventure*, a high-budget release that had opened around the same time, had done better.) Some fans called for *Ten More*, but Schlossberg knew that when it came to *Your Show of Shows*, they simply weren't there. *Ten Others from*

"Caesar's Hour" might have worked, but that would have meant more direct dealing with Caesar, a prospect Schlossberg wasn't ready to face.

Though Coca had lost an eye in a car accident eight months earlier, in August 1973 she managed to appear with Caesar in Simon's *The Prisoner of Second Avenue* in Chicago. The next year she and Sid returned to Chicago as Charlie and Doris Hickenlooper in a play Tolkin and Kallen had stitched together from old sketches (with Liebman directing). The experience was harrowing for Coca. "Sid went through a maniacal (? crazy) period—for about five performances," she wrote to Kallen. "Frankly he scared the hell out of me." She'd sent him a note about his mistreatment, she'd said, but been too gentle; "I should have written 'if you continue your obvious hostility I'll walk off stage.'" Though Caesar had no respect for either theater or anyone connected to *Your Show of Shows*, she wrote, everyone, including Liebman, pampered him. "I don't understand sids and maxs relationship at all," she went on. "I feel they really don't like—don't respect—, each other, but are somehow tied together."

Caesar's Hour, she reflected, had swollen Caesar's head beyond even what she'd known; "one kneels and basks in his genius + asks to be kicked + thanks him for his effort." "You know, Lucille, I look back on 'Show of Shows' + wonder how you + I existed in the midst of this male, mad with power, atmosphere," Coca wrote. "We all had success—we all made more money than we'd ever made—but did it have to be that agonizing[?]" She nonetheless asked Liebman about additional collaborations. "I know he thinks I'm talented—I think he likes me—I know he wishes for me the best—but it could be I represent a period of his theatrical life that he feels is better to keep as a lovely memory + move on to new and more exciting things," she wrote. Even doing the one-person show she performed periodically, Caesar's shadow still enveloped her. "I mind it most of all when they refer to my having been in the 'Sid Ceasar [*sic*] Show,'" she wrote to Liebman. "That really does it,—+ to smile + sign the programmes, + not to throw myself on the floor + start screaming takes great control."

To keep working, Caesar pushed NyQuil and Mogen David

wines. In May 1974, he booked a two-week engagement back at the Rainbow Grill. Again, there were complaints about his stale material; goodwill and nostalgia took him only so far. And always, there was his appearance. "A man who has lost that much weight," the man from *Newsday* wrote, "just doesn't seem like someone you ought to be laughing at, even if he is Sid Caesar." Gone from Caesar, at least for Albert Goldman, was the "Jewish adrenaline" that "makes Jews manic and crazy and jumpy and lunatic"; in its place was someone who talked like a saint, wore a medal around his neck, and wanted to be liked. But when Kallen took in the show with Liebman, even her jaundiced old eyes teared up. "He did the young boy in a dance, which I had not seen in twenty years, and I *swear,* I almost cried, it was so perfect," she wrote. "There are certain things even now that he can do that nobody on earth can do."

Reporters labored to open him up. "At a time when television talk shows are glutted with actors breathlessly unloading inane trivia about themselves, Caesar keeps to himself," wrote Mort Sheinman of *Women's Wear Daily.* William Raidy of the *Newark Star-Ledger* asked Caesar what he'd have been were it not for show business. "A field marshall," Caesar replied, prompting Raidy's first laugh in an hour. "I'm serious," said Caesar, showing him his bedside reading: J. F. C. Fuller's *Military History of the Western World.* To Maurice Zolotow, Caesar circa 1974 was an "utterly altered human being" from the man he'd profiled twenty years earlier; only the unhappiness endured. "Imprisoned in this new slender Caesar," he wrote, "the old fat crazy-genius Caesar is wildly signaling to be let out."

At home Caesar "could be very terrible at times," Florence recalled, going into rages, traipsing around half stoned and disheveled. Occasionally he'd go out and work; should he go off the rails on the road, she would come and rescue him. In Milwaukee for a five-week run of *The Prisoner of Second Avenue* in early 1975, Caesar, who'd patronized call girls at least three times (and smoked pot with one of them), got swept up in a prostitution sting; beyond the local press, though, no one noticed—obscurity had its blessings— and with the authorities out for bigger fry, he wasn't prosecuted.

Four things, Florence later explained, led her to stick with Sid: her memories of the romantic young man she'd married; her faith that things would eventually improve; her belief that marriages were for keeps; and her fear that, were she to leave him, he'd die. "Like most comedians, Sid was another child," she observed. "He needed me more than my others did."

He took bit parts in films like *Airport 1975* and *The Munsters' Revenge*, and roles in what Tom Shales of *The Washington Post* called "has-been get-togethers" like *The Love Boat*. "It didn't bother me when people would say 'What's the great Sid Caesar doing in *that* piece of shit?'" Caesar was to write. "All that mattered was that I could get it over with quickly and go home to my friend, the bottle." "People didn't know what to do with him," said Reiner. "People writing minor movies would say, 'Ooh, let's try and get Sid' because Sid wasn't doing much and he wanted to work. So he did a couple of movies that were not really very dignified . . . not *dignified*, that's not the word—'*elegant*.'" Fresh from watching a very unfunny Caesar in the film *Fire Sale* in the late 1970s, the writer Patrick McGilligan asked Reiner, then directing *The One and Only*, the usual question about Caesar: *What had happened to him?* "Reiner drew me aside, sat down in his director's chair, put me in a chair next to him, and said in a low voice, 'The real problem is he stopped being funny,'" McGilligan remembered. "'For more than a decade, he was the funniest man in the world. All of a sudden he stopped, and he wasn't funny anymore. He was still talented, just not funny.'" McGilligan asked him why. "'Most people are only funny for a period of time,'" Reiner told him. "'His time was up.'" "Maybe it's just me, but I didn't feel he said it as sympathetically as I would have expected," McGilligan recalled. And, he noted, "Carl and Mel stayed funny for the rest of their lives."

Though he, too, considered Caesar a has-been, Max Liebman dashed off angry letters to NBC and CBS, imploring them to use Caesar for *something*. "With all the junk that you're packaging," he'd asked, "is there not some place on this *whole planet* for a show with Sid Caesar?" He got no reply. The veteran newsman Sander Vanocur asked Larry Gelbart whether Caesar would ever be given another TV show. "Not in the world of Captain and Tennille," Gelbart replied, referring to an ephemeral husband-and-wife singing act that got its own TV program. Gene Wilder yearned to tell Caesar how much he'd meant to comedy but, afraid it would only make him feel worse, never did. "We'll talk about his diet, about the weather, about everything except what's in my heart," Wilder said.

Though the film famously featured a man punching a horse, Brooks hadn't cast Caesar in *Blazing Saddles*, which came out in 1974. But he appeared in Brooks's short-lived sitcom, *When Things Were Rotten*, in 1975, and in 1976 Caesar played a bewildered studio executive in *Silent Movie* with "surprisingly humorless intensity," according to Vincent Canby of the *Times*. (Bewilderment, Brooks recalled, "was Sid's natural state in those days.") "He was a little on the sauce. Not sauce . . . more heavy syrup," recalled Rudy De Luca, who co-wrote the screenplay. Laid up by a car accident, Caesar spent time off the set in a hospital bed. For Barry Levinson, who'd loved Caesar's show as a kid and was now working with De Luca, it was heartbreaking to see his childhood hero lying immobilized on the set while everyone else dashed off for lunch.

Liebman felt there was something impertinent about Brooks casting Caesar in a silent movie of the sort Caesar had once so lovingly re-created, and in so minor a role. Fairly or not, Caesar felt Brooks had ripped him off, first with the 2000 Year Old Man— "Instead of being the Professor over here," Caesar said, "he wants to change the accent a little bit and he was a two thousand year old Jew"—and later in his films; he spotted five or six instances of expropriation in *Blazing Saddles* alone. But Brooks at least threw him work. When he was asked in 1977 how Caesar was doing, the best Reiner could do was "still funny" and "making a living." Caesar appreciated the nods from Brooks, and thanked him for them. "He wasn't thanking me for being nice," said Brooks. "He was thanking me for recognizing his talent. Mostly it was 'you still see that I've got it.' It was very important to him." As *Silent Movie* opened in Hollywood, Caesar opened in *Last of the Red Hot Lovers* in Gilford, New Hampshire. His co-star, Carolyn Michel, watched him go through a month's worth of sleeping pills in a week. She feared he'd collapse during a performance, or maybe even drop dead.

In 1977, Caesar went to Australia for a bit part in a film called *Barnaby and Me*—and remembered nothing about it afterward. Around that time, he paid an uninvited return visit to his old house in Kings Point, where the present owner, spotting someone crawling around in the bushes, went out, baseball bat in hand, to investigate. (When he recognized Caesar, he invited him in. Caesar disapproved of the changes he'd made to the place.) Caesar caught a break when he was cast as John Travolta's high school coach in *Grease*, filmed in the summer of 1977. His part was small and his performance innocuous; coming during what he later called "the darkest of my Dark Period," he'd barely remembered doing it. Watching him in it, one critic wrote, you wondered what the fuss always around him was all about. But his role in so beloved a film familiarized him to a new generation of viewers.

In June 1977, Caesar and Coca had a two-week gig at the Sahara hotel in Las Vegas, opening for the country singer Eddy Arnold. Taking in their show was Frank Rich, then of *Time* magazine and soon to become chief drama critic of *The New York Times*, who hoped to write the kind of group portrait of Caesar and his collaborators that Roger Kahn had just done of the Brooklyn Dodgers in *The Boys of Summer*. He found their show— "Caesar and Coca doing *The Bicycle Thief* for uncomprehending autoworkers"—profoundly sad, and Caesar himself unresponsive and unreflective, prone to long riffs on the biography he was reading or his son's physics textbook. When Rich talked to Caesar's colleagues, all he heard was how much they loathed one another. "I thought it would be another glorious *Boys of Summer* and instead it was a bunch of 'Angry Jews in Winter,'" Rich recalled. He soon abandoned the project.

Caesar happened to be in New York when Coca was in the Broadway production of *On the Twentieth Century*, which opened in February 1978. Though her role was small, it won her new admirers. ("You have clearly got the part by the 'balls'" was how one of the show's stars, Madeline Kahn, inscribed a picture to her.) Though Coca offered Caesar tickets, he never came. "But that's like Sid," she said. "It isn't that he doesn't want good things to happen to me—it's just that if it doesn't involve him, it doesn't exist." Two months later, Caesar and Coca appeared in an HBO special featuring famous comedy teams, including Rowan and Martin, the Smothers Brothers, and the two surviving Ritz Brothers. "Meeting this rather shy, thin, drawn man who appears not to have aged, I think I probably poleaxed him with my effusiveness," another of the participants, Michael Palin of Monty Python, later wrote.

CAESAR SOON FELL INTO a funk: For four months he never left his Beverly Hills house and barely left his room, plotting how best to kill himself without inconveniencing anyone unduly. "I didn't live too far from Mulholland Drive," he wrote. "How easy it would be to get into my car and just let it roll gently over one of those cliffs." As Larry Gelbart once put it, Caesar was "not having a great third act." Only his lifelong frugality—he'd always put aside 10 percent of whatever he made, even when, as he once said, he'd had to put out the lights to do it—kept him on his feet.

He steeled himself for another go at Simon's *Last of the Red Hot Lovers*, this time in Regina, Saskatchewan. He arrived aggrieved and befuddled; he refused to rehearse and was rude to the company. He seemed sleep deprived and high and had difficulty focusing. A few nights into the run, he froze on the stage, unable to remember anything. At intermission they called off the performance and took him to the hospital. "It was not one of his *Show of Shows*," a local columnist wrote. "And for the many Reginans who had wanted to see the star who more than any other represents television's Golden Age, it was not exactly *Caesar's Hour* either." The official fig leaf was a "fever," plus exhaustion from his multifarious projects. But as he later related, this was when he stared into the dressing room mirror and asked himself whether he wanted to live or die. The doctor treating him made him go cold turkey, and a rough week later Caesar returned to the show and completed his run.

He began exercising and adopted a regimen of cereal, yogurt, fruits, and nuts. He also gave up smoking his cigars, though he continued to greet, fondle, and talk with them periodically in his humidor. "Sid had a lot of walls around him, and you didn't see so much humanity out of him," the musician Elliot Finkel, who collaborated with Caesar on one show, recalled. "But I saw a brief moment of it there. It was over a cigar."

While Caesar's routine changed, his attitude didn't, at least at first. A disastrous appearance in Simon's *The Prisoner of Second Avenue* in Miami Beach helped sink the local theater company. "He was surly, uncooperative and even rude," complained one critic, who then addressed Caesar directly. "What's worse, your performance in the Simon play was rotten." Shortly after that, Caesar went to Paris for a small role in *The Fiendish Plot of Dr. Fu Manchu*, with Peter Sellers. There, through a cassette recorder, he began a twenty-two-year-long dialogue between the two halves of himself: "Sid" (his newly sober self) and "Sidney" (the self-destructive guy who'd brought him so much pain). The machine provided better therapy than all of his psychiatrists, who he now thought had just ripped him off. "Once the shrinks get you addicted to drugs, they own you lock, stock and barrel," he said. "They keep you coming back day after day, year after year, putting their kids through college on your neuroses and drug dependence."

One night at a Chinese restaurant in Paris, Caesar encountered Jonas Salk, the man who'd conquered polio. Salk, for whom watching Caesar on TV had been a ritual, spotted Caesar off in a corner, eating by himself, looking forlorn, and invited him over. ("He's *so* admiring of my dad, so deferential," recalled Salk's son Jonathan, who was there that night. "And I'm going, '*You're* the genius, man! You're meeting Jonas Salk, big deal, but I'm sitting next to *Sid Caesar*!'") Simply by recognizing Caesar, Salk gave him a boost. "Sidney, you schmuck, what did I tell you about your self-worth?" Caesar dictated into his machine afterward. "Tonight you meet a man who is one of the greatest medical minds in the whole world. You're in awe of him and afraid to approach him, and he's in awe of *you* and afraid to approach you. Self-worth, Sidney. Keep that in mind the next time you feel that you're nothing."

A new and ebullient Sid Caesar—to some, *too* new and *too* ebullient—now emerged. Howard Rosenberg of the *Los Angeles Times* resisted pleas from Caesar's new publicist to talk to him; Caesar, he knew, had always been a lousy interview. "He's a new man, an extrovert, loves to talk," the publicist promised. And so he was: Caesar, Rosenberg wrote, had "shed his introversion like an overcoat on a hot day" and become "the lampshade-wearing life of the party." "I decided I wouldn't be morose anymore," Caesar told him. "The new Caesar never shuts up," Rosenberg noted. "He snaps his fingers a lot and reminds you of a caricature of a jazz musician, almost as if he were a character in one of his own sketches." (Tolkin related something similar to Kallen, describing the new Caesar as "flitting about, very much up, talkative and quite incoherent.")

Caesar resumed his television career at rock bottom with *Pink Lady*, a bizarre, short-lived series that eventually landed on *TV Guide*'s list of the fifty worst shows ever. It was built around two Japanese actresses who spoke little English. The program's head writer, Mark Evanier, recalled the ritual around Caesar: People approached him to say he was the greatest comedian who ever lived, then asked him why he didn't have his own show; then Caesar mumbled something about idiotic network executives. He also appeared briefly on a variety show with Coca. "Sid has found a Happy Pill—actually, it's a state of mind where he loves everyone, and is madly happy 24 hours a day,—I found myself wishing for the old really lousy Sid," Coca reported to Kallen.

> This new "I love—I love" Sid is even more self involved than the Scrooge Sid. True he doesn't suspect he's surrounded by enemies,—he just knows everyone loves him, + he's so happy they have such good taste. He arrives at rehearsal—embraces everyone in sight,—does all of his dialects in his greetings,—dances a bit, rubs his hands in glee,— + yells "Let's Go" + I had to grab the arms of the chair to keep myself from bolting the room. However,— everyone is delighted with this new Sid, & if he is really as happy as he seems, I am happy for him.

"They made such a thing about our working together—so many interviews,—I know we were really not doing things really together, so each interview I felt like such a liar,—it was just awful," Coca said. The experience was "such a downer—it took weeks to get over."

In 1981, Brooks gave Caesar a bit part in *History of the World, Part I*. Brooks had long tailored Caesar's scripts to his capacities—giving him foreigners to play, inserting those choreographed coughs—and so he'd made Caesar a caveman, with no lines, only grunts. Long afterward, he recalled a Chinese lunch (apparently deviating from his new diet, Caesar had dim sum with egg drop soup) they'd shared at the Formosa Cafe during filming, with Caesar still dressed as a Neanderthal:

> He stopped and he said, "Mel, what happened? Who was I, what did I do? Tell me what happened! I don't know what happened!" And I said, "What happened is, you lived your life on demand, so you couldn't see it. You were asked to do things every day and you did them, so you didn't have time to breathe and say, 'Well, wait a minute. What am I doing?' You were too busy doing them. You were too busy spending twenty years of your life doing what other people needed from you, making money from you, getting laughs out of you, and because of that, you were like a chipmunk in a cage. You never stopped and said, 'Wait a minute. Stop it all. I want to find out where I am and who I am.'"
>
> I couldn't believe it, but he actually stopped eating for five minutes—and he was an animal if there was food—and he just nodded his head, and he said, "Why don't we know what's happening when it's happening?" I said, "Well, some of us can because we're not being paged every two minutes to do something for the world. You *were*. It's a black and terrible reward when they stop asking you to do it, and that's the time you don't want to think about where you are. You want to think about where you are when you're on top, and you can't, 'cause you're too busy.

And then later, when you're heading downhill, you don't want to know."

Later that year, the desperate producers of a national tour of Cole Porter's musical *Anything Goes* needed a leading man opposite Ginger Rogers, and plucked Caesar out of a directory. By this point pot had become Caesar's salve of choice. He smoked after each performance while taking care to hide it from Rogers, a devout Christian Scientist. According to his daughter Karen, pot helped keep Caesar calm but "wouldn't knock him out for a week or make him a crazy lunatic." It also helped explain Caesar's new mellowness—how, as his son, Rick, put it, he'd evolved from "an aggressive, almost neo-Fascist-type American" into "a delayed flower child." Pot was also a staple of the "laugh nights" that Rudy De Luca, who'd directed *Pink Lady*, held weekly (largely for Caesar, though there were always others there) at his house. "He found a guy he could smoke grass with and talk to," said De Luca.

Gene Shalit of *Today* became the latest old fan to try to engineer a Caesar comeback now that, as Caesar put it, he had his "brain back." Caesar nonetheless told a group of television critics that nothing was cooking for him, and then, sounding both embittered and beaten down, explained why: The "shrimp cocktail" he'd feed viewers would only remind them of the slop they were currently being served. Along with the usual culprits, he blamed remote controls, which made viewers impatient. In his own mind he was still enough of a star to drive a hard bargain. "If someone comes to you with a part and says not a word can be changed, tell them to shove it up their ass," he said. "There isn't a part in the world that you can't make a little better."

In the fall of 1981, Les and Glen Charles were searching for someone to play a former baseball coach named Ernie Pantusso on the program they'd co-created with James Burrows: *Cheers*. They doubted Caesar was right for the part, but they, too, had watched, and revered, him as kids, so when Caesar's agent asked them to see him, they enthusiastically obliged. But Caesar hated the part ("pure cardboard," he called it) and began dictating how the show would have to be revamped (that is, built largely around him) for him to consider the role. "It was almost as if he were doing us a favor," Les Charles remembered. "He was going to rescue us." Unsurprisingly, Caesar wasn't offered the job. But afterward, he insisted *he'd* rejected *them* and dismissed the Charles brothers as "twenty-five-year-old boys who were brought up on *Gilligan's Island.*" (Neither Charles had ever watched it.) *Cheers* ran for eleven seasons, collecting twenty-eight prime-time Emmys.

Caesar (and Coca) were among what Kallen called "the sad little number of mourners" at Frank E. Campbell's, the celebrity funeral home on Manhattan's Upper East Side, when Max Liebman died in July 1981. Usually a master of timing, Liebman had had the bad sense to die shortly before his lease was up; his office was soon cleaned out, with several filing cabinets' worth of showbiz history thrown down a chute and into the dumpster on the street below.

Liebman's cache might have come in handy for Caesar's first memoir, *Where Have I Been?*, ghostwritten by the veteran Hollywood journalist Bill Davidson and published in October 1982. As bad as things had been for Caesar, he now made them sound still worse. He enlisted his wife and kids to trash him even more, in long italicized passages detailing what a rotten husband and father he had been. Even the charming tale about hanging Brooks out the window in Chicago was repurposed into a parable about Caesar's abusiveness when drinking. "Do you realize what you nearly just did, you crazy son-of-a-bitch?" he said his brother Dave had asked him after pulling them both back in. "I was so out of it, I didn't have the slightest idea," Caesar now remembered. ("*Little Mea Culpa,*" Albert Goldman said the book should have been called.)

The book was sloppily done and filled with errors, but once more the goodwill and happy memories he'd generated muted any criticism. "He has survived the double-barreled ordeals of success and prolonged self-destruction, and the book has the inspirational quality of any good recovery tale," wrote Dick Cavett. "Give it to the alcoholic, the drug addict, and the comic genius on your Christmas list." Lou Reed asked for it in a Greenwich Village bookstore; the book was excerpted in, of all places, the *National Enquirer.* ("NEXT WEEK: What happens when Sid blacks out in a restaurant—and his head falls in the coleslaw," it teased after the first installment.)

Reiner said he cried reading it. "It was so honest, and so human," he said. Brooks said he laughed *and* cried, though there was nothing funny about it. Kallen read the book—"Portrait of the Artist as Monster Turned Evangelist," she called it—in one gulp, and confessed to knowing nothing of Caesar's vices at the time. "I must have been very self-centered, incurious, or immature," she told Tolkin. "Sid's been talking like the book suggests for months," Tolkin replied. "The Born Again schmuck." "Honestly, I hope Sid has really come through the fog—is emerging as a more or less whole person," Coca—who wasn't interviewed for the book—told Kallen, but with all its omissions and mistakes she had her doubts. Still, ever the loyalist, she'd helped him flog the book on TV. "I added whatever I could, but it was stupid," she said. "Even his press man knew that I shouldn't be there."

Howard Morris confessed he hadn't read what he called "that fucking book." "He said to me a short while ago, 'You know, Howie, I don't really know you too well,'" Morris remembered. "Now, we were crotch-to-crotch for a long time. That *really* is knowing somebody. And he said, 'You have to remember something. I've been on a twenty-seven-year nervous breakdown.' Wow." But Morris saw Caesar as better for his ordeal. "He doesn't look as much like a Jewish god, but he looks like a nice fellow, a fellow you could say hello to and he'll remember who you are, maybe," he said. It was great to have Caesar "back on this planet with us again," Gelbart told Dick Schaap. Publicists hawked it as a tale of redemption. "Caesar now is totally recovered mentally and physically," they boasted.

"You know what it is to be able to walk out and just sit in the sun?" Caesar asked Schaap, who profiled him for the television program *20/20.* "And to talk to somebody? And have them listen to you and realize that you're making sense? That you're not talking nonsense?" He'd lost twenty years, Caesar told Schaap, but he now hoped to get some of that back. "I have more to say," he said. "I would like to do more—much more."

"But you like you now," said Schaap.

"Oh, I'm getting to like me," said Caesar. "I'm not in love with myself yet."

But he was with his wife. "You deserve the medals, you really do," he told Florence as the cameras rolled.

"Everyone's giving me medals," she replied.

"If I, I never said this before, I'm gonna say it on camera. I love you."

"Well, I love you, too," she replied. "You've said it before."

"Not on camera," Caesar pointed out. "That's for everybody to see."

The sight of Caesar "schlepping his way from one TV talk show to another" describing his rejuvenation "seems beneath the dignity of an idol, even a toppled one," Tom Shales wrote in *The Washington Post*. But Caesar found the book tour eye-opening. "I didn't care about people before," he said. "Now I do." A book signing at a Caldor store in Yonkers was a far cry from the ticker-tape parade he'd received there thirty years before, but the locals still loved him. Catching a glimpse of Caesar at the store, Claude Riddick, formerly of the Billy Williams Quartet, wondered "what in the heck happened" to the handsome dude he remembered.

With its stark account of a drinking life, the book earned Caesar new admiration from the comedian Richard Lewis, a budding alcoholic himself, who'd watched Caesar as a kid. The book also inspired an eight-week Caesar retrospective at the Museum of Broadcasting in midtown Manhattan. "He seemed to be a very deep man, like someone who suffered a lot," recalled the playwright Arthur Miller, who encountered him there. The columnist Murray Kempton likened Caesar to a dinosaur "struggling to free himself from the Ice Age of television comedy." Caesar came to forgive Brooks for making off with his stuff. "I used to be paranoid about material I originated, but now I figure, it's not mine, it's everybody's," he explained.

Brooks's colossal success had inflamed some of his former colleagues. In 1977, Kallen told William Holtzman (who was writing a book on Brooks and his second wife, the actress Anne Bancroft) that she'd seen three of Brooks's movies—*Blazing Saddles*, *Young Frankenstein*, and *Silent Movie*—and laughed once at each. "Saw Mel's movie," Tolkin wrote to her about *History of the World: Part I.* "Moments of brilliance, in a sea of shit." Coca found that film "an extravaganza of bad taste." Max Liebman was more balanced, but only a little bit. "The world twisted and turned and made room for Mel Brooks," he told Holtzman. "He is a man who met his time and conquered it. Mel Brooks met the time when bad taste became good showmanship."

Brooks created additional resentment with the 1982 film *My Favorite Year,* the purported love letter to *Your Show of Shows,* for which he was executive producer. Partly it was because Benjy Stone, the wisecracking, nebbishy junior writer (played by Mark Linn-Baker) widely seen as Brooks's stand-in, was so central to the film. Stone squired around and babysat Alan Swann, the dissolute Brit (played by Peter O'Toole and thought to have been modeled after Errol Flynn), for the week Swann was guest-hosting the show. Brooks himself later said the film was based on the three days that he had spent with Flynn (and two redheaded Cuban sisters) in the Waldorf Astoria. "Max Liebman assigned me to him and said, 'Get him into rehearsal! Make him learn his lines! Work with him on the sketch!'" Trouble is, Errol Flynn never guest-hosted *Your Show of Shows.*

Now here it was thirty years later, and, as Tolkin and Kallen saw it, Brooks was still hogging all the attention. As a portrayal of Brooks's coming-of-age, *My Favorite Year* was, Tolkin said, "abject shit." "Actually, Mel never got a job to look after a drunk," he wrote Kallen. "What happened was, he volunteered to assume the role of clown to Sid the alcoholic." As the head writer, Tolkin was miffed by the film's insinuation that *Your Show of Shows* had ever been thrown together. And even worse was its portrayal of that head writer (played by Adolph Green) as what Tolkin called "a sniveling, cowardly asshole."

For her part, Kallen was exercised by the film's portrayal of women, which she called "the most totally male chauvinist, self-aggrandizing piece of work I've ever seen." She complained that it ignored Coca altogether and reduced Kallen herself to what she called "a nonentity who just passed messages from one man to another." To her, *My Favorite Year* perfectly encapsulated the sexism of Jewish men of that era, for whom "every woman was either in bed with somebody or running for coffee or being a disgusting Jewish mother in shrill terms." Not surprisingly, she blamed Brooks, whom she predicted would torment them forever. "He will never be out of the public eye," she said. "Even if he ends up in an old actors' home, he will be producing the show. He's going to go on and on and on, he will be intolerable for as long as he lives, and it'll probably be another fifty years."

Slighting Caesar in a purported homage to him wasn't easy, but King Kaiser—the film's Caesar character, depicted by Joe Bologna as what the *New York Post* called "a big dumb ox"—was actually the film's *third* banana, behind Swann and Stone. Publicly, Caesar was a good sport about it all, saying nice things about the film. But he spoke more candidly with Bill Diehl of ABC News. "When you put a big cigar in somebody's face and you put [on] big shoulders and a lot of hollering, you got Sid Caesar—supposedly," he said. He added that he'd related less to King Kaiser than to O'Toole's character, because he played "a compulsive and perpetual drunk." "Forget about Sid," Kallen counseled Tolkin. "The person who now inhabits his body bears no relation to the hunk of raw talent we used to know." "My true thoughts on Sid, you know pretty well," Tolkin wrote back. "No other comedian needed material to open his mouth as much as he did, being an uneducated lout." In Tolkin's defense, it's not clear he ever sent that letter; after his death, it was found in a file labeled "Anger."

TO MANY, *SATURDAY NIGHT LIVE*, which had launched in 1975, was the closest heir to Caesar's shows. "We want to do comedy-variety that harks back to the quality of the old Sid Caesar *Your Show of Shows*," said Dick Ebersol, NBC's director of late-night programming when it made its debut. "I remember us revering it," Al Franken, one of *SNL*'s first crop of writers, said of Caesar's show. But apart from presenting live sketch comedy on Saturday nights on NBC, the two programs had little in common.

Caesar and his colleagues, almost all of them Jews, were hardworking, giddy, grateful, tentative, aspirational; *SNL*'s writers were more diverse, entitled, jaded. "You want to know what I think is missing from comedy today? Jews," Gelbart told the writer Mike Sacks. Not Jews per se, of course—there'd always be lots of them in comic circles, including on *SNL*—but Jews like him, Jews who'd been "*hungry.*" *Caesar's Hour,* he noted, was written by the children of immigrants, largely self-taught; the newer show, staffed by college grads, was "more corporate, more smart-ass." The writer Michael Tolkin, Mel Tolkin's son, captured the difference after visiting the *Saturday Night Live* set in 1976. *SNL's* people, he wrote, "avoid the Mel Brooks spritz in favor of a more relaxed, prep-school cleverness and bright sarcasm."

Far from avoiding topicality, *Saturday Night Live* embraced it—within limits, of course. But the show was less ambitious and erudite, and proudly so. Caesar boasted of never dumbing down what he did; he and his colleagues relished the culture they'd picked up largely on their own. *SNL's* producer, Lorne Michaels (like Kallen and Tolkin, a Canadian Jew), vowed to do just the opposite. "We don't intend to deal in reference points our audience wouldn't understand," he said. He took pains to say there'd be "no satires on esoteric foreign films." Caesar didn't impress Michaels all that much anyway. "A lot of Sid Caesar just wasn't funny anymore," he said after reviewing kinescopes of *Your Show of Shows* for NBC's fiftieth anniversary special in 1976. Michaels believed "*basic* comedy" like Berle's held up better. He wasn't alone; John Belushi found Caesar's work "too long, drawn-out, overdone," while Joe Piscopo preferred Jackie Gleason and the Three Stooges.

Perhaps because they were freer to try whatever tickled them, *SNL's* creators lacked the discipline and ingenuity that working within strict confines imposed. Rather than select and hone a few sketches every week, they started innumerable ones, picking the ones they'd use at the eleventh hour, thereby guaranteeing their lack of polish or craft: Rarely, if ever, did they progress beyond what Brooks called the "colloidal." No longer was the goal partly to impress, as it had been for Liebman and Caesar; now it was simply to amuse.

One Saturday night in Cambridge in the spring of 1976, Peter

Kaplan of *The Harvard Crimson* toggled between Channel 7, which aired selections from *Your Show of Shows*, and Channel 4, which showed *Saturday Night Live*. Unusually for someone of his generation—he was born the year *Your Show of Shows* was canceled—Kaplan had exhumed and studied enough of Caesar's work to call it "the best comedy on television, ever." And Caesar shone even more brightly to him when stacked against *SNL*. What animated *Your Show of Shows* was elation born of novelty, of Jews breaching the American mainstream via a brave new medium. "You can almost see the shock and the exhilaration on the actors' faces at what they are doing," he wrote. Then you'd turn the channel, and behold *SNL*'s "wicked, cynical edge": Chevy Chase joking about the Italian earthquake, a drunk "Pat Nixon" griping about lousy sex with Dick.

During his Dark Period, Caesar had viewed all younger comics as enemies, stealing from him the laughs he no longer got himself. But his bitterness and jealousy congealed around *Saturday Night Live*. Apart from its success, of course, he resented its greater freedom, broader comedic palette, and cushier circumstances, loathed its laziness (going for cheap laughs) and its lack of discipline, conviction, and craft. "I think they are what they say they are: 'The Not Ready for Prime Time Players,'" he said. Imagine people saying he and Coca resembled Belushi and Gilda Radner, rather than the other way around! He didn't find Belushi any funnier than Belushi found him, especially since he'd ripped off his Japanese shtick; he'd erupt if his children watched him or, worse, laughed when they did. The sunniness of the new, blissed-out Caesar stopped at *SNL*'s stage door.

But when, in early 1983, Caesar was asked to guest-host *Saturday Night Live*, he put all that aside. That the show was in a creative trough (when Ebersol displaced Michaels for a time) hardly mattered; no other show offered a more direct route to rehabilitation. The idea of inviting him came from the actor Brad Hall and Paul Barrosse, a writer. Along with his future wife, Julia Louis-Dreyfus, Hall had just joined the show from Second City, which, favoring sketches over stand-up, really *was* Caesar's legitimate heir. Who, Hall asked, could more appropriately host

Saturday Night Live than the guy who'd invented the form? Caesar could goose a show that, to Hall at least, didn't feel "live" at all. His impending appearance generated an excitement that only a few other guest hosts (like Ringo Starr) previously had. "You're about to meet a comic giant," Ebersol told the staff. It would be Caesar's first encounter with live TV in more than twenty years.

While most guest hosts were smart enough to know their fate and the show's were intertwined, Caesar kept his distance from everyone. "He wasn't chummy," said Hall. "He was trying to re-create himself, and I think he was nervous. This was a big deal for him." Caesar also behaved like someone who'd been there before, as of course he had. As another writer, Nate Herman, put it, "Being on *SNL* wasn't exactly the crowning achievement of his career." He'd brought his own proposed sketch: a twin takedown of *Rocky* and *Tootsie* that never got anywhere. Instead, he had to go with the program's smorgasbord of ideas, none of them polished. In the old days, he'd told his staffers that the more they fought over a sketch beforehand, the better they'd feel when the show came off: They'd done everything they could. But in the lackadaisical world of *SNL*, where indiscipline was a virtue, everything was destined—*designed*—to be half-baked. He considered the process insane, and went nearly insane over it. "You think you know everything because you're a college boy!" he shouted at the writer Barry Blaustein, before throwing a chair at him. Caesar's moments of pleasure were equally extreme. "He couldn't contain his anger or delight," another cast member, Tim Kazurinsky, recalled. "It was almost like a bipolar thing." Caesar might be an asshole, people thought, but he was also a legend, so, like so many others before them, they made allowances.

Out Caesar came on Saturday night, February 5, 1983. He looked lean and buff, especially for a man of sixty—"easily the healthiest-looking member of the group," wrote Frank Prial of *The New York Times*. (And, as Louis-Dreyfus remembered, also reeking of cologne.) He was dressed like someone a third his age from some outer borough: jeans (with an enormous belt buckle), tight red shirt with open collar, gold chain around his neck. "Could easily pass for a deck hand on *The Love Boat*," went one contemporaneous description of his look.

The applause was loud, but not loud enough for someone of Caesar's stature as far as Eddie Murphy, then a member of the *SNL* cast, was concerned. "Everybody up!" he bellowed to the audience. "Up! Up! Up! Up! Up! Up!" Louis-Dreyfus shouted, gesturing as if flinging open a window. The frenzy grew. As Caesar shook his head in wonder, she patted him gently on the back. After a break, Don Pardo (a genuine link between the two shows) formally introduced Caesar. Sid strutted out once again and basked in more love—bowing, shaking his head, clenching his fist, throwing a left jab, as if punching his way out of his long, unhappy exile. "I can't tell you how much I appreciate being on this show," he said. "It's a new era of my life."

"Warmly welcomed as Role Model and Father Figure," Caesar "seemed to think this was the boost his career needed," one reviewer wrote. "What he needed was his old 'Show of Shows' writers." He'd been given several sketches' worth of newly minted junk. But the curtain call was as emotional as the opening, with another cast member, Mary Gross, awarding him a plaque declaring him an "Honorary Member of *Saturday Night Live*," a gesture the television writer David Bianculli likened to a Little League team honoring Pete Rose. "Thanks for making the juices flow again," Caesar wrote in the copy of his book he gave the show's producer, Robert Tischler. If there was anything left from Caesar's truckload of couth, now was the time for him to spread it around, and sprinkle in some tact, too. But rather than celebrate his appearance, in interviews and public events afterward he apologized for it, ostensibly blaming himself but in fact foisting fault on others.

They'd placed him in a straitjacket, he complained. "I was told, 'Don't move, don't make any noise, and be funny.' That's a new technique to me. You got the pupils of the eyes to work with, and that's about it. They forgot body language; they *forgot* it." When he was playing the Professor, they'd stuck him behind a desk. "I was cut off at the legs. I couldn't use my body." And he'd let them! "I didn't insist heavy enough. I didn't say, 'Look, I want to do this. I want to do that.'" "He seemed so unhappy—just agitated and angry at life," Blaustein recalled. "Even though he was a pain in the ass, I wound up feeling sorry for him, because

he couldn't help it." The experience further soured Caesar on
the state of television comedy, and the smart kids who he felt had
hijacked it. "They have Ph.D.'s so they know what's funny," he
said. "They graduated with doctorates of philosophy on humor,
magna cum louder, louder, and louder."

Caesar played an Orthodox Jewish garmento in *Over the
Brooklyn Bridge*, a film starring Elliott Gould and Margaux
Hemingway. For someone who'd always avoided Jewish material, let alone dealt in Jewish stereotypes, it marked another
departure. Once off-limits to him, Yiddish words, some embar-
rassing or offensive, now came gushing out. "Give 'em a couple
of drinks, maybe they'll get *shikkered*" is his advice on how to
deal with Japanese businessmen. Later, he calls Blacks "*schvar-
tzes*." On the set, Gould, who'd long admired Caesar and knew
his history, both guided him and calmed him down. In the film's
climactic scene, the two come to blows—the most dramatic acting he'd ever attempted, and an oddly affecting moment in an
otherwise awful film. When the Friars roasted Caesar in New
York in October 1983, his old pal Jan Murray said Sid had been
in a coma for thirty years—"the Jewish Rip Van Winkle," he
called him—and joked that when he finally came to, in his hand
were two tickets to the Joe Louis–Tony Galento fight (which had
taken place on June 28, 1939). Even here, Caesar was somehow
upstaged, this time by Phyllis Diller, who, disguised as a man,
crashed the stag event.

Whatever bounce Caesar got from *Where Have I Been?* didn't
last long; his agents at William Morris couldn't, or didn't, find him
much work. But shortly after the roast he hired a new personal
manager named Larry Spellman. Spellman not only discovered
new comic talent—he'd spotted Rodney Dangerfield when he
was still selling aluminum siding—but resuscitated the old: He'd
brought back Joey Bishop and Frank Gorshin. He quickly got
Caesar on talk shows, signed him up with a lecture bureau, and,
through Columbia Artists Management, arranged for appearances with symphony orchestras, narrating pieces like *Peter and
the Wolf*. He also got him to spring for first-class publicists and
gave them his message: to sell Caesar as "a legend and a genius."

And it became clear that for all his baggage Caesar could still draw crowds. Four weekends in 1984 at the Playboy club in Atlantic City—his first nightclub appearances both in five years and since emerging from what one paper called his "dope-and-booze fog"—earned him nearly $180,000.

Caesar's health kick got him on the cover of *Parade*, and on *The Tonight Show* Joan Rivers told Caesar that at age sixty-one he looked fabulous. He appeared in more forgettable films (in *Stoogemania* he played a German shrink trying to wean a patient off Moe, Larry, and Curly), exercise videos, and commercials. He created the video compilations of old sketches that appeared late at night. All this activity didn't make Caesar any easier to deal with; Jack Thomas of *The Boston Globe* found him "impatient, obsessive, compulsive, waspish, bitter, insecure, frustrated, often selfish, easily irritated and frequently angry at *them*" when he came to town in 1984.

The producer Marty Bell hired Caesar to do the voice-over for a documentary about the Brooklyn Dodgers in their dotage based on Roger Kahn's *Boys of Summer*, only to watch him stray from the script, interjecting jokes and foreign accents. "I laughed a lot, but I couldn't use any of it," Bell recalled. Sometime in 1987, Ralph Edwards played "This Is Your Story" for Jimmy Stewart and his wife. "They were absolutely hysterical," he recalled. Late that same year, despite breaking his hip, Caesar began two seasons playing the drunken jailer Frosch in the Metropolitan Opera's production of *Die Fledermaus*. This, plus talk from the producer Allan Carr of a Broadway version of *Your Show of Shows* and a possible sitcom for Caesar (directed by David Steinberg and co-starring Dorothy Loudon) and the Smithsonian adding the Professor's outfit to its collection, led Larry King to tell Caesar on his radio show in February 1988 that he was "hot again."

Maybe not *hot*, Caesar replied, but at least functional. "For twenty years, I didn't even know my own name," he said.

"You were brain dead," King interjected.

"Oh, yeah," said Caesar. "I was just walking around going through the motions."

Later that year Caesar, though only sixty-five, appeared with

Milton Berle (seventy-nine) and Danny Thomas (seventy-six) in *Side by Side*, a cloying made-for-television movie about three retired executives in the rag trade plotting a comeback, which evolved into a touring show packaged as the *Three Living Legends of Comedy*. (One reviewer described Caesar as "bewildered.") But appearing at the Village Gate in New York in 1989, he got a much warmer reception. The historian Arthur Schlesinger Jr. brought some friends with him to the show, though it had taken some doing. "Steve Smith,[*] who shares my fond memories of the brilliant *Your Show of Shows*, was all in favor," Schlesinger wrote in his diary,

> but Betty Bacall was reluctant, fearing it would be a sad evening, and Alexandra[†] was too young to recall the glories of Sid and Imogene. . . . I shared Betty's concern that he might be a ghost vainly trying to renew the past, but I felt that in any case we owed a visit to a man who had once given us much pleasure.
>
> We could not have enjoyed ourselves more. Sid Caesar did mostly old numbers, it is true, but he did them with the same mimetic brilliance, the same verbal dexterity, the same antic imagination as he did them a third of a century ago; and he seemed to add to that a dimension of sweetness that perhaps resulted from the vicissitudes of life.

Afterward, they all went backstage to congratulate him. "He looked fine, seemed much moved by the audience reaction and was charming," Schlesinger wrote. "It is cheering to watch such a smash comeback."

But moving the show to Broadway proved disastrous. The production was underfinanced, too intimate for a big theater, and plagued by discord between Caesar and the producer, Martin Charnin, who'd pushed him to update his material. ("He's trying

---

[*] John F. Kennedy's brother-in-law and manager of his 1960 presidential campaign.
[†] Schlesinger's second wife.

to tell me how to make love to my wife of forty years," Caesar complained.) "When, at the curtain call, Sid stands there in what the program calls his 'legendary German Professor costume,' and thanks the audience for helping him complete his resurrection from a boozing and pill-popping has-been, even as he fumbles with his collapsed stovepipe hat (which you half expect him to start passing around), you may well feel that his kind of comedy has outlived its amusefulness," wrote the famously savage critic John Simon, who dismissed Caesar's co-stars as "second bananas to an overripe plantain." The show closed after five performances. Albert Goldman's brief attempt to revive his dormant Caesar book came a cropper when Caesar demanded $100,000 for his cooperation.

But Caesar (joined by Coca, now walking with a cane) rebounded in April 1990 with a well-received show at Michael's Pub in New York. Ed Koch arrived one night with a party of twelve; on another, Woody Allen came in with Dick Cavett. "They were both very funny and very brilliant," Allen remembered. "It was not some dinky little comedown." Afterward, they went backstage, which was when Caesar told him, "Funny that I'm going to be a footnote in your life story," and Allen replied that that was "completely untrue." "But he'd felt that he had come upon harder times and that he had been forgotten to a large degree," Allen recalled. "That wasn't so with those of us who knew him." When the show went to Chicago, Studs Terkel was equally moved—not out of nostalgia, he told Caesar and Coca when they appeared on his radio program, but quite the opposite: Their humor, he said, was "eternal."

But over time, Caesar, basking in all those "legend and genius" press releases, became increasingly high-maintenance, picking and choosing gigs, then canceling them on a whim. A triumphant winter appearance for him and Coca at the Fontainebleau in Miami Beach, one that would have had the Jews lining up all the way from Boca Raton, fell through when he demanded a room with a balcony, where, Spellman assumed, he could smoke his pot undetected. It was behavior Spellman had seen before from stars: "They have a button next to them called 'self-destruct,' and when things go too well, they can't help but press it." Spellman and Caesar soon parted ways. As did Caesar and Coca; once he stopped asking her to tour with him, he stopped talking to her altogether, including over her last five years. She died, at age ninety-two, in June 2001.

Neil Simon offered his sentimental take on the Caesar years in *Laughter on the 23rd Floor*, which reached Broadway in November 1993. When Nathan Lane, who played the Caesar character (Max Prince), introduced Caesar (seated near Barbara Walters, David Geffen, and Mike Wallace) after the curtain on opening night, he got a long standing ovation. (Later, Caesar offered Lane some advice about success: "Try to enjoy it while it's happening. Don't be like me. Enjoy it now.") The next day, accompanied by Gene Shalit of NBC, Caesar returned to Max Liebman's old quarters at City Center; just walking into the lobby brought back the knot in Caesar's stomach. "Sid is active [and] fit, having been through a life that would have killed three ordinary men" was how Dick Cavett introduced him on his talk show.

In March 1994, Reiner, Coca, Fabray, and Weaver, along with an assortment of Sid's writers, saluted Caesar during a program at the Museum of Television and Radio in Los Angeles, in which Howard Morris was relegated to the audience rather than given his proper place onstage. While he'd had a respectable career post-Caesar—directing, doing voice-overs, gaining cult status as the mountain man Ernest T. Bass on *The Andy Griffith Show*—he'd never approached his former fame or craft. He'd never stopped resenting Caesar, though publicly he was mostly gracious.

"Sidney, I have so much to thank you for," he said during the program. "From Sid I learned so many things . . ."

"Anger!" Brooks interjected.

". . . Comedy," he continued, not rising to Brooks's bait. "Timing. I learned about humanity, truth, honesty, where the laughs are . . . sometimes. Sidney, if you ever want to start up again, call me."

In 1995, Caesar watched Neil Simon collect a Kennedy Center Honor, something he would never receive, or ever even be considered for, himself.* The following January, eight writers for *Caesar's Hour*, along with Carl Reiner, assembled for what Tom Shales called "a comedy Last Supper" at the Writers Guild in Beverly Hills. Only at the last minute, and at the insistence of Larry Gelbart, who'd organized the event, was Caesar invited; Gelbart had initially not included him, because, as he put it, on any given night it was always "a crapshoot" which Sid you got. Caesar turned out to be in fine form. He'd actually grown more lucid and articulate in old age; while never exactly eloquent, when freed from the awkwardness and intoxicants, he could be pithy. Better than anyone else there, he summarized the complex biosphere of the writers' room, what he called "this mayhem that was going back and forth, the electricity—and hate."

"Everybody thinks that Sid waited to be pumped up with intelligence and with material from his writers," Brooks said that night. "They thought he'd sit there like a crazy empty balloon and then we would come in and we would pump him up, that we would make a human being out of him and his tongue would stick out and he would talk and be funny. But believe it or not, Sid was one of the funniest guys, even away from the writers and the writing room." The program—it could have been "a spoof on a Jewish burial society," Walter Goodman wrote in the *Times*—found eternal life on public television (the place to which Caesar's fans had migrated en masse), a powerful laxative during pledge drives.

"I don't know how many time's [*sic*] over the years I've thought of sitting down and writing to you and telling you what an inspiration you've been to me and what a genius you are," Jonathan Winters wrote to Caesar in early 1997. A month later, Caesar gave his oral history to the Archive of American Television. In it he likened his writers to Renoir, Van Gogh, Pissarro, and Seurat, and recalled how they'd tried to shield him when he plunged into what he called the "salad" at Blair House.

"Well, they loved you," said his interviewer, the producer and programmer Dan Pasternack.

---

* A great injustice, as the man who administered the awards, George Stevens Jr., later acknowledged.

"Sure," Caesar replied softly. "I loved *them*."

It was pretty to think so, but though Caesar's writers and Caesar cherished everything they'd shared, what they'd said to Pasternack simply wasn't so. Caesar pronounced his career officially over. "There's a time to say 'enough,'" he said. "There's a time to say you're never going to do it as well as you did." He still avoided most television comedy, he said; better to watch the *Bismarck* sink yet again or Archduke Ferdinand get re-assassinated on the History Channel. How would he like to be remembered? "I brought laughter to the world," he replied.

To mark his half century in television, the Friars roasted Caesar again in 1999, this time in Los Angeles. The comedy writer Hal Kanter described him as "a man some of you remember from the Catskills, some remember from the Coast Guard, and others with long memories remember when he was popular." It was an older crowd, or as the comedian Jeff Ross put it, "I've seen younger faces on cash." Ross, who'd grown close to Caesar, championed him among younger comics, but, as he put it, "it was very hard to explain to a thirty-year-old how funny this seventy-year-old used to be."

Still, a group of younger self-styled "comedy nerds"—Phil Rosenthal, Judd Apatow, and Larry Wilmore among them—threw a dinner in Los Angeles for Caesar; Caesar burst to life when Rosenthal reenacted the boardroom sketch, his glasses case simulating Morris's pickle. Caesar was also there when Rob Reiner screened some of Caesar's old sketches at his home for Billy Crystal, Jon Lovitz, Tom Hanks, and the comedy writer Alan Zweibel, among others. "What you kids did for Sid last night added ten years to his life," Carl Reiner told Zweibel afterward.

The big-shot journalists and Broadway columnists who'd once stalked Caesar were nowhere to be seen in December 2000, when he collected the Alan King Award in American Jewish Humor at the Pierre. Though initially out of sorts that night— "You can be Jewish and be bad," he snapped when asked whether his background helped explain his comedic gifts—he was pleased to be in New York. People (and maybe the penguins) around the Penguin House at the Central Park Zoo recognized him. "It's a different world," he said of the city. "People here in New York are *alive*."

Only a few brand names—Jerry Stiller and Anne Meara, Susie Essman—had shown up at the award ceremony, and from Caesar's old crowd only Tolkin was on hand. In the video tribute he sent, Reiner called Caesar "the *most* brilliant comedian that lived on television in the history of time." In his video, Gelbart said he missed seeing Caesar on TV. "Although to me he's still there," he went on. "Just as the light from a distant star takes eons to reach us, Sid's light is still in there. The light from this brilliant Jewish star is still an inspiration and challenge to us all." Alan King introduced Brooks, who reminisced about the "young blond god" he'd met backstage at the Copacabana. "Do I lie, Florence?" he asked. "Shoulders out to there. The strongest man that ever lived." At one point while speaking about Caesar, he choked up, and put his hand to his chest. "It's not the chicken; it's a feeling," he said.

The release in May 2001 of a made-for-television version of *Laughter on the 23rd Floor*, which ventured some into Caesar's private life, helped kill off a Caesar biopic championed by the actor Noah Wyle. Caesar became an emblem of old age: One of Ted Williams's pals told a reporter he avoided seeing the Red Sox legend in his final years because, well, he "looked like Sid Caesar."

EPILOGUE

Despite his worsening infirmities, in May 2002 Caesar flew to New York to take part in NBC's seventy-fifth anniversary celebration at Rockefeller Center. A host of stars, including Ted Danson, Tina Fey, and Jimmy Fallon, sought him out. He brought down the house paying tribute to Coca, Berle, and Steve Allen in double-talk. But his world was shrinking and he went ever more silent, even at a semiweekly lunch with old cronies at a local delicatessen; Reiner passed along the little Caesar had to say, as he'd once done for Neil Simon in the writers' room. "Sid, it was wonderful seeing you again and watching your lips move," the director John Rich wrote to him after a meal together.

In 2003, Caesar published a second memoir, co-written by Eddy Friedfeld, a journalist and scholar on American culture. While not overlooking his struggles, the book, *Caesar's Hours: My Life in Comedy, with Love and Laughter,* was far more a celebration of his life and work than *Where Have I Been?* "You learn nothing from success; you only learn from failure," Caesar wrote in it. "Failure teaches you about life. Success without ever tasting failure ultimately teaching you only one thing: how to be a jerk." An appearance in New York to promote the book proved so popular that it had to be moved to a larger venue. But of the thousand or so who attended, only nine bought books. All those years, after all, they'd gotten him for free.

One by one, the stalwarts of Caesar's shows passed on. In May 2005, it was Howard Morris. At his funeral, as he had specified, "This Is Your Story" was played on a giant screen above his casket. Never, Reiner said afterward, had he heard such laughter at a mortuary. Caesar didn't attend, though he was much on people's minds. "You know, we're going to be doing this for Sid any day now," Aaron Ruben told Andy Griffith during the ceremony. (In fact, Caesar outlived them both.) Morris ended high up in a crypt. "That's nice. Howie gets to be tall for a change," someone remarked.

Mel Tolkin died in November 2007. At his funeral, which Caesar attended with the help of two caregivers, an ambulance could be heard in the distance. "Sid's ride," Brooks whispered. Caesar, by then in a wheelchair, fumbled when asked to say something at Larry Gelbart's memorial service, in the summer of 2009. "Do it in Italian!" Norman Lear shouted. And so Caesar did. And, even though they'd just played a clip of Caesar doing pretty much the same thing, it was, as the actor Richard Kind recalled, "as if the lights went on in the theater."

Though increasingly bedridden, Caesar occasionally got out. When Billy Crystal's one-man autobiographical show, *700 Sundays*, ran in Los Angeles in early 2006, Crystal invited Caesar to a matinee, sent a car to pick him up, and held the curtain until he was in place. "It was a thank you for coming into my life, for inspiring me to want to be funny," he later wrote. Caesar continued to give interviews, in one of which he blamed three new culprits for his reversals: Elvis Presley, the Beatles, and Woodstock. On entering the house that day, the interviewer had been struck by the smell of pot. Also striking was how stale and static Caesar's house seemed. Sid and Florence had never paid much attention to the place, and it showed. "Once swinging but now sadly bedraggled" was how *Variety* later described it. When I visited Caesar in 2008, I smelled no marijuana, but sensed the same stasis. Occasionally, Florence Caesar, wearing a housecoat, trundled by silently. "She has been living with Caesar's enormities since 1943," the writer Richard Gehman had written in 1963, and forty-five years later the toll seemed even clearer. She'd once been asked whether she really *knew* her husband. "I know *him*," she replied.

I found Caesar keen and animated. "No!" he'd declare with great vehemence (and more than a touch of disdain) when I asked something silly, and "Of course!" when I said something obvious. He laughed at some of his own antics, like buying a gun powerful enough to kill a tiger. "What are you going to do with that?" he asked. "Nothing! I'm not going to go to Africa, go on a safari. And I didn't like killing animals anyway." He denied ordering a flunky to unwrap a stick of gum for him, then rinse off the sugar, before he'd put it in his mouth. He said how much he missed the aroma of fresh halvah and the taste of Barney Greengrass's sturgeon. And how, fifty years earlier, that very sturgeon was proof to him that he had arrived. "Sturgeon was *$5 a pound*—$5 for a pound of sturgeon!" he said. "And I don't care, I'm going to buy it. And I did."

He had no unkind words for anyone. He was happy to watch for the umpteenth time his youthful self—vital, fleet of foot, totally in command—outrunning all those young ushers at the Center Theatre, before they finally corralled him and dragged him up onstage for "This Is Your Story." At first, he was matter-of-fact about what he'd pulled off that night. "It was just another sketch," he said. "It's a satire. That's what I did." But seeing it again, breaking into the silent laughter of the very old, he changed course. "Boy, that's some sketch," he said quietly when it was over. Had he spotted something he'd not seen before? "No, I knew every inch of it," he said. "It's just that you see it again and say, '*My God*, it's good.'"

Another figure from television, the writer Rocky Kalish, was with us that day, and said something about the freedom everyone involved in the sketch had enjoyed. Caesar set him straight. "It was freedom, but they were all in the same groove," he said, freedom within well-established and mutually respected rules. A few moments later, watching Morris dress up his German General, Caesar was pleased anew. "You don't see stuff like that anymore," he said, seconds after watching himself blow his whistle and collect his tip. "It's one of a kind. We did it. We didn't copy anybody."

Caesar rarely went out after Florence died in March 2010. Instead, his friends Lou and Fran Zigman organized dinners at his house. The regulars included Monty Hall, Lou Gossett Jr., and Joe Bologna; Nanette Fabray came a couple of times, as did Larry King, Dick Van Dyke, Billy Crystal, and Richard Lewis. Watching Caesar when he was given a lifetime achievement award from the Television Critics Association in 2011, the screenwriter Aaron Sorkin thought at first that Caesar had had a stroke. But when Caesar launched into his "French," Sorkin wrote, "you can't remember the last time you were with a group of people laughing this loudly and this sincerely." With his "German," all the people at Sorkin's table, colleagues from *The West Wing*, "completely lost control." But double-talk, too, was now on the way out— too touchy for modern sensibilities, too dangerous in the wrong hands. After being attacked for mimicking the Chinese president in Asian-sounding singsong, Rush Limbaugh pleaded that Sid Caesar had done the same thing, and they'd called *him* a genius!

Jerry Lewis, Woody Allen, and Robin Williams sent in taped greetings on Caesar's ninetieth birthday in 2012. Jay Leno had the studio audience at *The Tonight Show* stay over a few extra minutes, then asked everyone to give Caesar a standing ovation, which of course he never saw. Brooks and Reiner came by more regularly, sitting alongside him, Jeff Ross wrote in his journal, "like dutiful sons." His house smelling of "mold, brisket, and Shalimar," Caesar hosted several Passover Seders, led by the folk singer and actor Theodore Bikel. Among the assembled comics there, getting Caesar to laugh was the ultimate challenge, and validation.

One of Brooks's visits, a year or two before Caesar's death, stuck with him. "He didn't talk for five minutes and I sat there," Brooks recalled. "And then finally he said, 'So you went from me to Hitler,'" referring to *The Producers*, by then a hit musical. What Brooks called Caesar's "brushstroke of dementia" was actually a blessing, because it filtered out things that no longer mattered to him and allowed him to focus on things that did, like food and the History Channel. "But I would bring him back a lot," said Brooks. "I'd say, 'I've got $5, and it's burning a hole in my pocket,' and he'd start, we'd sing it together."

Brooks was back at Caesar's house, holding his hand, on the afternoon of February 11, 2014. Early the next morning, Caesar died, at ninety-one. On the front page of the next day's *New York Times*, under the headline COMEDIAN OF COMEDIANS FROM TV'S EARLY DAYS, the paper described him as "a comedic force of nature" who'd "influenced generations of comedians and comedy writers." On television, commentators struggled to make him matter. "Younger viewers may remember him in *Grease*" was how someone on ABC News did it (that, and by describing *Your Show of Shows* as "the original *SNL*"). George Stephanopoulos said Caesar had a simple philosophy: "When it comes to humor, never take yourself too seriously." Of course, when it came to humor, taking himself too seriously was precisely what Caesar had always done.

Lots of people gathered four days later at the Mount Sinai Memorial Park in Hollywood Hills for Caesar's funeral, but the place still felt sort of empty. Caesar had outlived most of his peers, and some of those still around, like Simon and Reiner, weren't well enough to come, or were back in New York. Because the service hadn't been publicized, there weren't many fans. Had she known where to go, said Vikki Dougan, the model in "This Is Your Story," she'd have been there. The brightest star was Billy Crystal, who'd paid tribute in a piece in that morning's *Times*. The death of Sid Caesar, along with Mickey Mantle's nineteen years earlier, were the bookends on his childhood, he'd written.

Caesar was finally certified—by Rabbi Jerry Cutler, who presided—as a "Jewish" comic. That the references weren't explicit didn't matter, he said, "because the Jewish humor permeated every script, every joke, every nuance"; whenever Caesar was on the air, "every single Jew walked around with a smile on their faces, *kvelling*." Caesar would have felt proud, and slightly mystified, by the rabbi's words.

The first eulogy came from Karen Caesar, the youngest of Sid's children and the only one of them to speak. Born in 1956, she acknowledged she'd not known her father in his prime, but she'd grown up with the consequences and, she said, "a lot of it

wasn't pretty. He had addictions, and anger, and so many demons.
Although it was easy to appreciate his talent and comic genius, he
could be ornery and self-involved and immensely difficult. But he
could also be generous and empathetic and a great big softy." Joe
Bologna and Richard Lewis both recalled how watching Caesar
every week had eased their troubled Brooklyn adolescences. Only
when *Your Show of Shows* was on, Lewis recalled, did the anger in
his family momentarily abate. "There was something very magical
about this guy," he said. "He was *so powerful* . . . he was like the
center of the universe. When the show was over, I heard my family
yelling in the kitchen, doing the exact sketch—without the jokes."

In a taped message, Reiner described Caesar as "all talent,
drive, energy—and appetite." But he'd foolishly superimposed
his remarks over the clips of Caesar in action—over buckets of
water landing on him and Coca on a "beach," and the clanks and
buzzes of a busted Bavarian clock, and the chaos of "This Is Your
Story"—and two layers of laughs, sixty years apart, overwhelmed
his words. But it didn't really matter. It was Mel Brooks everyone
wanted to hear.

Only Brooks had all of the elements—the size, and passion, and pizzazz, and depth of feeling—to do Sid Caesar right.
Brooks's Caesar had *never* shrunk. All the good taste, generosity,
and modesty Brooks possessed, Sid Caesar was uniquely able to
summon. It didn't matter that Brooks's stories had been tweaked
or embellished or fabricated; what greater homage can a story-
teller give you than more, and more outlandish, stories about
you? Besides, the reverence and gratitude were real. Brooks now
recounted their improbable beginnings: how these two incon-
gruous yet strangely complementary young Jews, the hulking
one from Yonkers who couldn't talk and the diminutive one
from Brooklyn who couldn't shut up, had come, then hung, then
stayed together. He talked again about those graven images, and
the $40 that Caesar gave him out of his own pocket every week,
at a time when Brooks's older brother Irving, with a family to
feed, was making only $35.

I didn't realize then that a comedian could not only meet
your material but actually *lift it*. Sid taught me not to

write *jokes* but to write *people*. And to find out what made them tick. And to find the common denominator in all people so that the humor would actually be lovely, translatable, and understandable.

And I'd throw curves, and I'd throw sliders and fastballs. . . . There was *nothing* that he couldn't hit out of the park. And it was a thrill to sit there in the greenroom on the *Show of Shows* . . . it makes me cry . . .

He paused and wiped his brow.

. . . and watch this guy take a sketch and *send it to the moon*. We *couldn't believe* this genius. We use the word too loosely, but Sid . . . was . . . a genius. He was a genius. He was born to interpret humanity and send it back to us in delicious and different forms.

He then pivoted, at least for a moment, to the tragedy of the man, which he blamed on television. All the perils of its impermanence, those things he'd spotted sixty years earlier, those things to which he'd tried to alert Caesar, had come to pass, and had denied him the recognition he so clearly deserved.

Television is not a safe harbor. It's nowhere: you're out at sea. And movies seem to have a permanence, especially comedy giants like Harold Lloyd, like Chaplin, like Keaton, all of these people, Laurel and Hardy, all of these people before Sid, and they're still trenchant, palpable, *with us*, and you ask kids about Sid Caesar and they don't know who he is. It's . . . it's terrible.

"Anyway, he'll always be with me," he added, quickly, almost cheerfully, as if to keep things from getting too heavy, which a comedian's funeral should never be, because for a comedian a somber funeral is really a rebuke. "He was an unforgettable guy!" he said. "He was unforgettable, he was unique, he was the greatest comedian who ever plied that trade, and he was . . . a great man."

. . .

CAESAR'S AFFAIRS WERE SETTLED quickly and amicably. A trust
divided his estate among his children.* Beleaguered though his
house was, because of its pedigree, panoramic views, and zip
code (the much-coveted 90210), it fetched a premium price—
$5.5 million—only to be torn down and replaced with something
else that soon sold for three times as much.

Regarding his worldly goods, Sid had traveled light. Aside
from his kinescopes, guns, cigars, and a set of outsized scrapbooks of clippings, he'd left most of his past behind, providing
Julien's, Hollywood's celebrity auction house, only a motley sam-
ple of Caesarabilia to sell. There was lots of art, but the master-
works that had once hung along the stairway up to his office had
been either deaccessioned or discredited: The Vlaminck Caesar
had pointed out so proudly to Ed Murrow turned out to be a
fake. There were a few books of note, like a collection of Sholem
Aleichem's short stories inscribed by his grandson, telling Caesar
that his grandfather would have admired him; a souvenir key
chain from *Grease 2*; a serving tray from *The Love Boat*; and a
pitcher from Hugh Hefner. Caesar's Emmys had disappeared,
but he'd held on to the plaque Charles Berlitz had given him for
popularizing foreign languages. For all his ire at *Saturday Night
Live*, he'd also kept the certificate making him an honorary member of the cast, along with a black nylon *SNL* jacket with "Sid"
stitched in red on the front.

The gaudy gold chains and necklaces that Sid favored later
were amply represented, but more important baubles, like the
pinkie ring retrieved from the gutter in front of Milgrim's, were
not. A Browning Olympian bolt-action rifle, one of ten pages'
worth of firearms in his catalog, went for $5,000. The priciest
item was the Marini sculpture Coca had given him, which sold
for more than $200,000. Caesar's 1985 El Dorado convertible
attracted no buyers, and was driven off by a charity.

Nestled among the furniture, dishes, and "event-worn"
clothes were two objects of note. Item 353 was a mustard-yellow

---

* Following a long illness, his son, Rick, died six months after his father.

"Sid Caesar Performance Worn Military Costume," comprising a jacket (complete with epaulets, gold tassels, rope belt, and medals), trousers, and cap. It was in this that Howard Morris dressed him in the German General sketch; Caesar had held on to it, in all likelihood, because the routine remained a staple in his act. It sold for $1,200. But far more significant was item 461, described as "a rusty saxophone, accompanied by a hard-shell case in a travel bag." It was a Selmer Super Cigar Cutter tenor sax dated back to 1932, making it, in all likelihood, the very instrument the delinquent lodger had left behind at the St. Clair Lunch. Caesar hadn't played it in ages. It had been fished out from beneath a pile of old clothes in his closet on his ninetieth birthday, but proved too heavy for him to lift. It was appraised at between $300 and $500, but embarrassed that something so foundational in Caesar's life would go for so little, Caesar's pal Lou Zigman bid preemptively for it, taking it home for $1,600. He couldn't play it himself, but vowed one day to give it to someone who could.

Why *had* Caesar held on to it? Maybe he'd hoped to pick it up and play it again at some point. Or maybe he realized that without it he might have wound up like his brothers, taking bets at the back of a candy store. But as someone who'd never stopped believing in the souls of everyday objects, who'd even apologized to a trash can, maybe he feared hurting its feelings, or appearing ungrateful. After all, that simple piece of brass had given him more unalloyed happiness than anything, or anyone, ever had.

The New York Times, September 9, 1957.

The "Committee for Caesar's Longevity," aka Harry J. Macklis, Esq., of Jamaica, Queens, placed notices in the New York papers protesting Caesar's disappearance from the airwaves (top) and, four months later, celebrating his happy—but short-lived—return (bottom).

New York Post, January 26, 1958.

ACKNOWLEDGMENTS

Sid Caesar was a great student of history but a poor custodian of his own. There are almost no Caesar papers—contemporaneous letters or journals—and his first memoir was filled with errors. (Fortunately, he was more informative, and accurate, and easier on himself in the second.) Most of his greatest work survives, but it's scattered and, thanks in part to his desperate efforts to keep it alive, not always intact.

So my first thanks go to those very special people who helped me gather and watch Caesar's programs. The indefatigable and resourceful Jane Klain of the Paley Center for Media in New York is crucial to anyone writing television history. Never did she tire of my endless requests. Nor did Mike Mashon, formerly of the Library of Congress, and Mark Quigley, television curator at the UCLA Film and Television Archive (who also, at the eleventh hour, miraculously found the missing half of Caesar's precious scrapbooks of clippings). I was blessed to work with them all.

Television, too, has been careless about its past, and I'm thankful to those who took care to preserve pieces of it, and then to share those pieces with me. There's no way Jeff Kisseloff could have included all of the gems he collected from his interviews of early television personalities for *The Box*, his vital oral history of the industry. I'm grateful to him for preserving those recordings, then donating them to the Television Academy, then letting me listen to and quote from them. The academy's fine oral histories were also indispensable to me. Thanks to Jenni Matz for all of her good work with them.

My old friends John and Susan Edwards Harvith, both great students of American cultural history, did their own important set of interviews, now preserved at Syracuse University, with many of the principals in this story. They have been keenly interested in my project from the outset, and generously read several drafts of this book. Thanks, too, to Willy Holtzman for sharing his interviews with Max Liebman and Lucille Kallen for *Seesaw*, his 1979 joint biography of Mel Brooks and Anne Bancroft. Craig Horwich and Jon Sotzing generously provided videos of Caesar's appearances on *The Jackie Gleason Show* and *The Tonight Show*, respectively.

Bob Waldman shared the transcripts of the many interviews he did for his 1994 documentary, *A&E Biography: Sid Caesar: Television's Comedy Genius*. He is also a great television savant. Jeremy Schaap made sure I got to hear the interviews his father, the legendary Dick Schaap, did for his Emmy-winning *20/20* profile of Caesar in 1983, and Anthony Perrone of ABC News retrieved the ancient tapes and played them for me on his ancient East German equipment. Tom Laura shared with me the documents he rescued from the dumpster outside Max Liebman's office. I'm only sorry he didn't get there earlier.

Wendy Swanberg, Jane Anne Morris, and George Ferencz went through the invaluable NBC papers for me at the Wisconsin Historical Society (and when I finally went there myself, George shared with me the great pleasure of a Wisconsin "supper club"). Michael Schmidt found wonderful Caesar-related material from the *Newsweek* archives in the Harry Ransom Center at the University of Texas at Austin.

I'm grateful, too, to Andrea Grimes of the San Francisco Public Library for sharing the interviews the late Gerald Nachman did for *Seriously Funny*, his important book on the rebel comics of the 1950s and 1960s. The devotion that Mark Basile and Steve Schnepp bestowed on Imogene Coca in her final years has continued posthumously, when they found for her papers a fine home at the Smithsonian Institution.

With everything else he had to do, Mel Brooks was exceedingly generous with his time, his memories, and his thoughts. I thank him and Shelby Van Vliet, vice president of Brooksfilms, for arranging our interviews. Woody Allen was equally forthcoming; I'm grateful to him for seeing me, and to Daphne Merkin for helping make that happen. I was fortunate enough to talk with both Sid Caesar and Carl Reiner; each received me graciously. Sid's daughter, Karen, and her husband, Tim Carroll, were unfailingly helpful, especially by entrusting Caesar's scrapbooks to me. I'm also grateful to Max Liebman's nephew, Ronald DeCook, for his help and support.

Edith, Michael, Stephen, and Emma Tolkin helped me understand Caesar's most loyal and long-serving writer, Mel Tolkin, and Hillary Swett at the Shavelson-Webb Library of the Writers Guild Foundation was a wonderful guide through his papers. Frank Rich generously unearthed and lent me the materials he collected on *Your Show of Shows* decades ago; Jenni Lyn Bader arranged for me to meet her ageless stepfather, Joe Stein, a keen student of Caesar from his time writing for both *Your Show of Shows* and *Caesar's Hour*. Like so many others I interviewed—including Florence Baum, Michael Dann, Herbert Engel, Jules Feiffer, Bill Hayes, Al Jaffee, Len Kanter, Frances Keane, Pat Marshall, and Leonard Stern—Joe died before I finished this book. I feel so lucky to have caught them all.

I'm indebted to all of the comedians and writers—Judd Apatow, Carol Burnett, Billy Crystal, Larry David, Al Franken, Richard Kind, Nathan Lane, Louise Lasser, the late Richard Lewis, Conan O'Brien, Phil Rosenthal, Jeff Ross, Larry Wilmore, and Alan Zweibel among them—who shared their thoughts on Caesar and his impact on their lives and work. The folks at *Saturday Night Live* in 1983—Anne Beatts, Barry W. Blaustein, Mary Gross, Brad Hall, Nate Herman, Tim Kazurinsky, Andrew Kurtzman, Tom Schiller, David Sheffield, Andrew Smith, and the late Bob Tischler—summoned for me vivid memories of Caesar when he guest-hosted the show.

My pal Jeff Roth shared with me the matchless treasures of the *New York Times* morgue—including the handsome photograph of the Center Theatre opposite the title page of this book—along with his boundless friendship and wisdom. With her endless knack for ferreting out information that has eluded everyone else—me included—Sandy Zwyer, creator and curator of the "Sid Caesar: More Than Double-Talk" Facebook page, has been a steady source of material.

I want to thank the endlessly patient staff at the New York Public Library for the Performing Arts, the Dorot Jewish Division of the New York Public Library, and the wondrous New York Public Library generally for retrieving books from its astonishing collection and delivering them virtually to my door. And the Internet Archive, for existing, and persevering. Also helpful in my work were the Rare Book and Manuscript Library at Columbia University; the Tamiment Library and Robert F. Wagner Labor Archives at New York University; the Studs Terkel Radio Archive at the Chicago History Museum; and the Ziegler and Ross Agency Collection at the University of Wyoming's American Heritage Center.

I'm indebted to Eddy Portnoy, Sam Glauber-Zimra, and—in an amazing fertile burst at the end—Abe Gold, for opening for me the often-untapped riches of New York's Yiddish press, which *kvelled* over

Caesar. Eve Jochnowitz and the late Mimi Sheraton helped me understand what it is about Jews and food. The co-author of Caesar's excellent second memoir, *Caesar's Hours*, Eddy Friedfeld, has been a constant source of friendship and help to me, just as he was to Sid and Florence Caesar. Betty Katkov graciously hosted me during my repeated research trips to Los Angeles.

I'm thankful to everyone who reviewed this manuscript during its long gestation, offering their suggestions and corrections. They include David Andelman, Jerome Chanes, Jeremy Dauber, Eric Fettmann, Sara Fishko, Bill Goldstein, Bruce Goldstein, Tony Guida, John and Susan Edwards Harvith, Sherrye Henry, Robert Kaiser, Adam Kirsch, Joe Margolick, Howard Markel, Budd Mishkin, Michael Morris Sr., Dan Okrent, Peter Osnos, David Ostwald, Monroe Price, Howard Rosenberg, Connie Rosenblum, Mike Sacks, Jeff Shandler, Marvin Siegel, Ron Simon, Enid Stubin (multiple times), Bob Waldman, Jonathan Winer, and Julian Zelitzer.

I'm greatly saddened that several of my keenest readers—Richard Bernstein, Warren Hoge, Jack Schwartz, and Stephen Silverman—didn't live to see the finished product, or to accept my appreciation. I'm also sorry my friend Stuart Schoffman never got to read this book; I know he'd have enjoyed it, but he'd also have made it better.

Though my years on this project were hardly as desperate as Al Duncey's childhood, many other people "helped and encouraged me," just as Duncey's beloved Uncle Goopy did with him. Among them are the late Patricia Bosworth, Dick Cavett, Les Charles, Bob Claster, Rudy DeLuca, Vikki Dougan, Jacob Edelman, Mark Evanier, Elliot Finkel, Rodman Flender, the late Natalie Goodman, Elliott Gould, Karen Herman, Peter Jaysen, Michael Kantor, Stephen Karcher, Garrison Keillor, Denis Kitchen, Robert Klein, Richerd Kleinberg, Stephen Koundakjian (and Chuck Hobin), Bambi Linn, Martha LoMonaco, Laurence Maslon, Patrick McGilligan, Carolyn Michel, the late Newton Minow, David Morris, Bill Persky, Robert Pinsky, Fred Plotkin, Claude Riddick, Jonathan Salk, Julian Schlossberg, Larry Spellman, Jeff Sweet, Rich Tackenberg, Robert Thompson, John Thorn, Joel Thurm and Randal Kleiser (both from *Grease*), Calvin Trillin, Kenneth Turan, Donald Weber, Stephen Whitfield, Margaret Winter, Noah Wyle, and Lou Zigman.

Jonathan Rosen was kind enough to sign me up for this project, and until her much-deserved retirement, Altie Karper at Schocken oversaw it, liberally dispensing her reassurances along the way. Jon Segal came forward providentially to edit this book and, blunt-tipped pencil in hand, did his customary splendid job. (That he came out of retirement to do so made me feel like a valued part of the incredible group of writers with whom he's worked over the years, and I'm grateful for that, too.) Mary Engel and Stephen McCamman ably shepherded the photos into print, and Paul Engel, Elena Radutzky, Karen Caesar, and Larry Schiller contributed to them. I thank Ben Hyman, editorial director of Schocken, and Jordan Pavlin of Knopf for giving this book life. And Chip Kidd for blessing it with its jacket. And Soonyoung Kwon for designing the text, and Ingrid Sterner for copyediting, and Kathleen Cook for managing the production. And Zuleima Ugalde for bringing all of the pieces together and actually *making it happen*, always with consummate professionalism and good cheer. And, finally, to Kathryn Zuckerman, Angela Rose West, and Abigail Endler for telling everyone about it.

Even as she approaches her hundred and third year, my mother retains all of her curiosity, enthusiasm, and showbiz knowledge. And though her efforts to take out at least a few of the book's vulgarisms and curse words were largely unavailing, her kindness and courage, wisdom and moxie, inspire me more than ever. And almost from the beginning of this project, Amy Morris has been by my side, appreciating whatever gifts I have, loving me and cheering me on. It's to her that I dedicate this book.

NOTES

EPIGRAPHS

vii "I'm proud of you": Interview, Brooks.

vii "To be Jewish": Norman Mailer Papers of Peter Manso, Harry Ransom Center, University of Texas at Austin.

vii "My boy, you will some day": Ben Hecht, *A Guide for the Bedevilled* (Garden City Publishing Company, 1945), 69.

INTRODUCTION

3 "Your 'Shine of Shines'": *Your Show of Shows*, April 3, 1954.

4 "the greatest sketch ever, ever done": Reiner at funeral.

4 "Such a glorious muddle": *New York Times*, Feb. 24, 1973.

4 "That sketch *says it all*": Interview, Persky.

5 "I have no doubt there is more": *Chicago Tribune*, May 5, 1954.

5 "You are young and talented": Weaver to Caesar, Feb. 19, 1954, box 122, folder 70, National Broadcasting Company Inc. Records, 1921–1969, U.S. MSS 17 AF, Wisconsin Historical Society.

5 "Much too front-loaded": Mike Sacks, *And Here's the Kicker* (Writer's Digest Books, 2009), 508.

5 "No Sid Caesar, no Mel Brooks": Interview, Brooks.

6 "the only comedian": "Albert at the New School: Sid Caesar," April 23, 1975, box 69, tape 13, Albert Goldman Papers, Rare Book and Manuscript Library, Columbia University.

6 "You're Sid Caesar": Interview, Allen.

6 "He was just somebody": Interview, Crystal.

6 "easily the best sketch": Email, David to the author, Aug. 20, 2024.

6 "My dad would watch": Interview, Lasser.

7 "Dr. Ludwig von Snowcap": *Your Show of Shows*, Jan. 3, 1954.

7 "Extremely smart but completely inarticulate": *TV Guide*, Nov. 18–24, 2000, 2.

7 "the most quiet man I know": *Newsweek*, Nov. 26, 1962.

7 "The first thing I noticed": "Sid Caesar: Master of Comedy" (1982), Paley Center for Media, New York.

7 "Comedy comes from animosity": Sid Caesar interview, Aug. 30, 1967, Goldman Papers.

7 "Like seeing a new country": *Esquire*, May 1972, 192.

8 "had a radar for truth": "Sid Caesar: Master of Comedy" (1982), Paley Center for Media, New York.

8 "He knew intuitively": Unedited transcript of Reiner interview for *Let 'Em Laugh*, April 6, 2006.

8 "Sid was a great mimic": Brooks to Albert Goldman, July 27, 1967, box 46, folder 8, Goldman Papers.

8 "mini-plays about mankind": Interview, Brooks.

8 "Zero," he'd replied: Gelbart interview for "Sid Caesar: Television's Comedy Genius," *A&E Biography*, April 12, 1994.

8 "*meshugana* energy": "Sid Caesar: Master of Comedy."

8 "walking across Niagara Falls": *Emmy* magazine, March–April 1982.

9 overcome his size: Interview with Liebman, Feb. 28, 1951, *Newsweek* records.

9 "could be taken for a U.S. Senator": *Forverts*, Dec. 30, 1957.

9 "He didn't know who Sid Caesar was": *Lancaster (Pa.) New Era*, Feb. 14, 1976.

10 "The pioneer TV set owner": *Alamogordo (N.M.) Daily News*, Nov. 3, 1955.

10 "Satire is what closes": *Boston Globe*, Jan. 7, 1973.

10 "newscasts, documentaries, late-night movies": Burton Bernstein and Barbara B. Haws, *Leonard Bernstein, American Original: How a Modern Renaissance Man Transformed Music and the World During His New York Philharmonic Years, 1943–1976* (HarperCollins, 2008), 92.

10 "In a world in which": Shelley Berman, "Comedy and Its Reflections in History," Santa Barbara Writers' Conference, June 26, 2003.

10 "I was on the most important": Kallen, interview by Sunny Parich, April 25, 1998, Television Academy Foundation (hereafter cited as TAF).

10 "Except for the fact": Gelbart, interviewed by Dick Schaap, undated.

10 "There was something more": Michael Stewart Papers, box 102, folder 22, New York Public Library for the Performing Arts.

11 "in a different ballpark": Brooks to Goldman, Aug. 9, 1967, box 46, folder 8, Goldman Papers.

11 "Absolutely the happiest and worst time": *New York Times*, Nov. 14, 1982.

11 "We used to sit around": *Newsweek*, Nov. 26, 1962.

11 "His knowledge and intuition": Reiner to Frank Rich, Nov. 22, 1978.

11 "We rode for eight hours": Caesar and Coca, interviewed by Dick Schaap, undated (ca. 1983).

11 "because he had the nerve": Morris interview for "Television's Comedy Genius."

11 "Zany, frustrated, unhappy, tragic": *TV Guide*, Feb. 19, 1955.

11 "shy, introverted, extravagant": *TV Guide*, Jan. 25, 1958.

12 "I seemed to be waiting": *New York Journal-American*, Nov. 30, 1956.

12 "Go make a fool of yourself": *Hail Sid Caesar! The Golden Age of Comedy*.

12 "As the price of sets": Gelbart, interview by Michael Kantor for *Make 'Em Laugh*, April 15, 2007.

12 "he was funnier than Sid": *New York Times*, Aug. 19, 1996.

12 "These people would have much": Sacks, *And Here's the Kicker*, 508–9.

12 "Nobody's talent was ever more used up": *Esquire*, May 1972, 192.

13 "It sounded funny then": *New York Times*, Jan. 30, 1966.

13 "It hurt more to fall": Interview, Reiner.

13 "Gentlemen, gentlemen, we've got to get": *New York Times*, Nov. 27, 2007.

14 "wave to the folks back home": Irving Howe, *World of Our Fathers: The Journey of the East European Jews to America and the Life They Found and Made* (Harcourt Brace Jovanovich, 1976), 569.

14 "Jews and our non-anti-Semitic Christian friends": Reiner interview, June 22, 2006, courtesy of David Grubin Productions.

14 "We wanted more universal humor": Interview, Brooks.

15 "the smartness of it, the smartassery of it": Interview, Feiffer.

15 "the model of the handsome": Untitled and undated, box 46, folder 10, Goldman Papers.

16 "was very afraid to offend": Reiner interview, Aug. 11, 1986, William E. Wiener Oral History Library of the American Jewish Committee, Dorot Jewish Division, New York Public Library.

16 "Smarter," she said: Kallen interview, April 25, 1998, TAF.

16 "No one can estimate": Brooks Atkinson, *Once Around the Sun* (Harcourt, Brace and Company, 1951), 64.

17 "very, very gifted neurotic young Jews": *Hail Sid Caesar!*

17 "probably the greatest comic talent": *Herald Statesman*, March 8, 1958.

17 that working with Caesar: *New York Times*, Nov. 15, 2000.

17 "underneath a hovel": *Caesar's Writers*, Writers Guild, Beverly Hills, Calif., Jan. 24, 1996; event produced by Bob Claster; Video/DVD produced by Michael Hirsh and Michael Hirsh Productions.

18 "Bonjour, Mesdames et Monsieurs": Taped recording of dinner, National Foundation for Jewish Culture, Dec. 11, 2000, collection of the author.

CHAPTER I ORIGINS

19 "It was the first time": Unedited transcript of Caesar, interview by Kantor, April 6, 2006.

19 "I used to worry": *Redbook*, Nov. 1956, 55.

19 "We used to call him": *Redbook*, Nov. 1956, 55.

20 "Hey, Dopey!": *New York Herald Tribune*, Feb. 8, 1957.

20 "Caesar himself feels": *Redbook*, Nov. 1956, 55.

20 the family name was Ziser: *Mishpacha* (Spring 2014).

20 "I was what they called": Sid Caesar, *Where Have I Been? An Autobiography*, with Bill Davidson (New American Library, 1982), 22.

20 "The first lesson": *Newark Star-Ledger*, June 26, 1966.

21 "If my mother and father": *Look*, Oct. 2, 1956, 49.

21 "he didn't develop those social skills": Reiner interview, March 25, 1998, TAF.

21 "It was like being in solitary": *Newark Star-Ledger*, June 26, 1966.

21 "Working both sides of the street": Sid Caesar, *Caesar's Hours*, with Eddy Friedfeld (PublicAffairs, 2003), xiii.

22 "has its own song": Caesar to Peter Jaysen, Jan. 18, 2001, for *Hail Sid Caesar!*

22 "I knew '*poulet*' was chicken": Caesar interview, Sept. 9, 1982, MS 3009-RG 13, microfilm reel B68, Time Inc. *Time* Research Center Files, New York Historical.

22 "It's a gift": *Charlie Rose*, Nov. 24, 1993.

22 "this tremendous pressure building up": "Sid Caesar," n.d., box 46, folder 10, Goldman Papers.

22 "I don't want to make fun": *Forverts*, Nov. 25, 1950.

22 "Is that nice": *Redbook*, Nov. 1956, 110.

23 "He showed no marked ability": *New York Journal-American*, Nov. 27, 1956.

23 "While the rest of us": *Redbook*, Nov. 1956, 111.

24 "in stitches": *Richmond (Calif.) Independent*, May 7, 1953.

24   "These people didn't laugh easy": Caesar interview, June 23, 2006, Courtesy of David Grubin Productions.

24   "A sax player in the family?": *New Rochelle Standard-Star,* Feb. 7, 1962.

24   "like a showgirl out of the Copacabana": Interview, Edith Tolkin.

24   "I couldn't think of anything": *TV and Screen Life,* May 1957.

24   "He was a tall, quiet fellow": *TV and Screen Life,* May 1957.

25   "the finest Jews come to eat": *Jeremiah's Vanishing New York,* Nov. 29, 2010.

25   "Sid was the Apollo": *New York Times,* Jan. 30, 1966.

25   To warm him up: *Forverts,* Nov. 28, 1950.

26   "wised up and intelligent": *Variety,* May 14, 1941.

26   "would forgive bad service": *TV Guide,* Oct. 14, 1950.

26   "Emergency theater": *New York Times,* Nov. 19, 1950.

26   "bird-like hands and feet": *Newark Star-Ledger,* March 18, 1951.

26   "The theater at Tamiment": *Variety,* May 14, 1941.

27   "He was the oracle": *Los Angeles Times,* Oct. 7, 1973.

27   "to banish forever the conception": *Variety,* May 14, 1941.

27   "I Play Hamlet in the Catskills": Tamiment Playhouse Records, TAM 107, box 7, Max Liebman file, Lyric Notebook 2, I-L, folder 1, Tamiment Library/ Robert F. Wagner Labor Archives, New York University.

28   "Sadie Salowitz likes to play bridge": Tamiment Playhouse Records, TAM 107, box 7, Max Liebman file, Lyric Notebook 2, I-L, folder 1, Tamiment Library/ Robert F. Wagner Labor Archives.

28   "Now Adolf and Benito": "Downing Street," Tamiment Playhouse Records, TAM 107, box 7, Max Liebman file, Lyric Notebook 1, A–D, folder 1, Tamiment Library/Robert F. Wagner Labor Archives.

28   "I didn't understand": Coca interview, March 13, 1986, Tamiment Playhouse Oral History Collection, box 1, folder 12.

29   "Miss Imogene Coca is a young lady": *Collier's,* Dec. 23, 1939.

29   "He made a lot of sounds": Liebman to Rich.

30   "on fire with talent": Liebman to Goldman, July 26, 1967, box 46, folder 10, Goldman Papers.

30   "writers on writers on writers": "Sid Caesar," n.d., box 46, folder 10, Goldman Papers.

30   "Caesarize": Liebman to Goldman, July 26, 1967.

30   "Wings over Bombinschissel": *Los Angeles Daily News,* Dec. 20, 1944.

30   "tears of laughter": *Miami News,* March 30, 1944.

30   "Complete newcomer, but surefire": *Variety,* May 10, 1944.

30   "I smoked a twenty-five-cent cigar": *Cosmopolitan,* Jan. 1951.

30   "After the war, I want": Caesar, *Caesar's Hours,* 55.

30   "I was building up": Caesar, *Where Have I Been?,* 73.

31   "All they were talking about": Caesar, *Where Have I Been?,* 74.

31   "I *told* you this one was a yellow Jew": *California Magazine,* July 1986; Caesar, *Where Have I Been?,* 74–75.

31   "Cute, tall, and blond": *American Weekly,* Oct. 14, 1956.

31   "All I could do was stand": *New York Post,* Dec. 23, 1957.

32   "likable blond zany": *Time,* Jan. 28, 1946.

32   "four-way threat": *Los Angeles Times,* Jan. 14, 1946.

32   "Sid Caesar is the boy": *Latrobe (Pa.) Bulletin,* Feb. 5, 1946.

32   "a young blond boy": Tynan to Julian Howard, Sept. 17, 1946, in *Kenneth Tynan Letters,* reprinted with kind permission of Kenneth Tynan Estate.

32   "Sid Caesar, funny the first time": *Chicago Tribune,* March 16, 1946.

32 "as exhausting to watch": *Los Angeles Times*, April 3, 1946.

32 "Like the first time you see": Simon to Schaap.

32 "whose mouth moved like nobody's mouth": Reiner interview for "Television's Comedy Genius."

32 "Extra-planetary": Gelbart interview, May 26, 1998, TAF.

32 "Every gag that can possibly be told": *PM*, Feb. 27, 1946.

33 "a little house in Bel Air": *Washington Post*, Feb. 2, 1946.

33 "Ron Roland": *Cosmopolitan*, Jan. 1951, 98.

33 "Highly entertaining": *Chicago Tribune*, Dec. 7, 1946.

33 "Boffola": *Variety*, Jan. 8, 1947.

33 "Sid had this terrific anger": *Playboy*, Feb. 1975, 56.

33 "Sid viewed him as an amusing kid": Interview, Baum.

34 "I always thought I was destined": Alan Sepinwall, *What's Alan Watching?*, Dec. 10, 2012.

34 "Mel began to burn up": Memo, Mary Cronin to Time Showbiz, July 20, 1976, Private collection of Robert Waldman, New York.

34 "The best looking young comedian": New York *Daily News*, March 6, 1947.

34 "Some guy comes in with a dame": *Cosmopolitan*, Jan. 1951.

34 "heavy mitting": *Variety*, Oct. 29, 1947.

36 "You'll never have another poor day": *New York Sun*, July 17, 1948.

36 "Vending machines, he implied": *New Yorker*, May 27, 1950.

36 "Do for Max what you did for me": Sennett, *Your Show of Shows*, 23.

36 "Hello, hello, hello": Ted Sennett, *Your Show of Shows* (Applause, 2002), 23.

37 "Who is this *meshuggener*?": Caesar, *Caesar's Hours*, 77.

37 "You get the idea": *Mamaroneck (N.Y.) Daily Times*, April 19, 1948.

37 "Comedian Sid Caesar is nursing": *Bangor Daily News*, Feb. 7, 1947.

37 "Look at me now": *New York Sun*, July 17, 1948.

38 "I don't know why": Caesar interview, April 1, 1997, TAF.

38 "Be careful": *Madison (Wis.) Capital Times*, April 25, 1957.

38 "flickering mess": Mel Tolkin, *Where Did I Go Right?*, unpublished memoir, 166, Tolkin Papers, Writers Guild Foundation, Los Angeles.

38 "television was a seedling": *New York Herald Tribune*, May 2, 1950.

38 "We are fighting for a new age": *American Israelite*, Oct. 23, 1947.

39 "mostly Jews and a few strange people": *Atlantic*, July/Aug. 2023, 32.

39 "persona grata": Reiner interview, Aug. 11, 1986, Dorot Jewish Division.

39 "Hitler made anti-Semitism disreputable": *Look*, Nov. 29, 1955, 34.

39 "highly spiced beef plate": *Collier's*, March 31, 1951.

39 "immoral," "ruining": *Jewish Advocate*, May 10, 1951.

40 "Were the Jews a totally extinct race": Hecht, *Guide for the Bedevilled*, 207–8, 204.

41 Professor Mischa Gos and Princess Latke: *Texaco Star Theater*, Oct. 25, 1949.

41 "Mom, it's not the same Kahns": *Texaco Star Theater*, May 24, 1949.

41 "Is television an electronic Jew?": Transcript of *Open End*, Feb. 14, 1960, Tolkin Papers.

41 "If I can't be the greatest": Liebman to Rich.

41 "Your husband is going to be": Caesar, *Where Have I Been?*, 101.

CHAPTER 2   ON TO TELEVISION

42 "Television only goes from here": Caesar interview, April 1, 1997, TAF.

42 "about what a courier gets": *Theatre Arts*, May 1953, 75.

42   "We were the most coordinated": Liebman to Reiner, June 28, 1977, box 2, folder 10, Max Liebman Papers, New York Public Library for the Performing Arts.

42   "a tall, immaculately dressed goy": Interview, Herbert Engel.

42   "Don't do it!": *New Yorker*, Oct. 30, 1978, 87.

43   "If you're an insider": Tolkin, *Where Did I Go Right?*, 10.

44   "The pressures made heroes": *Los Angeles Times*, Sept. 20, 1992.

44   "The war, for me": Sam Tolchinsky to Cyril Endfield, July 13, 1944, Cyril Endfield Papers, courtesy of Eden Endfield and Brian Neve.

45   "beautiful seductive": Tolkin, *Where Did I Go Right?*, 157.

45   "Come on out, the sun is hidden": "Night Life," Tamiment Playhouse Records, TAM 107, "Mel Tolkin Sketches," box 8, Tamiment Library/Robert F. Wagner Labor Archives.

45   "Anchorless. Rootless": Tolkin, *Where Did I Go Right?*, 8.

45   "If you like what's going on": Michael Elkin, Supplement to *Jewish Exponent* (Summer 1996).

46   "This was what you lived for": Kallen interview, April 25, 1998, TAF.

47   "And he looked out the window": Taped recording of dinner, National Foundation for Jewish Culture, Dec. 11, 2000, courtesy of Eddy Friedfeld.

47   "Mel was everything he hated": Interview, Baum.

47   "he saw an arrogant, obnoxious little shithead": "Caesar's Writers."

47   "Sid's private court jester": Liebman to Willy Holtzman.

47   "stalk the corridors": Liebman to Holtzman.

47   "sweaty jockstraps and discarded tights": *New York Times*, Nov. 29, 1992.

47   "We need three jokes": *Playboy*, Feb. 1975, 56.

47   "glorious and majestic": Interview, Brooks.

48   "I was either going to do that": Jeff Kisseloff, *The Box: An Oral History of Television, 1920–1961* (Viking, 1995), 308.

48   "a Jewish god": Morris to Schaap.

48   "Max! Him. Get": Morris interview, Feb. 27, 2004, TAF.

48   "When in doubt, rip Howie's clothes off": Kisseloff, *Box*, 313.

48   "Hi, Howie! How're they hangin'?": Kisseloff, *Box*, 308.

48   "*The Admiral Broadway Revue*": All quotations from *Admiral Broadway Revue*, Jan. 28, 1949.

49   "If it flopped": Caesar, *Caesar's Hours*, 73.

49   "Admiral Bows Sock Revue": *Variety*, Feb. 5, 1949.

49   "any nightclub and many theaters": *Time*, March 14, 1949.

50   "forceful, versatile, agile": *New York Post*, Jan. 31, 1949.

50   "A Caesar Rises in Television": *Chicago Tribune*, March 27, 1949.

50   "the fountain from which we all drank": Liebman to Rich.

50   "a hard-working gentleman": *New York Times*, Feb. 6, 1949.

50   "as malleable as wax": *New York Herald Tribune*, June 16, 1949.

50   "for an hour's entertainment": *New York Herald Tribune*, March 3, 1949.

50   "Sid Caesar, who is twenty-six": *New York Herald Tribune*, June 16, 1949.

51   "built entirely upon Broadway humor": *Televiser*, Oct. 1950.

51   "Get me some *writers*!": *Admiral Broadway Revue*, April 8, 1949.

51   "I ain't nuts!": *Admiral Broadway Revue*, March 4, 1949.

52   "Sid was like a Jungle Boy": Brooks interview for "Television's Comedy Genius."

52   "Could you brief the talent": Helffrich to "Ray," Aug. 15, 1951, box 151, folder 42, NBC Records.

52 "He was very conscious": Kallen to Jeff Kisseloff, Jeff Kisseloff Collection, Archive of American Television.

53 "cough, cough": Mel Brooks, *All About Me! My Remarkable Life in Show Business* (Ballantine Books, 2022), 98.

53 "That was a psychological thing": *New York Times*, March 19, 1950.

53 "Welcome to the Sid Caesar show": *Newsweek*, Sept. 27, 1954.

53 "Desi Arnaz" shouting "Loo-see": *Montgomery Advertiser*, March 5, 1955.

53 "one of the few things": *New York Journal-American*, Dec. 5, 1951.

53 "we forget what he's been funny about": *New York Journal-American*, Oct. 14, 1952.

54 "shortchanged on charm": Interview, Reiner.

54 "I thought 'Dear God'": Coca to Kallen, Sept. 15, 1982, box 1 folder 9, Kallen Papers.

54 "One of the subliminal sources": "Sid Caesar," n.d., box 46, folder 10, Goldman Papers.

54 "She wasn't *acting* poor": Coca to Kisseloff, Kisseloff Collection.

55 "knew where the fun was": Morris interview, Feb. 27, 2004, TAF.

55 "They were great before they knew me": Liebman to Holtzman.

55 "Sid Caesar is a fine pantomimist": *New York World-Telegram and Sun*, Nov. 21, 1951.

55 "People *loved* Imogene": Morris interview, July 30, 1999, Harvith Collection.

56 "If, a year ago, some guy": *Variety*, July 27, 1949.

56 "We're being dropped": Caesar, *Where Have I Been?*, 100.

56 "capacious instrument": *Variety*, June 1, 1955.

56 "make the average man": *New Yorker*, Oct. 16, 1953.

56 "intellectual yoga": *New York Times*, Nov. 21, 1954.

56 "Whenever your TV set": *New York Herald Tribune*, Jan. 21, 1953.

57 "Operation Frontal Lobes": *New York Times*, Dec. 4, 1950.

57 "somewhat starry-eyed attempt": *New York Herald Tribune*, Feb. 3, 1952.

57 "Used for good": *Philadelphia Inquirer*, Dec. 3, 1951.

57 "the day of the hinterland": Matthew Murray, "NBC Program Clearance Policies During the 1950s: Nationalizing Trends and Regional Resistance," *Velvet Light Trap* (Spring 1994).

57 "dog night": *Variety*, Nov. 17, 1954.

57 "There is a vast tendency": *New York World-Telegram and Sun*, Oct. 14, 1950.

58 "We had *matured* to the point": Morris to Kisseloff, Kisseloff Collection.

58 "Barnum-like bravado": *New Republic*, June 13, 1964.

59 "optimistically and somewhat arrogantly": Caesar, *Caesar's Hours*, 85.

59 "Greatest Show on Earth": *Chicago Tribune*, April 25, 1954.

59 "The camera can get": Caesar, interview by Elizabeth Forsling, Feb. 23, 1950, *Newsweek* Archive.

59 "Tonight! Premiere of the biggest show": *New York Times*, Feb. 25, 1950.

59 "In about a minute": *New York Herald Tribune*, March 3, 1950.

CHAPTER 3 *YOUR SHOW OF SHOWS*

60 "Stars over Broadway": *Your Show of Shows*, Feb. 25, 1950.

61 "great galaxy": *Your Show of Shows*, Feb. 25, 1950.

61 "The vast majority of people": *New York Times*, Nov. 19, 1950.

62 "a truly natural comic": *New York Herald Tribune*, March 3, 1950.

62 "to eventually replace even wrestling": *Daily Compass*, March 1, 1950.

62 "operating in a vastly uncrowded field": *New York Times*, March 19, 1950.

62 "terrified": *Your Show of Shows*, March 11, 1950.

62 "ad lib or add any": Contracts courtesy of Tom Laura.

63 "Some of my friends said": Liebman to Rich.

63 "all I did was sing": Bill Hayes and Susan Seaforth Hayes, *Like Sands Through the Hourglass* (Penguin, 2006), 109.

64 "Don't kiss me with the beard!": *Your Show of Shows*, March 11, 1950.

64 "You know, in almost every marriage": *Your Show of Shows*, Feb. 10, 1951.

64 "I'll kill you, you rat!": *Your Show of Shows*, Dec. 9, 1950.

64 "The world is a little sick": Unprocessed CART report 6, Feb. 28, 1951, box 1, folder 4, NBC Records.

65 "You give me your word of honor": *Your Show of Shows*, Sept. 13, 1952.

65 "agonizing accuracy": James Brussel to Sarnoff, Sept. 15, 1952, box 121, folder 36, NBC Records.

65 "I learned that from Sid": Morris interview for "Television's Comedy Genius."

66 "they couldn't build a castle": Caesar to Studs Terkel, Sept. 26, 1990, Studs Terkel Radio Archive, courtesy of Chicago History Museum and WFMT/WTTW Chicago.

66 Television was called a "medium": *Cosmopolitan*, Dec. 1957.

66 "A casual observer": *Collier's*, Nov. 11, 1950, 25.

66 "For the birds": *Los Angeles Times*, Sept. 19, 1954.

66 "Caesar seems to be the ideal comic": *Daily Compass*, April 9, 1950.

67 "Woolkim to the shoo": Tolkin, *Where Did I Go Right?*, 257.

67 "Our star tonight has just finished": *Your Show of Shows*, Oct. 13, 1951.

67 "His feeling is": *Atlanta Journal*, Nov. 27, 1954.

67 "the way I practice being me": Caesar to Peter Jaysen, Jan. 18, 2001, for *Hail Sid Caesar!*

67 "the stark, evident terror": Hugh Downs, *On Camera: My 10,000 Hours on Television* (Putnam, 1986), 63.

67 "fluffs": *Detroit Free Press*, Jan. 23, 1955.

68 "their opening nights were": *Television Quarterly* (Summer 1973): 50.

68 "Better a good old thing": Liebman, interview by Holtzman, n.d., ca. 1977.

68 "tired and pedestrian": *Variety*, April 12, 1950.

68 "clown of majesty": Sennett, *Your Show of Shows*, 38.

68 "depends on how funny Caesar": *Cue*, April 22, 1950.

68 "Ticket demand is almost": *Chicago Tribune*, March 30, 1950.

69 "one of the two or three funniest": *The New Yorker*, May 27, 1950.

69 "The big boys are too late": *TV Guide*, April 1, 1950.

69 "Now we own Saturday night": McGarrett to Weaver, April 19, 1950, box 119, folder 31, NBC Records.

69 "be ready for the guy": *St. Louis Post-Dispatch*, April 27, 1952.

69 "NBC oughtta build": *Billboard*, March 11, 1950.

70 "Our comedic attack was human behavior": Interview, Brooks.

70 "We were snobs": *New York Times*, Aug. 18, 1996.

70 "the husband of Congresswoman": *Your Show of Shows*, March 18, 1950.

70 Sam the Centaur: *New York Daily Mirror*, Sept. 25, 1949.

70 "back in the nineteen hundreds": *Your Show of Shows*, May 6, 1950.

71 "The people at NBC": Coca to Martha LoMonaco, March 13, 1986, Tamiment Playhouse Oral History Collection, box 1, folder 12.

71 "its complete absence of red-baiting": *Daily Worker*, Oct. 11, 1953.

71 "Does Sid Caesar have to worry": *New York Journal-American*, June 1–4, 1950.

71   "monster" tips: Email, Oshinsky to the author, Jan. 11, 2021.

71   "You can go nuts": *Daily Compass*, June 27, 1950.

72   "was as much a writer": Liebman, interview by Holtzman, n.d., ca. 1977.

72   "When you fire somebody": Liebman to Holtzman.

72   "Do the introduction number": *Daily Compass*, June 27, 1950.

CHAPTER 4   WEEKLY RITUALS

74   "It worked": *New York Post*, Oct. 10, 1950.

74   "The U.S. Steel of television": Kallen interview, April 25, 1998, TAF.

75   "the beginning of a comfortable bulge": *Cosmopolitan*, Jan. 1951.

75   "My, Sid Caesar's been putting on weight": *New York Journal-American*, Feb. 8, 1951.

75   "avoirdupois problem": *New York Journal-American*, Feb. 14, 1951.

75   "Tubby": *Hartford Courant*, Sept. 9, 1951.

75   "Oh, Sid just came in": Interview, Joe Stein.

75   "a great foil": Saul Kahan, "Too Many People Were Laughing: Carl Reiner and Mel Brooks Talk to Saul Kahan," 1994, on Kahan's blog (site discontinued).

76   "a Southern boy who": Interview, Hayes.

76   "I heard Sid Caesar": Reiner, interview by Susan Stamberg, *Weekend Edition*, National Public Radio, April 17, 1993.

76   "sturdy supporting oak": *Poughkeepsie Journal*, Jan. 23, 1958.

76   "Without him, the show": Interview, Persky.

77   "He measures himself out": *Los Angeles Times*, Dec. 20, 1985.

77   "It means to have extra antennae": Reiner interview, Aug. 11, 1986, Dorot Jewish Division.

78   "Carl acts mostly off-stage": Gelbart, interview by Dan Harrison, May 26, 1998, TAF.

78   "writer without portfolio": *American Film*, Dec. 1981, 14.

78   "so long as Mr. Caesar is around": *New York Times*, Sept. 17, 1950.

78   "one of the wonders": *New York Herald Tribune*, Sept. 19, 1950.

78   "there's no business like 'Show of Show'": *Your Show of Shows*, Feb. 16, 1952.

79   "probably the foremost lure": *York (Pa.) Daily Record*, June 10, 1954.

79   "How many times have you heard": *Brooklyn Eagle*, March 30, 1951.

79   "Now I have to introduce a guy": *Your Show of Shows*, Nov. 25, 1950.

79   "some figurative throwing of hats": *Des Moines Register*, Feb. 17, 1952.

80   "This is for the benefit": *Your Show of Shows*, Oct. 21, 1950.

80   "A few years ago": *Your Show of Shows*, May 10, 1952.

80   "In private conversation": *Cosmopolitan*, Jan. 1951.

81   "created solely to prove": *New Republic*, Oct. 9, 1950.

81   "The Jack Carter Show": Sarnoff to Weaver, Oct. 16, 1950, box 119, folder 31, NBC Records.

81   "I'll be OK": Caesar to Schaap.

81   "everyone for everything": *Variety*, Jan. 3, 1951.

81   "Maybe I liked Harry Ritz": *Emmy* magazine, Jan. 1984, 72.

82   "two very funny people": *Saturday Review*, Nov. 4, 1950.

82   "When I took a look": *Your Show of Shows*, Jan. 20, 1951.

82   "shelectricity": *New York Daily Mirror*, Jan. 28, 1951.

82   "Color-blind and quality obsessed": Caesar, *Caesar's Hours*, 88.

82   "sing, emcee and do a sketch": *Variety*, Dec. 27, 1950.

83   "The singing of 'Love'": *Variety*, Jan. 24, 1951.

83 "The Bill Williams Quartet (colored)": Program Cards for *Your Show of Shows*, Sept. 6, 1951, Paley Center for Media.

83 "A bunch of little Jewish girls": Interview, Riddick.

83 "mixed indiscriminately": *Statesman*, Jan. 3, 1952.

84 "Let's forget": Handwritten addendum by Fred Wile Jr. on note from Manie Sacks to Pat Weaver, July 27, 1950, box 118, folder 66, NBC Records.

84 "There would probably be some mention": Weaver to George McGarrett, Feb. 13, 1951, box 120, folder 35, NBC Records.

84 "If you must have negroes": Unprocessed CART report, Sept. 10, 1951, box 1, folder 4, NBC Records.

84 "Arthur was a better dancer": Interview, Linn.

84 "pseudo-comedy": *Brockton Enterprise & Times*, March 22, 1951.

84 "without malice": Unprocessed CART report, April 5, 1951, box 1, folder 4, NBC Records.

84 "Sid Ceasar [*sic*] may not know it": *Brooklyn Eagle*, Oct. 30, 1951.

85 "and not a word made sense": *New York Herald Tribune*, May 13, 1951.

85 "Every race wants to claim": *Forverts*, Nov. 25, 1950.

85 THE JEWISH TELEVISION ACTOR: *Morgn Zhurnal*, Nov. 13, 1950.

85 "like an old hand": *Morgn Zhurnal*, Dec. 7, 1950.

86 "No area of American life": *Forverts*, March 3, 1971.

86 "Sid Caesar is what people": *Forverts*, March 11, 1950.

86 "Sid Caesar's humor is not based": *Forverts*, March 23, 1950.

86 "can all shine his shoes": *Forverts*, April 25, 1950.

86 "He looks like a completely 'normal' person": *Forverts*, May 3, 1950.

87 "a balm for the soul": *Morgn Zhurnal*, Nov. 13, 1950.

87 "My mother came all the way": *Forverts*, Nov. 28, 1950.

87 "hold it any longer": *Admiral Broadway Revue*, March 11, 1949.

87 "They would all gather": Pat Weaver, *The Best Seat in the House*, with Thomas M. Coffey (Alfred A. Knopf, 1994), 196–97.

87 "He'd come to watch rehearsals": Morris interview, Feb. 27, 2004, TAF.

88 "From a polite conference": Liebman to Holtzman.

88 "a stork that dropped a baby": *Playboy*, Feb. 1975, 61.

88 "our living-in-the-world": Interview, Brooks.

88 "We coulda had a group rate": "Conversations on the Arts and Letters," *Nightcap*, Oct. 18, 1983.

88 "they looked at me": Kisseloff, *Box*, 312.

88 "Yes," he replied. "Being Jewish": "Conversations on the Arts and Letters."

88 "Tolkin and I would arrive": Kallen to Holtzman.

89 "Dot's a classic": Handwritten notes from "A Tribute to 'Your Show of Shows,'" UCLA, May 21, 1978, courtesy of Frank Rich.

89 "more in the vein of": Caesar, *Caesar's Hours*, 125.

89 "the screaming": "Caesar's Writers."

89 "things needed when we changed": Handwritten notes from "A Tribute to 'Your Show of Shows.'"

89 "Guys were coming up with": Reiner to Kantor, April 6, 2006.

89 "Sometimes he caught your energy": Transcript of *Open End*, Feb. 14, 1960, Tolkin Papers.

89 "a pile of cigar butts": Bill Hobin, *Window on the Stars: 35 Years of Television from a Director's P.O.V.*, with Stephen J. Koundakjian, unpublished memoir, 96.

90 "Had you been able to see": *New York Times*, Nov. 29, 1992.

90 "a shimmering strawberry blonde": "Show of Shows," box 11, folder 5, Kallen Papers.

90 "colloidal form": Brooks to Goldman, July 27, 1967, box 46, folder 8, Goldman Papers.

91 "I don't think I remember": Stein to Kisseloff, Kisseloff Collection.

91 "vomiting between parked cars": *Museum of Television & Radio's 11th Annual Television Festival in Los Angeles: A Salute to Sid Caesar,* March 2, 1994, Paley Center for Media.

91 "*Two hundred and fifty?*": Tom Teicholz, "Q. and A. with Mel Brooks," *Jewish Journal of Los Angeles,* Feb. 23, 2010.

91 "Every night when I left": Alan Sepinwall, *What's Alan Watching?,* Dec. 10, 2012.

91 "The fears, at least in my own mind": Tolkin, *Where Did I Go Right?,* 171.

91 "An ulcer business": *Newsday,* June 10, 1952.

91 "You didn't contribute anything": Flender to Goldman, April 7, 1965, box 46, folder 11, Goldman Papers.

91 "The decibel count in that room": "Show of Shows," box 11, folder 5, Kallen Papers.

92 "this male, mad with power": Coca to Kallen, Nov. 2, 1974, box 14, folder 1, Kallen Papers.

92 "They had three categories": Kisseloff, *Box,* 315.

92 "like the great chef": Interview, Baum.

92 "All shit!": *American Film,* Dec. 1981, 14.

92 "See, you don't have to be on time": Jay Malarcher, *The Classically American Comedy of Larry Gelbart* (Scarecrow Press, 2003), 30.

93 "The one who typed": *New York* magazine in *New York Herald Tribune,* Dec. 12, 1965.

93 "this overpowering need to dominate": Kisseloff, *Box,* 310.

93 "He was going to prove": Interview, Engel.

93 "Suppose you're in a jungle": Kallen, interview by Holtzman.

93 "I was ready for Mel Brooks": Tolkin interview for "Television's Comedy Genius."

93 "Lucille and I worked for days": Tolkin, *Where Did I Go Right?,* 183.

93 "seldom, if ever, smiled": Hobin, *Window on the Stars,* 92.

93 "by the window, contemplating suicide": *Los Angeles Times,* Jan. 18, 1987.

93 "When we wrote sketches": Kallen to Kisseloff, Kisseloff Collection.

94 "You mean the show is not AD LIB?": *Variety,* Jan. 7, 1953.

94 "I'd like to have seen Edison": *Television Magazine,* Jan. 1951. Also *New York Journal-American,* Feb. 2, 1951.

94 "Bloody Monday": Caesar, *Caesar's Hours,* 126.

94 "bleeding-to-death day": *Saturday Evening Post,* May 16, 1953, 108.

95 "see the miracle happen": Sennett, *Your Show of Shows,* 1.

95 "As soon as I'm lying there": *Chicago Tribune,* June 25, 1986.

96 "The big theater fills": *Atlanta Journal,* Nov. 22, 1953.

96 "that ninety-minute chasm": *Theatre Arts,* May 1953, 77.

96 "The world could have caved in": *Theatre Arts,* May 1953.

96 "Talk about stupid timing": Winchell, ca. March 10, 1950.

97 "The depths of poor taste": *Variety,* March 8, 1950.

97 "Sid Silver": *Your Show of Shows,* Oct. 28, 1950.

97 "like your first sexual experience": Garrison interview, Oct. 8, 1998, TAF.

97 "there would be a moment": "Sid Caesar: Master of Comedy."

97 "I used to stand": *Parade*, Dec. 16, 1984.

97 "Sunday was the one day off": Interview, Brooks.

97 "As soon as it was over": Garrison interview, Oct. 8, 1998, TAF.

97 "every other domestic farce": Weaver, *Best Seat in the House*, 199.

98 "To Edith, the inspiration": Tolkin, *Where Did I Go Right?*, 180.

98 "I never saw such carrying-on": *Your Show of Shows*, Feb. 10, 1951.

99 "our new-found middle-classity": David Zurowik and Christina Stoehr, "Hail Caesar!," *Memories*, April–May 1990, 44.

99 *Mother and Child Descending*: *Your Show of Shows*, Feb. 3, 1951.

99 "Merci": *Your Show of Shows*, Oct. 4, 1952.

99 "Pathetic" Symphony: *Your Show of Shows*, Nov. 1, 1952.

99 "I have more pot holders": *Collier's*, Feb. 23, 1952.

99 "I wonder if Imogene knows": Coca to Schaap.

99 "a woman is considered": *Your Show of Shows*, Sept. 9, 1950.

99 "Marry a stupid woman": *Your Show of Shows*, Oct. 14, 1950.

100 "What an eye he had!": *Your Show of Shows*, Feb. 10, 1951.

100 "How much you like": Karen Harvey, *Sid Caesar and "Your Show of Shows": The Birth of the Television Sketch Comedy* (McFarland & Company, 2021), 81.

100 "Well, you're wearing a battered": *Your Show of Shows*, May 3, 1952.

101 "They gave him a kind": Brooks to Goldman, Aug. 9, 1967, box 46, folder 8, Goldman Papers.

101 "The same majestic fraudulence": *New Yorker*, Oct. 30, 1978.

101 "That must be something deep": "Sid Caesar," n.d., box 46, folder 10, Goldman Papers.

101 "Just smashing authority": Brooks to Goldman, Aug. 9, 1967, box 46, folder 8, Goldman Papers.

101 "We loved that character": Interview, Brooks.

101 Actually, *characters*: Jet von Propulsion: *Your Show of Shows*, Jan. 24, 1953; Ludwig von Liebestraum: Dec. 30, 1950; Ludwig von Loophole: Sept. 15, 1951; Hocus von Pocus: Sept. 29, 1951; Kurt von Supper: Nov. 25, 1950; Ludwig von Heartthrob: Oct. 13, 1951.

102 Just about every Professor: *The Human Body and How to Avoid It*: *Your Show of Shows*, Jan. 20, 1951; *I Remember Mama—but I Forget Papa*: May 3, 1952; *Don't Be a Slob*: Oct. 27, 1951; *Animals: Their Habits, Habitats, and Haberdashery*: Jan. 27, 1951; *The Prince and His Papa*: May 2, 1953; *Children Are People, Only Smaller*: May 26, 1951; *Archeology Made Simple, or Don't Lift Heavy Rocks*: March 10, 1951; *The Dream House or When You Build Castles in the Air, Make Sure the Foundations Are Solid*: March 31, 1951; *Love: Its Cure and Prevention*: April 28, 1951; *Money Talks, So Listen!*: Jan. 26, 1952; *Wake Up and Sleep*: Oct. 18, 1952; *What Do You Need It For?*: Sept. 20, 1952.

103 "his eyes were always laughing": Hayes and Hayes, *Sands*, 115.

103 "How many crazy German professors": Tolkin, interview by Bob Claster, Nov. 4, 1997, TAF.

103 "nice, relaxing drive": *Your Show of Shows*, April 21, 1951.

103 "Caesar Yens Straight Drama Role": *Variety*, Jan. 24, 1951.

104 "This simply comes down": Fred Wile Jr. to Weaver and Sarnoff, May 28, 1951, box 119, folder 66, NBC Records.

104 "Do you want to *go out?*": The story has been told in many places, for example, an interview for *A&E Biography*.

104   "He didn't *hang him* out the window": Florence Caesar to Peter Jaysen, Jan. 18, 2001, for *Hail Sid Caesar!*

105   "Mom, let's go home": *Cosmopolitan*, Aug. 1955.

105   "Hundreds of communities": *Chicago Tribune*, April 15, 1951.

105   "who refused to underestimate": Memo, Feb. 19, 1952, box 386, folder 17, NBC Records.

106   "What am I going to do?": *Los Angeles Examiner*, Aug. 22, 1951.

CHAPTER 5 A "JEWISH" SHOW?

107   "Broadway, the big night": *Your Show of Shows*, Sept. 15, 1951.

108   "Get your ass on the first goddamn plane": Hobin, *Window on the Stars*, 61.

108   "seemed like something": *Billboard*, Sept. 22, 1951.

108   "more tired than a night watchman": *New York Journal-American*, Sept. 19, 1951.

108   "Can we stand another season": *Chicago Herald-American*, Oct. 14, 1951.

108   "I was an only-lonely": *TV Guide*, July 25, 1963.

109   "all the bad places": Morris interview, July 30, 1999, Harvith Collection.

109   "Slowly some lights came up": Morris interview, Feb. 27, 2004, TAF.

109   "Violence was [Caesar's] basic medium": Albert Goldman, *Ladies and Gentlemen—Lenny Bruce!!* (Random House, 1971), 200.

109   "There was a time": *Chicago Tribune*, Oct. 20, 1956.

110   "was often out of control": Morris to Kisseloff, Kisseloff Collection.

110   "in the very best form": *Chicago Tribune*, Sept. 10, 1951.

110   "I like my eggs sunny-side up": *New York Journal-American*, May 25, 1952.

110   "I guess if you ain't got no liquor": *Your Show of Shows*, Dec. 1, 1951.

110   "My only fear": *New York Herald Tribune*, Sept. 30, 1951.

110   "Sid Caesar makes you laugh": *Variety*, Jan. 2, 1952.

111   "pathologically jealous of other comics": Flender to Goldman, April 7, 1965, box 46, folder 11, Goldman Papers.

111   "You're not worth the nickel": Flender to Goldman, April 7, 1965, box 46, folder 11, Goldman Papers.

111   "Sid was as jittery": Robert Merrill, *Between Acts: An Irreverent Look at Opera and Other Madness* (McGraw-Hill, 1976), 191.

111   "A hello from Sid": *Saturday Evening Post*, May 16, 1953, 108.

111   "crossing his eyes, grimacing": *Daily Compass*, Dec. 4, 1951.

111   "sleazy anatomical jokes": *New York Herald Tribune*, Oct. 19, 1951.

111   "falls down for every laugh": *Uniontown (Pa.) Evening Standard*, Feb. 26, 1952.

111   "stark, raving TV crazy": *Wall Street Journal*, Aug. 15, 1952.

112   "Cyclops of the living room": *Chicago Tribune*, Sept. 28, 1952.

112   "Think of it!": *Ogden Standard-Examiner*, Oct. 19, 1952.

112   "Don't figure to wait": *Ogden Standard-Examiner*, Nov. 12, 1952.

112   "We can stand only so much": *TV Today*, Nov. 3, 1951.

112   "May I ask you to discontinue": *St. Louis Post-Dispatch*, Nov. 12, 1950.

113   "As long as movies continued": Tolkin, *Where Did I Go Right?*, 172.

113   "We were a product": Harvey Kurtzman interview with John Benson, Sept. 7, 1985, in *The Complete Mad* (Russ Cochran, 1986), vol. 2, page unnumbered.

114   "psycho music": Coca to Kisseloff, Kisseloff Collection.

114   "A Place in the Bottom of the Lake": *Your Show of Shows*, April 19, 1952.

115   "At heart, Caesar was himself": Nachman, *Seriously Funny*, 103.

116 "When he did a silent movie": *Hail Sid Caesar!*

116 "tuxedo-clad percussionist": *Christian Science Monitor,* May 7, 1960.

117 "wired for high-fidelity sound": *New York Times,* March 4, 1973.

117 "We often worked out twists": *Indianapolis Times,* March 10, 1962.

118 "Let's make this one program": *New York Times,* Dec. 30, 1952.

118 "It's a fear-ridden industry": *New York Herald Tribune,* Jan. 4, 1953.

118 "some hinterland TV trade": *Variety,* June 6, 1952.

118 "that crowded little island": *Berkshire Evening Eagle,* Feb. 28, 1951.

118 "TV gold can be panned": *Variety,* April 13, 1949.

119 "Operation Lox": *Billboard,* April 21, 1951.

119 "Dozens of Broadway shows": *Richmond Times-Dispatch,* June 25, 1952.

119 "He never said a Jewish word": Liebman interview, Feb. 1978, William E. Wiener Oral History Library of the American Jewish Committee.

119 "A pet he brings to school!": *Your Show of Shows,* Sept. 22, 1951; "A finer girl you couldn't find anywhere": Nov. 10, 1951; "From my plate he has to eat!": Dec. 30, 1951.

119 "Jack Benny, George Burns": *Modern Maturity,* March–April 1999, 47.

119 "those fucking Jews": Interview, Reiner.

120 "waiting and watching for her reaction": *TV Digest,* Dec. 22, 1951.

120 "J. Moraiarty of the Bronx asks": *New York Journal-American,* Oct. 18, 1952.

120 "Herculean male genitalia": Hayes and Hayes, *Sands,* 116.

120 "Basic security being unavailable": Isaac Rosenfeld, "Adam and Eve on Delancey Street," *Commentary,* Oct. 1949.

121 "Why complain that delicatessen": Letter from Samuel Persky, *Commentary,* July 1946.

121 "Without pastrami sandwiches": *Commentary,* July 1946, 90.

121 "Because we were Jews!": Interview, Reiner.

121 "better appreciation": Reiner interview, Aug. 11, 1986, Dorot Jewish Division.

122 "four gigantic corned beef sandwiches": *Forverts,* May 3, 1950.

122 "I'll give you something": *Forverts,* Nov. 27, 1950.

122 "let off steam": *TV People,* June 1956.

123 "Double Caesar": *TV-Radio Life,* Oct. 12, 1951.

123 "He once said to me": Interview, Brooks.

124 "Eating with a guy": *Boston Traveler,* Oct. 18, 1954.

124 "The vivacious Mrs. C.": *Chicago Herald-American,* Dec. 23, 1951.

124 "We'd start doing the scene": Garrison interview, Oct. 8, 1998, TAF.

124 "She takes such tiny bites": *Los Angeles Times,* July 5, 1953.

124 "Why does Sid Caesar": *New York Post,* Feb. 6, 1958.

125 "Sid would order in 'Chinese'": Interview, Stein.

125 "Why? Where is it written?": *Your Show of Shows,* Nov. 8, 1952.

125 "What do you mean *eat*?": *TV Guide,* June 29, 1974.

126 "You got any food in the house?": *Your Show of Shows,* March 4, 1950.

126 "Very, very bad": *Your Show of Shows,* April 5, 1952.

126 "tutti frutti": *Your Show of Shows,* Oct. 27, 1951; "What gave them the idea": Nov. 29, 1952; Judge John Poundcake: Oct. 4, 1952; Ludwig von Dumpling: Dec. 29, 1951; "lot of lettuce": Feb. 27, 1954.

127 "You're eating as if there's no tomorrow!": *Your Show of Shows,* Feb. 9, 1952.

127 "Coming to America with my parents": Interview, Thorn.

128 "Dad worked six days a week": Interview, Edelman.

128 "We got a television set in 1949": Interview, Margaret Winter.

129 "Zey takeh batsoln far dem?": Interview, Stein.

CHAPTER 6 RESTLESSNESS

130 "Yonkers Stages Own 'Show of Shows'": *Herald Statesman*, Nov. 19, 1952.

130 "I will never forget it": Hobin, *Window on the Stars*, 115.

130 "a wholesome tonic": *Herald Statesman*, Nov. 19, 1952.

131 "I am still a little dazed": *Herald Statesman*, Dec. 2, 1952.

131 "the great gift of making you glad": *New York Herald Tribune*, Sept. 26, 1952.

131 "When you've got a winning formula": Hayes and Hayes, *Sands*, 119.

131 "Even the motor companies": *Advertising Age*, Oct. 6, 1952.

131 "Lindy's Law": *New Republic*, June 13, 1964.

131 "Dark Noon": *Your Show of Shows*, Oct. 18, 1952.

132 "By the time I got backstage": *New York Times*, April 1, 1995.

132 "kills flies instantly": *Your Show of Shows*, Oct. 18, 1952.

132 "Ancient House of the Golden Lamb": *Your Show of Shows*, Oct. 4, 1952.

133 "gears began to slip": Hayes and Hayes, *Sands*, 120.

133 "remains an island of engaging literacy": *New York Times*, Sept. 8, 1952.

133 "and who isn't?": *Chicago Tribune*, Oct. 30, 1952.

133 "We needed a Gentile": Handwritten notes from "A Tribute to 'Your Show of Shows.'"

133 "He always complained": Kallen to Kisseloff, Kisseloff Collection.

133 "be as bright": Handwritten notes from "A Tribute to 'Your Show of Shows.'"

133 "Promises, promises": Tolkin, *Where Did I Go Right?*, 215.

133 "That's the only thing": Morris to Kisseloff, Kisseloff Collection.

134 "like being in another world": *Radio & Television Mirror*, July 1951.

134 "pistols, revolvers, automatics": *Radio-TV Mirror*, April 1954.

134 "I can't understand it!": *Forverts*, Nov. 28, 1950.

134 "Please throw me back": *Saturday Evening Post*, May 16, 1953, 112.

135 "essence of life into his art": Caesar, *Caesar's Hours*, 35–36.

135 "He just sits there": *Toledo Blade*, March 14, 1954.

135 "first thing you know": *TV Digest*, Nov. 8, 1952.

135 "Oh, it's just a hat and coat": *Boston American*, Jan. 19, 1953.

136 "The main disadvantage": *St. Paul Recorder*, Dec. 12, 1952.

136 "That was different": Isaac Asimov, *In Memory Yet Green* (Doubleday, 1979), 587, 642.

136 "Move the TV set": *Winston-Salem Journal*, Dec. 5, 1953.

136 "Mom and Pop maintained": *New Yorker*, Dec. 26, 2013.

136 "A lot of time when I was watching": Interview, Jaffee.

137 "I thought, Jesus!": Interview, Cavett.

137 "There was nothing in there": Interview, Klein.

137 "Without ever having seen": Review of *Ten from Your Show of Shows*, April 24, 1973, on RogerEbert.com.

137 "but once a week a great American artist": Interview, Pinsky.

138 "Speaking French and Japanese": Robert Pinsky, "To Television," *New Yorker*, Aug. 10, 1998, 34.

138 "impatient for them to scram": Email, Rosenberg to the author, May 29, 2023.

138 "dietary phantasmagoria": *TV Guide*, June 29, 1974.

138 "You know, if all of us knew": *Your Show of Shows*, Oct. 11, 1952.

138 "anything," Caesar later said, "to relax": *New York Journal-American*, Nov. 30, 1956.

138 "When a show came off good": *New York Journal-American*, Nov. 30, 1956.

139 "What, 'every show'?": Morris to Schaap.

139 "a little intramural vomiting": Morris to Schaap.

139 "We had to be ready": Howard Morris interview, Feb. 27, 2004, TAF.

139 "The treatment of such a subject": Unprocessed CART report, Oct. 27, 1950, box 1, folder 3, NBC Records.

139 "drinking and drunkenness": Unprocessed CART report, April 26, 1951, box 1, folder 4, NBC Records.

140 "A disturbed alcoholic": *Your Show of Shows*, March 29, 1952.

140 "the usual": *Your Show of Shows*, May 3, 1952.

140 "light-pedal": CART Report 6, April 22, 1953, box 153, folder 1, NBC Records.

140 "A Drunkard's Fate": *Your Show of Shows*, Dec. 19, 1953.

140 "Flippancy about drinking": Unprocessed CART Report 2, Feb. 1954, box 1, folder 7, NBC Records.

141 "My analyst told me": Tolkin, *Where Did I Go Right?*, 246.

141 "a few too many": *Uncensored*, May 1957.

141 "What's his name?": *New York Post*, Jan. 3, 1952.

141 "like to make it a yearly thing": *Your Show of Shows*, Jan. 24, 1953.

141 "We were entertaining ourselves": Reiner to Kantor, April 6, 2006.

142 "pricing themselves right off": *New York Times*, Feb. 8, 1953.

142 "geldings": *TV Guide*, March 29, 1953.

142 "The Show of Shows Problem": McGarrett to Barry, Margraf, McAvity, and Weaver, March 12, 1953, box 397, folder 59, NBC Records.

143 "subjected to some drastic 'rethinking'": *Variety*, March 25, 1953.

143 "Lotsa Problems Beset Liebman": *Variety*, April 15, 1953.

143 "His box-office potential": New York *Daily News*, Jan. 28, 1953.

143 "Don't sign, Sidney": Alan Sepinwall, *What's Alan Watching?*, Dec. 10, 2012.

144 "about half a mile away": Caesar, interview by Dan Pasternack, April 1, 1997, for *The Interviews: An Oral History of Television*, TAF.

144 "a bright new format": Telegram, May 13, 1953, box 392, folder 40, NBC Records.

144 "We're conscious of the ravages": *Los Angeles Daily News*, June 16, 1953.

145 "a ruthless step": *New York Times*, Sept. 6, 1953.

145 "give our blood the plasma": *New York Herald Tribune*, July 18, 1953.

145 "After reading it": *Your Show of Shows*, May 16, 1953.

145 "TV Gives Him Nightmares": *Saturday Evening Post*, May 16, 1953.

145 "And the strain is showing": *New York Times*, May 3, 1953.

145 "Why don't Sid, Carl, Howie, and I": *Esquire*, May 1972, 146.

146 "Let's just tell the audience": Reiner interview for "Television's Comedy Genius."

146 "British parasites": *Daily Worker*, March 23, 1956.

146 "On Monday morning, I ask myself": *Saturday Evening Post*, May 16, 1953, 26.

146 "spent the summer with his therapist": Imogene Coca Diary, Coca Papers.

146 "He sits next to": *Connecticut Post*, Aug. 23, 1953.

146 "Don't even look in her direction": Tolkin, *Where Did I Go Right?*, 195.

147 "totally unprepared": Tolkin, *Where Did I Go Right?*, 196.

CHAPTER 7　THAT CHAMPIONSHIP SEASON

148 "Hail to balding trees": *New York Times*, Sept. 23, 1953.

149 "a couple of sizes larger": *New York Times*, Oct. 15, 1950.

149 "putting a painting": Coca to Kisseloff, Kisseloff Collection.

149 "we had *five* responses": Liebman to Rich, June 9, 1978.

150 "$1,356,000 buys *Your Show of Shows*": *New York Times*, Aug. 27, 1953.

150 "Well, Joe, so you've finally hit": Interview, Stein.

150 "Mel Tolkin and Mel Brooks": Interview, Stein.

150 "The television news of the moment": *Your Show of Shows*, Sept. 12, 1953.

151 "What kind of a lay": Tolkin interview, July 24, 1999, Harvith Collection.

151 "They were people who were getting": Tolkin interview, July 24, 1999, Harvith Collection.

151 "Kinda rough tonight": *Your Show of Shows*, Sept. 12, 1953.

151 "the entire stage was like a swamp": Hobin, *Window on the Stars*, 99.

151 "A famous producer watched": Tolkin interview, Nov. 4, 1997, TAF.

151 "hard-head": Defendant's Memorandum After Trial, *Columbia Pictures Corp. v. National Broadcasting Company*.

152 "Sid says he works best": *Scribe*, Prospect Heights High School, March 10, 1954, in Caesar Scrapbooks, vol. 7.

153 "you do at Camp Tonawanda": Morris interview, July 30, 1999, Harvith Collection.

153 "Imogene Coca made no friends": *Oregonian* (Portland), Oct. 1, 1953.

153 "It was great publicity": *Sacramento Bee*, Oct. 19, 1953.

153 "Anyone want to buy": *Your Show of Shows*, Sept. 26, 1953.

153 "Didn't throw off any sparks": Liebman to Holtzman.

153 "I want that brain": Neil Simon to Caesar, Sept. 20, 1994, courtesy of Karen Caesar.

153 "Why don't you eat": *Your Show of Shows*, Oct. 17, 1953.

154 "You're no wife for me": *Your Show of Shows*, Jan. 30, 1954.

154 "You're not the only one": *Your Show of Shows*, Sept. 26, 1953.

154 "any real pep or imaginative verve": *New York Times*, Sept. 28, 1953.

154 "perhaps the four most talented": Jenkins to Liebman, Oct. 12, 1953, courtesy of Barry Jacobsen.

154 "That's why the show": Liebman to Jenkins, Oct. 15, 1953, courtesy of Jacobsen.

154 "Comedy almost requires participation": *New York Post*, Feb. 2, 1958.

154 "Why does WSM-TV have": *Nashville Banner*, Sept. 29, 1953.

155 "If anyone wants ulcers"; "If it were only 30 minutes"; "I don't like"; "If all of TV": *Nashville Banner*, Oct. 1 and 2, 1953.

155 "The Grand Ole Opry": *Nashville Banner*, Oct. 1, 1953.

155 "Zippos" instead of "Sleepos": *Your Show of Shows*, Nov. 14, 1953.

155 Vitality Health Food Kitchen: *Your Show of Shows*, Nov. 21, 1953.

156 "*Gentlemen!*": *Your Show of Shows*, Dec. 19, 1953.

157 "schlepping stuff": Morris to Kisseloff, Kisseloff Collection.

157 "two behemoths": Morris interview, July 30, 1999, Harvith Collection.

157 "It was like a Jewish family": Morris to Kisseloff, Kisseloff Collection.

157 "fucking brilliant, a ge-ne-ius": Morris to Kisseloff, Kisseloff Collection.

157 "big gaps": Morris interview, July 30, 1999, Harvith Collection.

157 "Carl has an air-conditioned": Interview, Frances Keane.

157 "Howard was a malcontent": Interview, Reiner.

158 "young and resilient": Morris interview, July 30, 1999, Harvith Collection.

158 "As close to the perfect comedy": *New York Times*, April 15, 1990.

158 "NBC-TV pays Sid Caesar": *New York Post*, Dec. 16, 1953.

158 "With nerves all a-tingle": *Radio-TV Mirror*, April 1954.

159 "The press must have known": *Detroit Free Press*, Oct. 30, 1982.

159 "Sid's relationship with Max": Interview, Brooks.

159 "Caesar, his Cuban cigar": *Atlanta Journal and Constitution Magazine*, Nov. 22, 1953.

159 "Sid is a guy": Don Bishop to Childers, Oct. 9, 1953, box 164, folder 13, NBC Records.

159 "pinko leanings": New York *Daily News*, Oct. 5, 1953.

159 "It never—not even for a second": Email, Baum to the author, May 23, 2020.

160 "Without a character to play": Interview, Baum.

160 "as relatable as a jellyfish": Email, Baum to the author, July 16, 2022.

160 "Sid was a very classy guy": Email, Baum to the author, July 17, 2022.

160 "Over in Europe, a man writes": Washington *Star*, Oct. 25, 1953.

160 "The beginning of the rainbow": *New York Herald Tribune*, Sept. 10, 1954.

161 "an alarming loss of weight": *Miami Herald*, Dec. 25, 1953.

161 "Sid also wants an offer": Weaver to Gus Margraf, Jan. 7, 1954, box 123, folder 31, NBC Records.

161 "Rumors persist that Sid Caesar": New York *Daily News*, Jan. 25, 1954.

161 "It's now reached the point": Ernie Otto to Richard Connelly, Feb. 19, 1954, box 382, folder 16, NBC Records.

161 "a man of surpassing talents": *New York World-Telegram and Sun*, Feb. 5, 1954.

162 "Almost from the day": Weaver to Caesar, Feb. 19, 1954, box 122, folder 70, NBC Records.

162 "It was like a Marx Brothers movie": Coca to Kisseloff, Kisseloff Collection.

162 "big, bitter, reluctant crocodile blobs": *TV Star Parade*, May 1955.

162 "pale, glum, and a little sick": New York *Daily News*, Feb. 26, 1954.

163 "nervously clung to him": *New York World-Telegram and Sun*, March 9, 1954.

163 "It's really a heartbreaking thing": *New York Herald Tribune*, Feb. 26, 1954.

163 "Oh, I suppose that's quite true": *New York Herald Tribune*, Feb. 26, 1954.

163 "The truth is that Max": *New York World-Telegram and Sun*, March 8, 1954.

163 "certain things I want to say": *New York Herald Tribune*, March 31, 1954.

163 "like a hole in the head": Coca to Kisseloff, Kisseloff Collection.

163 "Sid wanted his own show": Morris to Kisseloff, Kisseloff Collection.

164 "A star must be king": Howard Morris and Daniel S. Broun, *King of the Hill*, I-20, I-77, Ziegler and Ross Collection, American Heritage Center, University of Wyoming.

164 "I don't prefer working again": *Boston Globe*, Dec. 28, 1954.

164 "simply had run its course": *New York Times*, March 1, 1954.

164 The Caesar-Coca "divorce": *New York Daily Mirror*, March 3, 1954.

164 "These are terrible times": *Greensboro Daily News*, Feb. 27, 1954.

164 "The program will not be": Edwin Vane to Thomas McAvity, March 5, 1954, box 122, folder 70, NBC Records.

165 "Right now, I'm making wonderful dough": *Atlanta Journal*, Nov. 27, 1954.

165 "Why should I want": *New York Journal-American*, Feb. 26, 1956.

165 "Caesar is never going": *New York Herald Tribune*, March 31, 1954.

166 "that lachrymose invasion of privacy": *New York Herald Tribune*, Dec. 14, 1953.

166 "What person in his right mind": Tolkin, *Where Did I Go Right?*, 174.

167 "I don't want to entertain": Morris interview, July 30, 1999, Harvith Collection.

167 "Welcome, America, and hi there": *Your Show of Shows*, April 3, 1954.

168 "He had the courage": Morris interview, July 30, 1999, Harvith Collection.

168 "I was used to the peaks": Interview, Brooks.

169 "Use your funny lenses": Morris interview, July 30, 1999, Harvith Collection.

169 "release from Jewish tension": Morris to Kisseloff, Kisseloff Collection.

170 "the first time really": *Hail Sid Caesar!*

170 "I think I matured comedically": Morris to Kisseloff, Kisseloff Collection.

170 "If *he's* getting laughs": Interview, Caesar.

170 "Mistakes were always good": "Conversations on the Arts and Letters."

170 "We related like I have never": Morris interview for "Television's Comedy Genius."

170 "You get a lot of strength": Interview, Caesar.

170 "Carl always pretended": Interview, Stein.

170 "The audience couldn't get enough": Interview, Reiner.

171 "Yes, after all these years": *Your Show of Shows*, April 3, 1954.

171 "on a cloud of euphoria": Caesar, *Caesar's Hours*, 255.

171 "the funniest sketch we have ever seen": *Chicago Daily News*, June 8, 1954.

171 "beating up Howie Morris sketch": Kallen to Kisseloff, Kisseloff Collection.

172 "The No. 1 Ted Williams fan": *Boston Daily Record*, April 8, 1954.

172 "Sometimes I think Sid Caesar": *New York Journal-American*, April 24, 1954.

172 Baron von Schmutzendangle: *Your Show of Shows*, Feb. 23, 1952.

173 "The show is ending": *San Francisco Examiner*, May 12, 1954.

173 "sniffled every 10 minutes": *Life*, June 21, 1954.

173 "This is the last one, Imogene": *Your Show of Shows*, June 5, 1954.

174 "We were five years ahead": Tolkin interview, Nov. 4, 1997, TAF.

174 "a funeral-parlor visitor": *Cincinnati Enquirer*, June 8, 1954.

174 "All hands looked as if": *Variety*, June 9, 1954.

174 "I panned close-ups of Max": Hobin, *Window on the Stars*, 116.

175 "We're off the air!": *York Daily Record*, June 10, 1954.

175 "And with that": Hobin, *Window on the Stars*, 116.

175 "I knew I damn well better": Coca to Mark Basile and Steve Schnepp, Nov. 26, 1997, Coca Papers.

175 "what's his name?": *New York Post*, Jan. 3, 1952.

176 "They quit while they were ahead": *The Sun* (Baltimore), June 8, 1954.

176 "there is a limit to human": *Cue*, June 19, 1954.

176 "Saturday night will revert": *Denver Daily Chief*, June 18, 1954.

176 "Very few television writers": *New York Herald Tribune*, March 27, 1955.

176 "TV's Overexposed Comics": *Variety*, June 16, 1954.

176 "don his toga as a solo": *Variety*, June 9, 1954.

176 "one of the major trade secrets": *Variety*, Sept. 29, 1954.

176 "own new laugh-a-minute show": *New York Times*, Sept. 27, 1954.

176 "format trap": *Los Angeles Times*, Sept. 19, 1954.

177 "They know what I like": *The Sun* (Baltimore), Aug. 8, 1954.

177 "Why disillusion them?": *Los Angeles Times*, Sept. 19, 1954.

177 "He says his six years on TV": *Pasadena Independent*, Aug. 25, 1954.

177 "People nowadays are too tightened up": *New York Journal-American*, Aug. 22, 1954.

CHAPTER 8 CAESAR'S HOURS

178 "If everything had gone": *Person to Person*, Oct. 1, 1954.

179 "not one to burble": *New York Post*, March 19, 1957.

179 "never said two words": Kallen to Holtzman.

180 "We were writhing on the floor": Interview, Stein.

180 "one of Caesar's closest friends": *Wisconsin State Journal*, Oct. 25, 1954.

180 "Sid Caesar was what you would call": *Forverts*, March 21, 1957.

180 "all the toys were mine": Caesar interview, Sept. 9, 1982, Time Inc. *Time* Research Center Files.

180 "Sid was like a racehorse": Roger Catlin, *TV Eye*, Feb. 13, 2014.

180 "Every day he came home": Interview, Baum.

181 he'd even had the pills: *New Yorker*, Oct. 30, 1978.

181 "At the beginning": Interview, Brooks.

181 "Funny is money": Tolkin, *Where Did I Go Right?*, 211.

181 "On the sybaritic side": *Plain Dealer* (Cleveland), May 19, 1956.

181 "perhaps the only Picasso-Rouault-Rodin": *Philadelphia Inquirer*, Jan. 26, 1958.

181 "Like something out of *Citizen Kane*": Ruben, taped interview, Kisseloff Collection.

181 "large enough to accommodate": *Good Housekeeping*, Jan. 1958.

182 "nearly full-time function": *Redbook*, Nov. 1956, 55.

182 "His valet would bring in a tray": Kisseloff, *Box*, 315.

182 "Sid looks like a little boy": *Modern Screen*, Dec. 1954.

182 "carpeted with expensive broadloom": *TV Guide*, May 25–31, 1957.

182 "garrulous parakeet": *Plain Dealer* (Cleveland), May 19, 1956.

182 "like the mayor of a small town": Interview, Baum.

182 "He was sitting in the back seat": *TV Guide*, Feb. 23, 1963.

183 "do justice to frozen beef": *New York Journal-American*, July 21, 1955.

183 "Sid Caesar is casting": *Washington Post*, June 13, 1954.

183 "Paddy is downstairs": *New York Herald Tribune*, July 31, 1955.

183 "Italian Marilyn Monroe": *NBC Trade News*, Sept. 16, 1954, NBC Trade Releases, Internet Archive.

183 "Eef his name is Caesar": *Brooklyn Eagle*, Sept. 27, 1954.

183 "tiresome old casserole": *New York World-Telegram and Sun*, Sept. 28, 1954.

184 "was hanging out all evening": *Providence Bulletin*, Sept. 28, 1954.

184 "A whole hour of Caesar": *New York Herald Tribune*, Oct. 17, 1954.

184 "of the thermo-nuclear variety": *Detroit News*, Feb. 28, 1955.

184 He "sort of" missed her: *Newark News*, Nov. 14, 1954.

184 "saved my ass": Coca to Basile and Schnepp, Nov. 26, 1997, Coca Papers.

184 "Caesar is one of those": *New York Herald Tribune*, Oct. 17, 1954.

184 "I'll be conventional at first": *Newsweek*, Oct. 11, 1954.

185 "On the Docks": *Caesar's Hour*, Oct. 4, 1954.

185 "Method mumbling": Caesar, *Caesar's Hours*, 220.

185 "Brando called me up": Caesar to Jane Collings, Session 4A, April 11, 2006, UCLA.

185 "left Humphrey Bogart howling": *Portsmouth Herald*, Oct. 16, 1954.

185 "one of the greatest bits": New York *Daily News*, April 19, 1955.

186 "I'm working on a tree": *The Tex and Jinx Show*, WRCA Radio, Dec. 12, 1955, Paley Center for Media.

187 "They jumped and screamed": *Down Beat*, Dec. 15, 1954.

187 "a fat F": *Army Times*, Nov. 13, 1954.

187 "among the biggest smiles": Will Friedwald, "When the King of Swing Met Caesar," *Slouching Toward Birdland*, Nov. 27, 2023.

187 "You're the world's greatest": *Caesar's Hour*, Nov. 1, 1954.

188 "Dragnyet": *Caesar's Hour*, Dec. 6, 1954.

188 Ted Burrows: *Caesar's Hour*, Dec. 27, 1954.

188 "My mind swirled": *New York Times*, Feb. 20, 2014.

188 *Caesar's Hour* "through": *Hollywood Reporter*, Nov. 18, 1954.

188 "I should have thot": Handwritten note from Sarnoff to Weaver, on memo from Robert Daubenspeck, Dec. 28, 1954, box 125, folder 24, NBC Records.

188 "French" chef; "Cleopatras": Outline of a Five-City Exploitation Tour Proposed for Sid Caesar, Oct. 12, 1954, box 125, folder 24, NBC Records.

189 "Sid is taking off": Kenneth W. Bilby to Weaver, Dec. 3, 1954, box 122, folder 70, NBC Records.

189 "What's happened to Sid?": *San Francisco Examiner*, Nov. 1, 1954.

190 "rake suburban life": Philip Roth, "The Hurdles of Satire," *New Republic*, Sept. 9, 1957.

190 "'The Honeymooners' with a station wagon": *Philadelphia Inquirer*, Feb. 8, 1956.

190 "Caesar's best characters always had": *Chicago Tribune*, Feb. 26, 1955.

190 "The vast majority of American viewers": New York *Daily News*, March 13, 1956.

190 "there is something uproariously funny": *The New Republic*, Sept. 9, 1957.

191 "really going down the tubes": Fabray interview, July 25, 1999, Harvith Collection.

191 "There was a madness": *Hail Sid Caesar!*

191 "She can dance and sing": *New York World-Telegram and Sun*, Feb. 23, 1955.

191 "Caesar seemed broader": *Television Quarterly* (Summer 1973): 53.

192 "nine-tenths" of *Caesar's Hour*: *Detroit Times*, March 6, 1955.

192 "the tiny capsule of Benzedrine": *Boston Daily Record*, June 23, 1955.

192 "peacherino": *Variety*, Nov. 23, 1955.

192 "royal indifference": *New York Journal-American*, July 27, 1955.

193 "Sid wasn't gay": Wild interview, June 4, 2001, Harvith Collection.

193 "unfunny after the first chorus": *Variety*, April 13, 1955.

193 "a nervous wreck": Washington *Evening Star*, May 25, 1955.

193 "I hope to live to watch it": *Long Island Press*, Jan. 5, 1956.

193 "Television Father of the Year": *Caesar's Hour*, June 13, 1955.

194 "Study in Succe$$": *New York Daily Mirror*, May 26, 1955.

194 "a discreet realization of a Hollywood fantasy": *New York Post*, March 19, 1957.

194 "a magnificent show place": *Holiday*, Sept. 1956, 71.

194 "my husband is the happiest": *New York Journal-American*, Jan. 31, 1951.

194 "a kind of baronial air": *New York Journal-American*, Nov. 25, 1956.

195 "like I was entering": Email, Turan to the author, Sept. 22, 2013.

195 "See that building over there?": *Milwaukee Journal*, Feb. 26, 1956.

195 "Sid often sits on his front lawn": *Redbook*, Nov. 1956, 56.

195 "If any of you like the show": *Long Island Press*, Jan. 5, 1956.

195 "tempestuous, mercurial, capricious": Interview, Richerd Kleinberg.

195 "the approximate size": *Plain Dealer* (Cleveland), May 19, 1956.

195 "He pulled up in a limousine": *New York Journal-American*, Feb. 18, 1955.

196 "big, knobby-looking pieces": Interview, Frances Keane.

196 "Not even Jackie Gleason": *New York Journal-American*, Nov. 25, 1956.

196 "was so big he thought it": *New York Herald Tribune*, April 25, 1957.

196 "Go ahead, eat the cake": *TV Guide*, Feb. 19–26, 1955.

196 "In liquids, his tastes run": New York *Daily News*, Nov. 20, 1955.

196 "Mr. Caesar is an abstentious man": *New York Herald Tribune*, Oct. 3, 1954.

196 "I had to be the big shot": *Boston Herald*, Nov. 1, 1955.

196 "The critics were right": *Boston Herald*, Nov. 11, 1955.

197 "Bullets over Broadway": *Caesar's Hour*, Sept. 26, 1955.

197 "With the preem as criterion": *Variety*, Sept. 28, 1955.

198 "eight comradely cowards": Gelbart interview, July 21, 1999, Harvith Collection.

198 "We had a lot of writers": "Caesar's Writers."

198 "Whatever the shit was going on": Morris interview, Feb. 27, 2004, TAF.

198 "that I couldn't produce": *Esquire*, May 1972, 149.

198 "I said, 'Sid loves you'": Email, Baum to the author, May 23, 2020.

199 "Sid, I want to come back": Interview, Baum.

199 "A pastiche of Jewish minds": Brooks to Goldman, July 27, 1967, box 46, folder 8, Goldman Papers.

199 "A roomful of screaming Jews": Morris interview, Feb. 27, 2004, TAF.

199 Caesar remained "addicted": *New York Times*, Jan. 20, 1957.

199 "Gallipacci": *Caesar's Hour*, Oct. 10, 1955.

200 "The pencil broke": Caesar to Peter Jaysen, Jan. 18, 2001, for *Hail Sid Caesar!*

200 "to the grave": "Caesar's Writers."

200 "I just came over": Caesar, *Caesar's Hours*, 258.

201 "There was some previous work": Interview, Brooks.

201 "It's hard to believe": Tolkin interview, July 24, 1999, Harvith Collection.

201 "Aggravation Boulevard": *Caesar's Hour*, Dec. 26, 1955.

202 "one of Sid's greatest": *The Sun* (Baltimore), Dec. 30, 1955.

202 "Sid Caesar is the only comic": *Look*, March 20, 1956.

203 "Are you going to pay money": *New York Post*, Feb. 29, 1956.

203 "Sid Caesar's 10 writers": *New York Journal-American*, Jan. 17, 1956.

203 "At the beginning there was nobody": Brooks to Goldman, Aug. 9, 1967, box 46, folder 8, Goldman Papers.

203 "didn't have the appetite": Interview, Brooks.

203 "everyone was happy": Transcript of *Open End*, Feb. 14, 1960, Tolkin Papers.

204 "All too often, comedy": *New York Times*, Jan. 15, 1956.

204 "Bright kids and educated people": *New Yorker*, March 3, 1973.

204 "There were no footprints": Gelbart to Michael Kantor, April 15, 2007.

204 "It went beyond street smarts": Larry Gelbart, *Laughing Matters: On Writing "M*A*S*H," "Tootsie," "Oh, God!," and a Few Other Funny Things* (Random House, 1998), 24.

205 "I looked at my writers": Interview, Caesar.

205 "figured out the physical equation": "Conversations on the Arts and Letters."

205 "Comedy is very hard to shoot": Caesar interview for "Television's Comedy Genius."

206 *Your Show of Shows* was a little": Tolkin interview, Nov. 4, 1997, TAF.

206 "We were a family": Simon to Caesar, Sept. 20, 1994, Caesar Papers.

206 "the kids took over": *Hail Sid Caesar!*

206 "the cell": *Philadelphia Inquirer*, April 12, 1956.

206 "Each morning the playroom": *Holiday*, Sept. 1956, 72.

206 "we were on some kind of high": *Emmy* magazine, Oct. 2001.

207 "I think we just ate": *Emmy* magazine, Oct. 2001.

207 "My card": *TV Guide*, Feb. 23, 1963.

207 "Sid would say, 'Dave'": Morris to Kisseloff, Kisseloff Collection.

207 "abusive, unappreciative shit": William A. Henry III, *The Great One: The Life and Legend of Jackie Gleason* (Doubleday, 1992), 250.

207 "Suddenly the double doors": Ruben, interview by Morrie Gelman, Feb. 25, 1999, TAF.

207 "a hand would reach out": Morris to Schaap.

208 "Everybody goofin' off again": "Caesar's Writers."

208 "He functions on two extreme levels": *Holiday*, Sept. 1956, 110.

208 "Sid, we're not married to it": *Salute to Sid Caesar*.

208   "Sid was very quiet": Fabray interview, July 25, 1999, Harvith Collection.
208   "Sid sarcasted you to death": Nachman, *Seriously Funny*, 111.
208   "came to accept his explosiveness": *TV Guide*, Feb. 23, 1963.
208   "Let's do a take-off": *Philadelphia Inquirer*, April 12, 1956.
209   "Thanks to me, the name": *Caesar's Hour*, April 16, 1956.
209   "The discarded idea": *Philadelphia Inquirer*, April 17, 1956.
209   "you can't argue with 'Naaah' ": Kisseloff, *Box*, 312.
209   "I think all of us": Interview, Stein.
209   "I never realized these guys": *Charlie Rose*, Nov. 24, 1993.
209   "Aside from his brilliance": Interview, Stein.
209   "For the next twelve minutes": Simon to Caesar, Oct. 1, 1982, Caesar Papers.
209   "produced with the abandon"; "They play interminably": *Holiday*, Sept. 1956,
          72, 73, 110.
210   "Inevitably, the writers clashed": *TV Guide*, Feb. 23, 1963.
210   "You had fourteen Jews": Morris interview, July 30, 1999, Harvith Collection.
210   "How did you do it": Kallen interview, April 25, 1998, TAF.
210   "I told him I didn't think": *New York Journal-American*, Nov. 25, 1956.
210   "butchered her": Keller interview, Jan. 10, 2000, Harvith Collection.
210   "It was madness": Simon interview, Jan. 1971, Dorot Jewish Division.
211   "You wanna do the snake joke": Caesar, *Caesar's Hours*, 135.
211   "Their statements about him": *New York Journal-American*, Nov. 25, 1956.
211   "Just a little anxiety attack": Tolkin, *Where Did I Go Right?*, 214.
211   "You have to understand": Keller interview, Jan. 10, 2000, Harvith Collection.
211   "He would tell Sid": Interview, Stein.
211   "After having felt in charge": Tolkin, *Where Did I Go Right?*, 238.
211   "There was anger": Tolkin interview, Nov. 4, 1997, TAF.
211   "It was all creative anger": *New York Times*, Nov. 14, 1982.
212   "It's almost as though Caesar": *Holiday*, Sept. 1956, 110.
212   "Caesar's one groupie": Interview, Stein.
212   a word rhyming with "rocksucker": Tolkin, *Where Did I Go Right?*, 227.
212   "Between hearing about his psychiatrist": Wild interview, June 4, 2001, Harvith
          Collection.
212   "I was going to places": Interview, Brooks.
212   "without question the best": Stein to Kisseloff, Kisseloff Collection.
212   "What he taught me": Stewart Papers, box 102, folder 22.
212   "I hate that guy": *New York Journal-American*, Nov. 25, 1956.
212   "We knew it was special": Sacks, *And Here's the Kicker*, 508–9.
212   "It was as though we all had a piece": Museum of Broadcasting Seminar Series:
          Larry Gelbart, Day 1: The Early Days and *Your Show of Shows*, Oct. 2, 1984.
213   "Sid was an appreciator": Gelbart to Schaap.
213   "Sid did not drink until after 6:00": Gelbart, *Fresh Air*, Aug. 19, 1996.
213   "You were one of many": Transcript of *Open End*, Feb. 14, 1960, Tolkin Papers.
213   "Don't let any second banana": *Akron Beacon Journal*, April 22, 1957.
213   "I was sort of building my raft": Gelbart interview, May 26, 1998, TAF.

CHAPTER 9 'S WUNNERFUL

214   "I've seen tons of lobster": *Holiday*, Sept. 1956, 111.
214   "We'd cater the sketch": Brooks to Goldman, Aug. 9, 1967, box 46, folder 8,
          Goldman Papers.
215   downing four steaks "at a time": *New York Daily Mirror*, Sept. 28, 1955.

215 "taking mincing little steps": Interview, Linn.

215 "I didn't think he was a drunk": Interview, Stein.

215 "Oh, sure! Are you kidding?": Reiner interview, Aug. 11, 1986, Dorot Jewish Division.

215 "On rare occasions when I spoke": Downs, *On Camera*, 62.

215 "within ten seconds": Interview, Milgrim.

215 "His assault on the Chivas Regal": Tolkin, *Where Did I Go Right?*, 252.

216 "he would have a tumbler": Gelbart to Jane Collings, tape 4, July 12, 2005, UCLA.

216 "the most inappropriately named": *New York Post*, April 26, 1959.

216 "From where all of us came from": Interview, Edith Tolkin.

216 "Manhattanites are learning": *Davenport (Iowa) Daily Times*, May 31, 1955.

216 "Sid would assume a role": Interview, Stern.

217 "Tolkin would say": Interview, Brooks.

217 "My heart would be": Florence Caesar interview, Sept. 9, 1982, in Time Inc. *Time* Research Center Files.

217 "Sid always got bombed": Interview, Marshall.

217 "One night he sat at": *TV Guide*, Feb. 16, 1963.

217 "After the show was over": *Salute to Sid Caesar*.

217 "A manic depressive type": Caesar interview for "Television's Comedy Genius."

217 "No one came to me": Caesar, *Caesar's Hours*, 116.

217 "It was not easy for a celebrity": Tolkin, *Where Did I Go Right?*, 250.

218 "I was afraid to go in": Callaway interview, Dec. 2, 1982, Studs Terkel Radio Archive.

218 "my drinking became one": Caesar, *Where Have I Been?*, 142.

218 "for promoting, through humor": *Caesar's Hour*, Jan. 16, 1956.

218 "A mea culpa was needed": Caesar, *Caesar's Hours*, 245.

220 "Sidney, this is *insane!*": "Caesar's Writers."

220 "publicly expose the dark corners": *Camden (N.J.) Courier-Post*, May 6, 1958.

220 "out-gag": *New York Evening Post*, Feb. 9, 1946.

221 "He is voluble": *Redbook*, Nov. 1956, 113.

221 "reached the end of his rope": *Theatre Arts*, Feb. 1954, 32.

221 "Everyone should have analysis": *Look*, March 20, 1956.

221 "A man who has made": *Look*, Sept. 18, 1956.

221 "What Psychoanalysis Did for Me": *Look*, Oct. 2, 1956.

221 "TV's Tortured Clown": *New York Journal-American*, Nov. 25–Dec. 1, 1956.

221 "a deeper feeling for the idiosyncrasies": *Look*, Oct. 2, 1956, 52.

221 "Seven years ago he seldom, if ever": *New York Journal-American*, Nov. 30, 1956.

222 "has come brilliantly true": *New York Journal-American*, Nov. 25, 1956.

222 "It's been six years": *Forverts*, March 27, 1957.

222 "The new trend is to bare": *New York Post*, March 19, 1957.

222 "hooted": *TV Guide*, Feb. 23, 1963.

222 "damned foolishness": Report from Shoemaker lsa to theater nyk, Nov. 8, 1962, *Newsweek* Archive.

223 "perceptive man who knows him well": *New York Herald Tribune*, Feb. 8, 1957.

223 "He was not very nice to anyone": Interview, Edith Tolkin.

223 "pathos-ridden" boyhood: *Richmond Times-Dispatch*, Dec. 26, 1956.

223 "thumping bore": *Davenport (Iowa) Daily Times*, Nov. 15, 1956.

223 "inside dope": *Washington Post*, May 22, 1957.

223 "Surely, over the years": *New York Times*, March 24, 1957.

223 "sounded good in print": *Exposed*, June 1957.

223 "Papa wasn't that bad": Report from Shoemaker lsa to theater nyk, Nov. 8, 1962, *Newsweek* Archive.

223 "He [Sidney] was such a pretty boy": Abraham and David Caesar interview, Nov. 8, 1962, *Newsweek* Archive.

223 "In Sid Caesar's presence": *Forverts*, Dec. 30, 1957.

224 "A long time ago I had": *Scribe*, Prospect Heights High School, March 10, 1954, in Caesar Scrapbooks, vol. 7.

224 "Lead Mountain": *Saturday Evening Post*, Feb. 16, 1963.

224 "The tins go up like Old Faithful": *New York Herald Tribune*, Feb. 8, 1957.

224 "guns, carburetors, and crops": *TV-Radio Mirror*, June 1955.

224 "It relaxed him": *California Magazine*, July 1986.

225 "If he occasionally leaves his office": *Holiday*, Sept. 1956, 111.

225 "He just never had": Interview, Frances Keane.

225 "felt unloved at home": New York *Daily News*, Nov. 26, 1967.

225 "ribbons of paranoia": Interview, Brooks.

226 "the only medium in the world": *Admiral Broadway Revue*, April 8, 1949.

226 "He said, 'Who are they?'": Interview, Brooks.

226 "You didn't connect with Sid": Interview, Baum.

226 "They were pretty scared": Caesar to Schaap.

226 "a little premature": Caesar, *Where Have I Been?*, 180.

227 "He may not have been able": Brooks to Goldman, Aug. 9, 1967, box 46, folder 8, Goldman Papers.

227 "U-bet-U": *Caesar's Hour*, Feb. 6, 1956.

227 "Tea and Samurai": *Caesar's Hour*, Oct. 20, 1956.

227 "The Brave and the Bamboo": *Caesar's Hour*, March 23, 1957.

227 "perhaps the boldest, most compulsive user": *Esquire*, Oct. 1965.

228 "*shpritzing* one-liners": Howe, *World of Our Fathers*, 568, 570.

228 "the greatest comedy actor": *San Francisco Examiner*, Nov. 11, 1957.

228 "one of the greatest mimes": *Variety*, Feb. 13, 1957.

228 "TV's brightest ornament": New York *Daily News*, March 13, 1956.

228 "People walk up to me": *New York Post*, Feb. 27, 1956.

228 "a used-wife lot": *Variety*, Oct. 24, 1956.

229 "Now when Sid walks along Broadway": *TV People*, June 1956.

229 "Sometimes you eat because": *Bristol (Pa.) Daily Courier*, Jan. 4, 1958.

229 "Dining and Dancing": *Dallas Morning News*, Oct. 29, 1944.

230 "Thank you, Lawrence": *Lawrence Welk Show*, July 2, 1955.

230 "The small town this generation": Memo, July 1955, box 152, NBC Records.

230 "East Cupcake, Iowa": *Broadcasting*, July 21, 1958.

230 "ram" Caesar "down our vision": *Chicago Tribune*, Jan. 22, 1955.

230 "cross the Hudson River": *TV Guide*, May 25, 1955.

231 "Champagne Music": *Newsweek*, March 18, 1957.

231 "I play the kind of music": *New York World-Telegram and Sun*, Oct. 9, 1956.

231 "is not made up of wise guys": *TV Guide*, April 6–12, 1957.

231 "the still Christian soul": *Belleville (Ill.) Messenger*, Aug. 2, 1957.

231 "North Dakota cornball": Coyne Steven Sanders and Ginny Weissman, *Champagne Music: "The Lawrence Welk Show"* (St. Martin's Press, 1985), 10.

231 "That accent may be one": *Chicago Tribune*, May 5, 1957.

231 "shy, clodhopper charm": *Detroit Free Press*, March 26, 1958.

231 "a toothsome man": *New York Herald Tribune*, Jan. 15, 1956.

231 "Welk may have discovered": *The Daily Times* (Mamaroneck, New York), Oct. 29, 1956.

232 "accoutered in padded shoulders": *Boston Post*, Jan. 27, 1956.

232 "To demonstrate": *Down Beat*, March 7, 1956.

232 "anything I take off on": *Chicago Tribune*, Oct. 20, 1956.

232 "He *was* the real enemy": Interview, Brooks.

232 "I don't think he'll give us": *Bennington (Vt.) Free Press*, May 8, 1956.

233 "danceable, singable music": *Caesar's Hour*, May 21, 1956.

234 "The touch of lavender": *New York Journal-American*, May 22, 1956.

234 "If I were Welk, I'd sue": *Columbus (Ohio) State Journal*, May 29, 1956.

234 "Satirizing a TV opponent": *Boston American*, May 23, 1956.

234 "Your skit was wonderful": *Cincinnati Enquirer*, June 6, 1956.

234 Ricky Tick: *Caesar's Hour*, June 11, 1956.

234 "I said to everybody": Interview, Brooks.

235 "I laughed myself sick": *Fort Worth Star-Telegram*, June 28, 1956.

235 "Caesar Reigns": NBC promotional booklet, Waldman Papers.

235 "the most coveted job": *Boston Herald*, April 8, 1956.

235 "'Cause she was the lead": Morris to Kisseloff, Kisseloff Collection.

235 "He was just a tall, skinny kid": *TV Guide*, June 2–8, 1956.

235 "Now with three strong female stars": Buell Herman to J. L. Killeen and Robert Carley, Aug. 17, 1956, box 394, folder 22, NBC Records.

235 "Best Comedian on TV": NBC promotional brochure.

CHAPTER 10 THE (NEARLY) FATAL BOWL OF COLESLAW

236 "a big, fucking 12-reel": "Sid Caesar," n.d., box 46, folder 10, Goldman Papers.

236 "It was like, really, a cyclotron": *Washington Post*, Dec. 23, 1982.

237 "Nobody ever called Pat": *Wall Street Journal*, Sept. 10, 1956.

237 "would I have time": *The Sun* (Baltimore), July 24, 1955.

237 "From the beginning, we have been": *Variety*, Dec. 14, 1955.

237 "an omen of sterility and dullness": *Variety*, Sept. 12, 1956.

237 "will be filled by the expert": New York *Daily News*, Sept. 13, 1956.

238 "Hi there, nice Americans": *Caesar's Hour*, Sept. 15, 1956.

238 "Caesar had himself a ball": *Newark Star-Ledger*, Sept. 22, 1956.

238 "Who's smoking in the palace?": *Caesar's Hour*, Sept. 15, 1956.

238 "too hep to his tricks": *New York Herald Tribune*, Sept. 26, 1956.

238 "That was it": Wild, June 4, 2001, Harvith Collection.

239 *Try Not to Die*: *Caesar's Hour*, Oct. 20, 1956.

239 "Blast" toothpaste: *Caesar's Hour*, Oct. 6, 1956; "His Majesty's TV Dinners": Nov. 3, 1956; "1957 Fiasco": Jan. 12, 1957; "Poop-a-Trol": Dec. 15, 1956.

239 *Tigers I Have Hunted*: *Caesar's Hour*, Nov. 17, 1956.

240 "Televac audience response boxes": William J. Millard Jr., A Research Study of *Caesar's Hour*, Jerome Barnum Associates, Dec. 28, 1956, box 194, folder 25, NBC Records.

242 "I imagined for a moment": *Minneapolis Star Tribune*, Dec. 3, 1956.

242 "One feels of his satire": Roth, "Hurdles of Satire," 22.

242 "The Dancing Towers": *Caesar's Hour*, Dec. 8, 1956.

243 "Break Your Brains": *Caesar's Hour*, Dec. 15, 1956.

244 "responsible for the most": *New York World-Telegram and Sun*, Jan. 28, 1957.

245 "Let's keep a sharp lookout": *Caesar's Hour*, Oct. 13, 1956.

245 "I could see the timing": *Chicago Tonight*, Dec. 2, 1982.
245 "Poor, poor Sid Caesar!": *Philadelphia Inquirer*, Dec. 27, 1956.
245 "Sid wasn't going to go": Reiner interview for "Television's Comedy Genius."
246 "For the first time in my life": Caesar, *Where Have I Been?*, 173.
246 "He was literally—*literally*": Interview, Brooks.
246 "I have to stay": *Herald Statesman*, Sept. 22, 1994.
246 "He didn't want to go home": Morris to Schaap.
246 "A horse is one thing": Sacks, *And Here's the Kicker*, 508–9.
246 "There was coleslaw, brook trout": Interview, Brooks.
246 "I was worried he'd drown": Caesar, *Where Have I Been?*, 156.
246 "And there's Sid Caesar": Morris to Schaap.
247 "rose out of the fish": Morris interview, July 30, 1999, Harvith Collection.
247 "It's funny": Morris, interview by Schaap.
247 "zonked out": Caesar, *Where Have I Been?*, 155.
247 "Why doesn't Sid Caesar": *New York Post*, Dec. 14, 1956.
247 "changed, rechanneled—or canceled": *Chicago Tribune*, Jan. 23, 1957.
247 "Anyone who can endure": *TV Guide*, Feb. 9–15, 1957.
247 "I know now that my failure": *TV Guide*, March 2–8, 1957.
248 "a distinct ray of hope": *New York Herald Tribune*, Feb. 25, 1957.
248 "May I say one thing": *Emmy* broadcast, March 16, 1957.
248 "'We didn't come to bury'": *New York Herald Tribune*, March 22, 1957.
248 "hillbilly band": *Forverts*, March 21, 1957.
248 "There was no category": *Arkansas Gazette*, March 19, 1957.
248 "hollow victory": *TV Guide*, May 25, 1957.
248 "what's trite is right": *New York Journal-American*, March 25, 1957.
248 "the inexorable law of overexposure": *New York Times*, March 24, 1957.
248 "one long egg roll": *Caesar's Hour*, April 6, 1957.
249 "Sid was in a panic": Gelbart interview for "Television's Comedy Genius."
249 "I have nothing to say": *Newsweek*, April 8, 1957.
249 "a new breed of writers": *Life*, April 15, 1957.
249 "I have no fears": *New York Herald Tribune*, April 23, 1957.
249 "got exactly nowhere": *Variety*, April 24, 1957.
249 "Audience-wise, SID CAESAR": Robert Daubenspeck to Sidney Eiges, April 19, 1957, box 177, folder 18, NBC Records.
249 "I think Caesar is the greatest": *Saturday Evening Post*, Dec. 7, 1957.
250 "Jesus Christ, wouldn't you think": Morris to Kisseloff, Kisseloff Collection.
250 "excruciatingly funny": *Variety*, May 1, 1957.
250 "That's how nuts I was": *People Now*, Oct. 10, 1982.
250 "They didn't put up any kind": Caesar, *Where Have I Been?*, 175.
250 "South American finger eater": *Caesar's Hour*, May 4, 1957.
251 "The Man Who Killed Caesar": *Chicago Tribune*, May 5, 1957.
251 "The Meatgrinder": *Look*, June 25, 1957.
251 "They would like to control me": Memo, Sulzberger to Bernstein, May 18, 1957, Time Inc. *Time* Research Center Files.
251 "He has the most intensely loyal": Memo, Sulzberger to Bernstein, May 18, 1957.
252 "Sure, my show is expensive": *TV Guide*, May 25, 1957.
252 "continue to try to bring": *Chicago Tribune*, May 17, 1957.
252 "even begun to scratch": *New York Herald Tribune*, May 17, 1957.
252 "things like guitars and long sideburns": *Boston Evening American*, May 15, 1957.

252   "by the men in the charcoal grey": New York *Daily News*, Jan. 26, 1958.

252   "CAESAR: MCMXLIX–MCMLVII": *Variety*, May 22, 1957.

252   "Sid Caesar's fans continue": Kathryn Cole to Michael Horton, June 13, 1957, box 179, folder 20, NBC Records.

252   "In the somewhat hysterical search": *Toronto Star*, May 25, 1957.

253   "Like a ball player coming to bat": *Pittsburgh Press*, May 20, 1957.

253   "Until we meet again": *Caesar's Hour*, May 25, 1957.

253   "Caesar may have been": New York *Daily News*, May 30, 1957.

253   "If you laughed your sides off": *Cue*, June 6, 1957.

253   "The Thing": *New York Herald Tribune*, May 24, 1957.

253   "Everything will be all right": *Philadelphia Inquirer*, May 27, 1957.

254   "The cost-per-thousand boys": *Television Quarterly* (Summer 1973): 53–54.

254   "There is something vicious": *New York World-Telegram and Sun*, May 22, 1957.

254   "You sit around in your pajama bottoms": *New York Post*, May 8, 1957.

254   "A negative landmark": *Variety*, May 29, 1957.

254   "Any rating that puts Sid Caesar": *New York Herald Tribune*, Sept. 2, 1957.

255   "That Lawrence Welk, a tenth-class": *Forverts*, June 3, 1957.

255   *"di shtime fun folk"*: *Forverts*, Dec. 26, 1957.

255   "social thinker": *New York Herald Tribune*, May 29, 1957.

255   "pure mildness, pure torpor": *New York Herald Tribune*, June 19, 1957.

255   "Humbug Hero of the Month": *Humbug*, no. 3 (Oct. 1957): 3.

255   "Dot's vy he's now kaput": *Variety*, July 10, 1957.

255   "During the final months": *Philadelphia Inquirer*, Sept. 22, 1957.

255   "If the public is so indignant": *Boston American*, July 28, 1957.

255   "By the time you got to": *New York Times*, Feb. 2, 1958.

256   "I never played down": *Newsday*, May 31, 1957.

256   "If we listened to the eggheads": *Saturday Evening Post*, Dec. 7, 1957.

256   "Committee for Caesar's Longevity": *New York Times*, Sept. 9, 1957, 54.

256   "an inspired, unadulterated genius": *Omaha Evening World-Herald*, July 29, 1957.

256   "I have the feeling that Mr. Macklis": *Washington Daily News*, Aug. 7, 1957.

257   "went literally crazy": Memo from R. Steinberg, July 2, 1958, Time Inc. *Time* Research Center Files.

257   "ever really operated on my wave length": *Boston Traveler*, Dec. 10, 1957.

257   "Sid and Imogene May Walk": *New York World-Telegram and Sun*, July 23, 1957.

257   "an air of desperation": *Washington Star*, July 24, 1957.

257   "DON'T BURY CAESAR!": *New York Times*, Sept. 13, 1957.

258   "I hope for eternity": *Philadelphia Inquirer*, Sept. 21, 1957.

258   "Now I can relax": *New York Herald Tribune*, Sept. 21, 1957.

258   "Shake my hand": *Newsweek*, Sept. 30, 1957.

258   "Don't tell him all": *Tide*, Oct. 11, 1957.

258   "We plan to assume a watchful": *New York Times*, Sept. 23, 1957.

258   "a commuting nebbish": *Philadelphia Inquirer*, April 14, 1964.

258   "I want to be able": New York *Daily News*, March 9, 1958.

258   "Why did Sid Caesar knock off": *Forverts*, Dec. 26, 1957.

259   "I'm not gonna bust": *San Francisco Examiner*, Sept. 30, 1957.

259   "I think there's a Civil War": *New York World-Telegram and Sun*, Nov. 5, 1957.

259   "Sid Caesar is not in favor": *Forverts*, Dec. 30, 1957.

259   "It isn't too corny": *New York Herald Tribune*, Jan. 26, 1958.

259   "RATINGS, SHMATINGS!": *New York Post*, Jan. 26, 1958.

259 "so long as they don't get egghead": *New York Times*, Feb. 2, 1958.

260 "For the first time since 1953": *Chicago Daily News*, Jan. 27, 1958.

260 "a hat-wearing, open-collared": *Philadelphia Inquirer*, Jan. 27, 1958.

260 "drawn, almost anemic": *San Francisco Examiner*, Jan. 28, 1958.

260 "There was hardly a dry eye": *New York Herald Tribune*, Jan. 29, 1958.

261 "Even drizzle is welcome": *Time*, Feb. 10, 1958.

261 "This must have been an ordeal": *The Sun* (Baltimore), Jan. 28, 1958.

261 "It seems to me unwise": *New Yorker*, March 29, 1958.

261 "Why is Sid such a pet": *Akron Beacon Journal*, Feb. 5, 1958.

261 "Here's hoping his health": *Chicago Daily News*, Feb. 3, 1958.

261 Luis Flamingo, an aged bullfighter: *Sid Caesar Invites You*, Feb. 9, 1958.

262 "It didn't end up with": Interview, Brooks.

262 "the thrashing about of a dinosaur": *New York Times*, Feb. 2, 1958.

262 "This was easy": 10th Primetime Emmy Awards, April 15, 1958.

263 "It was like the earth": *Late Night with David Letterman*, Nov. 1, 1982.

263 "about the only one who was cheered": New York *Daily News*, Nov. 7, 1958.

263 "at the mercy of dial-twirling philistines": *Variety*, June 25, 1958.

263 "almost everyone mentions him": *Sandusky (Ohio) Register*, May 5, 1958.

263 "Sid Caesar, probably the greatest": *New York Daily Mirror*, May 29, 1958.

263 "Hollywood wasn't that interested": Alan Sepinwall, *What's Alan Watching?*, Dec. 10, 2012.

263 "What a strange genius": *News Chronicle* (London), July 2, 1957.

264 "gave no impression of the qualities": *Times* (London), July 2, 1957.

264 "Television is his vocation": *New York Herald Tribune*, May 19, 1958.

264 "Without everybody, Sid": Gelbart to Jane Collings, tape 4, July 12, 2005, UCLA.

264 "You. You're hired": *Hail Sid Caesar!*

265 "had all the hallmarks": *New York Herald Tribune*, Nov. 5, 1958.

265 "A scarce Caesar": *Variety*, Nov. 5, 1958.

265 "What, one wonders, went awry": *New York World-Telegram and Sun*, Nov. 3, 1958.

265 "This was undoubtedly": *Washington Star*, Nov. 4, 1958.

265 "Art knew I was a drunk": Caesar, *Where Have I Been?*, 182.

265 "washed up": *Sandusky (Ohio) Register*, Nov. 15, 1958.

265 "to shy away from anything": *Passaic (N.J.) Herald-News*, Dec. 8, 1958.

265 "If it keeps up": *New York Post*, Nov. 23, 1958.

265 Anthony Stunning: "At the Movies," May 3, 1959.

266 "laughing so hard": *San Diego Union*, May 6, 1959.

266 "all he needs is": New York *Daily News*, May 5, 1959.

266 "He believed that I had a contribution": Interview, Allen.

266 "Best Cough in Television": New York *Daily News*, Sept. 8, 1959.

266 Milton Berle: not truly funny: *San Francisco Chronicle*, Aug. 2, 1959.

267 "What is *jazz*?": "Tiptoe Thru TV," May 5, 1960.

267 "Watching Sid Caesar's outing": *Washington News*, May 6, 1960.

267 "a stereotyped and cheap jest": *New York Times*, May 6, 1960.

267 "I want to move into realer": *San Diego Times-Union*, May 5, 1960.

268 "Such an important man!": "The World of Show Biz," June 2, 1960.

268 "Sid has slipped from a groove": *New York Journal-American*, June 3, 1960.

268 "Caesar had a lot to give": Transcript of *Open End*, Feb. 14, 1960, Tolkin Papers.

268 "less sophisticated mentor": *New Republic*, Oct. 31, 1960.

268 "too easy to come by": *Fort Worth Star-Telegram*, Oct. 18, 1959.

268 "Protestantized": *New York Post*, Nov. 8, 1975.

269 "When you walk in the clouds": *Los Angeles Times*, Jan. 24, 1962.

269 "It was a bad period": *Herald and Review* (Decatur, Ill.), June 14, 1965.

269 "a composite": *Los Angeles Times*, Jan. 24, 1962.

269 "You're a lousy human being": Morris and Broun, *King of the Hill*, I-80.

269 "Morris won't admit": New York *Daily News*, Dec. 4, 1961.

269 "majestic": Interview, Allen.

270 "have the vehicle": Brooks to Goldman, Aug. 9, 1967, box 46, folder 8, Goldman Papers.

270 "If anybody else could do the part": Brooks to Goldman, Aug. 9, 1967, box 46, folder 8, Goldman Papers.

270 "In ten years TV reached": *Los Angeles Times*, May 8, 1960.

CHAPTER 11 BOTTOMING OUT

271 "I can't blame them": Caesar, *Where Have I Been?*, 192.

271 "the golem": Carter interview, Nov. 12, 1962, *Newsweek* Archive.

272 "virtual unemployment": *Boston Sunday Advertiser*, Jan. 15, 1961.

272 "Hello, Sid": *New York Daily Mirror*, Nov. 18, 1962.

272 "at the end of the line": *Orlando Evening Star*, July 21, 1962.

272 "He worked hard": *Variety*, Oct. 18, 1961.

272 "warned by everybody": Report from Shoemaker lsa to theater nyk, Nov. 8, 1962, *Newsweek* Archive.

272 "People look up to you": Caesar, *Caesar's Hours*, 277.

272 "You don't have to copy him": Kramer to Caesar, May 28, 1974, Caesar Family Papers.

273 "like an oxygen tent": *The Sun* (Baltimore), Dec. 16, 1962.

273 "You're a *shtarker*": Caesar, *Caesar's Hours*, 277.

273 "My dear fellow": *The Sun* (Baltimore), Dec. 16, 1962.

273 "There is insecurity": *Chicago Daily News*, Oct. 17, 1962.

273 "stunted plant": *New York World-Telegram and Sun*, Oct. 17, 1962.

273 "When you saw that show": Garrison interview, Oct. 8, 1998, TAF.

274 "It was a bad night": *New York Post*, June 13, 1963.

274 "He wasn't always coherent": Simon to Schaap.

274 "The Last Hurrah of My Glory Days": Caesar, *Where Have I Been?*, 191.

274 "pie-throwing free-for-all": *Boston Globe*, March 22, 1963.

274 "We're all looking forward": *As Caesar Sees It*, June 10, 1963.

274 "the decline of Sid Caesar": John Malcolm Brinnin, *Sextet: T. S. Eliot & Truman Capote & Others* (Delacorte, 1981), 95.

274 "stalking through the split-level corridors": *TV Guide*, Feb. 16, 1963.

275 "doll-like Korean girls": *Jewish Advocate*, April 26, 1952.

275 "Sid Caesar's good-luck charm": *Hartford Courant*, May 13, 1963.

275 "I was too busy blazing": Interview, Brooks.

275 "He was moving on": Interview, Baum.

275 "Are you by any chance": *What's My Line?*, May 19, 1963.

276 "One for the books": *Philadelphia Inquirer*, Nov. 20, 1963.

276 "Caesar, whose nervousness": *New Republic*, Nov. 16, 1963.

276 "The most insecure man": Memo, Thimmesch to Applegate, May 15, 1963, Time Inc. *Time* Research Center Files.

277 "would have turned Chaplin": *New York Times*, Jan. 30, 1966.

277 "Aren't you going to say": Hobin, *Window on the Stars*, 500.

277 "the protective coloration": *Akron Beacon Journal*, Feb. 19, 1967.

277 "simply disgraceful": *What's My Line?*, March 26, 1967.

277 "the way Ralph Nader discusses": *Newsday*, April 4, 1967.

277 "Sid Caesar!": *The Sid Caesar, Imogene Coca, Carl Reiner, Howard Morris Special*, April 5, 1967.

277 "could kill a Buick": *New Yorker*, March 3, 1973, 94.

277 "It was wonderful": *New York Times*, Nov. 19, 1967.

277 "*The Beverly Hillbillies* and *Green Acres*": *Minneapolis Star*, April 7, 1967.

278 "He's more in touch": *Kingston Daily Freeman*, March 25, 1967.

278 "you didn't have time to think": *Houston Chronicle*, Jan. 16, 1977.

278 "an office building with slums": *Niagara Falls Evening Review*, June 27, 1968.

278 "Maybe it was the psychoanalysis": New York *Daily News*, Nov. 26, 1967.

279 "a not very bright thing": *Boston Record-American*, Oct. 13, 1967.

279 "the most brilliant comedy": "Sid Caesar," n.d., box 46, folder 10, Goldman Papers.

279 "like walking into Aladdin's Cave": "Sid Caesar," n.d., box 46, folder 10, Goldman Papers.

280 "He feels that if anybody": "Albert at the New School: Sid Caesar."

280 "lined up in military procession": "Sid Caesar," n.d., box 46, folder 10, Goldman Papers.

280 "I thought, 'I'm talking'": "Albert at the New School: Sid Caesar."

281 "Have you ever played Gaithersburg?": *The Tonight Show*, May 20, 1968.

281 "Once upon a time": *San Francisco Chronicle*, March 25, 1969.

281 "the best comedian on TV": *San Francisco Chronicle*, May 2, 1960.

281 "in trouble": Dick Cavett, "Caesar's Conquests," *New Republic*, Dec. 20, 1982.

281 "Totally aloof and totally preoccupied": *New York Post*, Nov. 30, 1982.

282 "Great Caesar's Ghost": *Esquire*, May 1972.

282 "Sid was a terrific person": *Esquire*, May 1972, 192.

282 "A species of nervous wreck": *New Republic*, March 17, 1973, 29.

282 "Given a few years of unemployment": *Atlanta Constitution*, June 4, 1972.

282 "house liberal for Bob Hope": *Emmy* magazine, Nov./Dec. 1984.

282 "The predilection of interviewers": Tolkin to Liebman, July 10, 1977, Tolkin Papers.

282 "a seminal mind behind YSOS": Tolkin to Liebman, July 10, 1977, in Kallen Papers.

282 "the white hopes of TV": Tolkin to Gelbart, May 2, 1977, in Tolkin Papers.

283 "If he were a larger talent": Gelbart to Tolkin, May 26, 1966, in Tolkin Papers.

283 "wandered off like atrophied": *New York Times*, March 30, 1975.

283 "a talented *tummler*": Tolkin to Gelbart, April 3, 1975, Tolkin Papers.

283 "as if he were Michelangelo": Email, Rosenberg to the author, May 29, 2023.

283 "only the certainty that if I": Kallen to Tolkin, April 26, 1972, Tolkin Papers.

284 "He promptly bent over": Email, Eisenberg to the author, Dec. 11, 2019.

285 "You think they make a move": Interview, Schlossberg.

285 "Get rid of the old guy": *Los Angeles Times*, May 9, 1973.

285 "with great anxiety": *Los Angeles Times*, April 22, 1973.

286 "Sid was starting to tell me": *The Tonight Show*, April 6, 1973.

286 "That woman screaming": Interview, Reiner.

286 "I was viewing it": Kallen to Tolkin, Jan. 28, 1973, Tolkin Papers.

286 "moved through the sketches": *San Jose Mercury*, April 14, 1973.

286 "It's as if what": *New Yorker*, March 3, 1973.

286 "Americans today have forgotten": *Sunday Herald Advertiser*, April 29, 1973.

287 "Sid went through a maniacal": Coca to Kallen, Nov. 2, 1974, box 14, folder 1, Kallen Papers.

288 "A man who has lost": *Newsday*, April 30, 1974.

288 "Jewish adrenaline": "Albert at the New School: Sid Caesar."

288 "He did the young boy": Kallen to Holtzman.

288 "At a time when television": *Women's Wear Daily*, April 22, 1974, 18.

288 "A field marshall": *Newark Star-Ledger*, April 28, 1974.

288 "utterly altered human being": *TV Guide*, June 29, 1974.

288 "could be very terrible": Caesar, *Where Have I Been?*, 199.

289 "Like most comedians": Caesar, *Where Have I Been?*, 200.

289 "has-been get-togethers": *Washington Post*, Dec. 23, 1982.

289 "It didn't bother me": Caesar, *Where Have I Been?*, 194.

289 "People didn't know what to do": Interview, Reiner.

289 "Reiner drew me aside": Email, Patrick McGilligan to the author, Sept. 22, 2022.

289 "With all the junk": Max Wilk, interview by Michael Rosen, Nov. 15, 2000, TAF.

290 "Not in the world of Captain and Tennille": *Washington Post*, Sept. 28, 1976.

290 "We'll talk about his diet": *New Mexican*, Feb. 6, 1978.

290 "surprisingly humorless intensity": *New York Times*, July 1, 1976.

290 "was Sid's natural state": Interview, Brooks.

290 "He was a little on the sauce": De Luca interview for "Television's Comedy Genius."

290 "Instead of being the Professor": Caesar interview, April 1, 1997, TAF.

290 "still funny": *Los Angeles Times*, June 20, 1977.

291 "the darkest of my Dark Period": Caesar, *Where Have I Been?*, 275.

291 "Caesar and Coca doing *The Bicycle Thief*": Interview, Rich.

291 "You have clearly got the part": Inscribed picture in Coca Collection.

292 "But that's like Sid": New York *Daily News*, July 9, 1978.

292 "Meeting this rather shy": Michael Palin, *Diaries 1969–1979: The Python Years* (Thomas Dunne Books, 2006), 452.

292 "I didn't live too far": Caesar, *Where Have I Been?*, 211.

292 "It was not one of his *Show of Shows*": *Edmonton Journal*, June 10, 1978.

293 "Sid had a lot of walls": Interview, Finkel.

293 "He was surly, uncooperative": *Miami News*, Feb. 1, 1979.

293 "Once the shrinks get you": *Atlanta Constitution*, Nov. 30, 1980.

293 "He's *so* admiring of my dad": Interview, Jonathan Salk.

293 "Sidney, you schmuck": Caesar, *Where Have I Been?*, 250–51.

294 "He's a new man, an extrovert": *Los Angeles Times*, May 9, 1980.

294 "flitting about, very much up": Tolkin to Kallen, Dec. 15, 1980, box 2, folder 3, Kallen Papers.

294 "Sid has found a Happy Pill": Coca to Kallen, June 30, 1980, box 1, file 9, Kallen Papers.

295 "He stopped and he said": Interview, Brooks.

296 "wouldn't knock him out": Interview, Karen Caesar.

296 "an aggressive, almost neo-Fascist-type": Caesar, *Where Have I Been?*, 264.

296 "laugh nights": Interview, De Luca.

296 "brain back": *Today*, Nov. 13, 1980.

296 "shrimp cocktail": *Minneapolis Star*, Jan. 21, 1981.

296 "If someone comes to you": Caesar, *Where Have I Been?*, 275.

296 "pure cardboard": Caesar, *Where Have I Been?*, 268.

297 "It was almost as if": Interview, Les Charles.

297 "twenty-five-year-old boys": *Washington Post*, Dec. 23, 1982.

297 "the sad little number": Kallen to Tolkin, July 28, 1981, Tolkin Papers.

297 "Do you realize": Caesar, *Where Have I Been?*, 127.

297 "*Little Mea Culpa*": Goldman to "Andrew," Oct. 4, 1989, box 100, folder 18, Goldman Papers.

297 "He has survived the double-barreled": *New Republic*, Dec. 20, 1982.

298 "NEXT WEEK: What happens when Sid": *National Enquirer*, September 28, 1982.

298 "It was so honest": Reiner interview for "Television's Comedy Genius."

298 "Portrait of the Artist as Monster": Kallen to Tolkin, April 13, 1982, Tolkin Papers.

298 "Sid's been talking like the book": Tolkin to Kallen, April 19, 1982, Tolkin Papers.

298 "I added whatever I could": Coca to Basile and Schnepp, Nov. 26, 1997, Coca Papers.

298 "that fucking book": Morris to Kisseloff, Kisseloff Collection.

298 "He said to me a short while ago": Morris to Schaap.

298 "back on this planet": Gelbart to Schaap.

298 "Caesar now is totally recovered": Promotional materials for *Where Have I Been?*, n.d., box 46, folder 10, Goldman Papers.

298 "You know what it is": Caesar to Schaap.

299 "schlepping his way": *Washington Post*, Dec. 23, 1982.

299 "I didn't care about people": Caesar at Museum of Broadcasting, Feb. 7, 1983.

299 "what in the heck happened": Interview, Riddick.

299 "He seemed to be a very deep man": Mel Gussow, *Conversations with Miller* (Applause, 2002), 84.

299 "struggling to free himself": *Newsday*, Feb. 8, 1983.

299 "I used to be paranoid": *Village Voice*, Nov. 30, 1982.

300 "Saw Mel's movie": Tolkin to Kallen, June 15, 1981, box 2, folder 3, Kallen Papers.

300 "an extravaganza of bad taste": Coca to Kallen, Sept. 15, 1982, box 1, folder 9, Kallen Papers.

300 "The world twisted and turned": Liebman to Holtzman.

300 "Actually, Mel never got a job": Tolkin to Kallen, June 2, 1992, Tolkin Papers.

300 "a sniveling, cowardly asshole": Tolkin to Reiner, Nov. 18, 1982, Tolkin Papers.

300 "the most totally male chauvinist": Kallen to Martha LoMonoco, March 6, 1987, Tamiment Playhouse Oral History Collection, 31, box 1, folder 32.

301 "He will never be out of the public eye": Kallen to Holtzman, May 29, 1977.

301 "a big dumb ox": *New York Post*, Nov. 30, 1982.

301 "When you put a big cigar": Caesar, interview by Diehl, ABC News Radio, Nov. 26, 1982.

301 "a compulsive and perpetual drunk": *Washington Post*, Dec. 23, 1982.

301 "Forget about Sid": Kallen to Tolkin, Nov. 17, 1984, Tolkin Papers.

301 "My true thoughts on Sid": Tolkin to Kallen, Nov. 16, 1989, "Anger" file, Tolkin Papers.

301 "We want to do comedy-variety": *Broadcasting*, Oct. 6, 1975, 43.

301 "I remember us revering it": Interview, Franken.

302 "You want to know": Sacks, *And Here's the Kicker*, 411.

302 "avoid the Mel Brooks spritz": *Los Angeles Times*, March 28, 1976.

302 "We don't intend to deal": *Broadcasting*, Oct. 6, 1975, 43.

302 "A lot of Sid Caesar": *Washington Post*, Nov. 20, 1977.

302 "too long, drawn-out, overdone": *Chicago Tribune*, May 14, 1983.

303 "the best comedy on television": *Harvard Crimson*, May 13, 1976.

303 "I think they are": *Los Angeles Times*, Aug. 15, 1976.

304 "He wasn't chummy": Interview, Hall.

304 "Being on *SNL* wasn't exactly": Email, Herman to the author, Nov. 22, 2019.

304 "You think you know everything": Interview, Blaustein.

304 "He couldn't contain his anger": Interview, Kazurinsky.

304 "easily the healthiest-looking member": *New York Times*, Feb. 4, 1983.

304 "Could easily pass for": *The Sun* (Baltimore), Nov. 2, 1982.

305 "Everybody up!": *Saturday Night Live*, Feb. 5, 1983.

305 "Warmly welcomed as Role Model": *Pittsburgh Post-Gazette*, Feb. 11, 1983.

305 "Thanks for making the juices": Interview, Tischler.

305 "I was told": Caesar at the Museum of Broadcasting, Feb. 7, 1983.

305 "He seemed so unhappy": Interview, Blaustein.

306 "They have Ph.D.'s": *Asbury Park Press*, March 21, 1984.

306 "Give 'em a couple of drinks": Quotations from *Over the Brooklyn Bridge*.

306 "the Jewish Rip Van Winkle": New York *Daily News*, Oct. 21, 1983.

307 "dope-and-booze fog": *Philadelphia Daily News*, Feb. 7, 1984.

307 "impatient, obsessive, compulsive": *Boston Globe*, April 12, 1984.

307 "I laughed a lot": Interview, Bell.

307 "hot again": *The Larry King Show*, Mutual Broadcasting, Feb. 26, 1988.

308 "Steve Smith, who shares": Journals of Arthur M. Schlesinger Jr., July 27, 1989, box 318, folder 1, New York Public Library.

308 "He's trying to tell me": Interview, Keith Sherman.

309 "When, at the curtain call": *New York*, Nov. 11, 1989.

309 "They were both very funny": Interview, Allen.

309 "They have a button next to them": Interview, Spellman.

310 "Try to enjoy it": Interview, Lane.

310 "Sid is active": *The Dick Cavett Show*, Dec. 17, 1993.

310 "Sidney, I have so much": *Salute to Sid Caesar*.

311 "a comedy Last Supper": *Los Angeles Times*, Aug. 19, 1996.

311 "a crapshoot": Interview, Bob Claster.

311 "This mayhem that was going": "Caesar's Writers."

311 "Everybody thinks that Sid waited": "Caesar's Writers."

311 "a spoof on a Jewish burial society": *New York Times*, Aug. 19, 1996.

311 "I don't know how many time's": Winters to Caesar, Feb. 10, 1997, Caesar Family Papers.

312 "There's a time to say": Caesar interview, April 1, 1997, TAF.

312 "a man some of you remember": *The Sid Caesar Collection: 50th Anniversary Edition, The Magic of Live TV*, vol. 1, Creative Light Entertainment.

312 "What you kids did": Alan Zweibel, *Laugh Lines: My Life Helping Funny People Be Funnier* (Abrams, 2020), 236.

312 "It's a different world": *New York Observer*, Dec. 18, 2000.

313 In the video tribute: Taped recording of dinner, National Foundation for Jewish Culture, Dec. 11, 2000, collection of the author.

EPILOGUE

314 "Sid, it was wonderful": Rich to Caesar, courtesy of Karen Caesar.

314 "You learn nothing from success": Caesar, *Caesar's Hours*, xvii.

315 "You know, we're going to be": Mark Evanier, *News From ME*, Feb. 12, 2014.

315 "Sid's ride": Interview, Stephen Tolkin.

315 "as if the lights went on": Interview, Richard Kind.

315 "It was a thank you": *New York Times*, Feb. 14, 2014.

315 "Once swinging but now sadly bedraggled": *Variety*, May 7, 2015.

315 "She has been living with": *TV Guide*, Feb. 16, 1963.

316 "I know *him*": Rudy De Luca interview for "Television's Comedy Genius."

316 "No!" he'd declare: Interview, Caesar.

317 "you can't remember": Aaron Sorkin, *Huffington Post*, Dec. 14, 2011.

317 "like dutiful sons": Email, Ross to the author, Oct. 1, 2019.

317 "mold, brisket, and Shalimar": Rena Strober, *Singing for Sid and Other Wow Moments*, forthcoming.

317 "He didn't talk for five minutes": Interview, Brooks.

318 "a comedic force of nature": *New York Times*, Feb. 12, 2014.

318 "Younger viewers may remember him": *ABC World News Tonight*, Feb. 12, 2014.

318 "When it comes to humor": *ABC World News Tonight*, Feb. 12, 2014.

318 a "Jewish" comic: These and the following quotations from Caesar's funeral, recording of the author.

321 "event-worn": *Property of the Estate of Sid and Florence Caesar*, Julien's Auctions, Beverly Hills, Calif., June 25–26, 2015.

INDEX

Page numbers in *italics* refer to illustrations.

ILLUSTRATION CREDITS

ii Center Theatre: Robert Walker/*New York Times* Archive

viii Cast of *Your Show of Shows*: Photograph courtesy of Paul Engel

INSERT

Page 1: (top left) Photofest, Inc.; (top right) ZUMA Press, Inc./Alamy Stock Photo; (bottom) Columbia Pictures/Photofest © Columbia Pictures

Page 2: (top) Photograph courtesy of Lucille Kallen Papers. Billy Rose Theatre Division, The New York Public Library for the Performing Arts; (bottom right) Courtesy of Florence Baum

Page 3: (top) Bettmann/Contributor; (middle left) New York *Daily News*/TCA; (middle right) New York *Daily News*/TCA; (bottom) Caesar's portrait courtesy of Photofest, Inc.

Page 4: (top) NBC/Photofest, Inc. © NBC; (middle) Photograph by Jack O'Connell/ *Boston Globe* via Getty Images; (bottom) PictureLux/The Hollywood Archive/ Alamy Stock Photo

Page 5: (top left) Photograph © Ruth Orkin Photo Archive; (top right) Photograph courtesy of family of Leo Friedman; (middle) Photograph © Esther Bubley Archive; (bottom) Photofest, Inc.

Page 6: (top left) Photograph courtesy of Elena Radutsky, © Harry Radutsky; (top right) Photograph © Milton Greene; (bottom) UPI Photo/Files

Page 7: (top left) TVGM Holdings, LLC; (top right) Photograph courtesy of family of Jack Davis; (bottom) Photofest, Inc.

Page 8: (top left) United Artists/Photofest © United Artists; (top right) Paramount Pictures/Photofest © Paramount Pictures; (middle) Broadway Video/NBC Productions/RGR Collection/Mary Evans/Alamy Stock Photo; (bottom) Photograph by Kevin Winter/Getty Images

A NOTE ABOUT THE AUTHOR

David Margolick is the author of several books, including *Beyond Glory: Joe Louis vs. Max Schmeling, and a World on the Brink; Strange Fruit: The Biography of a Song*; and *Elizabeth and Hazel: Two Women of Little Rock*. He was a longtime contributing editor at *Vanity Fair* and, prior to that, a legal affairs reporter at *The New York Times*, where he wrote the weekly "At the Bar" column. He lives in New York City.

A NOTE ON THE TYPE

This book was set in Janson, a typeface long thought to have been made by the Dutchman Anton Janson, who was a practicing typefounder in Leipzig during the years 1668–1687. However, it has been conclusively demonstrated that these types are actually the work of Nicholas Kis (1650–1702), a Hungarian, who most probably learned his trade from the master Dutch typefounder Dirk Voskens. The type is an excellent example of the influential and sturdy Dutch types that prevailed in England up to the time William Caslon (1692–1766) developed his own incomparable designs from them.

Composed by North Market Street Graphics
Lancaster, PA

Designed by Soonyoung Kwon